In Search of
Canadian Political Culture

In Search of
Canadian Political Culture

...... Nelson Wiseman

UBCPress · Vancouver · Toronto

16 15 14 13 12 11 10 09 08 07   5 4 3 2 1

Printed in Canada on ancient-forest-free paper (100% post-consumer recycled) that is processed chlorine- and acid-free, with vegetable-based inks.

Library and Archives Canada Cataloguing in Publication

Wiseman, Nelson, 1946-
      In search of Canadian political culture / Nelson Wiseman.

Includes bibliographical references and index.
ISBN 978-0-7748-1388-4

      1. Canada – Politics and government. 2. Political culture – Canada.
I. Title.

JL65.W586 2007   306.2'0971   C2007-903352-0

Canadä

UBC Press gratefully acknowledges the financial support for our publishing program of the Government of Canada through the Book Publishing Industry Development Program (BPIDP), and of the Canada Council for the Arts, and the British Columbia Arts Council.

This book has been published with the help of a grant from the Canadian Federation for the Humanities and Social Sciences, through the Aid to Scholarly Publications Programme, using funds provided by the Social Sciences and Humanities Research Council of Canada.

UBC Press
The University of British Columbia
2029 West Mall
Vancouver, BC V6T 1Z2
604-822-5959 / Fax: 604-822-6083
www.ubcpress.ca

Contents

Tables

Acknowledgments

I am grateful to Gad Horowitz for reading and commenting on the chapters as I produced them. Colette Malo typed the first half of the manuscript and taught me how to type the rest. Don Forbes and Graham White read and commented on Chapters 2 and 3 respectively. Grace Skogstad helped me address the comments of the anonymous readers. Their attention and constructive suggestions are appreciated. Thanks to Emily Andrew for her advice and editorial skills and to Peter Milroy who prodded me for over a quarter century to produce such a book. Research grants were not solicited nor were research assistants employed in the book's preparation. Errors of fact and interpretation are mine alone.

In Search of
Canadian Political Culture ....

Introduction

Political culture is the broad encompassing term used in this book to serve as a platform for a rumination on Canadian politics. It is a reflective inquiry rather than a venture into the frontier of research. Political culture is a long-established pivot in the study of Canadian politics, drawing the attention of some of the country's best scholars and subjected to some of their most high-powered analytic techniques. Canadian political culture is also the stuff of more popular treatments, as conveyed by tantalizing titles such as *Sex in the Snow* and *Fire and Ice*.[1] The arguments I pursue build on and directly contest some of the major contributions in the study of Canadian political culture. My effort is not intended to demythify or remythify Canadians' conceptions of their political culture by using benchmarks such as equality, inclusiveness, tolerance, freedom, and other democratic touchstones. It is intended to cast light on how Canada, its people, and political institutions came to be what they are today rather than what they ought to or could be in the light of contemporary norms and values.

A tension runs through much of this book, for it is of an atypical breed. It incorporates elements of a conventional research monograph, but it is also intended to be accessible to a general audience. It strives to be scholarly without being impenetrable. It is directed at non-professional as well as specialist students of Canadian politics, particularly those who wish to understand and make sense of its regional variations. This study takes an eclectic approach to research, teaching, and thinking about Canadian political culture. It adopts a pluralistic orientation to the subject without being jerry-built or amorphous. It seeks both to provoke the academic and to enlighten the general reader about who and what Canadians have been and are in the political world. I have pursued the luxury of writing on points that interest me, instead of trying to cover the whole field in a systematic way. Written by an academic gadfly and generalist in the study of Canadian politics, this study seeks to prompt discussion rather than agreement or conversion from other ways of seeing or dissecting the subject. It offers possibilities rather than prescriptions in ways of understanding Canadian politics. It is tendered as another tool for thinking about Canadian political culture.

The book is influenced by traditions in political theory, political economy, political sociology, and political institutional and historical studies. It is written by a social scientist dubious of the ascendancy of science, one who laments the deprecation of more traditional historical studies in the study of politics. It does not subscribe to the notion that the past is another country. The historian may frown on the lack of archival materials, and the behavioural political scientist may find it short on systematic analysis, quantification, and theory building. In bringing together the kinds of materials that historians and political scientists have separately used, it strives to help remedy a shortage in Canadian political studies, that of comparative provincial political cultures.

Political historians have not taken the trouble to compare Canada's regional political cultures: they have been busy telling the story of Canada at large or that of a specific province. They have a reasonable suspicion of generalizations that compare countries' or regions' political histories. They tend to dwell on the unique and specific, highlighting a particular case, place, or people. In contrast, comparative studies of political systems are a staple among political scientists, always in vogue and with a pedigree that runs back to the ancient Greeks. Canadians often, and sometimes smugly, contrast and compare themselves and their country to Americans and the United States. They spend less time comparing themselves regionally. Newspapers and broadcasts facilitate this; replete with political stories about the United States, they devote substantially less attention to what goes on politically in neighbouring provinces. Canadians may be more familiar with major political players in their neighbour to the south than in the Canadian jurisdictions to their west or east. Canadian political scientists have also expended more energy in studying how Canadians differ politically from Americans than in how, say, Nova Scotians differ from Albertans. Their findings and assertions reveal engaged debate: some argue that Canadians are becoming increasingly like Americans; others maintain that Canadians are becoming less like them.[2]

Regionalism is a predominant characteristic of Canadian politics, one of its axes or fault lines. The attention regionalism generates usually focuses on sectional grievances and the tug-of-war between regions and Ottawa rather than on comparing and contrasting what tugs politics *within* the regions. The high-water mark among political scientists for the enterprise of comparative provincial politics was at the turn of the 1980s.[3] Most of those studies were survey-driven.[4] Survey researchers generally inform us that, with the exception of Quebecers, Canadians are more similar than different in their values. Such studies, however, tend to be ahistorical because the survey instrument is of relatively recent vintage and the questions that surveys put and the nuanced meaning of words they use are constantly changing in relevance. Canada's political traditions and institutions, however, are old and firmly implanted. Although they too have changed, they continue to shape and resonate in today's politics. Canadians who dislike the way in which parliament works or the bickering engendered by the federal system still prefer the parliamentary to the congressional system and the federal to the unitary state. In any case, they are more or less stuck with them because such institutions as the monarchy are inherited and ingrained irrespective of the opinions Canadians endorse in surveys about what they believe or value.

Surveys suggest that Canadians outside Quebec have remarkably similar tastes, values, opinions, and beliefs, but their political behaviour – as opposed to their popular culture – differs remarkably when we examine their political preferences regionally. Institutional walls – provincial boundaries, provincial administrations, and the configuration of party systems and social forces they contain – reinforce these differences. One could look beyond the conventionally accepted regional and provincial boundaries to cluster Canada's regions into unusual categories such as "cosmopolitan Quebec," "rural and mid-northern," "manufacturing belt," "metropolitan Toronto," and so on, and suggest that they help to explain the most politically salient cultural distinctions.[5] This points to the ever-present challenge to political culture studies: how to relate sub-cultures to an overall societal culture.[6] We may also think in terms of the political cultures of concentric and overlapping communities.

Many have noted, beginning with Alan Cairns, that the federal electoral system favours regionally concentrated parties and penalizes upstart national third parties – something obvious since the 1920s, although no other political scientist had written about it. In Cairn's judgment, this magnifies artificial regional differences and exacerbates them.[7] His brilliant and much-cited single factor analysis, however, cannot account for the particularly blustery regional tensions that surrounded the rise and demise of the Meech Lake Accord in the late 1980s. It was precisely by that decade that the minor regional parties favoured by the electoral system, such as Social Credit and the

Ralliement des Créditistes, had disappeared from the scene, while the remaining three federal parties became more regionally representative than ever. The electoral system certainly handicaps erstwhile major parties that have been eclipsed, such as the provincial Social Credit and Conservative Parties in British Columbia and the Liberals in Manitoba and Saskatchewan. The federal Progressive Conservatives suffered the same fate, spectacularly, after 1993. Cultural factors and the workings of institutions such as federalism and cabinet-parliamentary government, however, are more important in fuelling regional identities and tensions than are the distorted outputs of the electoral system.[8]

This book is the product of a long gestation period. It builds on some of my earlier suggestive forays in the field.[9] In the social sciences, it is common – imitative as they are of the harder physical and natural sciences – to spell out at the outset the objectives, methods, and conclusions of one's enterprise. Once upon a time, some frowned on this form as "showing the works," telling the reader what to expect, think, and conclude before she had begun to study and evaluate the text. Social scientists generally opt to provide thesis statements, executive summaries, or synoptic conclusions. They tell the reader what he will encounter before his journey begins. This contrasts with the more literary styles of fiction, many histories, and writing in other humanities – ones that leave the reader to discover and encounter surprise along the way. Many of the constructions and connections made in this book will surprise.

The first chapter introduces some conceptions of political culture and its intimate connection to but distinction from ideology, which, in turn, is often misleadingly confused with policy prescriptions. Four generic paths – historical studies, survey research, institutional analysis, and socialization theories – are outlined as search engines for studying the multifaceted concept of political culture. Three historically complementary approaches proffered by others in pursuit of a panoramic understanding of Canada's political culture are dissected. These approaches draw primarily and respectively on political theory or philosophy, formative societal events and social indicators, and economic forces and structures. My contribution is to push the combined implications of these pathways for understanding Canada's political culture in the context of Canada's regions. I use the prism of distinctive historical waves of immigration to synthesize them.

In the focus on charter immigrant groups, their ideological superstructures, and their settlement patterns, I pursue the social rather than the individual psychological dimension of political culture. Unlike many who study electoral behaviour, I do not deeply probe what citizens at a fixed point in time think of specific leaders, issues, and policies as they come and go. Rather, the overriding concern here is with the dominant ideological and partisan tendencies expressed collectively by the five immigrant waves I identify: their views on the nature of society, their relationship to the state, and their concepts of the regime's proper role. I connect these waves of immigration with and within their regional settings. The object of study is the cultural collective: groups with distinct origins, characteristics, statuses, and ideological and partisan inclinations, and their regional manifestations.

The drive for specious precision characterizes much of the literature on political culture. Chapter 2 takes a critical disposition toward the widespread reliance on the public opinion survey, the tool now most commonly associated with studying political culture. This tool is used to compare Canadian political culture from without and within – that is, to contrast Canadians' values as reported in surveys with those of others and to look at the variations in the values held by residents of different Canadian regions. Surveys offer a straightforward strategy and a simple regimen. Nevertheless, they may artfully distort – however unintentionally – our understanding of the subject. Survey questionnaires probably reflect the issues and values that preoccupy surveyors more than respondents. I question the utility and reliability of surveys as gauges of political values but do not dismiss them categorically. Indeed, when they prove instructive, these high lords of political culture research are respected at points in this book.

An examination of the relationship between political institutions and culture reveals an unmistakable shift from British to American imprints in the evolving constitutional consciousness of Canadians. To be sure, indigenous elements have always modified both legacies and fed competing constitutional visions within the polity. Chapter 3 examines political institutions for clues about national and regional political cultures. Canada's three constitutional pillars – Westminster-style parliamentary government, federalism, and the Charter of Rights – exhibit a distinctly Canadian hierarchy of constitutional values. If one includes political parties, elections, and interest groups as part of the institutional infrastructure, the deepening and broadening over time of Canadians' democratic and egalitarian impulses becomes patently apparent. The operation of parallel institutional structures, such as legisla-tures with identical powers, gives voice to the regional political cultural dif-ferences played out within those institutions.

The issue of an overarching Canadian political culture is touched on in Chapter 4 and revisited in the Conclusion, which includes a collection of musings. Some attention is also given to prominent regionally crosscutting sub-cultural cleavages: the bilingual, multicultural, and Aboriginal dimen-sions of national political life. As Canada has become more culturally di-verse and its visible and other minorities have grown and become less deferential, more of them have participated in and been incorporated into national and provincial political life. The relatively new and heightened sig-nificance of Aboriginal title and self-government has contributed to an emer-ging Aboriginal cultural self-redefinition. Aboriginals are too few to drive the broader political culture but their recently elevated societal, legal, and political status contributes to reshaping it. That is evident in the images Can-ada offers of itself to itself and to others – from Native symbols on coins to the Queen's visit to Nunavut, to the choice of an Inuit *inukshuk* as the em-blem for the 2010 Winter Olympics.

This book is less bold about pronouncing on Canada's national politic-al culture than on its regional ones. The very notion of a Canadian nation is a highly contested one. No region, with the possible exception of Quebec, could conceivably qualify as a nation. To assert the Canadian nation as one entity is to reject the plausible dualistic and multinational conceptions of the country that are held by many Canadians. To dispute regional defini-tions (what are the boundaries of "central Canada" or the "West"?) is to deal with geographical demarcations. To determine the nature of westerners' col-lective values is a more substantial issue. Defining Canadians' collective ethos is a profoundly more disputatious and intractable matter.

Many studies deal with the Canadian political culture. Some ponder the political culture of individual regions. Few think about those regional polit-ical cultures comparatively. This book does so audaciously. The regional fo-cus in the latter half of the book deconstructs and marginalizes the pan-Canadian approach to Canadian political culture and politics. This study pursues a regionally specified composite portrait of Canada in which the country's political history is mined to stress difference rather than commonality among regions.

English Canada's political culture is not treated here as if it were cut from a single piece of territorial cloth. To be sure, no one seriously disputes that regional cleavages are critical factors in Canadian politics; regional considerations are conspicuous criteria in the appointment of public servants, from cabinet ministers to judges, and in the dispersal of federal monies. The three long-standing national political parties, however – the Liberals, Conservatives, and NDP – have shied away from directly addressing regional cleavages for fear of dividing their parties along regional lines. This study devotes more attention to the particular inclinations of those in the provinces, regions, and immigrant groups than to the common values and beliefs that cut across and conceal them. It deals more with broad regional social forces and the ideological currents that drive politics than with national institutions or the foibles and fortunes of towering personalities that captivate journalists and popular audiences.

By selecting a regional frame, this study makes a case for bottom-up provincial and regional analyses of Canadian politics. In this respect, it ventures into the terrain of political cultural geography. The attention drawn to regional politics, rather than the tensions among regions or the tensions between regions and the federal government, oscillates in the study of Canadian politics. Consider and compare successive editions of the established reader *Canadian Politics*. The first and second editions featured chapters on the politics of each region. By the fourth edition, there were none.[10] The politics of Quebec, the most distinctive region, were ignored. The framework in the latter half of this book should not imply that regionalism is a more fundamental cleavage in Canadian politics than language, ethnicity, or economic class and industrial structures. The objective is to illuminate such cleavages within the regions with a view to filling a lacuna in our thinking and writing about Canadian political culture.

The relationship between regions and political culture raises the issues of identifying and labelling the regions, as well as characterizing their values. Is every province to be deemed a discrete region, or are there sufficient cultural similarities that transcend some provincial boundaries and permit lumping some provinces together? Perhaps intraprovincial variations – the cultural contrasts between St. John's and Labrador, between Winnipeg and northern Manitoba – are more vital to a cultural analysis than interprovincial ones, for example, the differences between Newfoundland and Manitoba. These issues, and those of provincial identities and the popular imagery of politics in different regions, are addressed in Chapter 5. Voting results of the Charlottetown Referendum are deployed to demonstrate the powerful link between geography and political choice.

In traversing Canada's regions from east to west, this book makes one break with conventional regional categorizations. The West is partitioned in two, between the Midwest (Manitoba and Saskatchewan) and the Far West (Alberta and British Columbia), displacing the older and more common distinction between the Prairies and BC. The socio-economic makeup and history of each region raise issues and questions distinctive to it. To illuminate the singularity of each region, metaphorical images are offered, images that inventively conjure up the political dynamics of other societies. Newfoundland is cast as the offshoot of Ireland and West Country England; the Maritimes, the oldest and most socially homogeneous part of English Canada, are presented as a Canadian branch and homologue of New England. Chapter 6 questions whether the mythology surrounding Atlantic Canada's alleged traditionalist political culture is still viable. Perhaps the very idea of an Atlantic Canadian political culture is a chimera. Quebec and its predecessor, New France, inherited and long wore the cultural apparel of Old France. The trajectory from subjugation to sovereignty, the redefinition of *la nation québécoise,* and the outlines of the New Quebec are traced in the context of a historiographical debate in Chapter 7.

In Chapter 8, English Canada's political and cultural hegemon, Ontario, is characterized as America's counter-revolution. In Ontario, the founding American Loyalist wave of the late eighteenth century came to be challenged by a British liberal reform wave of the early nineteenth century, and both were augmented and upset by a British labour-socialist ripple at the turn of the twentieth century. Since mid-century, all three legacies have accommodated each other and the kaleidoscope of peoples from non-traditional immigrant sources. The Midwest's support for social democracy is then probed in Chapter 9. The wave of continental European and British immigrants that flooded the prairies a century ago was a pivotal factor in social democracy's fortunes in this region. Manitoba comes across as the Ontario of the prairies; Saskatchewan provides the unlikely agrarian setting for a replication of British Labour's success in an ideologically polarized two-party system in what was considered the mother country. In Chapter 10, the Far West is noted for a lack of tradition and an upstart and recalcitrant political character. Alberta is depicted as a splinter of the United States, specifically the Great Plains. In both Canada and the US, populist liberalism had its greatest traction on the plains. Finally, BC resembles Australia – a sister British colonial offshoot on the Pacific.

This book builds on and veers away from the established political culture literature in two respects. The first is in its primary emphasis on the ideological baggage and acculturation of immigrants and their impact in the regions at different stages of regional political development. The second and related theme is what has become known in the specialist academic literature as the ideological "fragment theory" or the "Hartz-Horowitz" interpretation of Canadian political culture. That framework, employing the ideological triad of conservatism, liberalism, and socialism, identifies the dynamic philosophical connections in their interaction in societies such as Canada's that are "thrown off" from older European societies.[11] It accounts for the pattern of politics in a New World society such as Canada's in terms of its colonial heritages and the ideological genetic codes implanted by founding pioneers. Although there is no single master narrative in this book, the connections between these two threads – the interplay and political expression of the distinctive ideological world views of immigrant groups – come nearest to providing a spine for this study. What is novel in this treatment is the pursuit and regional application of the fragment theory. Unlike that theory, however, it devotes less attention to ideological dialectics and more attention to political economy, social indicators, and electoral forces.

"Red tory" has become a term of wide and overvalued currency in both the academic and real worlds of Canadian politics. It first surfaced in the lexicon of Canadian politics in 1966[12] and since then has spawned the "blue tory" as a mirror image. Gad Horowitz argued that the strength of social democracy in Canada is a function of the strength of toryism, a traditional collectivist philosophical disposition whose communitarianism is shared by socialists. In this respect, both classical conservatives (or tories) and contemporary socialists (or social democrats) stand together and diametrically apart from classical liberals (such as those who dominate what is now the Conservative Party). However minoritarian a force it was in English Canada's primarily liberal political culture, the tory streak formatively differentiated Canada from the American, universally liberal behemoth to its south. That "tory touch," according to Horowitz, was the philosophic seed that permitted Canadian socialism to sprout. The United States, in contrast, rid itself at the end of the eighteenth century of whatever was left of its tory touch by symbolically and physically rejecting it and its vestiges in its revolutionary war and declaratory Constitution.[13]

In this book, I offer *an* interpretation of Canadian political culture. No claim is made that it is *the* only possible explanation or *the* definitive interpretation. I extend but also swerve from the Hartz-Horowitz approach by contextualizing some of its features regionally. I make no claim that social democratic strength in particular regional pockets is connected to the strength of Canadian toryism in those same regions. That there is a residue in Canadian political culture that marks it as more communitarian, tory, and social democratic than American political culture is neither contested by nor critical to my analysis. Horowitz's analysis draws particular attention to the toryism of the Loyalists. This cannot explain (nor does Horowitz try to do so) why Canadian social democracy has been most potent and viable in the West, the part of Canada where the tory Loyalist stamp was absent. Nor, conversely, can it account for why socialism has been weakest in those regions where the Loyalist tory imprint was formative and most profound, such areas as eastern Ontario and New Brunswick. It is in the treatment of Quebec's political culture that I play explicitly with the stimulating counterintuitive kernel at the centre of the Hartz-Horowitz hypothesis. It is there that I make an interpretive case for the dialectical dance between classical *ancien régime* conservatism and modern socialism and use it to account for Quebec's passage beyond its liberal Quiet Revolution and into the arms of a self-professed social democratic and *indépendantiste* regime. Like other fragment theorists, I treat Quebec as a national fragment, a separate European offshoot equal in dignity to the American and English Canadian fragments, making it no mere region within Canada.

The motive in this book is neither to identify a looming challenge in Canadian politics nor to proffer a cure for a perceived political malady. Neither Canada's recently alleged "democratic deficit" nor the perennial issues of Quebec's constitutional status and Western alienation are the subjects per se of this book. Nor are the more recent concerns regarding the place of Aboriginal peoples and multicultural communities and the workings of the first-past-the-post electoral system. This study treats Canada's "problems" and issues of identity and citizenship with a measure of intentional benign neglect. Of the Canadian political scientists who engaged with these issues, quite unlike the more circumspect and skeptical historians and lawyers, most were cheerleaders for the Meech Lake[14] and Charlottetown Accords. Those misadventures in institutional redesign proved impolitic for the politicians carrying the brief and disintegrative for the polity. Both the political class and those professional students of politics who abetted the dubious pursuit of constitutional "reform" were chastened in their ambitions to institutionally remake Canada. My view from the start was that the undertaking itself was folly, a quest for a false messiah.[15]

Unlike many, I am neither fearful nor welcoming of Canada's seemingly always-imminent disintegration or reconfiguration. The language of "crisis," so pervasive and long-standing in assessments of Canada's political condition – the alarm bells are constantly ringing – has been cheapened and rendered meaningless. By comparative international measures, Canada is remarkably stable, tempered, and blessed with prosperity. Political implosion, uncontrollable rioting, and the perpetual paralysis of governing institutions are not associated with Canada. The Canadian political cultural tradition is one of evolutionary change: gradual, incrementalist, and iterative. Certainly, the past is no infallible guide to the future, but neither is it simply over and done with. Grievances will persist and fissures may widen in Canadian political life, but an acceptance of working with what is feasible or practical will probably prevail among leaders and followers.

The understanding of Canadian political culture offered in the following pages is not intended to present the conventional social scientist's superficial patina of neutrality. In its dissection of Canadians' political values and behaviour, it selectively presents facts and avoids trumpeting the virtues of particular values. Selecting "facts," however, is always a matter of evaluation: deciding what is important and what is not. Consider Gerald Friesen's highly regarded history of the Prairies.[16] His book draws attention to the Métis on 70 of its 524 pages, yet it neglects to mention Tommy Douglas, North America's first and most successful and popular social democrat. Facts presented are judgments made. Many facts are permanently lost. Inevitably, this study moulds its facts to fit the author's interpretation of them. Modern physics, catching up with ancient Buddhism, has irrefutably demonstrated the interconnectedness of observer and observed; the student cannot be dissociated from what he observes.

Contemporary conditions and conundrums influence social scientists' and historians' views of the past. That is why studies of multicultural and Aboriginal issues have proliferated. Social scientists are products of their societies and their histories. I arrived in Canada as a six-year-old immigrant, born behind the Iron Curtain to Holocaust survivors. I immediately realized that my family was low on the Canadian ethno-political pecking order

described a decade later in John Porter's "vertical mosaic." Politically socialized in Winnipeg's North End, I pursued the study of Manitoba politics[17]
after witnessing the dramatic transformation of the province's political cultural and partisan landscape in the late 1960s and the 1970s. I came to reject
Porter's assertion that it was "hallowed nonsense"[18] to believe that Canada's
provinces and regions (with the exception of Quebec) have distinct political
cultures. When I was assigned to teach a course on comparative provincial
politics at the University of Toronto, I looked for transformative links between ethnicity, ideology, and party politics similar to those I had noticed in
Manitoba. In this respect, in the sense that political life, like personal experience, is constantly evolving, my discussion of Canadian political culture is
an exercise in creative plausible storytelling. Yet the story woven here, though
it is situated in my concerns and those of my society, endeavours not to be
locked into or totally beholden to them.

1

Pathways to Canadian Political Culture

Culture, broadly speaking, is a society's way of life. It is the primary but not exclusive domain of anthropology. Political culture, then, is the way of life of a political community or polity. The term "political culture" is of relatively recent vintage,[1] but the concept and its application are ancient. Plato, Aristotle, and Herodotus, who offered insights into the differences among societies, cities, and leaders, sought to explain their causes. During the Renaissance, Machiavelli continued in this tradition; during the Enlightenment, Montesquieu followed suit. The latter thought that political culture was governed by laws that could be discovered. To Tocqueville, a student of American political culture in the first half of the nineteenth century, political culture meant the habits of the hearts and minds of Americans."[2] Later in that century, as modern nation-states emerged, the term "national character" was commonly used. A leading European political sociologist's famous and now century-old study of English and French Canadian political cultures was entitled *The Race Question in Canada*.[3] In whatever way the term for political culture may mutate, the idea persists.

Culture is something like the air we breathe. It is all around and in us. We take it for granted. Culture changes slowly. Stable and enduring, it is more like climate than like the weather, whose buffeting storms are transient. Culture does not come and go, as does fashion. It is cross-generational: we inherit it from our forbears, teach it to our children, and transmit it to future generations. We are shaken into an awareness of our culture's nuances when we visit another culture. Never doing so renders us culture-bound. Culture enables us to see and make sense of our physical and social situations.

Culture is an abstraction. So too is ideology. Both deal with fundamental values and are related, but they are also fundamentally different. Culture is an ordered system of symbols; ideology is an ordering of symbolic terms. "Left" and "right," conservatism and liberalism, are shorthand ideological categorizations. Ideologies or political philosophies may be defined, dissected, and debated at a metaphysical level without reference to any specific group, society, or nation. Culture is no less a mental construct than is ideology. It, however, cannot be explored solely on a theoretical plane, for it refers to real and specific groups, societies, or nations. Culture is a group activity, a shared experience. No person alone constitutes a culture, but one is socialized by and absorbed into a culture. If we think of the culture of a corporation, union, government, or university, we think of its vision and ambitions. Its culture is how it defines and organizes itself on its mission.

To come to terms with Canada's political culture requires some grounding in Canadian history. Also necessary is an appreciation of the country's contemporary society, economy, and political institutions. To place Canadian political culture in perspective, we can look beyond our borders, comparing it to those of other states. We also gain from comparing it within, searching out regional political cultures and the politics of other sub-cultures. Comparing improves our sense of what makes Canada distinct and of how various groups of Canadians (Chinese Canadians, French Canadians, Maritimers, the rich, the poor, and so on) are different from each other politically.

In search of Canadian political culture, one must consider how to go about investigating it. Does the past or the present dictate it? Is it to be located in identifiable historical patterns and landmark events, or is it what Canadians think politically in the here and now? Is Canadian political culture typified and expressed by political and other elites, or is it to be found among the masses? These dichotomies are heuristically necessary and simultaneously limiting and false. The prudent answer to such queries is that each requires a both/and rather than an either/or approach.

Ideology, Policy, Practice

Culture is a big idea, one with many facets. It may be looked at in terms of three levels: fundamental abstract values or *ideology*, time-honoured *policies*, and ritualized *practices*. The first represents the ideational elements of political culture; the second represents its programmatic content; the third represents its operational elements. These three levels or categories constantly interact; the boundaries between them are blurred. The purpose of categorization is to diminish blur. Examples of ideological notions are freedom, equality, and patriotism. Examples of now time-honoured Canadian policies are medicare and equalization payments to "have-not" provinces. Examples of rituals or common practices are the Speech from the Throne and political party conventions. Ideology, the first category, is deployed to legitimate established and new policies. Ideas may also be used to justify emerging practices such as referenda and the recall of elected politicians. For some long-established practices – such as electing a disproportionate number of MPs who are male lawyers – there may be no ideological legitimation, yet they stubbornly persist.

Debate and contentiousness run throughout this trinity of categories. Even among ideological kin, such as modern conservatives, there are philosophical disputes. Libertarians, for example, reject the legislation of morality, whereas social conservatives demand it. Business liberals see government as an obstacle to individual advancement; welfare liberals see government as an instrument to facilitate it. The ideological level informs much academic analysis. Policies provide context for jousting between political parties and leaders. Ritualized practices represent the heart of political reportage. Like the climate, rituals and common practices generally change gradually.

The three categories or levels of political culture outlined here are nothing more than focal points for analysis. From different perspectives, policies may appear as practices, and practices as policies. This typology – of ideology, policy, and practice – makes no causal claims or claims of relative importance. The now-established practice of multipartyism in Italy and Israel may be contrasted to the established practice of two-partyism in Newfoundland and Prince Edward Island. The roots of multipartyism in the first two were consequences of strong ideological divisions; the roots of two-partyism in the latter two were less so. Multipartyism as an *idea*, however, arguably took on a life of its own in the first two societies while, paradoxically, the ideological differences between their parties narrowed. Hence, ideology contributed to the emergence of a practice that now, in turn, encourages the parties to insist on their lingering ideological distinctiveness. This contrasts with Newfoundland and Prince Edward Island, where ideological distinctions between the parties were less important to begin with and continue to be so. This does not mean that the end of ideology has arrived. That would mean the end of ideas. No shortage of them and their prescriptive implications is to be found in the financial press. All parties are ideological, even when the gaps among them are not starkly discernable. Pragmatism, when contrasted with ideology, is merely a euphemism for upholding the established ideological order.

Disputes may be intense at all three levels. The consequences, however, are greater if the ideological struggle is, for example, that of capitalism versus socialism. A long-established policy debate in Canada concerns free trade with the United States. It demonstrates that its ideological champions and adversaries may flip positions: in both the 1911 and 1988 federal elections, it was *the* issue; the Liberals backed it in 1911, but the Conservatives traded places with them in 1988. In both cases, the party in favour of free trade was in office and the party against it in opposition. Were their positions simply a matter of "ins" and "outs"? No doubt there is an inevitable element of that in an adversarial parliamentary system with a constitutionalized Loyal Opposition. Another way of looking at the partisan cleavage, however, is that Canadian conservatism and liberalism, as elsewhere, have evolved. Canada's classical liberals, like Britain's classical liberals, stressed negative liberty and business liberalism. They were fixated on market solutions for policy issues. Canada's classical conservatives, like Britain's conservatives, were more protective of established elites and more state-oriented than liberals. In recent decades, as in Britain, they became neo-conservatives, spouting what classical liberalism stood for. Modern liberals have tended toward positive liberty and the welfare state. These imply an expansive rather than constricted government orbit.[4]

Conflicting policy preferences may take root in a single region. In Saskatchewan, support for co-operative and compulsory grain pools is long established among farmers. They embraced them in the 1920s and again, in plebiscites, in the 1990s. In neighbouring Alberta, in contrast, farmers insisted on voluntary non-compulsory pools in both decades.[5] This suggests that political cultural traditions vary by province as well as region. As further evidence, Saskatchewan in the 1988 federal election returned anti-free-trade candidates in most of its constituencies; by contrast, in all but one of its seats, Alberta returned candidates who favoured free trade. Residents in both provinces have repeatedly demonstrated alienation from central Canada but in obviously fundamentally different ways. Artificial political geographic demarcations, like provincial boundaries, contribute to and reinforce the taking hold of differing traditions. The institutions of provincehood influenced the mobilization, expression, and strength of competing political forces.

Do not confuse or mechanistically link the ideological and policy realms. Bismarck, the German conservative, pioneered the welfare state; W.A.C. Bennett, the fervent anti-socialist, nationalized BC Hydro. What is vital at the ideological level is not a specific policy or program but the *rationale* for it.

Philosophic liberals, conservatives, and socialists in Canada, for example, have all embraced medicare. So too have all the federal political parties. Does that make it a non-ideological policy or a non-partisan issue? No. Ideologues in all three philosophic traditions may endorse medicare on the basis of three quite different motivations. A classical or tory conservative underpinning for medicare might be *noblesse oblige*, a sense that society's privileged classes should help underwrite it, via the state. The idea is to maintain the fabric of the entire community, including its desperately needy classes. A liberal may support medicare due to the belief that all individuals require an equal opportunity to prove themselves and get ahead, something tragically impossible if one is stricken by illness. A socialist might embrace medicare because it manifests our care for one another as equal members of a community in solidarity – medicare as an important component of socialist equality of condition. When a policy is cited as an ideological inclination or as evidence of "the end of ideology," be skeptical. Apply an ideological litmus test. Did the governing party nationalize an industry to redistribute wealth (socialism), to help other private industries prosper and profit (classical liberalism), or for the purpose of nation building (possible classical conservatism or toryism)?

Four Generic Approaches

Many paths may be taken in the search for Canadian political culture. There are as many interpretations as there are students. Many approaches, however, are related in their strategies. Four broad rubrics may be used to arbitrarily categorize them. They are not mutually exclusive. Social scientists generally use them in conjunction, even though individual scholars will have their own emphases. No single approach is inherently superior to the others. All offer insights and pose limitations.

The first is to *probe history*. Such an analysis entails reviewing the rise and fall of social forces and political movements. Which succeeded and why? Conversely, which withered and failed, and why? Historic milestones in political development are assessed. One then reads back from the present and explains what Canadians have valued, what Canada represented as a political culture. In brief, it is the study of the tribulations and triumphs of Canada. That some developments (such as repeated Liberal victories at the polls) prevailed over others (Communist, NDP, or Social Credit victories) suggests that certain values, mass beliefs, and sentiments have been more viable and sustainable than others. This is not to say that Canadians are trapped by their pasts any more than they are by their parents, their jobs, or their present circumstances. It merely acknowledges that history – the cumulative experience of the Canadian people to date – conditions contemporary political values and behaviour. History contributes to reading Canadians' current temperaments. Tentatively perhaps, it helps us project what they hope to become as a people.

A second approach is to *survey values* by asking directly about fundamental political beliefs. This strategy permits precision and exactness, whereas wading through historical tomes leaves one with fragmentary evidence and conflicting interpretations. Although the scientific measurement of attitudes is not foreign terrain off limits to historians, most historiography is impressionistic. The writing of history – Canada's is no exception – is driven by the historian's own cultural milieu, agenda, and background.[6] The interpretations, subject matter, and emphases of francophone historians will tend to differ from those of Aboriginal, feminist, or Atlantic Canadian historians. Survey research holds out the attractive prospect of dissociating the observer from the observed. It purports to offer scientific objectivity to counterbalance the historian's humanistic bias in style and subject matter. Of course, surveys and surveyors are also biased, but there is a conscious struggle with method. The survey researcher seeks through constant refinement of technique to overcome problems. Although historical studies have a long pedigree, the survey method is of relatively recent, but mesmerizing, vintage.

A third approach is to *examine constitutions and institutions*. Institutional structures reflect and contribute to moulding political culture. Formal political rules – how they are made, interpreted, and implemented – tell much of a society's values and norms. They are inherited but potentially changeable in the here and now. The language entrenched in fundamental laws generally does not change easily. This is quite unlike the coming and going of political generations, which must live with the laws and structures of their long-deceased predecessors. Some constitutional formulations resonate with the public, their platitudes universally popular (such as "life, liberty, and security" in the Charter of Rights and Freedoms). Other constitutional laws are fictional adornments neither particularly valued, significant, nor popularly known (such as the designation of the governor general as the commander-in-chief of the armed forces). Laws and formal rules are but one part of constitutions and institutions. In and of themselves, they may mislead (for example, does anyone really believe that it is the governor general, rather than the prime minister, who selects the cabinet?). The operative and conventional, rather than theoretically legal, principles of the Constitution are more important (could the prime minister select a cabinet of wholly unelected politicians?). Institutions such as parliaments, political parties, and the federal system are playing fields in which organized politics and policy making unfold. They process inputs, such as public opinion and lobbying efforts, converting them into public policy. In constitutions and institutions, and the debates that swirl around them, we encounter consensual and competing images of Canada.

A fourth approach to understanding political culture is *political socialization*, the learning of politics. Socialization is a lifelong process with discernible agents: the family, church, school, peer groups, media, the Internet, and political actors such as leaders and parties. Personal and social values are inculcated, absorbed, and systematically learned. The venues for socialization are varied: the kitchen table, the pulpit, televised newscasts, classrooms, and so on. Socialization's effects also differ by social group: men, women, the young, the old, the immigrant, the native, and so on. Generally, youth are more receptive, resilient, and radical than the old, who tend to be more fixed, cynical, and cautious.[7] These are tendencies, not absolutes. There are old political revolutionaries and young reactionaries in all societies. Women are generally more responsive than men to social issues and appeals (health care, education, social services); men are generally more receptive than women to military campaigns and radical economic prescriptions (troops and bombing, privatization/nationalization, taxation). Historically, men have been more encouraged to debate and engage in politics, women more encouraged to defer and follow.

The regionalized nature of the Canadian state, society, and economy also has implications from the perspective of socialization. Schooling in Quebec dwells on Quebec's history and underplays national Canadian themes, except where francophone issues are at stake. In Ontario, the curriculum downplays provincial history for broader Canadian history. Schools with large numbers of Aboriginals now give Aboriginal history a pride of place lacking elsewhere. Once, it was suppressed. Environment, geography, and demography contribute to socialization: local newscasts in Vancouver and Toronto are more likely than in St. John's to be anchored by a member of a visible minority and to convey an image of Canada as multicultural. Local newscasts in Newfoundland, almost certainly anchored by white Anglo-Celts, will feature more stories on the fishery. Such regional tendencies are logical. Socialization therefore contributes to instilling and reinforcing regional differences in perceptions and values.

Political culture is multifaceted; its study is many-sided. No one theory explains or accounts for all its facets. The view from one eye or one theory of reality will be dissimilar to that from another eye or theory. Simply adding up what the two eyes or theories see produces a two-dimensional picture, not the three-dimensional depth that theories, working like eyes together, offer. The applications of one approach cast light on another. They are not mutually exclusive, do not add up to a single theory, and should not be reductionist, claiming to explain everything.

Students of political culture are imbued by and immersed in their own culture, although they may strive for neutral, value-free science. They also bring their own disciplinary orientations. Political science, sociology, and economics are prisms through which to see or help make sense of Canadian political culture. One orientation is the macro-ideological "fragment" theory associated with political scientists Louis Hartz and Gad Horowitz. Another is political sociologist Seymour Martin Lipset's focus on formative events and social indicators. Yet another points to the cultural consequences of economic structures. This last orientation is associated with Harold Innis and Marxist academics. All three applications have historical dimensions and are best seen as complementary.

Canada's Fragment Cultures

Hartz argued that New World politics reflected that New World societies were the ideological offshoots of the Old World societies that had founded them. David Bell has likened Hartz's method to a search for a "genetic code," one seeking to identify the implanted ideological genes of a founding people.[8] Although Hartz's idea was not novel, he made it intriguing by inserting two twists. The first was that a narrow slice of the old society's ideological spectrum is transplanted – in the case of his subject, the United States, this was the ascending Lockean liberalism of Britain.[9] At the time, liberalism was eclipsing but still vying with conservatism, or what became labelled in Britain as toryism. From Hartz's perspective, early British North America's liberalism contrasted with New France's conservatism, the cultural spin-off of pre-revolutionary, pre-Enlightenment, pre-liberal France. Similarly, Latin America was a quasi-feudal, conservative Iberian splinter and Australia a fragment of late nineteenth-century radical and increasingly labourist

Britain. South Africa, in this comparative ideological relief, was a dual-fragment culture somewhat like Canada, but its Dutch liberalism and transplanted British socialism were quite unlike British America's liberalism and New France's quasi-feudal conservatism.[10] By "feudal," Hartz referred to an outlook rather than the literal institutions of feudalism. His frame of analysis rested on the chronologically Marxist-ordered triad of feudalism (or classical conservatism), liberalism, and socialism. These were heavily laden terms – Hartz was using "broad terms broadly"[11] – and he explained why he settled on them.

Hartz's three ideological constellations might be distilled into five principles, or elementary components, as plotted in Table 1.1. They refer to classical conservatism and classical liberalism, not their now popular and journalistic definitions. Classical liberalism is what modern-day neo-conservatives (sometimes termed neo-liberals) embrace. Classical conservatism is a fading echo of Europe's past, a view of society still vibrant in some Asian cultures but now quaint in the West. It harks back to the wisdom (or the curse, depending on one's ideology) of the ages. It warns and encourages people to think and behave as their ancestors did. Classical conservatism sees social institutions – family, church, corporation, university, military, government – as hierarchically structured and properly so. Its exponents treasure social order. They fear and loathe chaos, anarchy, and revolution. They see people as innately imperfect, limited, weak. Conservatism's elitism is melded, however, with a collectivist sensibility, so that conservatives will justify the restraint of the individual in the interests of the community as a whole.[12]

Hartz's second twist on ideological-cultural development was dialectical. It connected America's characterization of socialism as "un-American," before and during the Cold War, to the absence and rejection of classical conservatism. American culture had early on congealed a monolithic liberal

TABLE 1.1

Three ideological constellations

Conservatism/toryism	Classical liberalism	Socialism
Tradition	Reason	Reason
Authority (order)	Freedom to have	Freedom from want
Hierarchy	Equality of opportunity	Equality of condition
Priority of community	Priority of the individual	Priority of community
Cooperation	Competition	Co-operation

consensus. This, and only this, became the American way of life. It became America's cultural identity. In Europe, liberalism and then socialism arose in succession in reaction to the older established conservative or feudal ideology. The relationship of these ideologies in Europe was like that of parents and children. Liberalism emerged as the philosophic antithesis of conservatism. It offered reason, logic, and enlightenment. Science and technology could serve and improve man's lot. This countered conservatism's faith in tradition and the ways of old. For the liberal, the state is man's creation and servant, existing to protect the individual, not the reverse. The liberal sees human nature as creative and innovative; man is a good and original being who must be permitted to be master of his fate. His place in society is a function of his skills and wits, not, as stifling conservatism holds, the station in life into which he is born.

Socialism later appeared as a synthesis of and reaction to the two older ideologies. It shared some and rejected other of their principles. Equality and freedom, for example, mean different things to socialists and liberals, yet both claim these as principles. Unlike liberalism, however, socialism also shares some ideological space with classical conservatism. They both view society as an organic, holistic, and ideally a co-operative community. Both see society in terms of classes rather than as an agglomeration of atomistic individuals, as liberals do. However, though conservatives strive for class harmony, socialists agitate for class struggle and want to abolish class distinctions.

Hartz's 1955 book, *The Liberal Tradition in America*, won some of the highest professional awards in its field. His provocative speculations led to his being asked to testify in front of the American Senate's Foreign Relations Committee. He attributed America's nationalistic and reflexively irrational and fierce reaction against socialism at home and abroad to its own unfamiliarity with the feudal or classical conservative outlook. America could not fathom why anyone or any state would turn to socialism, because America had no conservative or feudal heritage itself. Some Marxists dismissed Hartz's formulation as hopelessly idealistic, far removed from the material economic base of society. However, a century earlier, others had reached conclusions that were not inconsistent with the fragment theory. Friedrich Engels noted that the United States, compared to Europe, was "purely bourgeois, so entirely without a feudal past."[13]

In the 1960s, both Gad Horowitz and Kenneth McRae, Hartz's collaborator in his comparative study of fragment cultures, applied Hartz's theory to

Canada. Horowitz was studying at Harvard with Hartz and Samuel Beer, who authored *British Politics in the Collectivist Age*, a book to which Horowitz contributed.[14] To McRae, English Canada was a smaller version of the hegemonic liberal pattern that Hartz identified as pervasive in the United States.[15] Horowitz's formulation of Hartz's dialectic differed from McRae's. He saw English Canada's founding fragment – Loyalists fleeing the American Revolution – as liberals who brought with them significant traces of Britain's lingering conservatism and collectivism. Intellectually provocative, like Hartz, he asserted that the strength of Canadian socialism was attributable and proportional to that of Canadian conservatism.[16] This conceptualization garnered both attention and skepticism. The portrayal of the Loyalists as tory-touched was assessed as imaginative but inaccurate. British toryism itself was dismissed as a spent force by the time of English Canada's founding.[17] Some set out to measure and compare Canada's alleged tory streak with that of the United States and found it lacking.[18] Others chafed at the idea that a political culture congeals, that its future is fatalistically determined at its point of departure from the Old World. A leading textbook in Canadian politics summarily dispensed with Horowitz's thesis as unverifiable.[19] Nevertheless, and oddly, the Hartz-Horowitz formulation – powered by its intellectual verve and the insight of its comparative approach – became something of the conventional wisdom on Canadian political culture. Subsequent editions of the textbook gave it more prominence. In the 1980s, having been in circulation for two decades, the thesis was the subject of an anniversary assessment.[20] Once again, it was found hopelessly flawed and wanting. By the 1990s, a book of essays was constructed around the assumption that Horowitz had peddled "bad history, poor political science."[21] Others concurred.[22]

Yet, Horowitz's interpretation stubbornly persists. One of his fascinating ideas, that of the "red tory," has leapt to the columns of journalists and the lips of politicians themselves. He did not invent the term, but it is impossible to locate it anywhere in the literature on Canadian politics before he floated it in 1966. It appears in *The Language of Canadian Politics: A Guide to Important Terms and Concepts.*[23] It is commonly referred to by the media's political analysts and among partisan denizens. Horowitz's academic critics would tell them that they, like Horowitz, know naught of what they speak. That they speak it, however, is testimony to its resonance in the real world of politics. It reveals the infiltrative power of academic ideas in political discourse.

Horowitz came of age politically in the 1950s and was swept up by Diefenbaker toryism. George Grant's best-selling *Lament for a Nation* and the classical conservative credo in W.L. Morton's *The Canadian Identity* in the 1960s helped Horowitz see the Canadian links between toryism and socialism.[24] The links were confirmed by personalities like Eugene Forsey, the toryish socialist researcher for the Canadian labour movement, the subject of Horowitz's doctoral dissertation.[25] Grant depicted socialism as a variant of conservatism's collectivism. Horowitz's nationalism, and the national question in the 1960s, helped convert him from toryism to socialism, testimony to the symbiotic tory-socialist dynamic he felt was at work in Canadian politics.[26]

A limitation of the fragment theory is its pan-nationalism. It treats national political cultures – in Canada's case, both the English and French varieties – as homogeneous. It stresses their monolithic character. Hartz and Horowitz, as well as their Canadian critics, write of English Canadian political culture as identifiable and coherent, a singular national one. They quarrel over its ideological characterization. The idea of a pan–English Canadian political culture, however, becomes problematic when one confronts the country's diverse regional legacies. If toryism feeds socialism with a complementary collectivist bond that contrasts with liberalism's individualism and competitive ethos, why has English Canadian socialism been strongest in the West, a region in which Loyalists and tories never settled? Conversely, why have the historical conservative regions – the Maritimes and eastern Ontario – been the least receptive to socialism? Where the Hartzian framework is most potent is in the case of Quebec: its once quasi-feudal order, exploded by the liberalism of the Quiet Revolution, quickly ushered in socialist voices by the late 1960s. They synthesized, as Hartz's dialectic required, conservatism's ideology of *la survivance* with liberalism's *rattrapage* to produce an *épanouissement* that promised *dépassage*, a step beyond the older two ideologies.

Canada's Formative Events

Seymour Martin Lipset's interest in Canada is related to his doctoral dissertation at Columbia University. *Agrarian Socialism* was his classic study of the Saskatchewan Co-operative Commonwealth Federation (CCF). It commanded a status at home and abroad that few accounts of any aspect of Canadian politics had attained. Until the 1980s, excerpts from it were reproduced in successive editions of the long-established textbook reader *Party*

Politics in Canada.[27] Before going to Saskatchewan in the mid-1940s for his field research, Lipset, a socialist, "had literally not been more than a few miles west of the Hudson [River]."[28] His point of departure is revealed in the title of his first chapter, "The Background to Agrarian Radicalism." A title such as "The Background to Canadian Socialism" would have revealed more of the phenomenon's British immigrant and labour-union urban character. His reference points were American: that first chapter has exclusive American citations on American agrarian politics but no documentary sources from Canada or Britain, although Lipset was certainly not oblivious to the British labour and socialist influences on the CCF, as other parts of his book attest. Canadian agrarian radicalism was presented as a small-scale version of American agrarian radicalism. What Lipset overlooked were the contrasts between Saskatchewan's brand of agrarian politics and those of the other provinces. Why, while Saskatchewan elected left-wing CCF governments, did Alberta simultaneously elect increasingly right-wing Social Credit regimes? Why was Manitoba governed for nearly four decades by an amorphous coalition of Liberals, Conservatives, Progressives, and others, while Saskatchewan opted for a polarized and competitive left-right party system?

Lipset, like Hartz and Horowitz, attached significance to cultural and ideological origins. He also perceived a connection between social democracy and statist conservatism. In many of his comparative studies of American and Canadian political cultures, Lipset pointed to their common defining founding moment, or formative event: the American Revolution. Like Horowitz, Lipset saw the Loyalists and Canada as representing the conservative counter-revolution to America's revolutionary liberalism.[29] Lipset spread his net to reach well beyond the macro-ideological to the macro-sociological. Using dimensions of polarity taken from Talcott Parsons, Lipset employed an impressive assembly of statistical indicators and other qualitative measurements through which to compare the United States and Canada. He concluded, on the basis of broad surveys of history, literature, economic and religious traditions, and other data, that Canada's value system was more elitist and less egalitarian than that of the US. Canada was more oriented to ascription and less to achievement than was America. Canada, by original design and the citizenry's temperament, would be more deferential to state and ecclesiastical authority. It would be more hierarchical and more particularistic; that is, it would tend to treat people more as group members and in terms of the position they held than as individuals subject to common community-wide standards.

Expanding his comparative ken, Lipset ranked Canada and Australia as falling between the United States and Britain.[30] The Canadian political tradition or value system was deemed more liberal than Britain's but more conservative than that of the United States. Others echoed this assessment.[31] Lipset reaffirmed his appraisal in the 1990s but noted the liberalizing, egalitarian implications of the Charter of Rights.[32] He remarked that "Canadians are more elitist, law-abiding, statist, collectivity oriented and group oriented than Americans."[33] Canadian literature, relatively, has focused on community survival, American literature on personal independence and freedom. Canadians have been more likely to belong to hierarchical churches (Catholic, Anglican); Americans have been more likely to affiliate with egalitarian, fundamentalist ones. Canada has had lower crime rates, higher levels of unionization, more corporate concentration, and more public enterprise. Canadians have been less cynical about their governments, more likely to vote, less likely to participate in riots and protest demonstrations, more likely to trust their police forces, and less concerned with civil liberties. They have also been less likely to insist that new immigrants assimilate. Canada was defined more as a mosaic than a melting pot. Canada's Constitution enshrines group rights (language, religious, multicultural, Aboriginal), but that of the United States shuns them. Such differences suggest that tory and socialist influences are stronger in Canada than in the United States.

A limitation of Lipset's macro-sociological comparisons is that they are national. His early pan-Canadian comparisons lumped English and French Canada together. He later adjusted for this bi-national cleavage (Hartz's dual fragments), but this begs other cross-provincial comparisons in values and behaviour. If founding moments are pivotal determinants of political culture, what was the relevance of the American Revolution to the Canadian prairies, settled more than a century afterward, or to Quebec, settled nearly a century before? An enlightening use of the formative event idea is to apply it within Canada. The founding moments of the provinces differ radically in their prevailing ideological currents. Although Ontario's formative event was the American Revolution, the province is not synonymous with Canada as a whole. In Quebec, the Conquest was the momentous event. In Alberta and Newfoundland – two provinces that Loyalists did not settle – it was something else again.

Formative events may act as casts for political cultures, but casts are subject to stress, assault, and modification. Sometimes they crack. Quebec's Quiet Revolution in the 1960s amply demonstrated that. Thus, the idea of

TABLE 1.2

Formative events and quakes

Province(s)	Formative events/ founding moments	Quakes
Newfoundland	Confederation debates 1860s, 1940s	Commission government 1934-49
Maritime	Acadians expelled 1755	American Revolution 1780s Responsible government 1848
Quebec	The Conquest 1760	1837 rebellion Quiet Revolution 1960
Ontario	American Revolution 1780s	War of 1812 1837 + resp. govt. 1848
Manitoba	Riel and CPR 1870s	Winnipeg General Strike 1919
Saskatchewan	Riel and CPR 1880s	Depression 1930s
Alberta	"Last best West" 1896	Oil 1947
British Columbia	CPR and Panama Canal 1885 and 1914	Social Credit 1952

the formative event might be augmented with that of "quakes." America's "quake" is its Civil War, a monumental tremor, and a landmark throwing a shadow on the future. Quakes in provincial and regional histories vary too. Table 1.2 suggests such formative events and quakes. Pursuing them requires analyzing Canada's political culture upward, from inside its regions or components. Perhaps the assumption of a national or English Canadian culture is unwarranted. Each province might be seen as a separate and small political world in its own right.[34]

Staples and Class
Throughout most of the twentieth century, the study of politics, economics, and sociology fell under the unifying disciplinary rubric of political economy. Many Canadian universities had such departments; the University of Toronto's was the most prominent. The centrifugal impact of disciplinary specialization led first to the spin-off of sociology and then the parting of

political science and economics. The political economy tradition in the United States is different, consistent with the country's own ideological underpinnings. It came to mean rational choice or public choice theory.[35] Imported from micro-economic theory, its key assumption is ahistorical and ideological. It takes a spare, unvarying, and individualistic view of human nature. In its cosmology, values or choices are driven by people's unflinching desire to maximize personal goals.[36] There is little room here for cultural origins and collective pasts.

The Canadian political economy tradition was best expressed in the 1930s in a nine-volume series, *Frontiers of Settlement*. In this tradition, Harold Innis – chairperson of the University of Toronto political economy department – and others became associated with the "staples" approach. Like Hartz's fragment and Lipset's formative events theories, the staples approach is historical, hinged to Canada's colonial legacy and status. It highlights Canada's development as the successive exploitation of raw natural resources, or staples, extracted from sea or land. The pattern and pace of Canada's growth was dictated by external demand and control. From this perspective, Canada has been a resource hinterland and cultural backwater to the metropolitan economies and cultures in Europe and the United States. Canada's businesses and labouring classes are at the colonial frontier, the margin or periphery of imperial economies. One line of analysis among the theorists who followed Innis is that not only do the metropolitan centres abroad retard Canadian economic development but also, in turn, core regions within Canada (Ontario, Quebec) underdevelop the outer Canadian regions (Atlantic Canada, the West).[37] A staple theory of economic growth was also developed, which pointed to the backward and forward linkages of staples and their spread effects.[38] Today, by historic standards, relatively few people work as fishers in Newfoundland or on the farms of Saskatchewan. Ontario's cash farm receipts exceeded those of any other province in the 1990s, yet only 3 percent of Ontarians laboured in the primary sector.[39] Nevertheless, if the demand for Canada's staples shrivels, the fallout goes far beyond those working in the sector. There is a multiplier effect: the secondary and tertiary industries that supply and service staples development – transportation networks, financial institutions, construction, manufacturing, refining, and so on – are affected too. Innis' focus was economic, but he noted cultural origins and their implications for staples development.[40] The underlying theme of his *History of the Canadian Pacific Railway* was the spread of Western culture and civilization.

Innis was not a radical, and certainly no socialist or political activist. Frank Underhill described him as one of the "garage mechanics" of Canadian capitalism.[41] For Marxists, political culture reflects the interplay of economic forces that envelop them. From this vantage point, the inputs of production – capital and labour – and the staples to which they are applied shape power relations and political consciousness or culture. Marxist scholars developed an interest in Innis' ideas, for he cast light on the mode of ideological production and reproduction, on the classes that sustained it, and on the character of media and communications. He is seen as a precursor of communications guru Marshall McLuhan.

From a Marxist perspective, the challenge is to account for the embrace by subordinate labouring classes of values and beliefs that serve not their interests but those of the dominant capitalist classes. To do so, Marxists use the notion of false consciousness. This is traced by some to socialization – media and propaganda, for example – that helps to perpetuate the economic elite's self-serving ideology. Marx saw workers as living the ideology of the capitalist wage labour market in their day-to-day lives. Many reasonably perceive a connection between their personal experiences and the principles upholding the dominant ideology. Thus, Atlantic fishers may subscribe to an individualistic ideology that is based in their individual ownership of boat and gear. Alternatively, they may have a historical memory of such, even though they are employees or deeply in debt and not real or effective entrepreneurs. Fishers and farmers differ greatly from each other. There are also stark regional variations in the types of fishing and farming. Maritime farmers have tended to be subsistence farmers, whereas those in the Western grain trade have been commercial farmers. The former have been less dependent on bankers, transport firms, merchants, and others who were identified as large common exploiters. Whereas Western farmers looked to co-operatives as alternative economic structures, Maritime farmers had less need for co-operatives, tended to spurn them, and were less affected by the volatile cycles in international commodity markets.[42] Political consciousness and values, and the political behaviour they engender, are also influenced by the type and conditions of subordinated labour. Diverse fractions – from small independent commodity producers to merchants, to large commercial, financial, and established landed interests – exist within the broad capitalist class. Such differences occur within the labouring classes as well – as much between well-paid union members and unorganized, less secure labourers as between wage labourers, commissioned employees, and piecemeal workers.

TABLE 1.3

Staples development by approximate period and region

Staples	Period	Province/region
1. Fish	18th-19th centuries	Atlantic Canada
2. Fur	18th-19th centuries	Quebec
3. Forests	19th century 20th century	Central + Atlantic Canada British Columbia
4. Farms	Early 20th century	Prairies
5. Fuels/minerals	Late 19th and 20th centuries Late 20th century	Northern Ontario + Quebec Alberta + British Columbia

From a fused Innisian-Marxist angle, differences in regional economic structures are the driving differences in regional political cultures. Staples and class development vary chronologically and regionally. Different eras had different reigning ideologies, and the regionally concentrated staples economies have had differential cultural consequences for class-consciousness. Table 1.3 broadly approximates the formative exploitation of staples and the regions and provinces most affected.

Synthesizing Applications: The Prism of Immigration

A way of melding fragment, formative events, and staples-class applications is through the prism of immigration. Successive and relatively discrete waves of immigration have occurred throughout Canadian history. Their backdrop is the Canadian culture that received them and the older societies that socialized them. "Canada," goes the adage, "is a country of immigrants." If so, it is a country of immigrants' ideas and experiences. There have always been regional variations in immigrant settlement. If formative events are critical to political culture, the varied concentrations of immigrants must be assessed and compared. Cross-national comparative cultural analyses fudge regional variations; their primary interest is to characterize a dominant cultural ethos or national outlook. Immigrants were once imported expressly to work in the staples industries, but they represented more than mere raw labour: they carried ideological-cultural baggage from their homelands. They were *pushed* out of their older societies by economic hardship and social turmoil. They were *pulled* into a newer Canadian society by the liberal promise of opportunity and relative freedom. Ideology and class migrated together. Immigrants helped to throw up differing political cultural traditions in various provinces.

Five distinct immigrant waves and broad periods of immigration have occurred in Canada. They require sub-national or provincial attention. For example, Loyalism's hierarchical, elitist, and ascriptive preferences for social order, stability, and continuity have been used to contrast Canada's political culture to that of the United States. These conservative hallmarks once rang true in Ontario and still resonate in Atlantic Canada, but they never have in the West. Moreover, the new polyethnic and multiracial social order of metropolitan Ontario seems far from exhibiting the characteristics of tory orderliness and deference to authority associated with the Loyalists. A remarkably diverse non-immigrant ethnic group has also arisen to political prominence in recent decades: Aboriginals. Their ideas once counted for naught in politics; they were disenfranchised from the legal and political systems until the 1950s and 1960s. Similarly, the Chinese in Western Canada, imported to build a staples conveyor belt – the CPR – had, like Aboriginals, low political status. Irish immigrants had fulfilled a similar infrastructure function earlier in the nineteenth century, building central Canada's canals and railways.[43]

The five immigrant waves identified in Table 1.4 shaped Canadian political culture generally and provincial political cultures more specifically. The first and oldest, from pre-revolutionary France, was transplanted to New France and Acadia. Those in this fragment represented, as Hartz suggested, quasi-feudal conservatism. Yet, they were also the pioneers, as Innis documented, in the more entrepreneurial fur staple. The Conquest, Quebec's formative event, reinforced French Canada's classical conservatism: a pre-Enlightenment Catholic clergy filled the vacuum of a decapitated middle-class lay leadership. Fewer than ten thousand French immigrants settled before 1759, but they had multiplied to over seven million French Canadians by the end of the twentieth century. Many others migrated in turn, becoming Franco-Americans. French Canada's reigning conservative ideology cracked only in the quake of the Quiet Revolution, two centuries after the Conquest. The contradiction between the subsistence agriculturalism of the nineteenth-century *habitant* and the industrial modernization led on its irrepressible march by anglophone Canadian and American corporations was not sustainable.

The second immigrant wave, the Loyalists, was expelled by America's liberal revolution.[44] They swelled Nova Scotia with nearly thirty thousand new settlers, and established New Brunswick. About ten thousand other Loyalists anchored what is now Ontario. Although these were fewer in number than in the Maritimes, their impact was greater because Ontario had no existing settlers as did Nova Scotia. Loyalists became English Canada's economic

Table 1.4

Immigrant waves by period, region, and orientation

Immigrant waves	Period	Primary region	Dominant orientations
France	To 1760	Quebec/Acadia	Quasi-feudal conservative
Loyalist	1780s	Maritimes/ Ontario	Tory-touched liberal
Britain	1815-51	Ontario/ Maritimes	Reform liberal
Britain/US/ Continental Europe	1890s-1920s	West/ Ontario	a) Labour-socialist b) Populist-liberal c) Deferential
Asia/Southern Europe Caribbean Latin America	1945-	Metro Canada	Individual/equality rights

and political elite. Politically tory, and Tory, they were relatively liberal compared to French Quebec's ideological leadership.

A half century after the Loyalist influx, coinciding with the growth of British reform liberalism, an even larger, third immigrant wave appeared. Between the end of the Napoleonic wars and 1851, the population of what became Ontario increased tenfold, from fewer than a hundred thousand residents to nearly a million.[45] Composed largely of labourers and artisans – few of them were middle class – this wave, more liberal than the Loyalists, reflected Whig and Reform ascendancy in Britain. These immigrants demanded and secured responsible government in the Maritimes and the Province of Canada in 1848. Their liberalism modified the authoritarianism of the Family Compact's political order. This wave had a greater impact in Ontario than in the Maritimes because embryonic Ontario was, relatively, a frontier society. Thus, Upper Canada's liberal reform rebellion of 1837 was led by a Scottish immigrant who arrived in 1820 to seek his fortune in the New World: William Lyon Mackenzie. That same year, future Tory leader John A. Macdonald emigrated too.

The fourth immigrant wave, at the turn of the twentieth century, was more diverse than the other three. It was composed of three overlapping ripples. The largest, from the mother country, reflected Britain's emerging labour-socialist politics. Many of these immigrants were British liberals, some more tory than others. Most were city-bred labouring folk; many of them were receptive to the new egalitarian and distributional promises of socialism.

Their greatest impact was in the sparsely settled West, where the wheat economy was burgeoning. Some settled in urban Ontario, fewer still in the Maritimes. Some British miners went directly into Cape Breton's mines, established a labour party, and launched labour wars there in the 1920s. By far, however, the new British impact was greatest on the new shifting frontier: the West. The radical British outlook was reflected in the leadership and personnel of numerous nascent Labour Parties and the CCF. These parties proved strongest and most resilient where institutions were rudimentary. The prairie population grew from about 100,000 in 1881 to 2 million in 1921, and that of British Columbia tripled in half that time.

A second, relatively small but regionally influential ripple in this fourth wave was a populist-liberal American one, flowing northwest from the American Great Plains. In 1911, nearly a quarter of all Albertans were Americans. Their dominance in rural areas dictated the shape of provincial politics. Their American plebiscitarian-democratic instincts were devoid of toryism, and though this outlook attracted some socialists, it rejected socialism itself. This populist strain, moving steadily to the right over the years, came to be expressed in a long string of unorthodox (by Eastern Canadian standards) parties: the Non-Partisan League, the United Farmers of Alberta (UFA), the Progressives, Social Credit, and the Reform Party.

The third and last ripple in this fourth wave was a diverse lot of continental Europeans: Ukrainians, Germans, Poles, Jews, Scandinavians, and others. They were not ideologically influential because their origins and outlooks were mixed and their languages foreign. In social status, Scandinavians were below those of British ethnic origins but above the others. In order to avoid suspicion and gain acceptance, the Europeans deferred ideologically. By the time the first generation learned English, it had bred a second generation that assimilated some of the prevailing Canadian values. As they acculturated, they came to the fore politically. In the early 1990s, for example, for the first time, none of the four Western premiers was of exclusively British ethnic origin.

The fifth immigrant wave comes from Southern Europe, Asia, the Caribbean, and Latin America, as well as from the more traditional sources. It is the most socially and ideologically variegated. Coming since the Second World War, it has been overwhelmingly urban and metropolitan, drawn especially to the largest centres and labouring in the post-staples economy. Many of the visible minorities in the fifth wave already speak English or French before they arrive in Canada, unlike the continental Europeans of the fourth and fifth waves. Those from Hong Kong and most from the Caribbean (the former British West Indies) tend to settle in metropolitan English Canada; many from Haiti, the former French Middle East, and Vietnam gravitate to Montreal. We may differentiate between two broad ripples within this broadest of waves. The Southern Europeans – Italians, Greeks, and Portuguese – arrived somewhat before and became better established than the Asians and those from the Caribbean and Latin America. More visible, multicultural, and multiracial than the other waves, this wave is loosely tied together in its stake in a recent ideological emblem: the Canadian Charter of Rights and Freedoms. Although this wave's numbers are large, its ideological and political impact is weak. The national and provincial political cultures are now too established to be overwhelmed by a new wave but are nonetheless influenced by it, as they in turn influence it. This wave has not created new political parties, preferring to attain status within the established ones; right wing and left wing, liberal, socialist, and conservative, this wave is the most motley.

Political culture has many facets. Cultural preferences exist. By themselves, however, they do not cause anything. Values generate preferences for certain types of political institutions. Institutions, in turn, help to shape values. The social sciences offer a variety of strategies to study political culture. Four broad approaches that overlap and have been used by political scientists are historical analysis, opinion survey research, constitutional and institutional studies, and political socialization.

Three specific applications that have garnered attention in placing Canadian political values in historical focus are the fragmentation and interaction of ideological currents, the formative events, or founding moments, in the country's regions, and the cultural implications of economic structures such as staples and class. Synthesizing these approaches is methodologically challenging and messy. But the approaches are mutually reinforcing rather than contradictory because each one, though emphasizing its own orientation, incorporates and does not preclude elements of the other two. The resulting synthetic interpretation of Canadian political culture is exploratory and, like much political history, impressionistic. It is suggestive rather than compelling or methodologically clear and precise.

2
Surveying and Comparing Political Cultures

Numbers are enticing. Offering precision, they facilitate comparison and gauge. They are handmaidens to progress and refinement in technique. In the twentieth century, students of political culture embraced sophisticated quantitative methods in their research designs. This movement complemented normative and impressionistic treatments with a plethora of empirical data. It reflected a mood change in political *science*. "Hard," precise data would complement and challenge "soft," lumpy data. As the physical and biological sciences consciously strove to formulate laws of interaction, so too did the imitative social sciences. The "behavioural persuasion" in politics came to the fore.[1] At the end of the century, however, no law of political behaviour could be pointed to as the product of quantitative analysis.

Politics and the media, more than ever, are driven by surveys. The media are awash with them. Political parties use them to mould their images and shape their campaigns. Pollsters and governments claim that surveys put them in touch with popular needs and wants, thus making government more responsive and democratic.[2] Interest groups use surveys to buttress their lobbying efforts. Corporations employ them for commercial market research. Courts, in a sharp break from their previous practice, now admit survey research that purports to report on community conditions and norms. Academics use surveys in sundry ways and more than ever. Some students of political culture look to surveys to directly tap people's fundamental political belief systems. Surveys are ubiquitous in Canadian politics and their study. Have they offered a deepened understanding of Canadian political culture? As surveys of opinions have proliferated, their value is increasingly questioned and denigrated. Skepticism regarding them is evidenced by respondents' higher rates of refusal to participate. As survey researchers inform us that the public has become increasingly cynical and distrustful of politicians and politics, the public has become increasingly cynical and skeptical about the purpose, sponsorship, and design of surveys.

Survey methodology represents a major advance in research design intended to probe political culture. Historical evidence leads us to infer values. Survey research leads to the rewriting or ignoring of history. It prompts us to process values directly rather than to deduce them. Surveys of opinions, values, and dispositions permit systematic search for and measurement of characteristics that mark off one group from another. Hence the lure of the survey technique. Individual-level data are the building blocks of surveys. They permit analyzing how, for example, women, farmers, or self-identified "leftists" think and behave, something that aggregated behavioural data – such as the raw results of an election – cannot. The movement to surveying political attitudes is the logical extension of commercial market survey research, which established its efficacy in the United States in the first half of the twentieth century. The logic is that just as attitudes toward brands of soap can be estimated by surveys, so too can they be in the political marketplace.

A challenge in political research is the work of separating the observer's values from those of the observed. The background, milieu, and agenda of the historian, sociologist, and political scientist influence the writing of history and the study of sociology and politics. That is also the case in the design of the public opinion survey. The questions asked impose a particular theoretical framework and particular assumptions. The lurking danger is that the survey researcher's interest in discovering respondents' values is subverted by the words that the survey instrument puts in their mouths. This problem is embedded in the nature of language itself and is inherent in survey technology. Language and context are not neutral. Survey analysis may misrecognize, if not misrepresent, other ways of looking at the political world. The survey questionnaire unavoidably translates and imperfectly interprets what the researcher is seeking to analyze. Asking whether religion is important to a respondent may appear to be a value-free and neutral query in some societies at some times; it is not in other societies at other times. It was not in Canada a century ago, when religious cleavages drove politics. Today, asking an Albertan about her preferred language at work may appear to her as a politically impartial question. It may not when asked of a Québécoise. The survey's architecture and field workers are infected by presupposition. So are respondents. Bilingual anglophones canvassing *pure laine* Québécois on issues of sovereignty elicit different results than do unilingual francophones conducting the interview. White male respondents may not be forthcoming or truthful in telling a female or a visible minority interviewer what they think of affirmative action programs to aid women and minorities.

There are many pitfalls in leaping from what people say to concluding what they actually think and, ultimately more importantly for students of politics, to what they do or how they behave. The efficaciousness of a survey may be marred by, among other things, its wording, question sequencing, timing, the effects of transitory political events, and a social desirability bias. That is, responses are skewed to what is deemed socially acceptable or proper behaviour. Surveys exploring political culture are interested in what people think, feel, and value because these serve as guides to political behaviour. Behaviour, however, is more accurately gauged than are values, opinions, or intentions.[3] Consider voter turnout. Every survey conducted by academics in the Canada Election Studies since 1965 has produced a gap, sometimes yawning, between reported participation in the political process and actual participation. Soon after the 1974 federal election, 80 percent of surveyed Newfoundlanders insisted that they had cast ballots. Only 57 percent had actually done so.[4] In the 1997 election, 82 percent of surveyed Canadians reported having voted. The chief electoral officer reported 67 percent. If reported behaviour is suspect, still less reliable are reported feelings, attitudes, and values. Discrepancies between reported and ascertainable realities therefore shake confidence in the survey technique when it is used to measure values. The most commonly cited methodological consideration is the survey's margin of sampling error, but it is usually the smallest source of error in a survey. It is not particularly pertinent to explaining the discrepancies between one's reported behaviour or values and one's actual behaviour or values. The limitations of the survey instrument are better appreciated by survey researchers than by others.

The Psychocultural Approach

The survey method of studying political culture is psychocultural, assigning to the mass culture the findings of individual-level data. This is problematic: Is Canadian political culture identical with the opinions of a majority of Canadians? Is it a statistical average? What if half the sample subscribes strongly to what a survey researcher defines as a collectivist set of beliefs but the other half equally strongly subscribes to an individualist set? Are we to conclude that a polarized political culture is absent because the cumulative data produce an average or mid-point between these two opposing belief systems? Can survey questions measure and fix anyone's values as individualist or

collectivist or anything else? The differences between individualism and collectivism are not illusory, but each implies and needs the other. Individual-
ists rely on collective authority to enforce individuals' contracts. Collectivists
require the energy of individualism to avoid stagnation. Collectivists may
embrace the collectivist path as the road to the individual's liberation and
dignity. Surveys presuppose choice, but the options are not often as separate
as supposed. Quantitative analyses purporting to capture and depict political culture are plagued by such issues. What is actually being measured, and
what, if anything, does it really mean?

The psychocultural interpretive tradition is a logical extension of Freud-
ianism and its insights a century ago: libido and psychological states are
related to the human propensity for war, conflict, and politics. The fall of the
Weimar Republic and the grotesque barbarity of the Nazis undermined both
Enlightenment theories of individual rationality and Marxist theories of class
rationality. Germany had a relatively educated, enlightened, and civilized
society. Its advanced capitalist economy boasted a well-organized working
class and the world's largest social democratic party. Then followed fascist
totalitarianism rather than a liberal or socialist democracy. Why? A host of
psychocultural studies interpreted the German "problem," contrasting and
comparing it to the politics of the United States, Japan, Russia, Britain, and
France. The analyzed variables were family structures, childhood socialization,
and subconscious processes. From these vantage points, the German patriarchal and authoritarian family was depicted as an explosive cocktail of servil-
ity, obedience, and hostility that produced an ethnocentric, anti-Semitic
nationalism. Such approaches ignored or downplayed political history and
the autonomous cognitive processes of adulthood. This approach to political culture, with its implicit reductionism, collapsed under the weight of
subsequent experience: it could not account for Germany's post-war democratic order.[5]

Canada was spared such political psychocultural treatment at the mass
level until the 1960s. The Canadian political science fraternity was steeped in
the institutional and constitutional analyses of British political science until
well into that decade. This meant highlighting Canada's British legacy, transplanted and reflected in the Westminster model of cabinet-parliamentary
government. The behavioural revolution in Canadian political science – concerned with the human conduct of politics rather than the mechanics and
processes of formal governmental structures – came, as so much else, by way
of the United States and at a later date.[6] Until the 1960s, Canadians who

went abroad to study politics tended to do so in Britain; afterward they were more likely to go to the United States. American voting studies based on surveys influenced Canadian political science in a psychocultural direction. They focused on what voters thought about politics rather than on their socio-economic conditions. The Canadian Election Studies, conducted by non-partisan academics, peer reviewed, and funded by public research granting agencies, counted among its initial architects Philip E. Converse, a member of the University of Michigan's pioneering survey research school.[7]

A celebrated breakthrough in political culture research was *The Civic Culture*, a cross-national survey of political attitudes in the United States, Britain, Germany, Italy, and Mexico.[8] Undertaken in 1959, it was published in 1963. The American authors, Gabriel Almond and Sidney Verba, were of course influenced by the biases of their own culture and the issues of their times. They examined what people knew of (cognition), felt about (affection), and judged regarding (evaluation) their political system and their proper role in it. One criticism of this approach is that it cannot account for changes over time. Values may be relatively stable but they are not static or immutable. They do change, however slowly, over time. In the aftermath of the Second World War and in the midst of the Cold War, American political science focused on conditions conducive to democratic stability and citizenship. America's triumphal war effort engendered rejoicing among Americans – social scientists and others alike – in their political and social system. Given this, American social scientists naturally wondered why some societies sustained, but others shunned, democratic government and politics. When Canadian social scientists adopted the survey orientation, this logically led to two kinds of investigation: examining and comparing political cultures without and within the country.

Comparing Canada from Without

S.M. Lipset depicted Canada as more hierarchical, particularist, and collectivist than the United States in its origins and institutions. This pointed to a people more likely to yield and submit to their betters and to those in power. Another American, Edgar Z. Friedenberg, pursued this theme of deference to authority a decade after the peacetime imposition of the War Measures Act and before the entrenchment of the Charter of Rights and Freedoms in the Constitution.[9] Deference to authority is consistent with Canada's characterization in America's popular imagination. By the 1990s, a contending thesis emerged in the work of expatriate Briton Neil Nevitte, labouring at a Canadian university as did Friedenberg. His theme was the decline of deference.[10] This is consistent with Canada's characterization in the British popular imagination. Friedenberg's book is devoid of surveys; Nevitte's is replete with them. That all three of these authors were born abroad, in the US or Britain, reminds us that Canadians are best understood in the twentieth century as living in a North Atlantic triangle.[11] They continue to reflect it in their spelling, dialects, and political institutions – particular mixtures and adaptations of British and American usage. An astute historian saw Canadian party politics as exhibiting the constant interplay of North American environment and British inheritance.[12]

Comparisons of two countries do not offer the benchmarks that are generated by multi-country comparisons. When comparing two cases according to any measure of data, one can conclude only that one case is "more" and the other "less." Neither case can be an outlier. It may be that they share similarities, that the differences between them are not as great as the differences between them collectively and those of a broader set of states. Comparing Canada and the US as distinctive singular cultures glosses over the glaring bilingual cleavage in Canada. Three-sided studies, in which francophone and anglophone Canadian attitudes are compared with each other and with American attitudes, reveal more. Language is the foundation of distinctive culture. Certainly, in some manifestations of popular culture – television, cinema, music, and some of the performing arts – anglophone Canadians and Americans share some touchstones relatively foreign to francophones.

Liberty and Equality

Freedom and equality are abstract but potent principles. What do anglophone and francophone Canadians think about them, and how do their attitudes compare to those of Americans? The age of democracy champions the principles of liberty and equality. Democratic order nurtures and extols them; pre- and non-democratic orders are menaced by them. Place names attest to America's historic embrace of liberty and Canada's relative reticence: twelve American states have towns or cities called Liberty. Another has a Libertyville, two have a Liberty Hill, and one a Liberty Reservoir. Canada has but Liberty, Saskatchewan.[13] Many American cities, but few Canadian ones, boast a Liberty Street.

On a scale with liberty at one pole and order at the other, the attitudes of anglophone Canadians are situated between those of Americans and

TABLE 2.1

Liberty, order, and equality: Canadian and American views

	Canadians			
	Francophones	Anglophones	All	Americans
1. "It is better to live in an orderly society than to allow people so much freedom they can become disruptive" (% agreeing)	77	61	65	51
2. "The idea that everyone has a right to their own opinion is being carried too far these days" (% agreeing)	45	33	37	19
3. "Too much liberalism has been producing increasingly wide differences in people's economic and social life. People should live more equally" (% agreeing)			41	32
4. "Certainly both freedom and equality are important, but if I were to make up my mind for one of the two, I would consider equality more important, that is, that nobody is underprivileged and that class differences are not too strong" (% agreeing)	38	29		20

SOURCE: Based on data reported in Stephen Brooks, *Canadian Democracy*, 4th ed. (Don Mills, ON: Oxford University Press, 2004), 52, 58.

francophone Canadians. Taking the survey responses to the questions in Table 2.1 at face value makes Americans appear collectively as more oriented to freedom than are Canadians. Conversely, more Canadians are oriented to order or authority than are their neighbours. Among Canadians, more francophones prefer order than do anglophones. The gulf between Americans and francophone Canadians on the prposition "It is better to live in an orderly society than to allow people so much freedom that they can be disruptive" is 26 percent. Is this a difference in degree – 51 percent compared to 77 percent – or one of sharp contrast? Is the difference partially a product of contextualizing meaning? The phrase "orderly society" may signify different things in

different languages. It may mean different things in the same language when
used in different countries. It may elicit different responses a day before and
a day after a terrorist attack.

In a democratic society, equality is the companion of liberty. A comparison of Canadians' opinions regarding equality with those of Americans shows
that here the survey findings are the inverse of those dealing with liberty.
Proportionately, more Canadians than Americans are supportive of distributional equality or equality of outcome (a social democratic or left liberal
principle). More Americans than Canadians are committed to meritocratic
competition or equality of opportunity (a classical liberal and now neo-
conservative principle). On the whole, Canadians appear more collectivist and
Americans more individualist when their preferences are compared. Once
again, anglophone Canadians are positioned somewhere between Americans
and francophone Canadians. The latter are the most concerned with class differences; the Americans are the most concerned with freedom. Even if the differences are seen as ones of degree, they are more than nuanced.

What do such differences reflect and what to they portend? They are culturally and institutionally consistent with Canadian and American origins.
America's liberal revolutionary past is bound together with its celebration of
individualism. Canada's pre-revolutionary French and counter-revolutionary
British pasts were relatively conservative, especially so in pre-liberal New France
and its fountainhead, the ancien régime. As modernization and the global
homogenization and bombardment of cultures proceeds, it is reasonable to
anticipate convergence in cross-national values. Significant differences stubbornly persist, however. Consciousness of globalization's pervasiveness feeds
conscious cultural resistance to it. This suggests continuing distinctive political cultures: American and Canadian and, within Canada, English Canadian and French Canadian. Among francophones, there are further differences
between those living in and outside Quebec. This was demonstrated during
Canada's constitutional dramas of the 1980s and 1990s. They are testimony
to the contradictions embedded in the Canadian political culture. Consider
the Canada clause in the Charlottetown Accord: an affirmation of the Charter of Rights and Freedoms sitting alongside a "distinct society" provision for
Quebec, Aboriginal rights, and assertions of the equality of individuals, provinces, two languages, and other groups. Trying to synthesize and bundle these
declarations into a single constitutional expression of Canadian identity fed
the tensions between them rather than mediating or resolving them. The

political elites discovered this at their expense. A referendum, like a survey, can determine if people agree or disagree, but it is a poor measure of their values or culture.

Left and Right

Categorizing political ideas in terms of "left" and "right" is another explicit and broad ideological approach to fathoming political culture. Such categorizations are convenient shorthand labels for conflicting belief systems. They are widely used, perhaps because they have simple and easily grasped spatial and visual dimensions. The terms "ideology," "left," and "right" all trace their origins to the French Revolution. The "ideologists" thought that a science of ideas could be pursued, as in the natural sciences.[14] Left and right initially referred to the seating arrangements in France's revolutionary parliament, with nobility on the left and clergy on the right.[15] The dichotomy evolved to be related to other groups and socio-economic classes, as well as the policy orientations identified with their interests. Right and left came to signify the ideological interests of society's haves and have-nots. On the political spectrum, the right now represents the concerns of the propertied, the established, the privileged, the wealthy. The left is associated with the landless, the less privileged, the downtrodden, the poor. For Marxists, the right controls the levers of capital, whereas workers who labour for capitalists are the left's natural constituency.

In democratic discourse, both the left and the right claim to further freedom and equality. Left and right perceptions of those principles, however, contrast. The right values negative liberty. It prescribes minimal government intrusion in the affairs of individuals. Contemporary rightists look at government as an expensive, obtruding, but necessary evil. The right sees markets as promoting the common good; in contrast, the left places its faith in the initiatives of government and collective planning. Leftists value positive liberty by way of activist government, so that bridled individuals and groups are liberated from oppressive conditions. Rightists prize freedom to accumulate; leftists pursue freedom from restraints such as illiteracy, hunger, and homelessness. Without shelter, health care, and adequate nutrition, contend leftists, what kind of liberty is there but the cruel freedom to suffer? Rightists decry dependence on governments as undermining personal dignity; leftists espouse wielding the instrumentality of government to secure dignity for all. Against the backdrop of changing working conditions in nineteenth-century

European industrial capitalism, Marxism crystallized the right-left divide into the struggle between capital and labour, between parasitic bosses and exploited wage labourers. In the latter part of the twentieth century, socialists came to see class as being lived as race, gender, ethnicity, and even sexual orientation. Leftists came to identify with social movements and "equity-seeking" groups. They pursue affirmative action initiatives, but rightists resist them as infringements of individual equality. Some other policy distinctions historically associated with the left-right divide revolve around minimum wages and cutting taxes, nationalization and privatization, regulation and deregulation, foreign aid and defence spending, environmental quality and economic growth, deficit financing and debt elimination. In all these simplistic pairings, the left is generally associated with the former, the right with the latter.

More significant from an ideological perspective, however, is not the policy choice but its underlying rationale, its philosophical underpinning. Are taxes being cut to spur private investment and return, or are they being progressively reduced to alleviate the burden of the poor? Rightists and leftists may both agree on a policy option, such as nationalizing or privatizing a utility, for fundamentally different reasons. The same, as we have seen, may be said of conservatives, liberals, and socialists. Those ideological constellations may be crosscut by a left-right dichotomy so that distinctions might be made, for example, between left and right liberals, between welfare liberals and business liberals.

Rightists and leftists – like conservatives, liberals, and socialists – have competing views of human nature and capacity. Rightists attribute great weight to an individual's will, ambition, and adroitness; leftists focus on an individual's social and economic background as a determinant of opportunity and achievement. Rightists give primacy to the individual, leftists to the collectivity. Rightists may embrace the collectivity, but see it as manifesting the triumph of individual will. Rightists tend to look up to their leaders; leftists tend to stress principle over personality. Within the modern panoramas of right and left, there are variations, some slight, others stark. Social or moral conservatives, along with libertarians, are rightists. They differ profoundly, however, on issues of personal morality such as abortion, homosexuality, euthanasia, and drugs. Leftists differ on the limitations and possibilities of competitive markets; some want to humanize capitalism (liberals), others to harness it for collective purposes (social democrats), and still others want to abolish it.

Elites and Masses

An effort to quantitatively measure left and right can employ a number of available strategies. One could survey and categorize the values of governmental and party leaders. One could ask leaders to categorize themselves. Alternatively, one could survey the values of citizens or followers. One could ask them to place themselves on a left-right continuum. When asked by one of the Canadian Election Studies to place the political parties, as well as an "Ideal" party, on such a scaled continuum, respondents positioned the Ideal party further to the right than any of the actual parties.[16] From a socio-cultural perspective, one could examine the socio-economic status of leaders and use the findings to classify them as left or right. Here the basis of classification is who and what leaders are, in terms of their education, income, and occupation rather than cognitions and opinions, the psychocultural approach. Nonetheless, if we wish to probe political values or deep dispositions, the ideas and beliefs of elites and prospective elites are particularly noteworthy. Elites inhabit the institutions – from political parties and parliaments to corporate boardrooms, labour unions, media, courts, and universities – that contribute to shaping mass political culture. A complementary thrust in research, as we have seen, is to probe mass values. Elite values are important because they help to channel and direct mass beliefs. If the disjuncture between them is too great, however, the contradictions may lead to a revolt of the masses, a routing in which the ruling elite is replaced by those whose values are more in harmony with mass sentiments. Elites are important articulators of political values and drivers of politics. Examination of elite beliefs is essential to understanding how a political system operates.

In the 1980s, Neil Nevitte and Roger Gibbins undertook to map the ideological terrain of "new elites" in five Anglo-American democracies (Canada, the US, Britain, Australia, and New Zealand) by surveying senior undergraduate students.[17] Youth elites are atypical of the general population, for they are relatively well informed and well educated. Nevertheless, they represent future national elites. Drawing on over thirty-one hundred respondents at fifty universities, Nevitte and Gibbins found that 90 percent of them had no difficulty in placing themselves on a left-right scale. The mid-point on the scale, combining all cross-national responses, turned out to be slightly left of centre. Oddly, the Australians were the most right wing, the Americans the most left wing. The Australian result was curious, in light of that country's long Labour Party tradition. The survey asked issue questions regarding the proper role and size of government, the status of women and minorities, perceptions of influential social groups, and notions of equality. Nevitte and Gibbins found that one's self-location on the left-right scale proved to be a stronger determinant than nationality of one's attitudes to these issues. They concluded that the political cultures of these five states were remarkably similar. When students were asked to name the parties with which they identified, rightists in Canada were most likely to choose the then governing Conservatives; leftists were most likely to opt for the Liberals and NDP. Similar patterns were found in all five states. In the US and Britain, leftists leaned to the Democrats and Labour respectively; rightists preferred the Republicans and Conservatives.

An illuminating finding was that within Canada, the left-right distinction was not particularly helpful in predicting the outlooks of francophones on the surveyed issues. Perhaps Quebec's national question – a debate not shared by those in the other states or English Canada – trumps the ideological discourse of left and right. Consider the history of a single Québécois family, the Johnsons. Between the 1960s and 1990s, Johnson senior and his two sons served as premiers of three ideologically distinct governing parties: the conservative Union Nationale, the social democratic Parti Québécois, and the liberal Liberals. Their common ideological thread was Québécois nationalism. National identity in the other states and English Canada is, relatively, a given, not a festering existential issue. In the other states, ideological discourse takes for granted the secure backdrop of the nation-state. In Quebec, it does not, thus making the national question itself an ideological issue.

Some fascinating counterintuitive patterns emerged in the Nevitte and Gibbins survey. Britons were the most supportive, and Canadians the least supportive, of interventionist government. On this issue, Americans were closer to Britons than to Canadians. Such findings are baffling in the light of policy debates of the 1980s. Privatization, deregulation, and free trade were much more contentious in Canada than in the US. Only in Canada did self-professed leftists as a group think that business ought to be more influential than labour unions. Such findings about national attitudes contradict the outputs of and observed behaviour in these states. Canadians, in their partisan voting preferences, parliamentary debates, media commentaries, and academic discourse, do not express themselves in ways consistent with such survey findings. For students of political culture, the interest in values cannot be dissociated from the deeper interest in the political – how people *behave* in politics. Survey findings may confound, helping neither to predict nor make sense of observable behaviours.

Comparing Canada Cross-Nationally

In a path-breaking and much-heralded study, Neil Nevitte analyzed cross-national surveys of political values against the backdrop of structural socio-economic shifts in recent decades.[18] Measuring value changes across time and boundaries, he related them to changing patterns of employment, education, and even divorce rates. He drew on Ronald Inglehart's theory of post-materialism and the World Values Surveys (WVS) of 1981 and 1990, which covered ten Western European and the two Anglo-American democracies. Nevitte found that post-materialist values were on the rise and that they were remarkably similar and consistent across all twelve states. Inglehart's post-materialism thesis rests upon the conjoined hypotheses of "scarcity" and "socialization." The former posits that individuals place a priority on whatever is in short supply; the latter asserts that individuals tend to retain a particular set of values throughout their adult life once this is established in their formative years.[19] If the formative years of older generations were ones of scarcity (the Depression and war), this fed materialist values. Since subsequent generations were socialized during times of relative prosperity, they were more likely to embrace post-materialist values. In addition, these values would become increasingly ascendant as older generations passed on and were replaced. Inglehart predicted that these cultural changes in advanced industrial societies, such as Canada's, would trigger changes in political party systems and voting behaviour.

Nevitte's demonstration of cross-national attitudinal commonalities based on surveys begs a number of questions. Why, given similar inputs (popular values), do political outputs differ so markedly? Why, for example, did the post-materialist Greens become a force in German politics but remain on the fringe in Canadian politics? Why did the Liberals govern Canada in 1900, in 2000, and in every decade of the century in between? One could depict the Liberals as having changed with the shift in political culture. If so, this reflects the political party system's adaptation and durability, not its dramatic transformation as Inglehart's theory implied.

Politicalness and Deference

An apparent incongruity between survey findings and actual behaviour appears in people's politicalness, that is, in how important and interesting politics are to them. The WVS revealed that, among the dozen societies surveyed, Americans, followed by Canadians, were the most likely to respond that politics were "very important" to them. Americans and Canadians also indicated substantially above-average interest in politics: for every Spaniard who was "very interested" in politics, there were three Americans; for every Italian, there were more than three Canadians.[20] Yet, voter turnouts in Canada and the US are lower than in Western Europe. Given the historical legacies of Italy and Spain, survey respondents in those societies may have perceived admitting to an interest in politics as undesirable. Nevitte suggests that citizens in all these states are participating more, not less, in political life but are choosing new ways of doing so. They are shunning, for example, traditional vehicles such as political parties. He does not provide any evidence, however, that political parties were any more vibrant or popular in the past than they are today. Indeed, political party membership – a measure of political activity – is a relatively recent development for the old Canadian parties. The evolution of the party leadership selection process in Canada, giving all party members a direct vote, has expanded party memberships dramatically. This suggests greater rather than lesser engagement in traditional political vehicles.

One of Nevitte's surprising findings is that in both 1981 and 1990, Americans were more deferential to authority than were either Canadians or Western Europeans collectively.[21] What explains this, given Americans' celebrated revolutionary roots and ethos of individualism? It is inconsistent with their political history and behaviour. Nevitte's findings showed that in all three societies, deference increases with age and declines with education and postmaterialist values.[22] Higher education feeds a critical disposition as a vital part of its function. But how do we account for the counterintuitive cross-national variations in deference levels? Nevitte indirectly recognizes the limitations of the survey technique: "It could well be ... that Americans are responding to questions about greater respect to authority not on the basis of some shared absolute standard of authority orientations, but on the basis of cultural experiences peculiar to the contemporary American situation. Thus, Americans may be more enthusiastic about 'more order' because they are more inclined than other publics to judge their own social order as chaotic."[23] He appreciates that his data and interpretations may be too narrowly focused on single broad indicators. If this is so, the survey method of uncovering political values or political culture is undermined. It throws into question the premise that "survey questionnaires provide *direct* measures of values or deep dispositions; they work from a simple principle, that the best way to find out about people's values is to ask them."[24]

If the WVS are reliable reflectors of deference or authority orientations or preferences for more or less order in society, how are they to be reconciled with the survey data reported earlier in Table 2.1? These revealed that Canadians are more likely than Americans to prefer "an orderly society." Perhaps the differing results are a product of the surveys' methodologies. Nevitte claims, "There is nothing to indicate that the priorities of Canadians are radically different from those of any of these other publics [in the WVS] ... Nor ... do Canadians appear to lag behind their American counterparts."[25] In brief, Americans do not show Canadians the "picture of their own future." However, intuition, experience, history, public policy debates and outputs, institutional structures, and voting behaviour do suggest Canadian retardation. Some examples in which Canada followed US precedent include federalism, a bill of rights, affirmative action programs, the methods of selecting party leaders, proposals for citizen-initiated referenda, a Triple-E Senate, flat income tax rates, and parliamentary review of Supreme Court nominees. All emerged as issues in Canada after their adoption in the US.

An example of differing value inclinations appears in party preference. If Canadians could vote in US elections, they would almost certainly vote Democrat more heavily than do Americans. Conversely, if Americans could vote in Canadian elections, they would probably opt for the political right more markedly than do Canadians. Why? Surveys on the divide between materialism and post-materialism cannot explain this. One could discount partisan choice as a signpost of political culture. Similarly, one could disregard the relevance of political culture – if surveys are offered as the basis of its assessment and measurement – to the behaviour and outputs of the Canadian political system. Nevitte's thesis, gracefully and rigorously constructed on the basis of two fixed-in-time surveys (1981 and 1990), is enshrined in his title, The Decline of Deference. However, his comparative figures do not function in aid of it. In 1981, 64 percent of Canadians indicated "support for the general principle of deference"; 75 percent did so in 1990. In the US, the percentage rose from 76 percent to 84 percent; in Europe, it increased from 57 percent to 62 percent. One could take from this, as the broader essence of the findings on attitudes to authority, that his book could have been titled Canadians: Less Deferential than Americans, more Deferential than Europeans. A corollary is that Western societies, with Canada in the lead, exhibited more deference to authority in the 1990s than in the 1980s. Such theses are not congruent with the received wisdom on Canadian and these other political cultures. Although there are grounds for believing that deference has declined in Canada, Nevitte's survey on the question does not reveal them.

Comparing Regional Political Cultures

Canada was not among the five states surveyed in 1959 by Almond and Verba in *The Civic Culture*. The book and its methodological sensibility had, however, a greater impact on the study of Canadian political culture than on most of the states surveyed. It was, for example, relatively neglected in Italy; no Italian translation of it appeared.[26] Although 94 percent of Italians voted in 1958, one-third of Almond and Verba's respondents reported not having done so, another 12 percent claimed not to know for whom they had voted, only 5 percent admitted to being a party "supporter," and only 18 percent admitted "leaning" toward a party.[27] These findings suggested a politically reticent culture. Unwillingness to talk about politics was an obvious, significant trait of Italian political culture that the survey instrument could not measure. In Mexico, the civic culture survey encountered other pitfalls. Nearly all respondents lived in cities, even though almost two-thirds of the population at the time were rural. Moreover, the questionnaire was plagued with problems of translation.[28] Political scientists in all five states were critical of *The Civic Culture*'s inability to examine sub-national or regional variations in culture.

In Canada, both the conceptual model and methodology offered by *The Civic Culture* were looked to and operationalized. They were harnessed in the search for discerning Canada's regional political cultures. Based on data from the Canadian Election Studies in the 1960s and 70s, two of the country's brightest political scientists, Richard Simeon and David Elkins, set out to measure provincial variations in Canadians' sense of their own political efficaciousness (whether they think they have influence in the political process), their levels of trust in their governments, and their degree of political involvement.[29] (See Table 2.2 below.) These Canadian Election Studies, involving thousands of survey respondents, have been elaborate and expensive: the 1974 study consumed just under 40 percent of the monies awarded by the Canada Council (later the Social Science and Humanities Research Council) for political science research that year.[30] Simeon and Elkins' effort, first published in the *Canadian Journal of Political Science*, was lauded, drawing considerable and uncritical acceptance; it became the second-most-cited article in the *Journal*.[31] Well into the 1990s, a leading textbook in the field used it to characterize regional political cultural differences within Canada.[32]

TABLE 2.2

Efficacy and trust scores: Canada and the provinces

	Efficacy					Trust		
	1968	1974	1979	Federal 1984	Provincial 1984	1968	Federal 1984	Provincial 1984
Canada	1.8	2.1	2.1	1.9	2.0	2.0	1.7	1.8
Newfoundland	1.2	1.6	1.7	1.6	1.7	1.4	1.6	1.7
PEI	-	2.0	2.2	2.0	2.1	-	1.9	2.1
Nova Scotia	1.4	2.3	2.1	2.0	2.2	1.7	1.8	2.0
New Brunswick	1.2	2.0	1.9	1.3	1.4	1.3	1.6	1.6
Quebec	1.5	1.8	2.0	1.8	1.7	1.8	1.9	1.6
Ontario	2.1	2.3	2.2	1.9	2.1	2.1	1.7	2.0
Manitoba	2.0	1.7	1.9	1.9	2.1	2.3	1.5	1.9
Saskatchewan	1.7	2.3	2.3	1.7	2.3	2.0	1.7	2.1
Alberta	1.8	2.1	2.2	1.9	2.1	1.8	1.7	2.0
British Columbia	2.3	2.6	2.3	1.9	2.0	2.3	1.6	1.5

NOTE: The numbers represent mean scores. The means are based on scores of "low" equals one, "medium" equals two, and "high" equals three. Three is the maximum score possible. The scores are based on responses to a number of questions related to efficacy and trust. Data compiled by Jon Pammett from the Canadian Election Studies.

Comparing their findings for British Columbia and Newfoundland with those of Almond and Verba, Simeon and Elkins concluded that the differences between the political cultures of those provinces with respect to political efficacy were greater than those between the US and Italy.[33] This bold and heady claim was subsequently demolished from without and from within as provincial levels of efficacy fluctuated greatly in the various Canadian Election Studies. With respect to "trust" in government, numbers of Americans who agreed that "you cannot trust the government in Washington to do what is right most of the time" increased from 22 percent in 1964 to 73 percent in 1980.[34] This suggested that US political culture of the 1980s resembled that of 1960s Italy more than it did its own 1960s version. Since political culture is stable, enduring, and cross-generational, such findings cast doubt on the efficacy and trustworthiness of concepts such as "efficacy" and "trust" in defining political culture. Within Canada the alleged differences among regional political cultures did not stand the test of time either: trust and efficacy appear inherently volatile, affected by current events. What people say on a given day does not necessarily or very well reflect their deeper, more stable values.

Ian Stewart catalogued a number of methodological shortcomings in the Canadian Election Studies' surveys measuring trust, efficacy, and political interest. Over the years and in the various surveys, the questions probing these variables were substantially modified, the order in which they were asked was not consistent, different cueing statements prefaced the questions, the format of the questioning was altered (sometimes asking respondents to agree-disagree to a single option, other times offering two or more forced choice options), some questions became more specific over time, and the scales coding the responses were changed.[35] In the early studies, people were asked if they trusted their "government," but no distinction was made between their federal and provincial governments. Even if errors of method are discounted, the "findings" did not hold up internally or over time.

Simeon and Elkins depicted British Columbia, Manitoba, and Ontario – in that order – at one pole and the Atlantic provinces collectively at the other. The former were characterized as either "supporter" or "critic" societies with relatively high levels of efficacy if not always trust; the latter were either "disaffected" or "deferential" societies exhibiting relatively low levels of efficacy and trust. Simeon and Elkins claimed nearly identical results from the 1965, 1968, and 1974 studies. However, in response to the efficacy measurement question, "People like me don't have any say about what the government does," 38 percent of the Newfoundland sample agreed in 1965. Significantly, exactly the same percentage of the British Columbia sample agreed with the statement in 1968. In one swoop, this undermines the interpretation of significant provincial differences. Moreover, the results go up and down like a yo-yo from one survey to the next. These differences put into question the results' compatibility with the concept of culture, which is relatively abiding. For example, the 38 percent of the Newfoundland sample that agreed with the above proposition measuring efficacy grew to 54 percent in 1968 and to 67 percent in 1974. Conversely, the opposite pattern occurred in New Brunswick: agreements with the statement diminished from 73 percent in 1965 to 61 percent in 1968 and then to 51 percent in 1974. In Nova Scotia, the drop was from 64 to 44 percent.[36]

Further evidence of the limitations of Simeon and Elkins' typology of provincial political cultures came in subsequent Canadian Election Studies. The 1984 survey, for example, produced scores for the largest Atlantic province, Nova Scotia, that showed it to be a leader on trust and efficacy; British Columbia went from polar leader to laggard. Simeon and Elkins' claim of distinctive political cultures came to be simultaneously embraced and challenged. One of the principal investigators of the Canadian Election Studies from which the data were drawn argued that provincial variations were a function of socio-economic variations among the provinces,[37] factors that Simeon and Elkins claimed they had controlled for. The methodological problems in the Simeon and Elkins landmark study do not extend so easily to Nevitte's use of the WVS.

Ideology and Region
Sociologist Michael Ornstein also challenged the Simeon and Elkins findings in terms of politicalness (efficacy, participation), but he went further in search of provincial political cultures in terms of ideology. He assessed *ideological* differences by measuring attitudes to *policy* issues, which he categorized as left and right.[38] His survey made light of the gap between opinions about policies and more stable ideological patterns. Of the differences between the anglophone provinces, he discerned that Atlantic Canadians were the most left wing and Western Canadians, especially those in Saskatchewan and Manitoba, the most right wing. He saw this as consistent with the relative class status of residents in the various provinces. Much of political culture research in Canada downplays social class, but Ornstein and Michael Stevenson highlight it to "argue that the importance of regionalism in Canadian political

culture has been exaggerated and that there *are* significant class divisions on key questions in popular ideology."[39]

From this perspective, relatively poor Atlantic Canadians are more likely to uphold social democratic or left values than are relatively wealthy westerners. This is an odd finding because it is Western Canadians, especially those in Saskatchewan and Manitoba, who repeatedly elect the social democratic NDP while Atlantic Canadians tend to shun it. Moreover, if, as Ornstein suggests, class status dictates values, how are we to make sense of his findings that British Columbians and Albertans, though more affluent than Saskatchewanians and Manitobans, were also more left wing than their Prairie neighbours? In many respects, those on the eastern prairies resemble Atlantic Canadians more than they resemble other Prairie westerners. In the early 1990s, per capita incomes in Saskatchewan were on average below those in the Atlantic region.[40] Residents of the Atlantic region, Manitoba, and Saskatchewan all have below national average incomes; their provinces, as "have-nots," are dependent on federal equalization payments. Ornstein's counterintuitive findings may, like those of Simeon and Elkins, be a function of methodological shortcomings. Ornstein's survey of Newfoundland and Saskatchewan was based on sample sizes of fifty-six and ninety-one.[41] Simeon and Elkins' 1968 data relied on sample sizes for Newfoundland and New Brunswick of forty-eight and seventy-six.[42] The margin of error for such sample sizes is great, too great to invest much confidence in the findings.

What Simeon and Elkins, Ornstein, and other survey researchers have in common, however disparate and conflicting their findings, is a dependence on quantitative rather than qualitative materials. In search of provincial political cultures, it might prove illuminating to read articles and books, newspapers, and political archives from each province and then to compare them rather than to rely wholly on surveys. The assumption that the survey technique offers a direct scientific shortcut to revealing a polity's culture is perilous. Surveys cannot account for historical factors, since they are single fixed snapshots of solicited opinions on subjects respondents might never have thought about. When longitudinal survey data are generated, they demonstrate further that the questions and responses are time-bound. The most salient aspect of the efficacy, trust, and political interest survey responses in the Canadian Election Studies is that there are but marginal differences at best between provincial political cultures. The trend lines tend to move together, unidirectionally up and down, across the provinces.[43] One knows experientially, however, in moving and travelling within the provinces, that this is not so. Provincial political cultures differ from each other in many respects, however similar they may appear in other respects. Historical studies and contemporary political formations suggest so.

Ornstein concludes that "differences in federal and provincial politics reflect institutional factors, such as party structures, and not fundamental ideological differences." These factors in turn "reflect the provincial histories of class and other social conflicts."[44] The survey method is not equipped to pursue such lines of research. To compare provincial histories of class and other conflicts requires a less symmetrical, less rhythmic, and less technologically sophisticated strategy than the survey instrument. It requires pursuing asymmetrical institutional and historical analyses. Ultimately, Ornstein acknowledges, such research is more fruitful too. The assumption that a survey on policy issues reveals "fundamental ideological differences" is a leap of faith cloaked in the guise of detached scientific observation. Ornstein's survey findings cannot account for the palpable outputs of a political system – such as which parties or political forces win elections and wield power. To explain such incongruities as why left-wing Atlantic Canadians elect right-wing parties and allegedly right-wing Prairie Canadians elect left-wing ones, he falls back on assertions that survey methodology cannot sustain. To explain the incompatibility between reported values and discernible political behaviour, Ornstein writes that "the provincial party systems conspire to limit the expression of regional economic needs," and concludes, "we have more to learn from the historical studies of the balance of class forces and the development of political institutions than from efforts to link the political structures to value systems or the climate of public opinion."[45] If this is so, survey research has not put us further ahead in the search for Canada's political culture.

Sub-cultural Variations
In the comparison of political cultures within Canada, cleavages other than those defined by the provincial geopolitical containers may be more significant. These are the divisions between young and old, rich and poor, men and women, the more and less educated, ethnocultural groupings, and so on. Such demographic and socio-economic categories may produce non-territorial sub-cultures. A 2000 survey on voter turnout in the 1997 election (in which 67 percent voted although 74 percent said they had) revealed a remarkable gap between young and old. Among those between eighteen and twenty-nine years of age, only 51 percent claimed to have voted. In contrast, 92 percent of

those over sixty did. This glaring gap of 41 percent is substantially greater than the one between the two provincial extremes, Alberta and Quebec. There the differential was but 14 percent. Noteworthy too, the wealthier (although not the wealthiest) participated more in the election than did the poor. So too did the more educated than the less educated. Such findings are consistent with established research on political participation in Canada and abroad.[46] The gender cleavage in political participation, which has attracted much more scholarship in recent decades than that for class or age, is a marginal one – 4 percent – according to Table 2.3.

This survey also probed satisfaction with how "democracy," "government," and "politics works in Canada." More than seven in ten were satisfied with Canadian democracy, and a majority were with the workings of Canadian government and politics. In none of the socio-economic or regional categories were more than a third dissatisfied with Canadian democracy. The least dissatisfied were the young, fewer than one in five. The young were also most satisfied with how Canadian government and politics work.[47] An apparent paradox emerges: young Canadians are the most satisfied with their country's democratic political order yet are the least likely to participate in the archetypal act of democratic expression, voting. Perhaps the relative lack of involvement, as exhibited by their lower voter turnout, is nothing to bemoan. It may reflect youth's belief that democracy is working well without their participation in this aspect of it. The relative detachment of youth, at least with respect to voting, may signal neither disaffection nor alienation from the political system but rather acceptance, trust, and support. Alternatively, it may simply reflect boredom. Surveys of attitudes or other quantifiable measures, such as voter turnout data, may not be able to capture adequately this reality.

Comparative differences generated by survey research such as those above are thought-provoking and puzzling. To neglect surveying opinions, attitudes, beliefs, and values in the search for understanding political culture would be remiss. To claim too much for surveys, however, would be misleading. As with the differences between Canadian and American attitudes to freedom and equality, one is challenged in determining when quantitative differences – however imperfect the methodology that generates them – are of sufficient magnitude to have qualitative implications. Quantitative data on non-territorial cleavages, such as age, gender, and class, aid in an appreciation of culture as not being rooted solely within provincial or national boundaries.

TABLE 2.3

Many people do not vote in elections; how about you, did you vote in the last federal election in 1997?

	Total (%)	Age (%)				Education (%)			Income (%)			
		18-29	30-45	46-60	61+	HS or less	Some post-secondary	University	$0-30K	$30-50K	$50-80K	$80K+
Yes	74	51	78	88	92	73	71	82	69	74	84	82
No	24	47	20	10	8	26	26	17	28	24	15	17
Don't know	2	1	2	3	0	1	3	1	3	2	1	1
Total	100	99*	100	101*	100	100	100	100	100	100	100	100
(N)	(1278)	(367)	(474)	(264)	(166)	(510)	(432)	(328)	(332)	(290)	(263)	(218)

	Total (%)	Region (%)						Gender (%)	
		Atlantic	Quebec	Ontario	Manitoba/ Saskatchewan	Alberta	British Columbia	Male	Female
Yes	74	75	82	72	74	68	68	76	72
No	24	23	17	27	23	29	28	23	25
Don't know	2	2	1	1	3	3	4	1	3
Total	100	100	100	100	100	100	100	100	100
(N)	(1278)	(146)	(307)	(393)	(137)	(150)	(145)	(601)	-(677)

* Rounding error.

NOTE: No explanation is offered by the authors for discrepancies; e.g., the Ns for Age, Education, and Income categories total 1271, 1270, and 1103, respectively, and not 1278 as indicated in the total.

SOURCE: Paul Howe and David Northrup, *Strengthening Canadian Democracy: The Views of Canadians*, Policy Matters 1, 5 (Montreal: Institute for Research on Public Policy, July 2000), table 21, 80.

Geopolitical boundaries, however, reinforce cultural differences. Within distinct political units such as states and provinces – unlike categories that crosscut them such as age, income, gender, and ethnicity – there operate concrete institutions. Such institutions consciously and unconsciously contribute to channelling values. They do so through school curricula, legislation, and governments whose focus and authority are bound by political borders. Governments and the politics they reflect and pursue are organized along spatial dimensions. Ian Stewart has used survey research to demonstrate that the boundary between Nova Scotia and New Brunswick is more than just a line on a map. It "has independently had a divisive impact on the area's political culture,"[48] producing quite diverse political orientations in a region, the Maritimes, whose provinces are often treated collectively. Whatever attitudinal differences exist between young and old, men and women, rich and poor, and so on, disproportionate shares of each of those categories of people are deeply influenced by their geopolitical setting. Thus, in the 1990s, Ontarians of all ages and levels of affluence and education were more likely to vote for the federal Liberals than were the same socio-economic groups in Alberta or Quebec. Similarly, Albertans and British Columbians – however old, rich, or educated – were more likely to vote for the Reform/ Alliance Party than were their socio-economic counterparts in other areas of the country. Saskatchewanians and Manitobans exhibited relative support, relative to other parts of Canada, for the NDP. Similarly, Atlantic Canadians were relatively receptive, whatever their socio-economic status, to the Conservatives.

States and provinces have governments, constitutions, and institutions. They impose themselves, allocate resources, and enforce laws in a way that non-territorial groupings cannot. The way in which a society negotiates, creates, and receives its constitution and political institutions reveals much about that society's values. In the pursuit of understanding Canada's political culture, one needs to understand constitutions and institutions, their structures and processes, and the values they reflect and promote.

3
Constitutions and Institutions as Culture

This chapter examines institutions as culture, undermining the conventional radical distinction between "institutions" and "culture." Culture and institutions have a symbiotic relationship. Like cultures, institutions are customary structures and practices. Constitutions provide for formal institutional structures; they contain a collection of rules and principles according to which an organization is governed. A polity's constitution defines the powers and relationships of the principal institutions of government. In the modern world, a constitution represents a badge of nationhood. It epitomizes the rights and duties of a state's citizens, including their rights to participate in governmental institutions. It is, however, more than that. A constitution's essence is also a product of imagination and consciousness. A constitution cannot be perceived, measured, or deduced independently of those who perceive it; it is not something external but, rather, internal to the observer.[1]

Political institutions may be contrasted with political processes. Realistically, institutions are processes in their own right, dynamic rather than static, less like a building with walls and measurable rooms and more like a flowing, meandering river. Like political culture, institutions are inherited. They are not commonly the products of contemporary will but of heritage and tradition. They cut across time in a way that individual lifespans do not; like cultures, they are constantly evolving, declining, forming, and being renegotiated.

To see culture as determining institutional form is too one-sided. The causal arrow points both ways because culture is a response learned from living under certain institutions.[2] In this light, institutions help to shape culture. After 1960, for example, Québécois youth were born into a setting in which revamped governmental and educational institutions reoriented their aspirations and expectations of the state. From this angle, institutions are more pivotal in explaining political culture than vice versa. Those with hierarchical preferences see people as innately imperfect; institutions make for stability and social order. Those with egalitarian preferences tend to see people as born good but soon corrupted by the institutions that envelop them. Tocqueville saw laws as institutional arrangements that, along with the manners and customs of a people, contributed to explaining why decentralized administration took hold in Anglo-America while centralized bureaucratic administration reigned in Quebec.[3]

Canada's Constitution and political institutions moved from their British grounding to adopting some American institutional principles. Accompanying this were changing relations between the three states. After the American Revolution, English Canadians defined themselves in terms of their "other" (the United States) and their mother (Britain). Dependent on Britain for defence, trade, and political modelling, Canada considered the US its foremost military threat until after the First World War.[4] In the 1920s, Americans replaced Britons as the primary investors in the Canadian economy.[5] Canadians came to see themselves less as British North Americans and more as North Americans possessing common interests with their southern neighbours. The Statute of Westminster in 1931 confirmed Canadian independence, and the 1940 Defence Production Sharing Agreement with the US signalled Canada's strategic reorientation. If Canadian institutions do indeed reflect political culture, their drift from the British to the American orbit must be a significant cultural indicator. In recent years, the global movement to liberal discourse has led to branding this development as the Americanization of political culture internationally. Against this backdrop, a distinctive Canadian orientation has developed with respect to the institutional structures of the machinery of government, federalism, and constitutional rights.

Evolving Constitutionalism

The legal and popular images of the Constitution have changed over time. They tell of how Canadians see themselves and what their country represents. The sacramental basis of constitutional authority comes from on high. It lies with the monarch, whose authority is symbolically consecrated in the coronation. That venerable coronation rite persists, but the sacramental expression of popular government comes from below, from the ballot box. Referenda express power directly; elections do so indirectly, anointing a select few to govern in the name of the realm. The tory conception of monarchy is that the office, rather than its occupant, is charismatic. Constitutionalism in colonial Canada meant parliamentary supremacy. There was equivalency in the terms "constitution" and "statute law." Both were products of a sovereign parliament. Neither trumped the other; both were woven of the same fabric.

The Constitution Canadians got was not imposed: it was what they negotiated among themselves and asked of Britain. It was consistent with John A. Macdonald's characterization of Canadians as "subordinate" people who, like the British people, were subordinate parts of a larger empire centred in Britain.[6] The Canada of 1867 was neither constitutionally independent of Britain nor the equal of sovereign states such as Haiti, Liberia, or France. Britain's Colonial Laws Validity Act (1865) ensured that no Canadian law could conflict with British law. Growing Canadian autonomy manifested itself in institutional practices that deviated from their British pattern in response to Canadian conditions.

Confederation modified constitutionalism. Canadians became subject to two parliaments, federal and provincial, each supreme in defined spheres of authority. Departure from Britain's unitary governmental system rendered Canada a jurisdictionally divided rather than a united kingdom. The preamble to the British North America Act (renamed the Constitution Act, 1867, in 1982), referring to "a Constitution similar in Principle to that of the United Kingdom,"[7] alludes to the principle of parliamentary supremacy but not to its federal modification. Federalism implies dual loyalties and identities: Haligonians in 1867 became newly minted Canadians but remained Nova Scotians. Torontonians became Ontarians but retained their Canadian appellation. Regional cultures persisted as they do in all states, but the foundation for a new distinctive pan-Canadian nationality was established.

Canadians fashioned the BNA Act against the backdrop of the American Civil War. They feared American "mobocracy" – the ballot box had yet to attain sacred status in Canada – and observed the devastation wreaked by the warring states. America's constitutional design provided for weak executive authority and strong states, whereas Canada's offered strong executive authority and weak provinces. The ironic historical upshot was a highly decentralized federal Canadian state and a relatively centralized American one. This mirrored the contrasting directions of the countries' judicial elites, who fleshed out constitutional language and purpose.

The Charter of Rights and Freedoms in 1982 further qualified parliamentary supremacy. One could no longer propound an "exhaustion theory,"[8] that the two orders of governments and legislatures – federal and provincial – monopolized constitutional rights and powers. The Charter grants "everyone" and "anyone" rights, including non-citizens and corporations, according to the courts.[9] In this, Canada's Constitution takes on more of the colour of the American Constitution, but with a culturally revealing difference: certain groups defined by language, religion, gender, age, race, and other distinctions now possess a constitutional status they do not in the US. The limited language and religious rights in the BNA Act – the right to English or French in a trial or parliamentary speech and the public funding of some denominational schools – were expanded. Canada's enshrined mini-bill of specific and narrow rights now brims with laudable rights like freedom of association and from discrimination. The courts, as in the US, spell out what these rights mean. Canadians enjoyed most of the rights and freedoms listed in the Charter – such as "freedom of conscience and religion" – before 1982.[10] They did so, as in Britain, by virtue of statutory and common law, but their explicit enumeration in the Charter contributed to a rights consciousness that was new.

The seeds of this consciousness were sown with Canada's social transformation. In English-speaking Canada, the British ethnic cast began to crack at the turn of the twentieth century, with new sources of continental European immigration. Technological developments in transportation and media, the eclipse of the British Empire, and the rise of American power shifted Canadians' gaze ever more southward. Much of the language and zeitgeist of the Charter is drawn from American constitutional jurisprudence – terms such as "unreasonable search or seizure," the right "to retain and instruct counsel without delay," and "cruel and unusual treatment or punishment."[11] Despite their insertion into Canada's constitutional order, Canada still exhibits sociological, institutional, and ideological particularisms that set it apart from the US. The bilingual/bicultural cleavages persist, Westminster-style parliamentary government continues, Aboriginal rights are constitutionally recognized, and both social democratic and tory impulses still resonate, however muffled, in policy debates and at the ballot box. Indigenous developments rather than foreign precedents and practice increasingly drive Canada's constitutional infrastructure and its legal system's philosophy. Indeed, some emerging and reconstituted states look to the Canadian experience for institutional modelling.

A modern rendering of the Constitution was articulated in the Quebec Secession Reference of 1998. The Supreme Court identified four principles as "animating the whole of the Constitution": federalism, democracy, constitutionalism and the rule of law, and respect for minorities. Significantly, popular will as expressed via referenda was elevated in status, and parliamentary supremacy was further compromised. Parliament and legislatures are now obligated to respond to referenda when they offer a "clear question" and gain "a clear majority vote."[12] This turns upside down the country's original constitutional framework by limiting parliamentarians' discretion.

Constitutional culture is found in the judiciary's ambient purpose. Pre-Confederation and early post-Confederation courts ensured no breaches of British imperial laws. Federalism rechannelled constitutional contention to delineating spheres of jurisdictional competence among Canadian legislatures. With the Charter, the courts are propelled into an era of full-blown constitutionalism. Ultimate authority now rests in the Constitution itself[13] rather than with a viceregal governor and her parliament. Governments have become not so much the moulders of the Constitution as they are the accessories, like their citizens, to it.

Constitutional conventions convey constitutional character and culture more than does the black-and-white letter of constitutional law. Examples are the legal powers vested in the queen, who is commander-in-chief of the armed forces and who has the authority to appoint cabinet ministers – powers actually exercised by the prime minister. Constitutional conventions represent a marriage of law and politics.[14] They are not court enforced but politically sanctioned via public opinion in election outcomes, media commentary, the behaviour of MPs, and potentially by the governor general. Conventions mirror and evolve with a polity's culture. They operate, according to the Supreme Court, "in accordance with the prevailing constitutional values or principles of the period."[15]

The use of referenda to trigger or halt constitutional amendment is an example of an emerging convention. There is, as well, some constitutional recognition of them: the BNA Act, 1949 (later renamed the Newfoundland Act), refers to the referendum preceding that province's entry to Confederation. The Charlottetown Accord referendum and Quebec's referenda on sovereignty – in conjunction with public insistence on them as legitimating processes – point to this practice as sinking ever-deeper conventional roots. In this respect, Canadian constitutional culture is also moving toward the American model, which explicitly provides for referenda as amendment

...vices. Referenda are a departure from the negotiated compromise of 1982, but within a decade, premiers, legislatures, and the public insisted on them as preconditions to constitutional reform.

Two of the Constitution's three pedestals – federalism and the Charter – draw imitatively on American practice. Popular and elite images of the Constitution have been quite dissimilar, however, in the two countries. Americans are apt to believe that their Constitution is perfect. If there is a problem in their eyes, it is that various parties to the Constitution – Congress, the courts, the president – have not lived up to its undisputed ideals. In contrast, Canadians have been quick to deprecate their Constitution. It is inconceivable (and would be deemed treasonous) for an American president to say, as Prime Minister Mulroney once did, that his country's constitution "was not worth the paper it is written on."[16] At times, Canadians have been obsessed with denigrating and changing, rather than celebrating, their Constitution. Five politically consuming bouts of attempted megaconstitutional reform were pursued between the 1960s and 1990s.[17]

Canadians have been less united than Americans in defining themselves and the principles that govern them. There has been greater uncertainty about what is "Canadian" and "un-Canadian," a term appearing only recently and tentatively in the language of Canadian politics, in contrast to the older, clearer use of "un-American." This is because Canadians negotiated their collective identity in a non-declaratory manner. Canada's history is littered with the messy and inarticulate but functional compromises of its elites rather than with ringing proclamations, as in the American Declaration of Independence. The Canadian way makes for ambiguity. The genius in the Canadian path of constitutional evolution has been to adapt, improvise, and muddle through as conditions and popular expectations demanded. The very notion of muddling through comes from Canada's British traditions. The declaratory route of articulating abstract principles of nationhood requires freezing concepts and terms in a document that is intended to persevere. The Charter is now the Canadian declaratory equivalent of the American Bill of Rights.

A notable parallelism exists in political institutions across provinces. Each province displays the trappings of parliamentary government, each exercises the same jurisdictional powers, and each is subject to the Charter's uniform national provisions. Such institutional co-extensivity contrasts with discernible differences in provincial socio-economic settings and political cultures. Although Eastern and Western Canadians may have differing cultural traditions, values, and partisan preferences, they act politically within almost identical

institutions. This gives them something in common across provincial boundaries. It contrasts them collectively with both Americans, who do not share
parliamentary institutions, and the British, who do not provincialize them.

Competing Constitutional Visions

The Constitution's multifarious evolution feeds a clash of competing visions,
each rooted in cultural sources that disagree regarding what Canada is and
how its national interest is to be defined. Four articulations of Canada appeared in the constitutional dramas of the 1980s and 1990s. The first, Pierre
Trudeau's pan-Canadianism, asserted that the national interest is expressed
only by the federal parliament as the sole representative and democratically
elected institution shared by all Canadians. Trudeau's Charter of Rights generates an image of Canada as a community of equal citizens governed by
majority rule and the rule of law. Its section 6 embodies this pan-Canadian
principle in asserting Canadians' mobility rights: to move, take up residence,
and seek employment in any province.

A counterpoint, presented by anglophone premiers since the 1960s, is
that the national interest is an ensemble, a consensus, of federal and provincial governments. In this perspective, Confederation is a contract between
legally equal provinces. Provincial legislatures reflect the public's will in their
jurisdictions no less than parliament reflects it collectively for the country as
a whole. This principle was displayed in the processes and products of executive federalism – the bargaining among first ministers – of the 1990s: the
Charlottetown Accord, the Agreement on Internal Trade, and the Social Union
Framework Agreement.

Quebec's view, a third vision of Canada, is also one of contract and equality, but with a focus on distinctiveness. It sees the 1867 bargain as a solemn
founding pact or "compact" of dual societies, with Quebec's legislature designated as the cultural guardian for the only jurisdiction where the French
language prevails. This was expounded at mid-century by a Quebec Royal
Commission (Tremblay) on constitutional issues.[18] In this light, the 1982
Constitution is a treacherous unilateral reversal. Supporting Quebec's bi-national perspective is section 94 of the BNA Act, a dead letter in practice but
weighty in symbol. It provides for potential uniformity in laws among the
original three English-speaking provinces, uniformity that excludes Quebec.

A fourth cultural perspective, that of Aboriginals, emerged in response
to the other three. First Nations trace their constitutional recognition to the
Royal Proclamation of 1763, which predates and thus detaches them from

both notions of provincial equality and Quebec's cultural distinctiveness. In this view, Canada is the product of a trilateral relationship between themselves and the tentacles of French and British imperialism. A problem this formulation faces is that the First Nations are fragmented as legally discrete bands, often with distinctive linguistic and other cultural traits. Aboriginals also lack independent constitutional authority, unlike federal and provincial parliaments.

All four of these viewpoints find some expression in the Constitution Act, 1982; Quebec's viewpoint is marginalized while Trudeau's is dominant. Grounded in a bilingual federal regime in a multicultural setting, the revised Constitution transfers powers from governments and legislatures to the courts; it does not acknowledge any special status for Quebec, save for one minor exception.[19] Quebec challenges the very legitimacy of the constitutional revisions of 1982 because it was not a party to them. Nevertheless, Quebec behaves in accordance with the Constitution. Provincial equality found expression in the constitutional amending formula. No province has a veto on constitutional change, a long-standing demand of Alberta. This departs from an earlier constitutional convention: both Ontario and Quebec possessed a veto. Aboriginal rights and recognition appear in sections 25 and 35. Confined to "existing" rights that are undefined, they continue to be disputatious. However, Aboriginals are acknowledged in a way denied in the BNA Act. They also secured the right to participate in any constitutional conference whose subject matter impinges on their status;[20] they are now more than wards of the state, but Ottawa continues to have fiduciary obligations to them. Aboriginals may be seen as "citizens plus":[21] they enjoy all the rights and freedoms accorded other citizens, but they also retain other sweeping and important rights and powers, as well as a special status in constitutional tampering.

Constitutional Pillars: Responsible Government, Federalism, the Charter

Canada's evolving political culture altered the relationships of the three pillars of the Constitution: responsible government, federalism, and the Charter. "Responsible government" requires the cabinet to have the confidence of the popularly elected legislature. Most contemporary Canadians would not recognize or use that phrase to describe their system of parliamentary government. For colonial British Canadians, Westminster served as the model. Responsible government was constructed atop three older elements of Canadian constitutionalism and, like them, had a British stamp: a system of law,

the right to representative institutions, and the principle of religious toleration.[22] An important difference, however, resulted from the two countries'
socio-economic settings. North America's frontier fostered individualism and
liberal values of equality and freedom. Cheap real property was available
and social relations were not as constrained as they were in the Old World.
Nevertheless, in practice the British political-constitutional system proved
flexible in British North America.

John Ralston Saul celebrates the coming of responsible government as
the most pivotal event in Canadian history. Depicting it as establishing a
regime that balances "personal freedom and public good," he favourably
contrasts it with America's democratic vision of unbridled individualism and
Europe's democratic dynamic of class tensions.[23] For Saul, the distinguishing
centrepiece of Canada's version of responsible government is the joint ministry of Robert Baldwin and Louis-Hippolyte LaFontaine, which established
a bicultural basis for national politics. Acknowledging responsible government as a keystone of the Constitution is at best only obliquely implied in
the Supreme Court's 1998 definition of the Constitution. The justices offered up the quite plastic terms "democracy" and "constitutionalism" – which
neither require nor intimate Westminster-style responsible government – as
two principles animating the Constitution.

Because the responsible government model concentrates power in the
executive branch, it does not fit well with the Court's treatment of referenda
as founts of democratic legitimacy. Nor does it sit well with evolving popular
notions of participatory democracy. Democratic "audits" of Canada's legislatures, cabinets, and first ministers – using criteria of responsiveness, accountability, transparency, inclusiveness, and participation – point critically at
legislatures' lack of institutional freedom and the localization of power in
first ministers' offices.[24] The prime minister's massive powers appear arbitrary. In theory, the prime minister is "first among equals" in the cabinet; in
fact, he or she is superior to the others, as they serve at his or her pleasure.
The prime minister appoints all the key positions in the vast bureaucracy of
government: deputy ministers, senators, the judges of all federal and superior
provincial courts, ambassadors, and the innumerable members of federal
regulatory boards, agencies, and commissions. He or she determines when
parliament convenes, prorogues, and dissolves. Until 2007, he or she also determined when elections are held. These are consequences of his or her control
of the governing party and parliament in a majority government situation.
Parliament appears as a rubber stamp and government MPs as supplicants,

fearful of losing the prime minister's favour, ever hopeful of gaining his or her approbation to advance their personal or constituents' interests.

Canadians may find the locus of power in one individual distasteful, but it makes for potentially robust government. They cannot decry, as can Americans, the gridlock and bickering among the branches of government as impediments to action. Such concentration of power in one person is incongruent with notions of checks and balances. It is consistent with the tory cast of the 1867 Constitution. The American Revolution rekindled Loyalists' faith in the executive's ascendancy. Most contemporary Canadians still wish to retain the monarchy but are leery of concentrated, centralized prime ministerial power.[25] That power stems from the Crown's prerogatives that the prime minister exercises.

Radically changing institutions is difficult once they operate over long periods. Canadians critical of the apparent overbearing power of their prime minister with a majority government see the parliamentary system, whatever its warts, as differentiating their country from the US. Although there is appetite for reforming it, there is virtually none for jettisoning it. Thus, in the tortured debates over reforming the Constitution, no opposition was expressed to maintaining the parliamentary system. It was listed as a valued "fundamental characteristic" of Canada – ahead of such principles as Aboriginal self-government, Quebec's cultural distinctiveness, racial and ethnic equality, and respect for individual and collective human rights – in the Canada clause of the ill-fated Charlottetown Accord of 1992.[26]

The Crown is the subliminal institution that permeates Canada's institutional infrastructure.[27] Contemporary Canadians, however, barely conscious of the monarchy's relevance to government, are largely ignorant of its status. In 2002, only one in twenty correctly identified the queen as Canada's head of state.[28] "God Save the Queen," once commonly sung, is now rarely heard; organizations such as the Imperial Order Daughters of the Empire and the Loyalist Association of New Brunswick have faded into history. A reason for the monarchy's continuing resilience is that it is decidedly un-American; a majority of Canadians agree that "the monarchy is one of those important things that provides Canadians with an unique identity separate from the U.S."[29]

The Crown is no mere icon. Largely invisible, it is the pervasive organizational feature of government. Canada and the US share a common democratic culture, but the bases of authority and legitimacy differ greatly from each other. This is due to the monarchical principle. American government is based at the bottom as a covenant of the people; it implies a uniformity of citizens, their collective separateness from the uncovenanted, and is infused with a messianic zeal. Canadian government is based at the top, by monarchical allegiance, with the monarchy as the symbol of national integrity.[30] Monarchy predates statehood; the state comes from the king, and the people are his people. Thus, the monarchical principle, which transcends the ideological chasm between conservatives and radicals, need not be bound up with wealth or aristocracy. Some of a people's sense of integrity and continuity comes from hereditary monarchy; in a presidential system – elected and, as in the US, subject to term limits – the people must derive their sense of integrity and continuity from elsewhere.

The Crown was converted into a compounded monarchy when Britain's Judicial Committee of the Privy Council (JCPC) ruled that the Crown in the right of one province was not subordinate to the Crown in the right of the federal government.[31] Canadians have but one monarch, but the Crown's institutional bifurcation is decidedly un-British. Moreover, unlike in Britain, where both the Crown and the civil service are perceived as lying outside the political realm – the former reigns above its fray, the latter labours apolitically below it – in Canada both are enmeshed in political calculations. Governors general in recent decades have often been protégés of the governing party. One, Jeanne Sauvé, intervened in the political process (verboten in Britain) by beseeching recalcitrant provincial legislatures to ratify the Meech Lake Accord. The "sponsorship" scandal that rocked the government in 2004 demonstrated to some that politicians had compromised the nominally neutral civil service. Crown prerogatives contribute to characterizing Canadian administrative culture as an amalgam of British institutions and conventions, American ideas and practices, and indigenous adaptations.[32]

Federalism was a response to the imperatives of geography, sociology, and the accommodation of elites. This institutional departure from the British pattern was American-inspired but consistent with Canadian realities. For most English Canadians, the British model of unitary, centralized, hierarchical, and relatively authoritarian government was understood and accepted. The unitary dimension, however, was impractical in a pan-Canadian context, given the reluctance of Québécois and Maritimers to have their regional institutions submerged. Between the 1840s and 1860s, the Province of Canada – governed by the convention of a double majority (English-French) principle – witnessed perpetual deadlock and the formation of at least eighteen different governments.[33] Such sociological sensitivity proved politically debilitating. Federalism permitted some autonomy to the colonial parties to it. It allowed the Upper Canadian English and Lower Canadian French some disentanglement. Ontarians saw Confederation as facilitating an east-west trading axis and the settlement of the west (threatened by American encroachments). Québécois saw their new provincial regime as shielding their cultural particularisms. Each party to Confederation saw in it what it wanted. Macdonald foresaw the provinces as king-sized municipalities whose relationship to Ottawa would parallel the subordinacy of the colonies to imperial Britain.

Macdonald's view of such parallelism was faulty: though he often wielded Ottawa's powers to reserve and disallow provincial legislation, Britain never disallowed Ottawa's legislation. Macdonald's quasi-federalist vision gave way to more classical federalism. Court rulings, challenges by premiers, and control over land and resources strengthened the provinces. Although Ottawa controls the Territories, only about 2 percent of the rest of Canada's land mass belongs to it. The provinces own about three-quarters, in the form of Crown land. This contrasts with the US, where most land is private. Garth Stevenson suggests that growing provincial power went logically with the growing democratic impulse in political life.[34] Provincial governments emerged with co-ordinate rather than subordinate powers in relation to Ottawa, although not principally because of public sentiment.

Dull, uninspiring, virtually devoid of symbolic aura, and with a tory sheen to its institutional underpinnings, the BNA Act nevertheless proved flexible and accommodative of change.[35] It became something bickered over rather than looked up to, unlike the US Constitution and the Charter. That Canadians did not look up to their Constitution was not unusual, for neither do citizens in most states. The mass of Canadians never much cared for the quarrels between their two orders of government. They have had, however, a keen stake in government services, as the charitable and educational functions of religious orders retreated and that of the modern welfare state came to the fore. Depression and war proved powerful catalysts for active government. Ottawa, with its unlimited taxation powers, has always had greatest access to revenues, but it is the provinces, with their expansive responsibilities for health, education, and social services, that gained increasing visibility. Provincial budgets collectively are now larger than the federal budget. Moreover, a good part of the latter is comprised of transfer payments to provinces, with few or no conditions attached.

Provincial governments, portraying themselves as the purveyors of sought-after public goods, depict distant Ottawa as the major confiscator of income through taxation. They "gang up" on the federal government in federal-provincial negotiations and have mounted advertising campaigns to make Ottawa, rather than themselves, appear as obstinate. Although other states have looked to Canadian federalism as a potential template for designing their own governing structures, in Canada federalism is strained by the pressures of Quebec nationalism, the claims of First Nations, and the popularly perceived inadequacies in the delivery of essential services.[36]

The machinery of responsible government is similar at both federal and provincial levels, but institutional parallels cannot submerge the regional political cultural differences played out in those institutions. Consider the chapter titles in an edited collection on provincial and territorial legislatures.[37] Nova Scotia's, "The Wisdom of Their Ancestors Is Its Foundation," conveys a sense of history and traditionalism entirely unlike the expectancy and prospects suggested by the Northwest Territories chapter, "Accommodating the Future." Manitoba's chapter is "The Role of the Legislature in a Polarized Political System," communicating ideological divisiveness; by contrast, Alberta's "From One Overwhelming Majority to Another" speaks to political consensus. New Brunswick's entry, "A Bilingual Assembly for a Bilingual Province," denotes linguistic cleavage; Quebec's "The Successful Combination of French Culture and British Institutions" explores the superimposition of one culture's institutional apparatus on another. The Yukon chapter, "Parliamentary Tradition in a Small Legislature," informs us that size, in and of itself, has implications for legislative behaviour.[38]

A difference between the Charter and the other two constitutional pillars is its relatively recent vintage. The Charter has had a profound impact on public consciousness. Canadians have been compelled to engage in a "rights" revolution.[39] This condition is not uniquely Canadian: a global rights discourse gained momentum in the aftermath of the Holocaust, boosted in 1948 by the United Nations' Universal Declaration of Human Rights. Political concerns broadened in recent decades to include more attention to human rights. With citizens and others as bearers of justiciable rights, the status of courts is elevated and the once unchallengeable powers of governments circumscribed. The relationship of citizens to governments has become less deferential and more contentious. This is consistent with the fading of toryism, always a secondary force in Canadian culture, and the widening triumph of liberal individualism.

The Charter conveys ideological content, more so than the federal principle and somewhat like responsible government. The monarchical principle underpinning responsible government is largely opaque to the public. The Charter more easily meets the threshold of conscious public perception and engagement. The media are replete with Charter-related issues and their relevance to people's lives. Stories related to the Crown, in contrast, focus on the foibles of the royals and regal fanfare rather than its pervasive institutional relevance. Canadians have come to revere the Charter as Americans do their Bill of Rights. There are, however, differences between the two: a distinguishing "genius" of the Charter, in some eyes, is that it generates a constructive dialogue between the judiciary and parliament.[40] Parliament may respond to court rulings by amending impugned laws, as the courts rarely reject the law's objectives. A legal observer of the Charter describes "a respectful conversation among those who have different abilities, concerns, and perspectives," and points out that "Section 1 of the *Charter* contemplates such a conversation."[41] Rights are not sacrosanct; unlike the Bill of Rights, the Charter makes this explicit by subjecting them to "reasonable limits."

The Charter centralizes the allocation of values; in this, it is the mirror opposite of federalism's decentralizing allocation of powers. Its provisions apply nationally. The BNA Act assigned "property and civil rights" and "all matters of a merely local or private nature" to provincial jurisdiction,[42] but the Charter effectively centralizes the meaning of these powers. The Supreme Court, at the apex of the judicial system, is the final arbiter in Charter cases. Despite differences in various provincial human rights acts and codes,[43] there is a de facto legal harmonization of such rights acts once the Supreme Court weighs in on the basis of a Charter challenge. When discrimination in hiring on the basis of sexual orientation was prohibited by the Court,[44] as it was on the basis of the Charter's equality clause (section 15), such discrimination became prohibited everywhere in Canada. This ruling applies notwithstanding some provincial human rights codes (such as Alberta's), which tolerate such discrimination by not listing it as proscribed. The Charter feeds Canadians' sense that their rights and freedoms are enjoyed jointly and nationally, rather than being province-specific.

Like federalism, and unlike responsible government, the Charter draws attention to the courts. Some academics and editorialists lambaste the judiciary for excessive activism.[45] Such censure is usually biased; critics do not object when judgments concur with their own opinions. Despite controversial rulings, the public expresses strong faith in both the Charter and the judges who are charged with fleshing it out. Public awareness and favourable impressions of the Charter grew from just over eight in ten Canadians in the late 1980s to more than nine in ten in 2002. Public satisfaction with and trust in the Supreme Court is also high, higher than for its counterparts in a number of countries, including Britain and the US. Nevertheless, Canadians are still evenly divided about whether the Supreme Court's right to decide controversial issues ought to be reduced.[46]

Public trust in judges and courts contrasts with the low esteem the public has for politicians and other institutions such as parliament, political parties, corporations, and the media. This is because the court system, unlike the parliamentary process and the workings of federalism, is perceived as transparent, devoid of corruption, and subject to meticulous review. Dishonesty, personal gain, and the misuse of office are not associated with the judiciary. The part of the Charter that has gained singular approval is the section dealing with equality rights. There is less enthusiasm for legal rights, which account for about nine-tenths of all Charter cases. They are seen by many as serving the interests of accused criminals. Indeed, more than half of Canadians are prepared to extend police powers, even if this means violating civil rights, and they are more likely than Americans to believe that their Supreme Court's power is too great.[47]

For Trudeau, the dual purposes of the Charter were the strengthening of national unity and providing a "guarantee" of civil liberties.[48] The Charter provides a common thread for all Canadians, one that counters the centrifugal pressures exerted by strong provincial governments in a decentralized federation. It has become a powerful symbol of national identity. Quebecers' approval of the Charter is no less strong than that of other Canadians – indeed it is stronger[49] – but the Charter exacerbates tensions between the two solitudes. The Québécois support most individual rights, as do English Canadians, but the Charter does not enjoy the transcendent status in Quebec that it does in the rest of Canada. This was spectacularly revealed when Quebec invoked the Charter's "notwithstanding clause" (section 33) to immunize its language law from legal challenge. Quebecers do not see the Charter or the Supreme Court as superior to their own political institutions.[50] Even Quebec's federalist provincial Liberals proposed (in their Allaire Report) that no legal appeal in Quebec, including Charter appeals, could proceed beyond the province's own courts.

How much the Charter has actually extended freedoms or the protection of rights is debatable. Canadians could not in 1982 joyfully cry, as American slaves had in the 1860s, "Free at last – oh Lord, free at last." Nevertheless, the Charter's values and symbolism have produced what have been labelled "Charter Canadians," peoples and groups that have been galvanized by it. Notwithstanding the nationalizing bent of the Charter, its treatment by the courts points to differences in provincial legal cultures.[51] Ontario's Court of Appeal upheld more than twice as many Charter claims in 1980s cases than did its Nova Scotia counterpart.[52] Such differences existed before the Charter and exist in non-Charter cases as well. Consider a study of 1970s criminal appeals cases heard by these same courts: the success rates in Alberta, Manitoba, Nova Scotia, and Saskatchewan ranged from 12 to 20 percent; in British Columbia, New Brunswick, Ontario, and Quebec, they ranged from 41 to 47 percent.[53] As the Charter contributes to the judicialization of politics, judicial verdicts inadvertently contribute to the politicization of the judiciary in public consciousness. As in the United States, scorecards of judicial rulings will infiltrate public debate regarding judicial appointees.

The political and policy implications of the Charter are numerous. One is that governments and legislatures must take care to draft laws so that they are Charter-proofed and do not run afoul of the courts. Another consequence is that interest groups may turn to the courts, and away from governments, in attempting to fashion public policy. Thrown to the courts, political and social issues are converted into technical legal questions. Legal verdicts have administrative implications that judges are not trained to appreciate. In the *Singh* decision,[54] thousands of additional cases were heaped onto an already burgeoning backlog of outstanding refugee claims. In *Askov*,[55] tens of thousands of criminal charges, including pedophilia, were dropped on the basis of the section 11(c) right "to be tried within a reasonable time." Courts are also weighing in on budgetary decisions. In 2002, the BC Court of Appeal reordered health care priorities by compelling the provincial government to provide intensive treatment for autistic children. Later, the Charter was used by a Quebecer to successfully assault the single-payer medicare system.[56]

An Americanizing cultural implication of the Charter is that core values of Canada's tory legacy – privileging certain group or collective interests over those of self-seeking individuals – are being further overshadowed by the liberal values of individualism and equality. Manitoba's Sterling Lyon, spokesman for the premiers in the 1980 constitutional negotiations, saw the Charter as representing "a republican system ... an experiment with a concept foreign to our traditions." It meant, he asserted, discarding the constitutional philosophy of 1867 and embracing that of 1776. Rather than empowering people, it would take power from them and their governments and transfer it to the courts. Saskatchewan's Allan Blakeney and Roy Romanow saw the Charter as a potential assault on social democratic traditions. The former foresaw conservative courts setting back the redistribution of power and wealth in Canadian society; the latter cautioned for the need to balance rights against social justice.[57] The contrasting views of government leaders pointed to similar disagreement among philosophical liberals and social democrats regarding what equality and justice mean in a democratic society and how an entrenched Charter may affect them.

An American influence in Charter jurisprudence was evident soon after its proclamation, but the Supreme Court has certainly been no captive of US decisions. It referred to them in 40 percent of its Charter cases in the 1980s, but it often took a differing policy orientation.[58] After the 1950s, Supreme Court references to JCPC decisions declined dramatically, and its American references became more pervasive. More striking, however, was the Court's increasing tendency to cite both itself and the lower Canadian courts, especially those of Ontario: by the 1990s, its citations of itself and lower Canadian courts outnumbered its US references by ten and five to one respectively.[59] This demonstrates that Canada is still quite unlike its neighbour in terms of the philosophy of law, just as it is politically, socially, and psychologically. Canadians may not share a consensus on who they are, but they are united on who they are not: Americans. America continues to serve as the requisite "other" for Canadian self-definition and identity.

Together or separately, Canada's three constitutional pillars may be seen as more alterable and dynamic than their American counterparts. Not as constrained by formal law, the machinery of Canadian government may evolve in ways prohibited by the more legally constricted American congressional system. Canadian federalism continues to be a more fluid institution too; federal-provincial diplomacy is relatively vibrant, American federalism is relatively quiescent. Due to its relative newness, the Charter leaves the courts with more interpretative roads and forks to explore than is the case for US courts, with their much older Bill of Rights.

A Hierarchy of Constitutional Values

Pierre Trudeau assailed the Meech Lake and Charlottetown Accords for creating a "hierarchy of citizens" related to which group or collectivity a citizen belonged. He decried the idea that collective rights would trump individual freedoms.[60] He feared the manner in which Quebec could wield the "distinct society" clause contained in those accords. Canada, however, has a tradition of group rights and restraints. They were reflected before and after 1867 in the privileged status of certain denominational schools and language groups. They were evidenced in the protected constitutional status (until the 1960s) of a dozen Quebec electoral districts that once had anglophone majorities. Laws operating under the Constitution discriminated against Aboriginals, immigrants, and citizens on the basis of their national origins. An example was the First World War act that denied the franchise to Canadian citizens who had immigrated from Germany or the Austro-Hungarian Empire after 1902. Simultaneously, the franchise was expanded to women who had a relative enlisted in the Canadian war effort. Trudeau's Charter acknowledged group rights in its provisions for language, gender, and "disadvantaged groups," as well as for Aboriginals and the country's "multicultural heritage." The notion of group rights – privileging some, such as Ontario's Catholics in education funding – is not new; nor has it been eliminated from the Constitution Act, 1982.

Until 1982, constitutional amendment was governed largely by convention. Since 1982, law has governed the amendment process. This is another example of how Canadian constitutional culture has moved from a British to an American mode. In both Canada and the US, the approval of 70 percent of the provincial or state legislatures is required for constitutional change according to the general amending formula. Along with the Charter, the amending formula is at the heart of the Constitution Act, 1982. It is consistent, more or less, with then provincial demands, just as the Charter more or less met Ottawa's requirements. Formula and Charter were a quid pro quo.[61] At the time, most Canadians accepted constitutional revision as the prerogative of government leaders, although some groups, especially those representing women and Aboriginals, insisted on public participation.

The five amending formulae point to the principle of the supremacy of legislatures. In practice, the amendment procedure is being modified by an emerging convention. This reveals again a fluid rather than fixed constitutional culture, one moving inexorably toward greater public participation. Under BC, Alberta, and Quebec legislation, referenda are mandatory prerequisites to any constitutional amendment considered by their legislatures. In 1991, Saskatchewan voters opted for such legislation in a referendum, and, effectively, so too did BC voters. Manitoba requires extensive public hearings before its legislature will proceed. The Charlottetown Referendum may have established a politically irresistible precedent for direct public input. Only a decade earlier, this was an unpalatable procedure to premiers. In changing provincial constitutions, the convention of wider public participation via referenda is not as clear or compelling. When Manitoba's government moved to amend its language regime in the 1980s, it resisted a provincial referendum, but municipalities mounted their own and effectively jettisoned the amendment. Newfoundland used two referenda to alter its denominational school system; Quebec did so without one. Content and history influence procedure; in Quebec there was a public consensus, in Newfoundland there was not.

The amending formulae suggest a hierarchy of values, in that some constitutional provisions are more deeply entrenched than others. Some amendments require approval from parliament and all provincial legislatures, some require parliament and seven legislatures representing more than half the national population, and other amendments may be executed trilaterally, bilaterally, or unilaterally. Subjects requiring unanimity are deemed most vital to the polity's self-perception. The short list includes the monarchical principle and the Supreme Court's composition. The formula is silent with respect to amending the Charter, except for language rights. This makes the rest of the Charter subject to the general formula (parliament and seven provincial legislatures). Via section 33, governments may also immunize some legislation from legal challenge. Thus, the right of a British Columbian (where fewer than half of 1 percent of the population speaks French at home) to deal with a federal agency in French (section 20) is more shielded than the right to liberty (section 7), the right not to be discriminated against (section 15), and those rights regarding freedoms of religion and expression (section 2).

The outcomes of constitutional referenda revealed an evolving constitutional culture of diminishing deference to governments. Having absorbed this fact, legislatures now hesitate to invoke the Constitution's section 33 (the "notwithstanding" clause). Section 33 balances the principles of parliamentary supremacy with court-enforced constitutional rights. Although it is intended to permit legislators' values to override Charter rights, governments have found it politically unsavoury in high-profile issues. Despite the Alberta government's determination to limit compensation to the forcibly sterilized and to give religious schools a free hand in hiring and firing on the basis of sexual orientation, in neither case did it proceed with section 33 after saying that it might. Nonetheless, the "notwithstanding" clause has operated in the shadows: Quebec's omnibus use of it on all legislation continued until 1985 and occurred in a controversial case regarding commercial signage; by 2001, it was also invoked in sixteen pieces of provincial and territorial legislation. When it was deployed, its use was invisible and inaccessible, dealing with matters not on the political agenda and with complex policy issues.[62]

The unanimity rule for tampering with the Supreme Court's composition reinforces the statutory requirement that three of its judges be Quebecers versed in its civil code. This acknowledges, yet again, Quebec's special cultural status. Ontario has three judges on the Court too, but that is a product of convention, not law. As for the monarchy, there is growing dissonance between its constitutional pride of place and public esteem for it. Public opinion outside Quebec still supports its retention but has become increasingly indifferent to it. Indeed, a deputy prime minister, an officer of the Crown, has advocated its abolition.[63] In 2005, more than seven in ten of Quebecers opposed retaining the Queen as head of state; in the rest of Canada, four in ten agreed with that sentiment.[64] It is increasingly doubtful that a British monarch will ever again address parliament (as the Queen did in 1957 and 1977, in reading the Speech from the Throne).

Elections, Parties, and Groups

In Canada's formative post-Confederation years, when democratic sentiments were relatively muted, the electoral system – its rules, management, machinery, and the franchise itself – was shaped by and manipulated by the governing party. A more deferential political culture tolerated egregious abuses. Canada's inherited British institutional legacy provided for the first-past-the-post, or single-member plurality, system (although a majority of provinces came to use multi-member constituencies to accommodate socio-cultural cleavages for partisan advantage or in response to reform demands). Electoral laws have been described as "constitutional statutes," and the Supreme Court once deemed the provincial ones as parts of provincial constitutions. Soon after that, however, with the coming of the Charter, electoral rules became like other ordinary statutes subject to constitutional challenge by the citizenry.[65]

Populist and American progressivist influences – in the context of the burgeoning agricultural economy of the early twentieth century – stoked demands for restructuring both the electoral and parliamentary systems. The Progressives, standard-bearers for institutional reform and the second-largest party in the 1920s, prodded parliament to consider departing from the first-past-the-post system. As they faded, so too did their cause, but not before Manitoba and Alberta adopted the single transferable vote (STV) for their largest cities. Manitoba also adopted the alternative vote in its rural ridings. These breaks with the norm ended in the 1950s. As urbanization proceeded, the new cries for "fair representation" were intended to counter the gross and growing overrepresentation of the rural areas.[66] Public and institutional attention then shifted nationally, between the 1960s and 1990s, to issues of electoral boundary readjustments and party and election finance.[67]

Elections are a democratic linchpin; most Canadians continue to see them as a means of expressing themselves, individually and collectively, concerning the shape of their government. The electoral system itself, however, has again come under increased critical scrutiny; as a result, in 2005 five provinces and parliament were examining their systems. A majority of British Columbians voted to revise theirs, even though 82 percent of them did not understand the alternative for which they were voting (STV).[68] The electoral system is important to the performance of political parties because it contributes to dictating their functions and behaviour. In pursuit of fairness, inclusion, and transparency, frequent revisions have been made to electoral laws in areas such as campaign finance, the registration of parties, partisan advertising during campaigns, and the publication of polls.

It is a paradox that as emerging democracies have looked to Canadian expertise in the conduct and rules of elections, some Canadians, especially in academic and media circles, as well as interest groups such as Fair Vote Canada, have been assaulting their own electoral system as democratically deficient.[69] Against this backdrop, in which pressures for reform increase and legal verdicts strike down various provisions of electoral law, voter turnout has declined in recent decades. So too, however, has it in other Western democracies. Diminishing turnout has been associated in the media with rising levels of cynicism regarding politicians and the responsiveness of government, but survey evidence in the 1990s suggests that levels of public cynicism declined in that decade as voter turnout continued to drop.[70] Much of the decline is confined to young Canadians. They are both less interested in and less informed about elections and politics than are their older counterparts.[71]

Canada's political parties began as clique-driven cadre parties but, with demands for more participatory democracy in later years, transformed themselves – at least nominally – into mass parties. Like the Constitution, they had a British cast but developed American affinities over time. The early Conservative Party considered itself a colonial equivalent of the British Tory party and as the specially appointed guardian of the British connection.[72] The early

Liberals also had some connection with British politics in that, like the British Whigs, they began as a reform party. They presented themselves, as in Britain, as more egalitarian and less wedded to vested interests than were the Conservatives. The Liberals, more than the Conservatives, defined Canada as a North American state, whereas Tory nationalism exuded British imperialist pride. Liberals who wished for more independence from Britain projected a stronger inclination to republicanism than did Conservatives. Conservatives who wanted independence from the US projected a stronger inclination to monarchism than the Liberals did. The King-Byng constitutional controversy of the 1920s – with the Liberals assailing the governor general's prerogative and the Conservatives defending it – encapsulated this dynamic. The social democratic Independent Labour Party–CCF, the NDP's forerunner, also drew on British antecedents. Paralleling the British Labour Party, the CCF-NDP provided for affiliated trade unions. The CCF's program and leadership were British-inspired too. Party leader M.J. Coldwell (a British Fabian) and Tommy Douglas emigrated from Britain; British Labour luminaries spoke in Canada on behalf of various Labour Parties.

British partisan inheritance was tempered by Canada's proximity to the United States. The party convention, a product of American Jacksonianism, spread northward in 1859; the Grits (a uniquely Canadian designation) held one. Their Liberal successors held another in the 1890s; in 1919, they broke with the British model, in which the caucus chose the party leader. Within a decade, the Conservatives followed suit. American parties became exemplars for policy innovations and the mechanics of electioneering. Early examples of American partisan modelling were the Non-Partisan League, the provincial United Farmers parties, and the Progressives. All used the language of American agrarianism; calls for direct democracy via the initiative, referendum, and recall swept across the plains and prairies on both sides of the border. Canadian advocates were derailed by the court's ruling that legislation by referendum was ultra vires because it circumvented the lieutenant governor, the sovereign's representative.[73] This was a reminder that authority in the Canadian political system flows downward from the Crown rather than upward from the people.

The pull between American and British partisan influences was strongest in the Conservative Party, but it affected all the federal parliamentary parties. It was weakest in Social Credit and the Progressives, both of whom owed little to Canada's Loyalist heritage and much to the frontier spirit of the American West. By the 1950s, a common assessment of the Conservatives and Liberals was that they were northern variants of the Republicans and Democrats. George Grant lamented that the Conservatives had become echoes of the Republican Party and that the Liberals saw Canadian independence threatened rather than sustained by the British connection.[74] The Liberals turned to Democratic pollsters in the 1960s; Conservatives soon followed with Republican advisors. The affinity of the Conservatives with the Republicans expressed itself in the policy and personal links between Brian Mulroney, Ronald Reagan, and George Bush. Pierre Trudeau's and Jean Chrétien's Liberals were more welcoming of and more welcomed in Democratic White Houses.

As with legislatures, provincial party systems reveal variations in political cultures. Examine the province-specific chapter titles in an edited collection devoted to them: the one for Saskatchewan, "Parties in a Politically Competitive Province," alludes to ideological fissures, but that for geographically adjacent Alberta, "Politics of Consensus," connotes electoral hegemony.[75] This polar contrast is striking in light of these provinces' common prairie and resource-based settings. The Nova Scotia chapter, "Tradition and Conservatism," suggests continuity; BC's "The Company Province" speaks to the discontinuities generated by industrial development. The New Brunswick chapter, "The Politics of Pragmatism," alludes to a patronage-driven system; Manitoba's "Ethnic and Class Politics" explores that province's mutually reinforcing social cleavages. Ontario's is "The Dominant Province," an attitude engendered by size; PEI's "Big Engine, Little Body" informs of the localism that comes with smallness. The Quebec entry, "Heaven Is Blue and Hell Is Red," communicates the historical link between partisanship and religion in that province. Distinct political cultures are also apparent in the leadership practices of governing parties. Contrast the subtitles of two chapters in a book on executive styles: Saskatchewan's is "The Centrality of Planning"; PEI's is "Managerial and Spoils Politics."[76]

Survey data point to a breakdown in partisan loyalty in recent decades.[77] On the surface, this implies a lessening of ideological politics. It may, however, intimate the opposite if party leaders – the focus of so much attention – are conceived of as engaged in ideological warfare. The appearance of federal leaders such as Stockwell Day and Stephen Harper, as well as premiers such as Mike Harris and Gordon Campbell, suggests as much. On the other hand, Liberal dominance in the twentieth century and beyond has been evident whoever the leader and whatever his ideological bent. The Liberal cavalcade of triumphant leaders has something of the apostolic succession about it:

Paul Martin served in Chrétien's cabinet; Chrétien himself served in Trudeau's, who served in Pearson's, who served in St. Laurent's, who served in King's, who served in Laurier's, whose first cabinet was in the nineteenth century. This speaks to partisan continuity, not dealignment or realignment.

If partisan loyalty has dissipated, what accounts for the federal Liberal Party's remarkable qualification as one of the most durable and successful political institutions in the world? It is that the Liberals are the clear favourites of those who continue to have a strong partisan identification, about one-half of the electorate. In 1997, for example, there were more Liberal identifiers than those for the Conservative, Reform, NDP, and Bloc Québécois (BQ) Parties combined.[78] In Ontario, in the 2000 election, almost 60 percent of partisans identified themselves as Liberal, but only 8 and 10 percent identified as Canadian Alliance or Progressive Conservative respectively.[79] This gives the Liberals a "natural advantage" in every campaign. A social base of Liberal strength is particularly discernible among those of non-European origins and the fast-growing visible minorities. Over 70 percent of those of non-European origins preferred the Liberals in the 2000 election; in the 2004 election, the ratio of Liberal-to-Conservative supporters among visible minorities was three to one.[80]

American-inspired notions propounded by some of Canada's parties and the British-modelled institutions within which they operate produce tensions. One example is the drive to transform the Senate so that its form and functions more closely resemble those of the US Senate than those of the House of Lords. Proposals to vest parliamentary committees with powers akin to those of their congressional counterparts, including the power to review and examine senior judicial appointments, represent a break with the Westminster model. Nevertheless, the British institutional legacy continues to influence parties. It privileges disciplined parties and their leaders. The congressional party system works with less discipline and more independence for representatives. Whether or not Canadians prefer a diminution of prime ministerial power and more freedom for MPs, the parliamentary system conditions party behaviour and culture in ways that the congressional system does not.

There are also political cultural differences in how Canadians and Americans relate to interest groups. Tocqueville, impressed by Americans' enthusiasm for voluntarily joining associations, noted how this contributed to deconcentrating power, to fostering democratic habits and civil society. Canadians historically have had less taste for voluntarism and joining groups.

Instead, they tended to look to their churches and then to their governments. Canadians, unlike the French and Italians but like the Americans, have not looked kindly on road blockades, mass demonstrations, and the disruption of public services as part of the normal course of democratic politics.

The past half century has witnessed the surfacing of new interest groups and social movements that are not driven by the traditional agendas of sectoral economic interests. Instead, they rally around civil rights and environmental, women's, peace, linguistic, ethnocultural, sexual orientation, and physical disability issues. The public's positive estimation of advocacy groups contrasts with its negative evaluation of political parties: 70 percent think the former are better vehicles for achieving change.[81] Some see such groups as fulfilling a compensatory role for interests neglected in traditional political institutions. Canadian governments in recent decades funded some of these groups on the rationale that they contribute to and nurture Canada's national identity. Ironically, and perversely, such efforts contribute to fragmenting rather than unifying national identity, for they perpetuate particularistic interests and identities.[82]

Just as the national interest is not the sum of all single or special interests, national identity is not the aggregate of particularistic identities. New interest groups and social movements tend not to trust the political leadership and to insist on direct participation on major policy dossiers. Sometimes the efforts of old private and new public interest groups superficially coalesce, each in pursuit of the same objective but motivated by differing values. American forestry interests, for example, made common cause with British Columbia environmental groups in efforts to stymie Canadian forestry corporations.[83]

Interest groups are not a formal part of Canada's institutional machinery of governance, but their behaviours are channelled by it. Responsible government, federalism, and the Charter all mould the manner in which organized groups press their interests. The concentration of power in the executive branch fits with the greater concentration of corporate and union power in Canada rather than in the United States. Interest groups are conditioned by the parliamentary system to focus their lobbying on the cabinet and its bureaucratic tentacles.[84] When interest groups urge Canadians to write to their MPs on a matter of policy, as Americans do their members of Congress, they communicate naiveté about the freedom and influence of the MPs. Since political authority in Canada is monopolized by cabinet in the context of tight party discipline, interest groups cannot exploit rivalries

among legislators as they can in the US. Long-established powerful groups
on both sides of the border, such as trade and medical associations, know
how to respond to the embedded processes of the political system's institutions. They pursue quiet diplomacy, using well-connected professional lob-
byists with governmental experience.

By contrast, single-issue and more transient interest groups are more
prone to seek media attention and engage in grassroots organizing. Often,
their approach reveals ignorance of how the political institutions operate.
Publicly visible campaigns mounted by the larger established groups in recent years reflect change in the culture enveloping the political process. Elite
accommodation between governments and influential interest groups, a
theme ensconced in the country's political history,[85] is being complemented
and now challenged in both the policy and political arenas. This was evidenced dramatically in the rise and demise of the Meech Lake and Charlottetown Accords. Products of the old process of elite brokerage, they were undone
by an emergent, more adversarial popular temperament.

Federalism offers interest groups dual pressure points. In the first half of
the twentieth century – when federal policy making and administration capacity exceeded that of provinces – Ottawa's ventures into regulating resource
industries were challenged by corporations as intrusions on provincial jurisdiction. The jurisdictional issue was used to negate the regulatory efforts of
the only government capable of exercising them. Corporations' interests were
to perpetuate a non-regulatory status quo rather than to protect or enlarge
the provincial sphere. In the second half of the century, peak interest group
associations such as the Canadian Manufacturers Association and the Business Council on National Issues faced more capable and activist provincial
administrations. This led to more corporate sympathy for overarching federal regulatory regimes as antidotes to a checkerboard of various provincial
regulations. Better to deal with and try to influence one master than ten. As
competition heightened between the two levels of government, and as once
unforeseen policy fields (like the environment) and older policy fields (like
health) became entangled, interest groups had incentives to lobby at both
levels of government.

Interest groups may attempt to influence public policy by turning to
courts and away from governments and legislatures. As an arrow in the quiver
of interest groups, the Charter contributes to fostering a more quarrelsome
culture. It provides incentives to litigate. "Rights" cases also arise where tan-
gential constitutional provisions are unsheathed to serve quite unexpected

interests. Winnipeg's Police Association, for example, argued on the basis of the language provisions of the Manitoba Act that a judicial report critical of police dealings with Aboriginals had no legal status because it had not been translated into French.[86] An environmental group used the same argument to challenge a legal agreement between Manitoba Hydro, a Crown corporation, and its Ontario counterpart.

In Canada, many interest groups are more closely linked to state institutions than in the US, in that they are to some extent extensions or dependants of government. Like Americans, Canadians may be distrustful of their politicians; unlike Americans, however, they express a certain level of faith in parapublic and parastate institutions, which are more prevalent in Canada than in the US. In 1999 – when the business cycle was at its apex and corporate leaders were hailed in the North American media as heroes and models – Canadians expressed much more trust in nurses, doctors, scientists, teachers, and not-for-profit organizations than they did in business leaders.[87] The business ethic has always been weaker in Canada than in the US. Conversely, the public sector and its institutions have been held in higher esteem.

A central theme emerges in searching for cultural signifiers in Canada's constitutional infrastructure: the gradual shift from old British conservative structures and processes of government to new, more proximate, American, liberal, and participatory ones. Tension exists between the three pillars of Canadian constitutionalism, between the prerogatives of governments and legislatures and the rights of their citizens. Strains are evident between past and present, between the historical values that shaped the institutions and the contemporary sensibilities expressed through them. Notwithstanding the parallelism of institutional forms across provinces, discernible provincial cultural differences endure and play out within those institutions. Although institutions may be inherited from or modelled on those of others, the trajectory of institutional form and values in any state is unique. The Mountie, a law enforcement officer, is a Canadian national symbol. The Beefeater, the monarch's guardian, stands for Britain, just as the ruggedly individualistic cowboy symbolizes America. In an age of converging popular cultures, lifestyles, and socioeconomic norms, the Mountie, Beefeater, and cowboy continue to be emblematic of persistent cultural diversity and national identity.

4
Culture, Biculture, Multiculture, Aboriginal Culture

Culture is all-encompassing. Culture is nothing less than the soul or way of life of a society. In his last public address, Northrop Frye, then Canada's most distinguished person of letters, spoke of culture's three dimensions: the culture of lifestyle, the culture engendered by a shared heritage of historical memories and customs, and the culture of creativity.[1] The culture of lifestyle is the way in which a society eats, drinks, clothes itself, and performs its social rituals; that of heritage and custom is expressed primarily through a common language; and that of creativity is a society's music, literature, scholarship, architecture, and applied arts.

In the first sense of culture, Canadians from coast to coast share common tastes in fast foods, cars, spectator sports, and vacation locales. Many of these tastes are North American or Western, not uniquely Canadian, yet paradoxically, globalization, modernization, and the homogenization of lifestyles have not mitigated the intensity of national identities. In the second sense of culture – history, customs, language – the Canadian state projects itself as bilingual and multicultural, composed of people drawn from over a hundred ethnic and linguistic origins and served by their federal government in two official languages. The polity, however, is also mobilized around provinces whose histories, societies, and language regimes differ. In the third sense of culture, as "creations," both the federal and provincial states promote "cultural industries," drawing attention to the wealth and employment generated by them. From this vantage point, culture is a marketable commodity, one providing a potential return on investment.

Auguste Comte portrayed societies as evolving through three stages: from the theological to the metaphysical to the scientific.[2] With imaginative licence, this triad may be used to frame the evolution of Canada's political culture. In the nineteenth century, religion, ethnicity, and language served as mutually reinforcing ramparts between English and French Canadians. Christianity differentiated them collectively from those whom they considered heathen Aboriginals. The cultural divide between the English and French was linked to the religious differences between Protestantism and Catholicism. Catholicism appeared as something like a state religion in Quebec, and Anglicanism played a somewhat similar role in English Canada. Until well into the twentieth century, religious affiliation was the strongest single indicator of party allegiance and voter behaviour. With the rise of industrialism, urbanization, and an influx of denominationally diverse Europeans, religion as a political force was overshadowed in the first half of the twentieth century. The nexus of politics shifted to an increasingly secular ideological plane. This movement occurred even on the Canadian left, where the Social Gospel tradition slowly gave way to social planning. The ideological constellations of conservatism, liberalism, and socialism were identified with differing class interests and differing views of human nature and the good society. They offered lenses alternative to religion for seeing politics, economics, and imperial connections. The state, as in Comte's evolutionary model, served as the basic unit of Canadian society. In the second half of the twentieth century, in the context of liberal ideological hegemony, Canadian political discourse increasingly fixed on individuals rather than economic or social classes. Once again, to draw with licence on Comte, in this third stage of societal evolution, the citizenry serves as the basic unit. The citizen is defined as a self-centred individual rather than as a member of a class or an organic member of a cultural community. The rise of survey research and rational choice economic theory is consistent with a view of political man as an autonomous actor, an atomized consumer seeking to maximize his or her utilities. The opinions and values of individuals, as with votes, are given equal weight by survey researchers. Political choice is assumed to be driven by an economic theory of democracy[3] rather than by communion, kinship, class, or other group bonds. In this cosmology, government is charged with fine-tuning macro-economic performance – defined as the sum of individuals' micro-economic behaviours.

Culture is transmitted and reinforced by communication. Social communications are stronger and more numerous among people within a national political system than across national boundaries.[4] The same may be said of provinces; people within one are more likely to communicate with each other about their province's politics than with people in other provinces. In Quebec, the societal shift from a subsistence rural economy to a technologically driven one with modern media and communications contributed to Quebecers' "social mobilization"[5] rather than their assimilation by English Canada. In the 1950s, Radio-Canada – a federal public institution – brought francophone Quebecers closer together while simultaneously reinforcing their separateness from anglophone Quebecers and French Canadians outside Quebec at a time when no equivalent modern francophone communications network existed for them.[6] Provincial cultures are less distinguishable outside Quebec (and, to some extent, New Brunswick) because of the commonality of English, even among francophones. Language and ethnicity provide a stronger basis for culture than do region or province. In this sense, Manitobans are not a distinct cultural group: they are English Canadians who live in Manitoba. Franco-Manitobans – francophones defined by mother tongue rather than ethnic origins – are a distinct cultural group, but they are bilingual and shrinking in numbers. Franco-Manitobans defined solely by their ethnicity are French English Canadians akin to Chinese English Canadians, Ukrainian English Canadians, and Jewish English Canadians.

Canadians, unlike Americans, have defined themselves in terms of who they are not – Americans – rather than as who they are. Lacking a founding myth and ideological consensus defining "Canadianness" and the Canadian Way, intellectuals have frequently questioned whether Canada has a national identity, or have prodded Canadians to embrace one. Historian Frank Underhill depicted Canadians as the world's longest-continuing anti-Americans.[7] Sociologists S.D. Clark and S.M. Lipset drew attention to the conscious will to resist absorption into the American Republic and the American Creed of melding diverse cultures into a unified whole national culture.[8] A positive twist on this is that Canada's toleration and promotion of cultural diversity make for national, pan-Canadian cultural enrichment. A negative twist is that Canada's recognized and sanctioned diverse cultures throw up irreconcilable political tensions. As in the case of Canada's institutional and political evolution, Canadian culture – however defined – has muddled along, interpreting and expressing itself with but one constant: its separateness from Americanness. What persists is Canadians' sense that national survival is tenuous and problematic. The theme of survival is embedded in Canadian literature,[9] in contrast to the individualism and freedom on which American literature is fixated. Canadians are perpetual pessimists about their country's prospects; most feel that it is doomed. According to a 2002 survey, seven in ten of them believed that their country would disappear within a quarter century.[10] It is this kind of survival anxiety that feeds organizations like the Council of Canadians, a group that had a membership of a hundred thousand in 2003, rivalling or exceeding the membership of four of the five parliamentary political parties.

As some decry the absence of a distinctly Canadian culture, federal governments have been financing its institutional expression. Both English- and French-speaking Canadians support their governments' active guardianship of national culture, although the English and Québécois may have differing ways of identifying their nation. Contrast this to the United States, where neither Washington nor the states see the need for cabinet-level secretaries and departments of culture or heritage. Governmental funding for culture is common in many countries; it expresses itself in the US, too, via public vehicles like the National Endowment for the Arts. It is at the most mundane level of culture, that of lifestyle, that Canadians are especially conflicted about the US. In the same 2002 survey referred to above, just over half of Canadians said they opposed the spread of US ideas and customs, but more than three-quarters of them said they liked American music, movies, and television. A vital difference between Canadian anglophone and francophone sensitivities to the American cultural behemoth is the francophone shield of language to deflect much of American popular culture. This offers cultural security vis-à-vis the US, even as the absence of a linguistic shield nurtures cultural insecurity in anglophone Canada. Thus, among the provinces, Quebec public opinion was the most favourable to the 1988 Free Trade Agreement with the US; in neighbouring Ontario – where English Canada's "national" cultural industries like the CBC are headquartered, and book publishing is concentrated – public opinion was the most opposed.

Talk of a distinctive national culture is perpetual, a historically circular phenomenon older than the country founded in 1867. Some historians identify the beginnings of a Canadian "national feeling" in the War of 1812.[11] Others draw attention to the battle of Vimy Ridge, a century later. Unlike American national identity and statehood, chiselled in consciousness at a fixed point (1776), Canadian identity evolved legally under the cloak of Dominion status until the country became wholly self-governing and an independent international actor. According to the political historical frame of Arthur Lower, it unfolded in popular consciousness from colony to nation.[12] Then, in the political economic frame of Harold Innis, it reverted to colony, with the imperial centre having tilted from Britain to the US.

Confederation's Georges-Étienne Cartier spoke of creating a "new nationality." Canadians, however, continued to live and work in two linguistic solitudes. Among British Canadians, an important variant of Canadian nationalism was "a master-race imperialism."[13] In this perspective, Canadian identity was proudly colonial, cut from a broader imperial cloth; it was simultaneously British and separate from Britain. By the 1920s, the relish for a "national culture" became the "master impulse" of Canadian intellectual life.[14] In 1920, the inaugural issue of the *Canadian Historical Review*, noting "the existence of a distinctive national feeling not French-Canadian or British-Canadian, but all-Canadian," proclaimed that Cartier's "new nationality" had taken root in a unique blend of British and French élans.[15] Yet, in the 1950s, Lower was still lamenting the absence of a common national feeling that transcended English and French Canadian identities. Canadians needed "to create a new culture – a native culture."[16]

Inherited British cultural symbols were modified: Canada's own flag, the Red Ensign – with the Union Jack prominent but relegated to the upper corner – made its debut in the 1880s. In the 1960s, it was replaced by the Maple Leaf flag, one with no hint of British legacy. The government's original proposed flag sported three maple leaves, each representing those of British, French, and other cultural backgrounds. The most British of the provinces, Newfoundland, kept the Union Jack until the 1980s; it is still evident on the Ontario, Manitoba, and BC flags. Provincial flags outside Quebec, however, do not evoke the emotions that the national flag does. Other expressions of dissociation from Britain were the patriation and retitling of the British North America Act and the disappearance of the Dominion of Canada. Dominion Day gave way to Canada Day, and Canadian passport holders were no longer deemed British subjects.

Against the backdrop of existential nationalist angst expressed by thinkers like Lower, the Royal Commission on National Development in the Arts, Letters and Sciences registered and aroused interest in Canadian culture in 1951. Canadian identity, in the view of the commission's Massey Report, was not so much compromised by Canada's British legacy as by an "American invasion." The report conveyed elite anxieties about national identity that had been dampened in the dirty thirties and the wartorn forties. The report's conceptualization of culture, essentially highbrow, was expanded over time by policy makers to include sports, recreation, and popular culture. In assuming the mantle of national guardian of culture, the Canada Council –

created in 1957 – represented a democratic and secular thrust; government became the major patron of the arts, a role historically played by church, royalty, and the wealthy. As with many Canadian institutions, there was a solid British precedent: the British Arts Council. The 1960s brought forth conscious efforts to produce Canadian works. In Canada the issue of national identity is commingled with support for the arts, whereas in the US it is not, because American identity is not perceived as threatened by outside cultures.

Culture became a field of public policy and public administration, subject to the jurisdictional turf wars of Canadian federalism. Culture's creative by-products came to be seen as something to be designed and directed in large part by the state for the purposes of achieving national unity and safeguarding sovereignty. One provincial minister of culture described the arts as creating "the thin thread that holds this country together"; another characterized them as vehicles that could be used to escape "the black hole called American culture."[17] Government "control" or jurisdiction over culture is worrisome and problematic, smacking of Big Brotherism and dictatorship. Government "control" may frustrate and undermine artistic freedom through censorship or may facilitate it through funding. Without government involvement, culture and the arts may be free of the state but not of other powers. The BNA Act contains no reference to "culture," but its references to "copyright," "telegraphs," and "education" embedded culture between the lines. Such terms sustained the constitutional basis for both federal and provincial cultural initiatives. Ottawa, for example, created the CBC and the National Film Board in the 1930s. In recent decades, the governor general has become a major patron sponsoring literary and performing arts awards. Provinces, under the "education" rubric, launched their own television stations. Through the Canada Council and provincial arts councils, the arts came to be financed aggressively, but no federal department of culture appeared. The Massey Report had recommended against it, for fear of state control of artistic expression. Nevertheless, culture fell under the purview of other departments, once the Secretary of State, more recently Heritage. The provinces, led by Quebec, began to create culture departments in the 1960s.

The political administration of "culture" is befuddled when governments, sometimes a single government, shift conceptions of what culture embraces. In the 1970s and 1980s, culture became one of many areas – including fishing, natural resources, family law, and immigration – on the negotiating table of constitutional reform. "Culture" makes two appearances in the Constitution Act, 1982, once in the anthropological sense ("multicultural heritage" in section 27) and once as something to be financially compensated for (section 40) when legislative powers regarding culture are transferred from the provinces to Ottawa. Ottawa voiced an ambiguous conceptualization of Canadian culture in its constitutional posture during the run-up to the Charlottetown Accord. It embraced "the duality of Canada's cultural milieux," qualified that with allusions to "aboriginal cultures," and juxtaposed those with the country's "multicultural experiences and traditions."[18]

Provincial governmental conceptions of "culture" are also diverse. Quebec explicitly connects it with social policy and the welfare state. To Quebec, mass media, the arts and letters, housing, health, leisure, scientific research, architecture, and education all fall under the "culture" rubric.[19] Quebec established two culture ministries: one funds the arts, the other attends to "cultural communities," their immigration, integration, participation, and francization in "a pluralist society," as spelled out in a Declaration on Ethnic and Race Relations by the National Assembly. Quebec also stands out from the other provinces in its pursuit of bilateral cultural accords on the international stage with a number of countries and cities. Other provinces generally lump together multiculturalism, sports and recreation, and the arts in one portfolio. PEI's Department of Community and Cultural Affairs refers to itself as a "department store" and groups together culture, sports, building standards, labour relations, multiculturalism, infrastructure, and the regulation of boilers and pressure vessels.[20] Most provinces designate francophone affairs as a separate dossier, suggesting a special status for the French language. Ontario – where more than half of national revenues in publishing, theatre, film, video, and sound recording are generated – promotes culture as an enterprise. It also expresses English Canada's nationalist streak. It has raised the spectre of "the constant threat of domination of the home market by foreign cultural markets" and has referred to its role to "protect Canadian sovereignty."[21] Sometimes, provincial policy and its administration point in opposite directions. On the prairies, where the plea for official recognition of multiculturalism first arose, it came to be denounced by the Reform Party and others. In the 1990s, while Alberta passed a Multiculturalism Act and established a Department of Culture and Multiculturalism, its premier was simultaneously arguing "let multiculturalism evolve and take whatever form it takes happen naturally. It should be taken out of the realm of legality."[22]

Biculture

André Siegfried has been referred to as "the Tocqueville of Canada."[23] Both men were inquiring French Europeans who shed penetrating light on the political cultures of the new North American civilizations. Tocqueville illuminated the democratic impulse as the heart of American political life; Siegfried ruminated on Canadian biculturalism and the delicate, shifting balance of British and American influences on Canadian politics. Unlike the Americans, who critically reflected on their new nationality and what it meant, Canadians proved tentative in engaging in self-definition. In part, this was a consequence of the fact that English and French perceptions of Canada had developed in separate universes with dissimilar discourses.

The bicultural idea of Canada has been buffeted by history, demography, and government policies. In the old Province of Canada (1841-67), francophones were at first a majority. The bicultural principle – defined as the equality of English- and French-speaking communities in political institutions – benefited anglophones, but as their numbers increased they came to insist on representation by population to capitalize on that advantage. By the time the province was divided and dissolved into the new Dominion, anglophones were more numerous than francophones. The post-Confederation estrangement of English and French Canadians – fuelled by the Métis uprisings, Louis Riel's execution, the Ontario and Manitoba Schools Questions, and conscription – has been well traversed. A common fanciful misconception is that if English Canada had been more receptive to the French fact, Canada could have flowered as a bilingual nation-state consistent with "the Trudeau vision"[24] in which two official linguistic groups enjoy equal status and thrive everywhere. The reality is that francophone Quebecers have always hesitated to trek beyond their province – more francophones appear to have migrated to Manitoba from Massachusetts than from Quebec[25] – because it meant exile. Quebecers' interest in the settlement of the West was in establishing an additional counterweight to Ontario's influence in the federal arena rather than in creating a potential bilingual region.[26] Paradoxically, Manitoba's francophone culture proved more vibrant after the suppression of French language and schooling rights in the first half of the twentieth century than after those rights were revived and promoted in the second half.[27]

In the 1960s, biculturalism served as a template for the most noteworthy Royal Commission of that decade. At the time, less than a third of Canadians were of French ethnic origins, about a quarter had French as a mother tongue, and fewer than one-fifth were unilingually French.[28] Since then, the French language has been on the rise in Quebec and in retreat outside it. By the 1990s, French was more commonly spoken in Quebec's public discourse than it was, as Quebecers themselves reported, in the private homes of the province. This is a contrast to the situation before the Quiet Revolution, when English had prevailed as the language of industry and commerce.[29] In the anglophone provinces, the assimilation of francophones into the dominant anglophone community shows no abatement. Every province outside Quebec has experienced French linguistic decline; in each passing decade, relatively fewer francophones, as defined by mother tongue, speak French at home.

In recent decades, the financial and symbolic resources of governments, courts, and the Constitution have been deployed to promote bilingualism. Despite Ottawa's Official Languages Act of 1969 and its constitutional reinforcement in 1982, twinned unilingualism – more French and fewer anglophones in Quebec, combined with more English and fewer francophones elsewhere – has prevailed rather than bilingualism. Quebec's government has resisted federal officialdom's efforts by regulating language, through its Charter of the French Language, in a more detailed, comprehensive, and controversial way than any other Western democracy. Outside of Quebec and the bilingual belts along its borders with Ontario and New Brunswick, French has been in retreat, even as the number of bilingual Canadians has grown steadily. In 2001, fewer than 23 percent of Canadians reported French as a mother tongue – the lowest percentage ever. Government inducements to inculcate bilingualism are faltering. English Canadian enthusiasm for French immersion programs peaked in the 1980s. It flatlined in the early 1990s and lost ground among anglophone youth outside Quebec in the late 1990s, although since then a small spike in demand for such programs has occurred in some provinces. Quebec's anglophone community is in steady decline, fuelled by outmigration. Quebec's unilingual anglophones are an aging, oft-dispirited lot. Bilingualism increased overall in Canada in the 1990s, with much of the increase in Quebec. In that decade, only 7 percent of anglophones but 84 percent of francophones outside Quebec were bilingual.[30]

When Cartier spoke of Canada creating a new "nationality," he meant "a political nationality independent of the national origin and religion of individuals." He did not suggest that "diversity will disappear. The idea of a fusion of the races in one is utopian; it is an impossibility. Distinctions ... [of races] will always exist."[31] In this scheme, Canadian identity represents a unity of diversity rather than the homogenization of two cultures. To the Royal Commission on Bilingualism and Biculturalism (B and B) – inaugurated in 1963 and charged with studying the "equal partnership between two founding races" – culture animates a group with common customs, habits, experiences, and language.[32] Identifying Quebec as the heartland but not exclusive home of Canada's francophone society, it pursued the idea of equality between two linguistic communities, which was consistent with Cartier's articulation and the compact theory of two equal peoples. Pierre Trudeau, minister of justice when the B and B Report appeared, feared that an equality of collectivities might imply a sovereign Quebec. His approach was to apply linguistic equality on an individual basis only. Trudeau and English Canada resisted asymmetrical federalism in the form of special status for Quebec to accommodate its linguistic reality. Asymmetrical federalism is quite different from asymmetrical citizenship – granting special privileges to Quebecers, ones not available to others – in the rest of Canada.

In the courts, French-language rights are now faring better than English ones but to little avail for the prospects of non-Quebec francophones. Consider two cases disposed of on the same day in 2001, with contradictory implications for minority language rights in Ontario and Quebec. The Ontario Court of Appeal ruled that, despite its undisputed provincial jurisdiction over hospitals, Queen's Park (the Ontario legislature) could not shut down a French-language hospital because doing so would violate an "unwritten" constitutional value: "respect for and protection of minorities." The Court affirmed the hospital's "important linguistic, cultural and educational role for the franco-Ontarian minority."[33] Simultaneously, the Supreme Court of Canada dismissed the appeal of thirteen mainly anglophone municipalities in Quebec that were fighting their forced merger with the francophone megacity of Montreal, an eventuality that would in effect strip residents of English-language services long enjoyed. The courts ruled in this case that the issue was a political not a legal question.[34] Neither case set off public remonstrations. This suggested a linguistic social peace inside and outside Quebec. On the other hand, the 1988 case in which Quebec invoked the Charter's "notwithstanding" clause to defend its commercial signage law – leading to the unravelling of the Meech Lake Accord – suggested that language issues might provoke political conflagration, and with little prologue. They could do so inside as well as outside the province, as the rise and demise of the English-language rights Equality Party demonstrated. Like the politics of

Quebec separatism and unlike the trends in linguistic demography, the politics of biculturalism are not unidirectional.

The French-English divide is complicated culturally by the presence of Acadians and, to a lesser extent, Newfoundlanders. L'Acadie was separate from New France; Newfoundland, settled separately from the Province of Canada and the Maritimes, was not part of Canada until the middle of the twentieth century. Acadians share French with the Québécois, but their dialects, and more importantly their histories and traditions, differ greatly. They have differing flags, hymns, and feast days. The 1755 expulsion of Acadians to Britain's southern colonies predates the Conquest of Quebec. Acadians were deprived of their civil and religious rights, whereas the Quebec Act of 1774 – two decades later – reinforced those rights for *les canadiens*. When the Queen toured New Brunswick in 2002, Acadians asked for an acknowledgment of Britain's historical exercise in ethnic cleansing – a grievance beyond the Québécois experience. None was forthcoming. Acadians developed their nationalism independently of the Québécois, but because of their minority status in New Brunswick, they had no provincial state to turn to or capture for cultural sustenance as did the Québécois. Only in the Constitution Act, 1982, were French linguistic rights in New Brunswick entrenched.

Acadian cultural interests are akin to those of francophones outside Quebec and divergent from those of the Québécois. Quebec's potential secession represents a threat to francophones outside that province, for in a Canada sans Quebec the rationale for a bilingual federal regime is undermined. Acadians make up a substantial third of New Brunswick, but the province is too small to have much impact on English Canadian national developments. Acadians are served by the bicultural vision of Canada, whereas many nationalist Quebecers are indifferent to or contemptuous of it. René Lévesque depicted the francophone minorities outside Quebec as "dead ducks."[35] The federal government's provision of French-language services in places where few francophones live is derided as "a cruel farce"[36] by Quebec nationalists preoccupied with developing a French provincial or national state. In this view, the bicultural idea of Canada is rejected by English Canadians beyond Quebec and New Brunswick who are waiting for French to fade away. In 2001, fewer than fourteen hundred unilingual francophones lived in Nova Scotia, Newfoundland, Saskatchewan, and PEI combined, easily outnumbered by those with facility in neither of the official languages. For Acadians and other non-Quebec francophones, however, the federal bilingual regime is a laudable sign of cultural respect and acceptance.

Newfoundlanders project a distinctive English Canadian culture due to their island separateness and relatively recent entry to Canada. Prince Edward Islanders also possess an island myth – one of an idyllic garden – but they are too few, too vulnerable, and too intimately and historically linked to the rest of the Maritimes to don nationalist apparel. One encounters references to Newfoundlanders' "emergent nationalism,"[37] but one does not encounter such references in the literature on the other English provinces. Although Quebec is thought of as the province with the strongest separate nationalist or provincialist identity, such an identity is not significantly weaker, and indeed is sometimes stronger, in Newfoundland.[38] It was the only province in which a majority felt so. At the beginning of the twenty-first century, it was Atlantic Canadians, much more so than Quebecers, who strongly agreed that they "feel profoundly attached" to their province.[39]

There is a religious, as well as linguistic, dimension to Canadian biculturalism. It was expressed in the 1867 constitutional protections for Protestant and Catholic schools in Ontario and Quebec. In Newfoundland it was reflected in a denominational basis for legislative representation until the 1960s[40] and in the constitutional provisions for the public funding of seven denominational school systems until the end of the twentieth century. Then, both Quebec and Newfoundland converted their religious-based school systems into public and (in the case of Quebec) linguistic ones. The deinstitutionalization of religion confirmed its declining role as a cultural force in politics and, in Quebec, reinforced the status of the French language independent of its historic connection with Catholicism. The continuing privileged status of Ontario's Catholic schools was censured by the United Nations' Human Rights Commission as discriminatory vis-à-vis other religious denominations;[41] nevertheless, that status was upheld in the courts so that the religious bicultural principle embedded in section 93 of the BNA Act continues to trump the anti-discriminatory and multicultural provisions of the Charter. An example of Anglicanism's continuing symbolic status appears in the fact that, when Governor General Ramon Hnatyshyn died, his funeral was held at the Ottawa Anglican church historically associated with the governors general, even though he himself was a member of the Ukrainian Orthodox Church. Although religious fault lines are not nearly as salient or inflammatory as they once were, they are not yet irrelevant. The extension of public funding to Ontario's Catholic high schools in the 1980s lit a political firestorm that contributed to the fall of the provincial Conservatives after four decades of uninterrupted rule.

Aboriginals borrowed the "distinct society" phrase from Quebecers at the time of the Meech Lake Accord to strengthen their own claims for cultural recognition, but the analogy is not apt. Quebec's French-speaking culture is composed of ever-larger numbers of immigrants of diverse traditions and origins. The emergent Québécois culture is linguistically French but increasingly removed from the historical political culture of French Canada, just as English Canada's culture is increasingly distant from Loyalist Canada's. Aboriginal cultures, in contrast, are not the sort that absorb outsiders; their prospects depend on the children and grandchildren of today's Aboriginals and on their ability to resist assimilation in the future. What Québécois and Aboriginal cultures have in common is that they are "nations within" or "national" groups.[42] This differentiates them from ethnic groups such as the Ukrainians and Chinese, whose Canadian origins lie in the act of immigration to post-Conquest Canada, and who make no claim to any kind of relatively autonomous political entity.

Multiculture

"Multiculturalism" has multiple uses and meanings.[43] It expresses an empirical fact (Canada is ethnically, culturally, and racially diverse) and an ideology (Canadians value diversity). Multiculturalism may also be understood as a policy (pursued by governments since the 1970s) and as a resource for attaining other goals. The multicultural ideals of a polity may not be congruent with its practices, and the intent of multiculturalism may not correspond to its reality. People in a multicultural society have the opportunity to appreciate cultures without judgment or favouritism in a way not available in a monocultural society. They may even aspire to a zero-cultural or post-multiculturalist vista, one that rises above exclusive immersion in Canadian or any national culture.

In the first half of the last century, the relatively few visible minorities – Chinese, Japanese, East Indians, blacks, and Aboriginals – were legally discriminated against in terms of voting and other rights. The Eastern Europeans who transformed Canada into a polyethnic if not multiracial society were also depicted a century ago, even by social progressives like J.S. Woodsworth, as visible minorities, on the basis of their languages, customs, dress, and foods.[44] Many were disenfranchised and interned in detention camps during the First World War, notwithstanding that they were Canadian citizens who had fled the very regimes with which Canada was at war. They were limited in the political process by extralegal conventions that held them ineligible for cabinet service or senior public administration posts. In the private sector, discriminatory racial pecking orders in employment practices contributed to a vertical mosaic of wealth and power.[45] Over time, however, acculturation, integration, assimilation, and the loss by subsequent generations of their forebears' mother tongues made the European minorities appear as established rather than "ethnic" or "new" Canadians, terms now most commonly applied to the non-European visible minorities that have recently come to Canada. At the beginning of the twenty-first century, Chinese was the third-most common mother tongue in Canada, and the more than 1 million Chinese Canadians outnumbered Aboriginals.

Multiculturalism defined by ethnic, racial, religious, and linguistic diversity has grown dramatically. The 2001 census revealed that the foreign-born proportion of the population was at its highest level in seven decades.[46] Until the 1960s, government immigration policies discriminated in favour of Europeans and white Americans. In recent decades, the majority of immigrants have been visible minorities – they increased threefold between 1981 and 2001 – coming from east and south Asia but also from Africa, the Middle East, the Caribbean, and Latin America. Three-quarters of them settled in Toronto, Vancouver, and Montreal, even though only a third of Canadians live there. This produces yet another gulf between urban and rural Canada. The large metropolitan centres are increasingly cosmopolitan and multiracial polyglots, but the rural regions are still overwhelmingly white and Christian. The northerly hinterlands of the provinces and the territories, in further contrast, are disproportionately populated by Aboriginals.

Perceptions of Canada's cultural composition have changed within officialdom and among the public. In the nineteenth century, the census' major ethnic categories were English, French, Irish, and "Scotch" (rather than Scottish). Relying on self-classification, the census until 1981 specified a patrilineal basis of ethnicity. Thus, the Canadian-born daughter of a Polish father and a French mother was deemed Polish, even though she may never have met her father or had any connection with Poland or the Polish language. "Canadian" was until recently excluded as an ethnic category, although "American" has long been acceptable. In rhythm with the rise of feminism and ethnic intermarriage, more recent censuses have provided for "multiple" origins. A respondent may now call herself "Canadian" or "Polish and French." This change in census classifications confounds delineating ethnic origins but reflects changing realities and values. Other societal changes have also compelled revisions in official terminology. The census once categorized "pagans";

few identified themselves as such, given its icily pejorative connotation. As the stigma of atheism and agnosticism faded and the more neutral "no religion" category appeared, the number of unbelievers mushroomed. More inter-religious marriages also meant cross-pressures in religious self-identification.

Biculturalism, expressed in the B and B Commission's very title, did not sit well with Canada's once deferential non-charter ethnocultural communities as they became more assertive and prominent in society and politics. In 1971, the Trudeau government sidestepped some of the commission's recommendations by rechannelling cultural dualism into a multiculturalism policy. This undermined the bicultural paradigm feeding Quebec's exceptionalism and quest for sovereignty.[47] "Third Force" (especially Slavic) Canadians[48] lobbied for the recognition of multiculturalism, arguing that the commission's framework of "two founding races" was inaccurate and insulting; on the prairies, Ukrainians and others had been more prominent than the French as pioneers. In relatively short order, however, the enthusiasm for multiculturalism among these European groups waned as new waves of visible minorities appeared and became the major beneficiaries of multicultural policy and programs. The "ethnic" appellation – long used to stigmatize Eastern Europeans – lost much of its relevance for them and others. By the 1980s, Slavs made up one-third of the Manitoba cabinet, and a Lebanese Canadian was elected premier of PEI. Then, in the 1990s, for the first time, all three Prairie provinces had premiers of non-British ethnic origins, and an Indo-Canadian became the premier of British Columbia. Aboriginals came to serve as lieutenant-governors in a number of provinces, and a Chinese Canadian of immigrant parents became governor general.

Official conceptualizations of multiculturalism shifted over time. The frame of reference in the 1970s was ethnicity; its program mandate was sponsorship of folkloric expression in an environment of perceived British Canadian ethnocentrism. By the 1990s, the frame of reference became one of equity, with a program mandate to foster race relations and combat racism in a perceived environment of systemic discrimination. Government policy went from emphasizing newcomers' adjustment, if not assimilation, to Canadian ways to restructuring Canadian institutions to accommodate them. The passive funding and celebration of cultural differences gave way to the proactive management of diversity. The key metaphor of multiculturalism was transformed from the older trope of "mosaic" to that of "kaleidoscope."

Critics of multiculturalism lambaste it as a wrong-headed policy, divisive rather than unifying as intended.[49] According to this critique, groups are encouraged to preserve rather than submerge their "tribalisms," risking the ethnic balkanization of Canada. The Reform Party promised to terminate funding for multiculturalism, leaving initiatives to private individuals and groups, as is the case with religion.[50] A sociologist characterized one way of seeing multiculturalism as "a form of cultural genocide aimed at the destruction of a pan-Canadian identity."[51] Whereas some see government policy as progressive, others decry it as regressive; whereas some see it as substantial, others dismiss it as merely symbolic. Some see multiculturalism, based on the praiseworthy egalitarian premise of equal-status cultures, as challenging the inequality engendered by capitalism, but others see "selling diversity" as a marketing ploy pitched to global corporate investors.[52]

Aging clichés are those of Canada as a "mosaic" and the US as a "melting pot." Constitutionally, Canada has always acknowledged group rights, whereas the US has not. The Constitution Act, 1982, explicitly providing for affirmative action programs for disadvantaged minority groups, includes race, religion, ethnicity, and national origin as criteria. Canada in this respect does what the US does not, although affirmative action programs appeared in the US before their importation by Canadian policy makers. Many Canadians smugly assert that, though America pressures its immigrant minorities to abandon their customs, Canada celebrates group differences. Prime Minister Joe Clark fondly defined Canada as a "community of communities," an implicit contrast to the US as a community of individuals. This distinction highlights Canadian tolerance of cultural diversity and American insistence on conformity. The contrast is questionable. According to survey research, more Canadians than Americans want immigrants to blend into the larger society.[53] More Americans than Canadians voice tolerance for immigrants' maintenance of their distinct cultural ways. Thus, as regards tolerance for cultural diversity, the similarities between Americans and Canadians may be greater than is suggested in the self-image of many Canadians. On the other hand, in the same survey, more Canadians than Americans were accepting of racial intermarriage among their children. Canada was spared a civil war, and its history of slavery is marginal rather than central. Racial strife continues to weigh on American politics and public consciousness in a way it does not in Canada.

French Canadian and Aboriginal identities persist, but "multicultural" Canadians are less wedded to their cultural origins and traditions. In the 2001 census, the biggest change in self-classification by ethnicity came in the explosive increase, by 3 million respondents, of those who chose the category of "Canadian." This suggests that multiculturalism itself may be a passing frame of reference in politics, or perhaps that "multicultural" is less potent than "Canadian" as a signifier of identity. Many members of visible and other minorities who continue to organize along ethnocultural lines are seen by themselves and others in terms of their forbears' groups; however, their group cultures, political and otherwise, are increasingly less discernible and less relevant to them. The common denominator for those individuals drawn from these groups of "ethnic" Canadians who list their ethnicity as "Canadian" is their Canadian identity and their individual opportunities, rights, and freedoms rather than their ethnocultural group membership.

Aboriginal Culture

Unlike those of the French, who have recognized rights and a Quebec provincial state to protect them, and unlike those of the ethnocultural groups who moved up the socio-economic ladder despite informal discriminatory codes, Aboriginal identity and culture were at first systematically and zealously suppressed. Aboriginal culture was derided and vilified as inhumane. Popular literature, films, and textbooks depicted Aboriginals either as sinister, bloodthirsty savages or as eternal children, naïve and resistant to civilization's ways.[54] Official authority – constitutionally charged in section 91(24) of the BNA Act with a fiduciary obligation for Aboriginal welfare – deemed Aboriginals as inferiors in need of enlightenment and refinement. This often entailed the forced separation of parents and children, the suppression of their languages, and the indoctrination of Aboriginal children with the exoteric trappings of religions and customs alien to their own esoteric spiritual, cultural traditions.

Parallels do exist between nationalist Québécois and militant Aboriginal analyses of their conditions and their quests for self-determination and sovereignty. Just as the older rural agrarian world of *les habitants* had largely evaporated by the 1940s – they became urban tenants and industrial labourers – the traditional hunter-gatherer Aboriginal economy had vanished in the Far North by the same time and in southern Canada in the nineteenth century. As far as their respective circumstances were concerned, Pierre Vallières' depiction of the Québécois as the white niggers of America would have been more fittingly applied to Aboriginals.[55] The decolonization of French West Africa in the 1960s was an impetus and ideological model for a redefined, assertive Québécois nationalism. The language of national liberation and anti-imperialism then influenced Aboriginals living on the impoverished periphery of an affluent society. It became commonplace in both Québécois nationalist and Aboriginal circles to define their group identities as victims of oppressive colonization by racist governments. That was the historical analysis put forward in the Parti Québécois' 1980 White Paper on Sovereignty-Association, and the frame of reference for leading Aboriginal figures. George Erasmus, for example, head of the Assembly of First Nations and later of the Royal Commission on Aboriginal Peoples, declared in 1975 that Frantz "Fanon's *Wretched of the Earth* is my bible."[56] In the struggles for self-government, Aboriginal leaders emulated Quebecers' language and tactics. They were students of what Quebec had accomplished in negotiating with Ottawa in matters such as the Meech Lake Accord, from which Aboriginals had been excluded.

There are of course important distinctions between the situation of the Québécois and that of Aboriginal societies. Unlike that of Quebec's francophones, but like those of the immigrant ethnocultural communities, Aboriginal languages have largely given way to English. Fewer than a quarter of the approximately 800,000 Aboriginals in the mid-1990s had an Aboriginal mother tongue; fewer still spoke it at home. Over two-thirds reported English as their mother tongue.[57] By 2001, the number of self-identified Aboriginals had grown by 22 percent (versus 3 percent for the non-Aboriginal population) to about 1 million. Although Aboriginals have a higher birth rate than the population as a whole, it does not fully account for their dramatic increase. It is, rather, due to the uplifted social, legal, and political status of contemporary Aboriginal cultures. They have gone from belittlement to being respectfully esteemed. The federal and some provincial governments, as one example, have investigated the possibility of allotting designated seats and constituencies, as in New Zealand, for Aboriginal political representation.

The embrace of aboriginalism by former self-identified non-Aboriginals raises the issue of cultural coherence and meaning. Culture is transmitted and learned across generations. Opting into a culture by declaring oneself a member of a group does not always reflect the continuity associated with culture. Many who are part Aboriginal and who once self-identified as descendants of other ethnic groups are now proud, rather than ashamed, to call themselves Aboriginals. Complicating the delineation of Aboriginal culture is that Canada's Aboriginal nations are composed of many micro-societies of

differing linguistic origins employing a variety of customs. Ottawa has designated over six hundred distinct Indian bands (to some extent, these are imposed bureaucratic categorizations). Unlike the francophones of Quebec, who
are concentrated in one province, Aboriginal communities are widely dispersed, relatively small, and sparsely populated; many are far from other
centres. The term "Aboriginal" itself is broad: constitutionally, it encompasses
status and non-status Indians, those on and off reserves, Inuit, and Métis. As
status Indians intermarry, progressively fewer of their descendants will inherit the guaranteed federal government obligations regarding their welfare.
The result in the longer term will be more Aboriginals as defined since 1982
but fewer Indians as defined before then. "Métis" is a particularly problematic category, for it is composed of those of mixed Indian-white descent who
are bereft of a land base (with some exceptions in Alberta). The most famous
Métis, Louis Riel, was but one-eighth Indian.

Aboriginal cultures are disproportionately afflicted with social pathologies: exceptionally high rates of incarceration, spousal, sexual, and substance
abuse, alcoholism, and suicide. As a group, Aboriginals are economic have-
nots: poorly housed, overrepresented among the unemployed, of below
average incomes and levels of educational attainment. Subject to shorter-
than-average lifespans, they suffer comparatively high rates of infant mortal-
ity, tuberculosis, diabetes, and HIV-AIDS. No one would argue that self-
government in and of itself would attenuate such conditions. The challenge
to Aboriginal culture and its renewal is developing human resources – as
Quebec did in its Quiet Revolution – to cultivate the skills needed to prosper
within a broader, largely non-Aboriginal world. In this respect, the Quebec
nationalist model – striving for sovereignty via the symbolically elevated
politics of constitutional revision – may not prove particularly helpful in
meeting Aboriginals' needs and aspirations.

Traditional Aboriginal political systems and their political cultures stand
apart from those familiar to most Canadians. Although all of them exhibit a
traditional hunter-gatherer society's predilection for consensus, there is no
single Aboriginal model of governance; collectively they generally feature the
pursuit of harmony, non-interference, persuasion, and unanimity.[58] They shun
the adversarial, confrontational, and narrowly majoritarian politics common
to Western liberal democracies. These differences point to dissimilar philosophical paths. In the West, the principle of egalitarianism arose as a reaction
to hierarchical doctrine. The Indian conception of equality, which predates
Western liberalism, derives from the classlessness of hunter-gatherer society

and is legitimated by "the creation myth ... that, from the *beginning*, all members of all tribes shared and participated *equally* in all privileges."[59] The Aboriginal perception of sovereignty is at odds with that of Quebec's sovereigntists, who, in the tradition of Western liberal thought, consider it an act of human agency. Drawing on a spiritual rather than rationalist tradition, the Aboriginal conception of sovereignty is one of a gift of creation – something that can neither be given, taken away, nor negotiated. It is, in the words of an Aboriginal chief, "the original freedom conferred to our people by the Creator rather than a temporal power."[60]

In submissions to the Royal Commission on Aboriginal Peoples, many First Nations intervenors called on their own band governments to revive traditional methods of decision making and accountability.[61] The Department of Indian Affairs, however, guided by mainstream conceptions of democracy and transparency, has pressed First Nations communities to adopt majority-based electoral systems displacing traditional family-based consensus processes. This has contributed to splintering communities, altering the traditional roles of elders and women, and breeding distrust of elected leaders and appointed officials, whose positions become a function of the domination of numerically powerful families.

Where Aboriginals have constituted a majority in a Canadian political system – first in the North-West Territories, then in Nunavut – an innovative operational melding of Aboriginal political sensibilities and parliamentary institutions has emerged. The Westminster model was modified; political parties did not arise with their attendant conventions of party discipline and leadership hierarchy. The government leader or premier and cabinet are collectively selected by the MLAs, all having run as independents. One upshot is that the Aboriginal-dominated legislature escapes "the raucous, rough-and-tumble standards of behaviour of other Canadian legislatures."[62] Nevertheless, non-confidence votes do take place and the cabinet centralizes power. The evolving system of territorial government has been criticized by some as falling short of traditional consensus politics, and chided by others as making for the inefficiencies and deadlock that a more conventional cabinet-parliamentary model overcomes. Whatever its merits or faults, the hybrid system's roots are tentative, its prospects uncertain. Accelerated economic development, infusions of corporate capital and management, shifts in Aboriginal-non-Aboriginal population ratios, increasing levels of educational attainment, and further exposure to Southern culture via television and the

Internet may dampen the territorial experimentation with open, participatory, non-partisan, and inclusive government.

A challenge to modern Aboriginal political cultures is reconciling consensual traditions with the subtly tenuous relationship of leaders and followers. The accepted style of Aboriginal political leadership is collective; leaders exercise authority with circumspection. Deliberation, co-operation, and constructive dialogue are touchstones; confrontation and oppositional posturing – prevalent in the dominant political culture as expressed in parliamentary institutions – are eschewed. Leaders and followers in the broader mainstream Canadian culture accept and operate with a majoritarian principle. Indians and Inuit have adopted it, with modification (60 percent required), for the selection of the national chief of the Assembly of First Nations, their peak association.

An example of the gulf between Aboriginal leaders and followers, one that parallels the gulf between politicians and general public, appeared in the response to the Charlottetown Accord. In the accord, leaders of four Aboriginal associations attained more than Aboriginals had ever before achieved in constitutional negotiations. When the referendum failed, federal and provincial first ministers immediately accepted the public's humiliating rebuff ("the people have spoken") and promptly swore off talk of future constitutional tinkering. By contrast, Aboriginal leaders vituperatively lashed out at the non-Aboriginal majority for trumping Aboriginal minority rights and frustrating Aboriginal aspirations. However, First Nations voting patterns greatly resembled those of mainstream Canada. For the first time, these had been tabulated separately, an innovation that ironically had been urged by the Aboriginal leaders themselves. Wishing to demonstrate what they believed would be the overwhelming Aboriginal preference for what they had negotiated, they had insisted that the chief electoral officer tabulate separate results for predominantly Aboriginal polls (as on reserves). In actuality, poll results subsequently revealed that Aboriginals had more resoundingly rejected the accord than had Canadians as a whole, indicating an even wider chasm than suggested between Aboriginal leaders and their followers. Why? There is no single reason: there are many, including the diverse needs, perspectives, and ongoing fragmentation of Aboriginal societies, the weak influence of Aboriginal leaders, and the preference of many Aboriginals for their established links with the Department of Indian Affairs. Breaking with Ottawa was tantamount to experimenting with the unknown. Aboriginal women's groups effectively fought the accord on the grounds that the insulation and guarantees it offered traditional Aboriginal cultures would detach Aboriginal women from accessing their equality rights under the Charter. Despite the reversal, First Nations leaders and first ministers pursued Aboriginal self-government as if it had been popularly endorsed. They did so in the Canadian vein of negotiated administrative arrangements and iterative legal change. In 2004, for example, Ottawa proposed legislation permitting First Nations, for the first time, to develop their own public institutions with the issuance of bonds.[63]

When Aboriginal, non-Quebec French, and other ethnocultural groups are compared, they display commonalties but also essential cultural differences. All are experiencing high rates of exogamy, cultural assimilation in the sense of popular culture, and linguistic discontinuity. Modernization, urbanization, and mass communication speed these up. On the vital issue of identity, however, the tendencies in these groups differ greatly. Notwithstanding their rejection of Aboriginal self-government in the Charlottetown Accord, Aboriginals have revived and celebrated their Aboriginal identity, something long repressed as painfully shameful. Placing the census in historical perspective reveals the revolution in Aboriginal identity. Although Manitoba was overwhelmingly an Aboriginal society when it entered Confederation in 1870, only nine people identified themselves as either Indian or Métis in the 1871 census of Winnipeg; only thirty did so in 1916, when the city was the country's third largest. Now, about 10 percent of Manitobans are Aboriginal. The multicultural minorities are the keenest to embrace the generic "Canadian" label of ethnic self-identification. French Canadian identity outside Quebec has perhaps fared better than that of the older European ethnic groups, but Frenchness as once manifested in language, observant Catholicism, and residentially segregated communities has faded. The same may be said of Aboriginal cultures. Their languages, spiritual practices, and once inaccessible and relatively self-contained communities are receding as ever more migrate to urban centres.

Unlike multiculturalism and like biculturalism, Aboriginal cultures have achieved a potent elevated status in legal jurisprudence. This has occurred despite the absence of explicit constitutional references to the culture of Aboriginals. The Constitution does refer to multiculturalism. However, its express section 27 direction, that the courts interpret it "in a manner consistent with the preservation and enhancement of the multicultural heritage of Canadians,"[64] has had little impact. Aboriginals do enjoy "rights and freedoms," including "treaty rights" (sections 25 and 35) – an indirect acknowledgment of culture or nation. The recognition of Aboriginal "cultural distinctiveness" in the anthropological sense has been pivotal in the Supreme Court's construction of the edifice of Aboriginal rights and title. Nevertheless, nothing the courts have done has abated intercultural assimilation and intermarriage of Aboriginals or others. According to a leading anthropological authority on Canada's Aboriginals, the courts have adopted a "naïve and outmoded conceptualization of culture," one that reflects "an ethnocentric frame of reasoning"[65] rather than conceptualizing Aboriginal rights as fundamental political rights.[66] That route would raise destabilizing questions about the existing jurisdictional arrangements between First Nations and Ottawa. Also, for instances of courtroom testimony that are based in Aboriginal oral history, the courts have removed the jurisprudential pride of place traditionally accorded to written evidence. Such recognition has obviously not been legally accessible to other Canadian cultural traditions.

The prisms of pan-Canadian culture, biculturalism, multiculturalism, and Aboriginal cultures indicate competing conceptions of equality and equity. The pan-Canadian perspective stresses the equality of Canadians as individuals. They share national institutions such as parliament, the Charter, medicare, and hockey. The bicultural and multicultural prisms highlight the principle of the equality of groups. The bicultural prism is that of the two founding "peoples," French and British, of the modern Canadian state. The multicultural one implies equal status for all cultures. The Aboriginals' claim of continuing structural impediments to their culture's development is the most striking. Leading Canadian political thinkers such as Charles Taylor, Will Kymlicka, Alan Cairns, and others have striven to reconcile the divergences that these cultural prisms present.[67] The prospect for a uniformly tidy individualist culture is weak and inconsistent with the Canadian tradition of collective group recognition. The path in the future, as in the past, will be one of cultural ambiguity. If multiple understandings of citizenship and culture are permitted to co-exist, Canadians – individually and as cultural groups – will continue to be free to define themselves as they wish rather than as is prescribed for them. For French Canadians in Chicoutimi, the compact dualism of the Confederation bargain may thus be perceived as an inherited covenant deserving of recognition. For Somalis in Toronto and Chinese in Vancouver, living in those multicultural milieux helps them to define their Canadianness. For Aboriginals, a broadly acknowledged recognition and respect by others for nativeness and natural belonging reinforces the pride necessary to sustain their culture.

The past has a vote on how Canada's multiple cultures evolve, but it does not have a veto. Canadians are capable of renegotiating for themselves their individual and group identities. When they attempt to do so collectively – as the Meech Lake and Charlottetown imbroglios demonstrated – Canada is in danger of implosion.[68] Those convulsions condemned the high politics of constitutional rewriting as dangerous folly because of the deep-seated emotions and powerful symbols they evoked. The less grandiose politics of muddling through the earthly, temporal, day-to-day world of political issues as they arise accomplishes more and risks less. This requires respecting, interacting with, and showing compassion for alternative cultural prisms. Tolerance, mutual respect, and goodwill among cultures cannot be constitutionalized on paper, only by praxis. Debates over whether Canada has, should, or can have a distinctive national culture will continue. They will persevere so long as there are Canadians of distinctly different cultural origins and as long as most Canadians share the language and many cultural icons of their potent American neighbour. Some will insist on Canada's essential duality, one driven and defined by language. Others will focus on the hyphens of multiculturalism. Still others will draw attention to Aboriginal cultures as the only genuinely native ones.

The Canadian way is one of cultural diversity and ambiguity. Canadians' peaceful co-existence amid their staggering cultural diversity makes their country of interest to others in the developed and developing worlds. Compared to the states that founded it and helped populate it, Canada's peaceable kingdom of co-existing cultures has developed in a malleable way. In those states, immigration and cultural distinctiveness are more potent political issues. For culturally diverse developing states such as South Africa and Sri Lanka, Canada's relative tranquility and harmony, combined with its institutional pillars of federalism and a Charter containing both collective group and individual rights, make it a source for ideas, emulation, and model building. Canada is now one of the world's oldest nation-states, but its enviable and evolving cultural features keep it a relatively new society.

5
Regions and Political Culture

In the 1960s and 1970s, a "modernization" thesis gained sway among social scientists; it postulated that as regionalized nascent national societies and economies age, they do so centripetally.[1] Integration and centralization would accompany the nation-state's maturation, its nationalization. In social policy fields such as education, pensions, and health care, modernization would imply steady movement toward common national levels of accessibility and criteria of quality. In the economic realm, modernization would intimate industrialization, urbanization, income increases, and, possibly, a more equitable distribution of resources and wealth. From a cultural modernization perspective, the evolution of Canada's national transportation, financial, and communications networks – railroads, highways, airlines, banks, the CBC, and self-styled "national" newspapers and magazines – would foster national consciousness and dampen regional identities. Political cleavages in the modernization scenario would be increasingly organized along territorially crosscutting horizontal functional lines such as social class, age, and gender. They would be decreasingly driven by the containerized vertical territorial lines of provinces or regions and their particularistic cultures rooted in language, religion, and ethnicity. The modernization thesis anticipates a unidirectional movement toward integrative nation-state building and consolidation. In it, national interest groups, for example, would come to overshadow regional ones. However, as the twentieth century unfolded, ethnocultural and regional movements gained and sustained momentum in both the developed and developing world – from Britain, Spain, Belgium, and Canada to Yugoslavia, Pakistan, Nigeria, and Moldova.

In recent decades another umbrella concept, "globalization," describes a process that contributed to thwarting the independent spheres of nation-states. National identities and cultures appear to be simultaneously falling apart and coming together. Globalization feeds the harmonization of tastes and standards. Movements in the direction of globalization include liberal-ized international trade and investment regimes, as well as instantaneous global communications networks and capital flows. Contemporaneously, peace, environmental, human rights, and anti-globalization movements have become more globally co-ordinated in their outlooks and efforts. Greenpeace, for example, was launched in Canada but operates as an international envi-ronmental movement. Anti-globalization demonstrations and protesters move from one national venue to another, following and harassing the ne-gotiators of global agreements. Globalization implies evermore porous na-tional boundaries and the seamless movements of people and products across them. However, security considerations in the aftermath of the 2001 terrorist attacks on the US highlighted, indeed elevated, the importance of national-ity and citizenship. Passports and visas – indicators of national identity – are now more scrutinized and vital than ever before in global travel. Liberalism's hub is the individual's distinctive qualities and efforts, but heightened secu-rity measures may shine brighter light on inherited traits – birthplace, ethni-city, religion, nationality, race – than on an individual's achievements and aspirations.

Paradoxically, as globalization has undermined the policy-making ca-pacities of national governments,[2] the significance of regional and local gov-ernments has grown. In most states, it is they who are responsible for delivering the requisite educational and social infrastructure that makes for successful competition in a globalized economic environment. One reason to pay at-tention to regional political cultures is that the drive for more regional au-tonomy and local self-government has itself taken on global dimensions. In the global communications village, devolution, decentralization, and decon-centration are rallying cries countering both nationalization and globaliza-tion. In this respect, the locally grounded resident and the globally conscious citizen are one and the same person. He cheers the rise of organic regional and city states whose internal coherence is rooted in a locally experienced culture rather than in an artificially conceived national or global one.

Canada is no exception in the push for more regionalist agendas in pub-lic policy and for regional power in public administration. Regional urban governments have emerged since the 1950s as intermediary structures be-tween older localized municipalities and central provincial authorities. In various policy fields, regional planning authorities have proliferated. Although many new regional governance arrangements have floundered, the dynamism of Canada's city regions, such as Toronto, Montreal, and Vancouver, is irrepressible.[3] The rationales for new regional political structures are not merely administrative efficiencies: they incorporate the premise that regional vehicles and forums are most responsive to local sensibilities and values.

Regional identities and interregional tensions in national politics have allegedly been fostered and exacerbated by the electoral system, a favourite whipping boy of Canadian political scientists.[4] The first-past-the-post system, according to a seminal article by Alan Cairns, conditions political parties to pursue regional rather than crosscutting nation-building strategies.[5] Courting regions enhances electoral performance; courting the country as a whole appears to dampen it. Between the 1920s and the 1960s, federal election results and their attendant regional cleavages made the Liberals appear as the party of Quebec, the Conservatives as that of Ontario, and the CCF-NDP as that of the West. A decomposition of the parties' popular vote, however, reveals more regional evenness in their support. In 1945, for example, the CCF won more votes in Ontario than in Saskatchewan, yet garnered no seats in the former and captured eighteen of the twenty-one seats in the latter. The Reform/Alliance Party experienced the same distortions in the 1990s and 2000. Partisan clashes in parliament could thus be seen in a distorting mirror as clashes between the values of regions and their citizens, as given voice and face by the regionally imbalanced caucuses of MPs. Scathing criticism of the outputs of the electoral system seemed justified in the 1990s, with their contortion of the Reform, Progressive Conservative, and Liberal votes to make them appear as parties of the West, Atlantic Canada, and Ontario respectively. The salutary premise of national parties – that they incorporate and mediate regional differences within their caucuses – is strained when regional lopsidedness prevails in all their caucuses.

In the late 1980s, two decades after Cairns' critique, the party system and its parties had become noticeably less regionalized: the Liberals held seats in nine provinces, the Conservatives in eight, and the NDP in five and one territory. The Progressives and Social Credit, voices and beneficiaries of sectional feelings of alienation, had faded and disappeared. Because the party system's regional skew was no longer obvious, the electoral system could hardly be faulted for producing a party system that thrived on exploiting regional suspicions of neglect. Notwithstanding the relative nationalization of the parties and party system, regional tensions exploded in the Meech Lake–Charlottetown debacle of the late 1980s and early 1990s. This confirmed

that distinctive and powerful regional feelings transcended the federal political parties. The Reform Party (contesting only Western seats in 1988) and
the Bloc Québécois (running exclusively in Quebec) represented not the
misbegotten offspring of the electoral system but the real, palpable political
clash of competing cultural visions and regional identities.

Recognition of the significance of distinct regional political cultures pro-
pelling federal parties must be tempered with an appreciation of the parties'
ideologically national, rather than regional, agendas. The Progressives' revolt
was more agrarian than it was Western; in their 1921 breakthrough, twenty-
four of their sixty-five seats were in Ontario, and one was in the Maritimes.
The CCF-NDP message was, originally, of a universal Christian social gospel,
then of national social planning, then of comprehensive social security, and
then of non-territorial social movements. Canadian socialism was never presented as a sectional agenda, to be erected behind a provincial or regional
wall. Social Credit's monetarist and populist messages were similarly intended
for national rather than regional application. So too for the Reform/Alliance's
fiscal and social conservatism, and its critiques of bilingualism, multiculturalism, and special status for Aboriginals. As for the nationalist BQ, it is a regional party from a federalist perspective only.

Regional or Provincial?

The case for the salience of regional political cultures is as necessary to make
as it is difficult to sustain. Regional grievances are undisputed features of the
national political terrain, but the notion that regional political cultures drive
them has not been well developed. Yet, regional political cultures beg for
magnification as there are good reasons to question the concept of a coherent
national political culture. To present Canadian political culture as an amalgam of its regional political cultures is akin to trying to tie a number of water-
melons together with a piece of string. Canada's vast regions are not easily
bound together. Nevertheless, appreciation of regional political cultures deepens understanding of Canadian identity. Like ethnicity and class, regionalism is a limited identity, but, as Ramsay Cook noted, "It might just be in
these limited identities that 'Canadianism' is found."[6]

There is a good case to be mounted in divining sub-national political
cultures as provincial political cultures. The much-cited 1974 article by Simeon
and Elkins, "Regional Political Cultures," was retitled "Provincial Political
Cultures" when they updated it in 1980.[7] The institutional infrastructure of

provincial governments – legislatures and laws, cabinets and courts, bureaucrats and budgets – feed provincially divergent development paths: legally, economically, socially, and culturally. As one example, exclusive provincial control over education (section 93, BNA Act, 1867) produces province-specific school curricula for the teaching of culturally laden subjects such as history, languages, and literature. Prairie residents whose education may have dwelled on the travails of the wheat economy and homesteading European immigrants will develop social and political narratives that differ from those of Quebecers schooled in issues of biculturalism and the 1837 rebellion. Both, in turn, will differ from those of Maritimers who study Loyalist landmarks and the chronicles of the fishery. Provinces have constitutionally mandated powers, identical spheres of policy jurisdiction, and their own electoral systems. Regions have none of these. Unless region is equated with province, regions per se have no institutional force.

To be sure, regions are not devoid of constitutional, policy, and political status. The BNA Act constructed a Senate with explicit regional divisions: twenty-four seats each for the Maritimes, Quebec, Ontario, and the West. The Supreme Court of Canada Act provides for three Quebec judges. It is otherwise unspecific about the Court's composition, but in practice an operative convention arose: an equivalent three judges from Ontario, two from the West, and one from the Atlantic region. The convention regarding the Western and Atlantic judges speaks to a regional rather than provincial requirement. Examples of cross-provincial, regional identity are the groupings of premiers in the Atlantic Provinces Economic Council and the Western Premiers Conferences. They serve as summit mechanisms co-ordinating regional policies and postures vis-à-vis Ottawa. The latter began as an assembly of Prairie premiers (the Prairies Economic Conference), later expanded to include BC, and was later yet further enlarged to incorporate the government leaders of the Yukon and Northwest Territories. During the 1980s, and into the 1990s, Ontario and Quebec formed something of a central Canadian entente operating offices in each other's capitals and having their premiers meet semi-annually.

Sundry structures reinforce regional identities rather than contribute to dissolving them. They imply that regional cultures are positive forces in need of nourishment. Examples of region-specific federal legislation are the Maritime Freight Rates Act of 1927 and the Prairie Farm Rehabilitation Act of 1985. In the 1960s, Ottawa created a Department of Regional Economic

Expansion (DREE), an acknowledgment of structural regional disparities. DREE represented a regional rather than a province-specific response, one more than simply cross-provincial; parts of certain provinces (such as north-ern Ontario) came under its program mandate, though other parts of the same province (southern Ontario) did not. Unemployment insurance and other programs such as the Agricultural and Rural Development Act and the Fund for Rural Economic Development have had express regional dimen-sions in their mandates (the former for the Prairies, the latter for the Mari-times). The federal cabinet in 2003 included one secretary of state responsible for the Economic Development Agency of Canada for the Regions of Que-bec, others for Western Economic Diversification and the Atlantic Canada Opportunities Agency, and yet another for Northern Development. Part 3 of the Constitution Act, 1982, titled "Regional Disparities," mandates federal equalization payments to poor provinces. The presence of such cabinet-level and constitutional focus on regions contrasts with its absence in the US. There, economic development policy strives to bring people to jobs, whereas Can-adian policy has tried to bring jobs to people in their regions. Provinces have also embraced their own regional initiatives. Many have Departments of Northern Affairs. With the view of giving "equal dignity and self-sustaining quality to each of the regions and all their people," Manitoba articulated a "stay option" as a guiding policy principle to provide people with opportu-nities to live and work where "they have roots."[8] Non-profit public policy research institutes like the Canada West Foundation introduce regional per-spectives into national policy debates. In addition, cross-border international regional associations of political executives have emerged since the 1950s:[9] Atlantic premiers meet with their New England counterparts, Western pre-miers with Western governors, and Ontario's with those of the Great Lakes states.

Canada has shifted from intrastate toward interstate politics, which el-evates the status of provincial states and identities at the expense of inter-provincial regional interests and identities. The case for provincial political cultures trumping regional ones emerges from an analysis of the evolution of the Canadian party system. Between the First World War and the 1960s, a time of "brokerage politics and ministerialist parties,"[10] prime ministers used "regional ministers"[11] as lieutenants to aggregate, articulate, mobilize, and reward regional interests. Regional bosses at the cabinet table – like Jimmy Gardiner for the Prairies – have since given way to provincial ministers. The brokering and mediating among regional ministers by the prime minister was also overtaken by the summitry of federal-provincial meetings of first ministers. Premiers came to the fore as both provincial and regional spokesmen. Designated provincial ministers in the federal cabinet now have relatively weak power bases compared to those of premiers and the regional ministers of old. Moreover, they are shuffled at the prime minister's whim.

Shifting from an institutional to a behavioural frame, one is hard pressed to deny that Canadians' popular cultural tastes are incontrovertibly similar (certainly in English Canada). Their political behaviour across provinces, however, has been remarkably dissimilar. This is noticeable, as we have seen, in the regional variations in national partisan support. It is also striking at the provincial level. Atlantic Canadians have never experienced – as have all other regions and provinces – a non-Liberal or non-Conservative provincial government. In contrast, Western Canadians in all four provinces have flirted with and embraced third parties that – like the NDP on the one hand, and Social Credit on the other – have been at opposite poles of the political spectrum. Ontarians stand out because, in three elections over eight years (between 1987 and 1995), they elected three majority governments led by three different parties, a feat of volatility unprecedented in Canadian politics. Quebec, in further contrast, has had a major nationalist party since the 1930s, whereas the other regions have had none. Parliament in the 1990s and at the beginning of the twenty-first century appeared – somewhat as it had in earlier decades – to be a forum for regionally based parties rather than national ones. When socio-economic and demographic variables are dissected, regionalism's imprint was equally unmistakable: women and the aged in Atlantic Canada were more likely to support the federal Progressive Conservatives than the NDP; the opposite applied to women in the Midwest (Manitoba and Saskatchewan). Business people in the Far West (Alberta and BC) were more likely to rally to the Reform/Alliance Party than were their counterparts in Ontario and Quebec, who proved more receptive to the Liberals and Conservatives.

Ideational versus Operational Norms

Sid Noel has deftly differentiated the ideational and operational elements of political culture.[12] The ideational elements are the high principles of ideology, contending philosophies circulating in a society's political discourse. They are competing perspectives on what constitutes ideals such as freedom, equality, justice, and democracy. The ideational elements in a political culture and their shorthand categorizations, such as "left" and "right," play out in the rhetoric of political debate. These attract media and scholarly attention. In contrast, the operational elements of political culture are the give-and-take of everyday political life. They are implicit rather than debated and promulgated as principles. These pervasive operational norms shape the manner in which leaders, political parties, and institutions behave because there is public expectation of such behaviour. They define what is acceptable and exclude what is not. Noel identifies five such operational norms in Ontario's political culture: the imperative pursuit of economic success, the assumption of the province's pre-eminence in Canada, the requirement of managerial efficiency in government, the expectation of reciprocity between leaders and followers, and the presupposition that governments will balance competing interests to maintain power. For Noel, these operative elements in Ontario's political culture have pedigrees, some dating back to the establishment of Upper Canada in the 1790s.

With the exception of presumed pre-eminence, these Ontarian norms may be said to operate in Canada's other regions/provinces. The challenge facing Noel's analysis is a comparative one: if the same principles underlie and drive the political cultures of other provinces (or, for that matter, of California and Catalonia), what accounts for differences in the politics of the provinces? It is here that political culture's ideational elements come to the fore. Identifying these elements entails pursuing the roots of socio-political forces in the provinces/regions and their political ideas rather than cataloguing the political system's day-to-day operational features. Moreover, other analyses of the operational components of political culture would throw up provincial differences if one looked at matters such as leadership styles, patterns of patronage, and the propensity to vote and participate in politics.

A potent example in which the ideational component of political culture explains more than does the operational one lies in the contrasts between the adjacent Prairie provinces of Saskatchewan and Alberta. These two provinces have had much in common – more than other neighbouring provinces – but it is their ideologically dissimilar traditions that are pivotal to explaining their very diverse paths of political mobilization. Both provinces were created in 1905, and both were led by Liberal administrations installed by Ottawa. Both began as frontier agrarian societies with homesteading pioneers drawn from older societies. The agricultural economies of both diversified over time with the exploitation of other natural resources. Both were ravaged by the Depression, and both benefited from the energy crisis of the

1970s. Both are distant from the national locus of economic and political power concentrated in Ontario and Quebec. From a number of angles, there are good reasons to lump these provinces together for the purpose of generalizing about political culture in the Prairie region.

Despite their commonalities, it is the political differences between Saskatchewan and Alberta that stand out. Saskatchewan developed and sustained a communitarian culture that contrasts with the individualist folklore that took hold in Alberta. Saskatchewan threw up a vibrant socialist party; Alberta threw up a party that took on a strong anti-socialist streak. Saskatchewan elected North America's first social democratic government, and that party became the province's natural governing party for most of the past six decades. Alberta elected and re-elected populist-conservative regimes that governed uninterrupted over an even longer period. Saskatchewan created a compulsory public health insurance scheme; Alberta was its leading foe.[13] In the 1990s, as another sign of their contrasting political orientations, Saskatchewan's farmers voted in favour of, and its government lobbied for, maintaining the Canadian Wheat Board's monopoly marketing powers, but Alberta's farmers and government voted and lobbied for dispensing with them. Saskatchewan became a voice for strong central government in Ottawa and for "positive" government, an active instrumentalist role for both the federal and provincial states. Alberta became a voice for decentralized federalism, for constructing a provincial firewall vis-à-vis Ottawa, and for decreasing the size and activity of government. Saskatchewan has had an intensely competitive and ideologically polarized party system, whereas Alberta has had an ideologically consensual quasi-party system, with opposition muted and marginalized. Both provinces have been exposed in recent decades to the same international and external forces – globalization, continental economic integration, the capriciousness of distant commodity exchanges, and the appearance of large transnational corporations in the agricultural and other resource sectors. Both have had to contend with the rising tide of neo-conservative thinking.

Yet, Saskatchewan and Alberta responded quite differently. With its government "acting as enthusiastic champions of globalization," Alberta embraced privatization, deregulation, and the logic of an internationalized market economy; it redefined citizens as "customers."[14] In contrast, Saskatchewan resisted neo-conservatism by seeking to embed rather than dismantle the provincial state: sheltering its substantial stable of Crown corporations and social programs. Albertans vociferously campaigned to open Canada's publicly administered health care system to for-profit corporations (as recommended in their Mazankowski Report), and its premier welcomed the 2005 Supreme Court decision permitting private health insurance in Quebec. Saskatchewanians sought to consolidate and expand the health care system's sphere of public, non-profit services (as recommended in their premier's Romanow Report).[15] Whereas Saskatchewan has "a highly politicized society which guards and protects its programs with particular vigilance,"[16] Alberta has endorsed the shrinkage of the state, the entry of the private sector into areas such as liquor and electricity distribution, and the opening up of the public health system monopoly. Nevertheless, it did not act on the Mazankowski Report, invested massively in its own system, and permitted fewer private health services than did Quebec. Saskatchewanians are more engaged with government and politics than are Albertans. Their provincial voter turnout rates are among the highest in Canada; Albertans have the lowest.[17] Evidence of differing provincial ideological tendencies related to the development of space is demonstrated in Lloydminster, a bi-provincial town straddling their shared border where "the housing market on each side of the border reflects the philosophy, the ideology, and the economic status of the corresponding province more than it does a commonly shared community."[18]

These policy, political, behavioural, and philosophical divergences between Saskatchewan and Alberta are functions of the ideational rather than the operational elements of political culture alluded to by Noel. To flesh them out, one needs to ask where the differing ideas driving Saskatchewan and Alberta politics came from, who carried and propagated them, and why they took hold and enjoyed success in one province but not in the other. These themes are pursued in Chapters 9 and 10. Lumping Manitoba, Saskatchewan, and Alberta together into an assumed common region called the Prairies confounds rather than clarifies both their provincial and regional political cultures.

Interprovincial and Intraprovincial

What parameters define the boundaries of a political culture? When a political scientist looks at a map, the political boundaries jump out at her. She assigns primordial status to territorial political cleavages. When a marine biologist or an agronomist looks at a map, other features rivet their attention. The topography of culture is challenging to chart: culture is social, nuanced, and abstract rather than physical and measurable. Political culture is conditioned by geography and history. Although it is logical to see the enveloping political boundaries sported by states and provinces as containing territorially constricted political cultures, such an approach is limiting because it places both politics and culture in conceptual straitjackets. Regional boundaries not coterminous with political boundaries are like culture: fuzzy, ambiguous, and amorphous.

If regional political cultures are pursued interprovincially rather than intraprovincially, what configuration of provinces is most appropriate? The one most used for the past century is that of five regions: the Maritimes (and then Atlantic Canada after 1949), Quebec, Ontario, the Prairies, and BC. A three-pronged categorization sometimes used is Eastern Canada, central Canada (combining Ontario and Quebec), and the West. The "East" in common parlance in Western Canada includes Ontario. In the Maritimes, "Upper Canada" is occasionally used for Ontario. A differentiation between "old" Canada and "new" Canada draws attention to historical settlement patterns, with the Ottawa River as a divider: to its east, "old" Canada's provinces are products of the seventeenth and eighteenth centuries; to its west, "new" Canada's provinces are products of the nineteenth and twentieth centuries.[19] The constitutional amendment formulae contained in the Fulton-Favreau proposals of the 1960s and the Victoria Charter of 1971 provided for four regions: Atlantic, Quebec, Ontario, and the West. The amending formula entrenched in the Constitution Act, 1982, is wholly provincial. The Regional Veto Statute on constitutional change adopted by parliament in 1996, however, returns to the common five-region configuration noted above.[20] According to the statute, constitutional change requires the support of provincial legislatures representing the majority of the population in each region. Thus, Alberta wields a de facto regional veto for the Prairies because its population exceeds that of Manitoba and Saskatchewan combined.

It is daunting to draw a satisfying all-inclusive map of Canada's political cultures. In fact, conceiving of a political cultural map of Canada that has some gaps and spaces in which significant distinguishing cultural features may not exist may be more instructive than thinking of one in which cultures must be situated in a precise spot in this or that province or territory. Culture and people are not spread evenly across a state or province, as jam is on bread. Canadian settlement has been discontinuous and disjointed, producing a series of cultural "islands" in what a distinguished historical geographer termed "the Canadian Archipelago."[21] Drawing on the cartographer's subjective notion of political culture, such a map may also feature overlapping circles of political culture seen from various perspectives. Any one place may mirror multiple cultures.

Since culture is an abstract social conceptualization, assigning it spatial dimensions renders attempts at locating sub-provincial cultures arbitrary and somewhat intimidating. Consider the political culture of Winnipeg's North End. Does it reflect Manitoban political culture, an urban political culture, contemporary ethno- and Aboriginal political cultures, or is Winnipeg's North End best understood as the home of a distinctive historical political culture defined by its immigrant working-class and labour-socialist traditions? It is all of these and more. Similarly, in whom is the political culture of rural southern Manitoba rooted? East of the Red River, French Canadians were formative influences. Just west of the river, significant German and Mennonite influences are detectable. In the 1960s, as a reflection of this divide, the east side of the river elected a Liberal Franco-Manitoban Catholic in La Verendrye; the west side returned a Dutch Mennonite Social Crediter in Rhineland. The names of these MLAs (Vilefaure and Froese) and those of their constituencies, as well as the candidates' religious affiliations and parties, point to contrasting intraprovincial cultures. Nevertheless, the generalization made here is limited, for there is a substantial Mennonite centre east of the river (Steinbach) and small, distinct Franco-Manitoban ones (Notre Dame de Lourdes) well west of it. Further west in rural southern Manitoba, the Anglo-Saxon Ontarian sources of the provincial state and society are most evident. This region has never elected a CCF-NDP MLA or MP in the province's history, even though the party has been a major provincial force. Does this make the political culture of rural southern Manitoba an amalgam of further geographically distinct sub-cultures? Must we pursue ever-smaller circles for analysis? Alternatively, which circle should get preponderant attention?

The same problems confront analysts fathoming the political culture of southwestern Ontario. Does it lie in the rural origins of its early nineteenth-century American and British pioneers or in its mid-sized cities of the late twentieth century? If it is located in the latter, is it better exhibited by Windsor, with its French-English and industrial working-class, unionized, and Liberal/NDP traditions, or by London, which projects a genteel, middle-class, English centre built around financial industries and which has Conservative/Liberal traditions? We may extend such forms of territorial analysis, frustratingly, to infinity.

Sub-provincial regions do not have obvious or universally recognized boundaries. In this respect, a region is like a political culture: what does it include and exclude? The varying efforts to define northern Ontario offer an example of such difficulties. What is central or marginal to this region? Few deny its existence, but differences of hundreds of kilometres are involved when they attempt to determine its size and location. This is compounded by differences in assigning significance to it. In Tom Courchene's prize-winning book on Ontario's political economy,[22] the north of the province goes unmentioned, although the provincial map on the book's cover makes it prominent due to its relative vastness. Geoffrey Weller writes of northern Ontario's three distinct sub-regions: a northeast, a northwest, and, above them, a far north beyond the fiftieth parallel.[23] The first contains large numbers of francophones, the second a large number of Finns once prominent in the Communist Party's fortunes, and the last has overwhelming numbers of Aboriginals. Rand Dyck settles for only a northeast and northwest subdivision of Ontario's North.[24] The Government of Ontario has put its own imprimatur on the region. Once, it defined it as lying north of the French River. In the 1980s, officialdom's North was extended southward to the District of Parry Sound; in 2000, it progressed even further south, to the District of Muskoka. This brings the North to less than a hundred miles from Queen's Park and nearer to Toronto than is London, Ontario. The regions of southern Ontario are no less arbitrary and murky: Dyck writes of four, Robert Williams of three,[25] and Randall White, drawing on a base map of the Ministry of Municipal Affairs, of seven.[26]

Provincial Identity

These differences in appellation reflect more than divergence in labelling. In titling an *Ontario History* article "Ontario – Does It Exist?" Arthur Lower posed a provocative existential query.[27] He observed that in Upper Canada, then in Canada West, and finally in Ontario in 1867, Ontarians did possess a separate identity. That Ontario, however, differed from the Ontario of later years: western Ontario then was London (the home of the University of Western Ontario) and its agrarian hinterland. By the 1890s, Ontario's boundary stretched beyond Kenora, which is a thousand miles west of London. Ontario grew again before the First World War, deeper into the Canadian Shield and up to James Bay. Before these expansions, Ontarians had, in Lower's estimation, "a collective will"[28] because their province was a small, coherent entity with a largely homogeneous society. Subsequently, the province became more varied geographically, economically, and culturally. Its eastern boundary is north of New York City's environs; its western boundary is north of Kansas. Vastness hindered the perpetuation of a collective provincial identity and contributed to building a national one. Ontarians are less likely to bask in their provincial roots than are Nova Scotians, Newfoundlanders, or Québécois. Fewer Ontarians than the inhabitants of these three provinces are native-born. Ontarians' view of their province, according to Lower, was refracted by an economic prism: historically it was but "a forest to be turned into pulpwood, a mine to be mined-out."[29] He did not believe that such an economic culture made for a collective will or separate identity. The pace of Ontario's social diversification accelerated rapidly in the latter third of the twentieth century. A new cosmopolitan Ontario is by definition not provincial.

Paradoxically, the one region of the province in which a sense of local identity has arisen is in the far-flung north. Northern Ontarians live in a region where the levers of political and economic power, the captains of industry and public administration, are far away. Spread out across immense distances, Northern Ontarians share a common self-image as dependent subjects in an empire rather than as full-fledged participants. In this, their outlooks have more in common with those of Western and Atlantic Canadians than with those of Southern Ontarians.

Territorial identification with one's province is noticeably stronger in Atlantic Canada and Quebec than in the westerly provinces. When people were asked whether they thought of themselves as Canadians "first" or as Ontarians, Nova Scotians, and so on "first," relatively high levels of primary provincial identification appeared east of the Ottawa River (from 27 percent in Atlantic Canada to 53 percent in Quebec), but low levels existed elsewhere (from 8 percent in Ontario to 18 percent in the West).[30] These are significant differences. Historical geography, more so than contemporary grievances with the federal government, accounts for them. The five provinces east of the Ottawa River were formed as political units before the creation of a national community. When immigrants settled in the westerly provinces, as contemporary immigrants now settle in metropolitan Canada, they came with a stronger sense of their new country than of their new region, province, or city. Logically, there is a more robust feeling of localism and parochialism in older regions – Atlantic Canada and Quebec – and a stronger feeling of nationalism and cosmopolitanism in newer regions, such as the West and the large cities that serve as receptacles for immigrants. The oldest regions/provinces have the longest-established traditions, institutions, and collective memories for residents to draw on. The newer regions/provinces and the remade, transformed urban centres contain more people with hopes, wishes, and aspirations tied to the future. They do not share a collective past. They are relatively more open to new ways, ideas, and experimentation. They are less averse to risk and political adventure – merely their emigration serves as evidence – than those in older provinces/regions who are relatively more secure with yesteryear's symbols and ways.

Urban and Rural

A spatial cleavage with cultural implications is that between the urban and the rural. One formulation of the dichotomy is "metropolis versus the rest."[31] Metropolis-hinterland or core-periphery analysis operates at a number of geographic levels. The metropole or heartland is where population, industry, finance, technical skills, affluence, and power are concentrated. The hinterland tends to be sparsely settled and dependent on resource extraction and extensive transportation networks. Its development is directed from the core or metropole. Compared to those of the core, those in the hinterland tend to be poor, disaffected, and powerless. The metropolis-hinterland framework may be used intraprovincially (as in Halifax, Montreal, Toronto, Winnipeg, or Vancouver versus the rest of their respective provinces) or interprovincially (the Toronto-Montreal-Ottawa triangle or the Quebec City–Windsor corridor or central Canada versus the rest of the country). It may also be applied continentally (Canada and Mexico as resource and labour hinterlands respectively to the US metropole) and globally (the G-7 states as the financial metropole versus the developing world). The search for Canadian political culture must also contend with the contrasting values of those in inner cities, their suburbs, and, beyond them, the exurban catchment area of labour-force commuters and consumers. Provincially imposed municipal amalgamations with metropolitan cities, unicities, and megacities – in Montreal, Winnipeg, Halifax, Toronto – exposed differences in the values and interests of those in the inner and outer cities.

The cultural breaks between city and country are old rather than new. They are expressed in popular literature, cinema, and politics. The overnight electoral successes of the United Farmers of Ontario (in 1919), the United Farmers of Alberta (in 1921), the United Farmers of Manitoba (1922), and the meteoric appearance of the federal Progressives in 1921 symbolized the awakened reaction of agricultural rural Canada against its eclipse by urban-labour-industrial interests. The agrarian revolt proved a failed reflexive lashing out at the intractable evolution from rural to urban society.

At the beginning of the twenty-first century, contrasting rural and urban outlooks were echoed in Canada's controversies over gun control legislation and same-sex marriage. They are also evident in voting patterns. The Reform/ Alliance and Conservative Parties have fared best in rural and small-town settings, whereas the Liberals and NDP have fared best in urban locales. In this division, which occurs in both the federal and provincial arenas, the conservative parties (in Ontario and the Prairie provinces) appear as rural parties; the Liberal Party and especially the NDP appear as city parties. The NDP has also had disproportionate support in northern and Native communities in Ontario and Manitoba. In 1960s Quebec, the Union Nationale and the Créditistes were disproportionally popular in the rural francophone districts. In contrast, the Liberals were disproportionately an urban party, and were thus penalized by a rurally skewed electoral map, one that denied them victory in 1944, 1966, and 1998, even though they won the popular vote. The bias in favour of rural areas stems from the belief, once common in both English and French Canada, that agriculture and a rural lifestyle are more wholesome and worthy of promotion than industrialism and city life.

Popular Imagery of Regional Politics

In 1978 the National Film Board released *The Art of the Possible*, a documentary on the governing style of Ontario premier Bill Davis. In a voice-over, the film encapsulated politics in Canada's regions: "It's been said that in the Maritimes politics is a disease, in Quebec it's a religion, on the prairies it's protest, and in B.C. it's entertainment. In Ontario politics is [the camera zooms in on Davis chairing a meeting of his prestigious advisory committee on economics, composed of fifteen of the nation's top business leaders, half a dozen labour leaders, and a couple of consumer representatives] business."[32] These one-word connotations resonate themes in the political cultures of the respective regions. In the Maritimes, more than in other regions, partisan identification has been familial, akin to an inherited congenital condition. Modernity is weakening the hold of the past, but cross-generational political loyalties have been more prevalent in the Maritimes than elsewhere. One participant at a Nova Scotia leadership convention, asked when he had joined his political party, responded, "At conception."[33] The link between religion and partisanship has been a prominent feature of both Atlantic and Quebec politics. Newfoundland and Quebec's denominational school systems were the vehicles for public education until the end of the twentieth century. Frank MacKinnon once noted that the PEI party system "has four political parties:

Liberal, Conservative, Catholic and Protestant."[34] As the twenty-first century began, weekly attendance at religious institutions and religiosity was higher in the Atlantic region than in any other.[35]

In Quebec the religion metaphor of the NFB film is apropos, for it refers to the existential anxiety elicited by the eternal national question: whether to keep or break the faith with Canada. The nineteenth-century efforts of Papineau's *patriotes* and the late twentieth-century struggles between sovereign-tists and federalists ate away, like a religious doctrinal dispute, at a culture that prides itself on societal solidarity. Although religious attendance in Que-bec (like that in BC) is now lower than elsewhere in Canada, language and the provincial state have attained something like the old spiritual equiva-lence of the church. The powerful religious past lingers visually in Quebec's grand cathedrals and its landscape, one dotted with aging Catholic church spires. Only in Quebec does the Christian cross hang above the Speaker's chair in the National Assembly. The spiritual nature of Quebec nationalism and its reverence for the distant past are expressed on provincial automobile licence plates: "Je me souviens" bridges the realms of nationality and religion.

The Prairies and protest politics have been synonymous throughout the twentieth century. This region gave birth to the Progressives, Social Credit, the CCF, Reform, and then the Alliance Party, as well as to a string of less successful but no less remonstrative parties including the Non-Partisan League, the Western Canada Concept, and the Confederation of Regions Party (CoR). In BC, entertainment, levity, and clownishness are conveyed by the very names of some of its premiers – from Amor de Cosmos in the 1870s to "Wacky" Bennett in the 1950s – and by the foibles of others: Bill Vander Zalm's Fan-tasy Gardens, Mike Harcourt's bingo scandal, Glen Clark's casino influence-peddling trial, and Gordon Campbell's Maui mug shot. BC political culture is detached and offbeat, partly on account of its physical and psychological isolation behind the mountainous Continental Divide and its distance from the Canadian heartland.

The NFB film's characterization of Ontario politics as "government is business" was reflected in the operational styles of Premiers Leslie Frost, John Robarts, and Mike Harris. For Frost, a small-town lawyer, the template for running government "was a prosperous family-run firm that was managed cautiously, invested wisely in future expansion, and paid close personal at-tention to details."[36] Robarts, almost certainly the first Canadian premier with an MBA, described himself as a "management man."[37] Harris renamed ministerial legislative estimates "business plans" and foisted performance

indicators common in the private sector onto the civil service. Governing
Ontario is viewed by Ontarians as an issue of sound business management
and stewardship. The NFB film projects Davis as governing Ontario in the
way that a chief executive officer or chairman of the board of directors runs a
major corporation. Contrast this to the relative tolerance for patronage and
nepotism in Atlantic Canada, for the historical corruption and then the am-
bitiousness of corporatist nation building in Quebec, and for the pungent
left-right ideological flavour of Western Canadian politics.

The film's portrayal of regional politics suggests regional biases in leadership styles. Imaginative licence permits heuristic comparative insights. More
than those of other regions, Atlantic Canadian politicians have been cast in
the traditional mould, disproportionately drawn from established political
families. In such societies, as in patriarchal and patrimonial systems, leadership rests on custom. Noting that for sixty-seven years within an eighty-three-
year span Nova Scotia had but four premiers, J. Murray Beck wondered whether
there was "something in the Nova Scotian character that makes the people
feel more secure when they have a father figure presiding over their destinies."[38] Atlantic leaders such as George Murray, Robert Stanfield, and John
Hamm projected comforting images of continuity, stability, and stolidity
rather than the vision, vigour, and ambition of the overtly self-made politician. Quebec, in contrast, has been somewhat more receptive to the charismatic personality – Maurice Duplessis, René Lévesque, and Lucien Bouchard
come to mind. Here, success springs from charming the masses, transcend-
ently inspiring trust and devotion based on the leader's presumed spiritual
genius. In further contrast, and consistent with the film's presentation of
Ontario politics as business-modelled, Quebec and the Prairies have been
relatively more oriented to a bureaucratic leadership type in whom organizational and managerial traits with a rational-legal basis prevail. To the Ontario examples cited above, one may add Manitoba's John Bracken and Duff
Roblin, Saskatchewan's Tommy Douglas and Allan Blakeney, and Alberta's
Ernest Manning and Peter Lougheed.

Geography and Political Choice

The 1992 Charlottetown Referendum suggested a national political culture,
in that Canadians united in rejecting the accord. Approximately equal percentages of Quebecers (57) and Canadians as a whole (54) said "No." As the
results highlighted, the greatest chasm lay between the parliamentary political parties on the one hand – all of whom endorsed the accord – and the

public on the other hand. One detects two "national" political cultures, in that Quebecers and Canadians elsewhere voted "No" for diametrically opposite reasons: "too little" for Quebec in the eyes of the former, "too much" for the latter.[39] Below the surface, the results pointed to the relevance of political geography. Patterns of support and opposition were far from uniform in either Quebec or the rest of Canada. The "Yes" side triumphed in the three smallest, clustered Atlantic provinces (Newfoundland, PEI, and New Brunswick), which make up only 5 percent of the national population. In Quebec, the accord found some support in Montreal but encountered overwhelming opposition outside it. In Ontario, each side received slightly less than a majority (with the balance being spoiled and with declined ballots). Noticeably, rejection of the accord was greatest in the West, ranging from 55 to 68 percent "No" in those four provinces.

What accounts for these uneven regional patterns? The hypothesis here points to the underlying cultures and differing tenors of regional politics. In Atlantic Canada, a "Yes" vote was consistent with a traditional society's outlook, one which, unlike that of modern societies, tended to defer to the judgment of leaders. That Nova Scotia was the exception in the Atlantic pattern is consistent with its identity as the most "modern" of the Atlantic provinces. Its residents' average incomes and years of schooling are higher than in the other three Atlantic provinces. In the West, populist, anti-elitist traditions are stronger than in the Maritimes. The Western-based Reform Party, unrepresented in parliament at the time, urged rejection of the accord. Geography's relevance to Atlantic Canadians is their vulnerability to Quebec's departure and their resulting physical separation from Canada. Westerners, on the other hand, are the most detached and distant from Quebec – physically, psychologically, and historically. They feel the least affected by Quebec's estrangement, yet are the most resentful of it. Ontario, the heart of English Canada, is Quebec's most intimate neighbour and by far its largest provincial trading partner. It is torn between these cross-pressures, and its vote was similarly split. In Quebec, anglophones and allophones, concentrated in Montreal, perceive themselves as losers in an outcome terminating their Canadian status.

An upshot of the accord's failure was the 1995 Quebec referendum. It too revealed the psychological role played by geography. Sovereigntists won the vote in all the ridings in Quebec's historic heartland – along the St. Lawrence River between Montreal and Quebec City, and beyond to the Gaspé Peninsula – but the federalist camp won all the ridings adjacent to Ontario,

New Brunswick, and New England. One lesson in the referendum was that physical proximity may generate sympathy. Those in New Brunswick and eastern Ontario were more supportive of Charlottetown's "distinct society" clause than were those not bordering Quebec. Quebecers who lived near their own provincial boundaries felt more kinship with non-Quebecers than did other Quebecers. Those bordering the regions of others, secure in their own distinctiveness, did not need to express it assertively.

Regional variations in political cultures are suggestively buttressed by some survey data. In 2002, an overwhelming majority of Atlantic Canadians (86 percent), but only a minority of westerners (49 percent), were satisfied with the Supreme Court's performance.[40] The opinions of Quebecers and Ontarians fell between these two poles. As regards authoritative institutions, Atlantic Canadians express greater deference than do westerners. Similarly, a majority of Atlantic Canadians had "trust and confidence" in both their federal (66 percent) and provincial (57 percent) governments, but in the West such levels were decidedly lower. They were generally minoritarian for both levels of government, with the exceptions of Albertans' confidence in their provincial government (64 percent) and Manitobans' and Saskatchewanians' confidence in Ottawa (56 percent). These differences may reflect Albertan affluence and eastern Prairie dependence on federal equalization payments. In the Far West, Alberta and BC, only 38 percent had "trust and confidence" in Ottawa. Again, Quebecers and Ontarians fell attitudinally, as they do geographically, between these Eastern and Western Canadian poles. English Canadian regions were uniform, united, and distinct from Quebecers on questions of freedom and equality. A majority in each of the English Canadian regions ranked "personal freedom" as "more important" than "equality," whereas in Quebec the reverse was the case. Ontario exceptionalism was evident in attitudes to the treatment of and respect for one's province in Canada. Only in Ontario did a majority believe that their province was "treated with the respect it deserves in Canada."

Some Comparative Perspectives

Political patronage may also be associated with distinctive regional political cultures. Borrowing the notion of "clientelism" from the vocabulary of social anthropology, Sid Noel constructed a three-stage model of the relationship of leaders or patrons and their constituents or clients.[41] In the most elementary stage, a direct and personal face-to-face link exists between the political patron or local notable and his client; in the intermediate secondary stage, brokers in the form of political machines or political parties – organized cliques of supra-local notables – arise to become mediating vehicles for dispensing patronage; and in the tertiary stage, large modernized governmental bureaucracies come to the fore, overtaking, but not totally displacing, local notables or party organizations in disbursing government largess. Bureaucracies dispense patronage impersonally, in programs favouring groups, interests, and institutions, rather than apportioning specific rewards to individual supporters, as in the first stage of patronage. Nor is it apportioned primarily to local communities for having supported the governing party, as in the second stage. The client beneficiaries in the third stage are more likely to be scattered throughout the province than to be local or regional. This move to a bureaucratically sanitized form of clientelism is consistent with the transformation of a rural society and economy into a technologically advanced urban world. Remnants of the first and second stages of clientelism persist in a modern setting but are dwarfed in the totality of public patronage.

In applying this model to provincial politics in the mid-1970s, Noel plotted a continuum: he placed the Atlantic provinces, followed closely by Quebec, at the end that represented the first stage of his model. At the other end – representing the third stage of clientelism in his model – he placed Ontario. The Western provinces were placed between these two poles. One may quibble with or update this classification – since the Quiet Revolution, Quebec has clearly advanced more rapidly than the other provinces as a prototypical bureaucratic state. However, Noel's framework points, as does the NFB film, to Ontario's business managerial culture in politics, policy making, and public administration, in contrast to Atlantic Canada's relatively more personal, cellular, and localized form of patronage. Generalizations regarding a national pattern of political patronage thus need tempering with an appreciation of regional variations. They must also fit with the differing socio-economic conditions, geography, and histories of Canada's regions.

Another comparative mid-1970s study of provincial political cultures, which appeared along with Simeon and Elkins' survey approach and Noel's "clientist" one, was that of John Wilson. Wilson identified three types of party systems that had evolved in the Western world. All three had two dominant parties and all three reflected stages of political development. In the first type, as in Britain and the US in their pre-industrial or early industrial eras, the two parties of the right and left were ideologically divided. Aristocratic and/or agricultural interests influenced one party camp and commercial and/or manufacturing interests the other. As modernization proceeded, a party of the industrial labouring classes arose. In the second type of party system, one of the old parties is marginalized by the new party (as Britain's Liberals were by Labour). In the third type of party system, as in the US, the older two parties adjust, accommodate, and incorporate the pressures exerted by the new industrial labouring class. Wilson's hypothesis was "that different political communities ... at different stages of development ... have different political cultures,"[42] as reflected in their party systems. Analyzing surveys and the popular vote garnered by Canada's two leading parties in federal and provincial elections, he suggested three distinct provincial political cultures, labelling them "underdeveloped," "transitional," and "developed." He placed all four Atlantic provinces in the first category and only Alberta and Saskatchewan in the "developed" category. He characterized the other provincial political cultures (Quebec, Ontario, Manitoba, and BC) as "transitional."

What is common to the analyses of Simeon and Elkins, Noel, and Wilson is their designation of Atlantic Canada as a political culture laggard, an identity that is consistent with its economic status. Where the three analyses diverge somewhat is in their placement of regional leaders. For Simeon and Elkins, these are Ontario, BC, and Manitoba; for Noel, it is Ontario; and for Wilson, it is Saskatchewan. Wilson's far-fetched, imaginative explanation of Saskatchewan exceptionalism – its appetite for the left-right cleavage reminiscent of British partisan evolution – is psychological but ageographic: that the Depression fostered a state of mind "so debilitating ... that it may be compared to the early experience of the urban working class in Great Britain."[43] A more direct and plausible explanation links the vitality and durability of Saskatchewan's social democratic inclinations to the transplantation of turn-of-the-twentieth-century British urban immigrants who brought socialist, labourist, and Fabian notions with them to rural Saskatchewan.[44] Wilson's explanation cannot account for why the farmers of neighbouring Manitoba and Alberta, impacted by the same Depression, opted for alternative paths of partisan evolution. Indeed, the psychological impact of the Depression has been used to account for the rallying of Manitoba's farmers to the banner of the status quo, for the Liberal Progressives,[45] for the retarded success of a socialist party in Saskatchewan,[46] and for why Alberta could never have embraced a socialist party.[47] What these conflicting interpretations, insights, and possibilities unintentionally throw up is a reminder of the importance of comparative analysis. We understand regional/provincial political cultures better by constantly placing them side by side, contrasting and confronting them with each other.

The two most lauded books in provincial politics since the 1950s are C.B. Macpherson's *Democracy in Alberta*[48] and Seymour Martin Lipset's *Agrarian Socialism*, on Saskatchewan. These studies are sophisticated, richly constructed, and detailed. Macpherson became the best-known Canadian in the international political science fraternity, and Lipset became the most-cited living sociologist writing in English. Their theories and explanations, however, are starkly different; culturally and politically, the two provinces appear as wholly detached and distant states rather than as adjacent Prairie provinces. Macpherson highlighted two variables underlining his analysis: the petit bourgeois values of small independent commodity producers – farmers and ranchers – and their perceived exploitation and neglect by central Canadian corporations and a distant federal government. Thus, Alberta had need of only one party, a strong hegemonic one, to confront its external nemeses. Both of Macpherson's variables, however, obtained in Saskatchewan, yet Saskatchewan threw up a competitive party system, one with an ideologically leftist rather than rightist regime. Once again, the contrasts between Alberta and Saskatchewan cry out for comparative analyses, especially in light of these provinces' divergent political paths, both before and since the 1950s. What Macpherson wholly ignored is the profound impact of the political ideas of transplanted turn-of-the-twentieth-century American farmers in rural Alberta. Their outlooks differed markedly from those of the British farmers populating rural Saskatchewan. Albertans' predilection for individualism and market liberal solutions to policy issues took hold; Saskatchewanians' preferences were for co-operative and state-centred solutions.

The remainder of this rumination on Canadian political culture pursues its search in the regions and provinces, their peoples, parties, institutions, and orientations. Suggestive veins do flow in regional/provincial political and historical studies, but they have barely been tapped for comparative purposes. The regions and provinces have been treated largely as unique small worlds or islands unto themselves. When they have caught the eye of social scientists and historians, they have been discussed mainly as reactants to and propellants of national politics and policy. The comparative forays by Simeon and Elkins, Noel, and Wilson have been exceptions that contain their own limitations. Province-specific studies do enrich our understanding of the provinces, but they need to be connected. Consciously reviewing regional/ provincial politics with a comparative sensibility deepens and broadens the picture of Canadian political culture. We need to continuously flesh out comparative regional/provincial perspectives at a time when provincial governments, regional parties, and regional forces are arguably more powerful, prominent, and popular than ever.

6
Atlantic Canada: Traditional Political Culture?

A crosscurrent flows through the literature about Atlantic Canadian political culture. A historical strand of thinking points to the region's traditionalism or conservatism, and to its social roots. This strand is generally subscribed to by outsiders, those "from away." Buttressing this frame of analysis is the region's economic retardation, as compared to the economy of its pre- and immediate post-Confederation past and to that of the rest of Canada in the twentieth century. Self-styled progressives see its constantly shrinking population and its lagging economic welfare as brakes on political cultural development. This rendition of Atlantic political culture harps on the status and power of long-established families and churches, a pervasive localism, and the continuity and dominance of relatively closed and self-perpetuating political elites. It notes the seeming irrelevance of ideology, the punishment of party mavericks, and the stability of a long-established two-party system featuring Liberals and Conservatives whose taproots and names lie in Britain and the pre-Confederation era. Atlantic Canadian governments have been depicted as servile in their relations with Ottawa; Atlantic Canadians have more commonly been presented as cynical about politics and untrusting of politicians than have other Canadians. Lineaments of this traditional political culture have been the glue of political patronage and its blameless acceptance, as well as of mischievous and dubious electioneering practices such as the widespread use of liquor and money to sway voters and the wily employment of pre-marked ballots.[1] According to this current of thought, Atlantic Canadians have looked at politics as a "sport," with graft and entertainment being the norm rather than the exception.

A complement to this analysis is a certain understanding of the region's dependence on Ottawa. Atlantic Canada relies more heavily than any other region on federal largesse in the form of equalization payments and other transfers to provincial treasuries. There have been years in which nearly two-thirds of PEI government revenues came from federal coffers. In the 1990s, each of the Atlantic provincial governments received more than a third, and sometimes near to one-half, of their revenues from Ottawa.[2] Dependence on public funds whose sources are outside the region raises the question of what public stewardship and fiscal probity mean for those in the region: is this "their" money that is being either husbanded or squandered by those whom they elect, or is it merely something over which claimants squabble? Atlantic Canada has received more government income supplements for individuals and handouts to struggling industries than have the other regions. As well, a plethora of publicly funded regional development programs have been insti-gated. The region, especially Newfoundland, is also associated with deficien-cies in democratic representation, deficiencies "rooted in a political culture affected by the late maturing of representative institutions [that] can only be rectified by a *prise de conscience.*"[3]

Another aspect of the Atlantic Canadian experience is the region's social homogeneity; visible and non-French minorities are less numerous there than elsewhere. Newfoundland's first infusion of central Europeans, for ex-ample, came only in the first half of the 1950s; they numbered fewer than a thousand.[4] The presence of Acadians and the names of former French forts (Louisbourg) and fishing ports (Portuguese Cove and Port aux Basques) communicate an old European world transplanted to America. To be sure, European-origin place names such as New Westminster, Berlin (now Kitch-ener), and Ukrainia (in Manitoba) were and are also found in other prov-inces, but the Atlantic place names cited here refer to an earlier and less technologically developed European presence in North America. It was one connected to France's ancien régime and an offshore foreign fishery that did not entail settlement. Atlantic Canada is the oldest and most British region in English Canada. Its founding settlers were a melange of English, Scots, and Irish whose origins lay in Britain and the New England states. On their heels came the United Empire Loyalists, more of whom settled in this region than in any other. What they shared was Anglo-Celtic descent, in contrast to the Acadians, the region's relatively few Aboriginals, and its even fewer blacks. St. John's is literally nearer and in some respects still spiritually and cultur-ally closer to Ireland than to Vancouver.

A recent thread in thinking about Atlantic Canadian political culture, one woven by academics from the region, points to its convergence with national norms and the Canadian mainstream.[5] This perspective fits with the region's new human and natural resources – from bilingual telemarketers and advanced technology workers to recent mineral discoveries and the off-shore oil and gas industries. In this economic frame, the fishery, agricultural, and forestry sectors are the industries of the old economy – respected and glorified by some but irretrievably eclipsed. The income gaps between Atlantic Canadians and Canadians as a whole, although still present, have been steadily shrinking over the past few decades. Concomitantly, the hallmarks of a traditional political system are attenuating: patronage is in retreat, public administration staffing is now more commonly merit-based, and political leadership is more open to outsiders than in the past. PEI, for example, was the first and only province to elect a female premier. It also elected another of Lebanese heritage and yet another who hailed from Saskatchewan. The region is now more receptive than in the past to parties and ideological currents flowing in from elsewhere in Canada: in the 1990s, the NDP came to serve as Nova Scotia's Official Opposition and – for the first time ever – elected MLAs in all four provinces. In the 1997 federal election, the party captured a quarter of the seats in the Atlantic region (and a third of those in the Maritimes), whereas in the West, the NDP's historical bastion, it won less than a tenth of the ridings. At the other end of the political spectrum, the CoR Party served as New Brunswick's Official Opposition in the 1990s. A 2003 survey of federal partisan preferences revealed that the NDP was more popular in Atlantic Canada than in any other region,[6] a dramatic change for both the party and the region. Atlantic Canadians today are also as likely as other Canadians to acknowledge, celebrate, and promote their minority cultural communities – the Acadians in New Brunswick, the blacks and Mi'kmaqs in Nova Scotia. One Nova Scotia riding has been designed, in an act of affirmative gerrymandering, to help elect a black; another was proposed by a government commission to ensure Aboriginal representation. No other province has ventured this far. For Atlantic Canada, this suggests leadership rather than laggardness on the issue of representation mirroring social diversity.

The old mythology of Maritime and Atlantic political culture has been assailed.[7] In a newer analytical frame, the influence of the political orientations of the Loyalists is minimized, and evidence is furnished of a growing appetite for contestation with Ottawa. Once upon a time, Atlantic Canadians appeared as humble, beseeching supplicants in the federal system; voters displayed a striking tendency to install provincial administrations that flew the same partisan banner as the federal government. Remarkably, that happened in PEI's fifteen elections between the late 1920s and the late 1970s;

the chance of that occurring in a perfectly competitive two-party system is about one in thirty-three thousand![8] In sharp contrast, at the end of 2003, while the Liberals held sway in Ottawa, all four Atlantic governments were Conservative. The new view of Atlantic Canadians presents them as no more or less cynical about politics or trusting of politicians than are Canadians elsewhere. It contends that Atlantic Canadians recognize, appreciate, and re-spond to ideological differences between the Liberals and Conservatives; they do not view these two parties, as the old school of analysis would have us believe, as Tweedledum and Tweedledee.

Old or New?

Which interpretation of Atlantic political culture is more cogent? Is it the historic or the more contemporary version? Each is worthy, and their complementarity emerges in the light of a comparative approach. The con-trast between old and new is highlighted in comparing Atlantic and Western historiographies. Carl Berger's award-winning *The Writing of Canadian History*[9] does not mention a single major historical work on the Maritimes for the post-Confederation period. In contrast, the late nineteenth and first half of the twentieth centuries are at the heart of Western Canadian historiog-raphy. The West's frontier was associated with dynamism, progress, egalitari-anism, democracy, and nation building, whereas the Maritimes – serving as a foil for the frontier thesis that drove Western studies – signified timidity, social stratification, stagnation, and cultural immobility, if not regression.[10] In a flippant and disdainful overstatement of Atlantic political quiescence, Frank Underhill asserted, "As for the Maritime provinces nothing, of course, ever happens down there."[11] To be sure, the Western-propelled Progressives were in full flight in the 1920s, but simultaneously something *was* happen-ing down East: there was a vociferous Maritime Rights Movement, and talk of secession from Confederation was circulating.[12] The region's Antigonish Movement – established in the 1920s and vital into the 1950s – also stands out because it was both Catholic and liberal; its focus on using adult edu-cation as a means toward social improvement and economic organization became well known in other parts of Canada, the US, and overseas.[13]

It is only in the context of broader, momentous national developments that Atlantic Canadian protest stirrings seemed less salient, enduring, and menacing to the established order. One reason for this lies in the fact that they never sought expression outside the traditional Conservative and Liberal

Parties. In this respect, Atlantic Canadian protest was more restrained and less robust than Western Canadian protest. Similarly, on the labour front, the stereotype of the region as torpid – one where paternalistic inclinations were reflected in company unions – is undercut by an analysis of working-class mobilization in the early years of the twentieth century. It suggests nothing backward: "Most of the issues raised in the workplaces of the Maritimes could as easily have been raised in England ... [including workers'] struggles for job control, their eagerness to press for such general objectives as nine (and even eight) hours [of work, and] their rethinking of religious traditions."[14] Again, however, unlike in England and the West, these sentiments did not express themselves in the formation of lasting labour or socialist parties, or in general strikes.

Compared to that of its past, contemporary Atlantic political culture appears to have been revolutionized, akin to Quebec's in the 1960s. In that decade, Louis Robichaud launched New Brunswick's own Quiet Revolution with its Program for Equal Opportunity – the uploading of long-established health, education, and welfare services, which had operated with widely divergent standards and capacities, from local governments to the provincial government. The province also adopted, more than two centuries after the systematic ethnic cleansing of its Acadians, a bilingual administrative and policy regime – one much more wide-ranging than that of any other province outside Quebec – which was constitutionally entrenched in the 1980s. This new regime was shepherded by the historically anti-French Conservatives, another sign of apparently changing times and values. In the areas of socio-economic development, the Liberals in the 1990s engaged in futuristic economic thinking, innovative social policy initiatives, and restructured public administration.[15] In New Brunswick and elsewhere in the region, genuine efforts have been made to learn from other jurisdictions, to adopt "best practice" standards, for example, in public service staffing. Nevertheless, on the question of what degree of success such efforts at institutionalizing reform practices will attain in the Atlantic region, "the jury is still out."[16]

In classifying Canada's twelve social values "tribes" at the end of the millennium, Michael Adams identified two of them as "traditionalists."[17] One was disproportionately concentrated in the Maritimes, the other in small communities across the country. Of the latter category, the Maritimes, as the least urbanized of Canada's regions, also had a disproportionate share. Key values shared by both groups of "traditionalists" were respect for historical tradition, religiosity, and duty. One group exhibited respect for authority, the other for institutions. This reinforces the old view of Atlantic Canadian culture and its values. Recent developments, however, suggest some thirst for modernization, but they must also be balanced against the region's comparative position. Unemployment levels remain chronically higher and incomes persistently lower than elsewhere in Canada. Provincial outmigration continues to exceed inmigration, and the region attracts fewer immigrants from abroad than other regions. Elected politicians are still viewed as "cash cows" whose pork-barrelling ways are lauded as the natural and just fruits of power.[18] Indeed, after John Savage took office in Nova Scotia in 1993 with a platform promise to terminate patronage in public administration, party loyalists challenged him. He nearly lost his party's leadership and the premiership precisely because he was failing to conform to established expectations of spoils. In the 1990s, contrasting attitudes to nepotism and partisan patronage were expressed in PEI and Saskatchewan government practices regarding the hiring of summer students: the former left it to the discretion of cabinet ministers, who chose relatives, acquaintances, and partisan loyalists; the latter relied on a lottery.

Another way to think about the recent discontinuities in Atlantic politics – such as the brief meteoric rise of the CoR Party – is as new twists on old themes. CoR's ideological core, its founders and followers, simply consisted of recast Conservatives drawing heavily on New Brunswick's Association of English Speaking Canadians (formerly the Loyalist Association) and on long-standing anti-French attitudes. To be sure, populist, co-operative, militant agrarian, and radical labour traditions have existed in the Maritimes – as expressed by the Antigonish Movement, the United Farmers, and Cape Breton's miners – but, when compared to such traditions in Ontario and especially the West, they pale in size and significance. Similarly, if CoR is depicted – as it has been[19] – as a Maritime provincial version of the populist, anti-multicultural, and neo-conservative federal Reform/Alliance Party, it proved to be a much weaker and more fleeting phenomenon than its federal counterpart. One of its provincial presidents came to serve as a Conservative cabinet minister. In 2005, all four Atlantic provinces and Alberta had Conservative regimes. However, Atlantic Canada's choice of party may be taken as a sign of the region's continuing strong preference for both traditional toryism and conservatism, which are quite unlike the market liberalism championed by Alberta's neo-conservatives. An example of the tory values of stability and continuity in the New Brunswick Liberal Party lies in the fact that it grants lifetime memberships to those with whom it has had any familial or past association. Thus, in 2003, the New Brunswick wing of the federal Liberals boasted 148,000 members.[20] This meant that the 148,000 members were the numerical equivalent of over a fifth of New Brunswick's population (including children), that they accounted for more than a quarter of all Canadian Liberals, and that they outnumbered the national Conservative, NDP, and Alliance memberships of the time.

In some respects the Atlantic region is the most homogeneous in Canada; in other respects it is the most diverse. The roots of this apparent paradox may be traced to the fact that two of the region's provinces are islands. Isolation and insularity reinforce solidarity, localism, and community. Only one in ten Newfoundlanders and about a quarter of Prince Edward Islanders refer to themselves as Canadians first and foremost; well over half of Canadians outside Quebec do so.[21] Pejoratively, outsiders may see such islands as feeding cultural "inbreeding." Over the course of a century, for example, all but three of St. John's mayors were city natives.[22] The lure of an Intercolonial railroad and its potential markets enticed Nova Scotia's and New Brunswick's entry into Confederation, but this was an irrelevant consideration for the other two British Atlantic colonies, so they initially remained aloof. Many Prince Edward Islanders, suspicious of integrative forces and fearing disintegrative consequences for their island community, felt regret rather than gratification when the Confederation Bridge linked them to the mainland. Bridges and other such linkages in non-insular locales – between Montreal and Laval and Longueuil, Winnipeg and St. Boniface, Vancouver and West Vancouver – are eagerly and universally welcomed rather than greeted warily. Even when natural boundaries are not impediments to interaction – as is the case for Nova Scotia and New Brunswick, which are linked by the isthmus of Chignecto – the presence of a political boundary facilitates divergent political outlooks.[23] Borders provide a source of power and status independent of size. In the case of Atlantic Canada, its four small provinces make up only 7 percent of the national population, but if they act collectively they can thwart constitutional amendments endorsed by the six other and larger provinces, which collectively account for 93 percent of the population.

Newfoundland's rugged terrain compounded its geographic isolation from Canada. Outports, typically unapproachable by land, relied on the sea for intercourse with each other. Fishing hamlets in which a handful of family surnames prevailed for hundreds of people were distant socially, psychologically, and practically from neighbouring, but difficult to access fishing villages in which a different handful of family names prevailed. New-foundland has yet another cultural "island" in the form of Labrador (once claimed and still eyed enviously by Quebec). Small in population – about 5 percent of the provincial total – it is rich in mineral and hydroelectric re-sources but bedevilled by the social pathologies of suicide and substance abuse afflicting its Innu and Inuit communities. Labrador expressed its sepa-rate identity in the 1971 election of a New Labrador Party MHA who briefly held the balance of power. In 2001, Newfoundland reinforced its link to Labrador by altering its constitutional identity to "Newfoundland and Lab-rador"; in the 2003 election campaign, the winning Conservatives promised to build a tunnel between the island and Labrador. Nevertheless, the two are cut from quite different cloth, as the fate of their respective Aboriginal com-munities attests. Newfoundland's Beothuks were hunted and exterminated nearly two centuries ago; Labrador's Aboriginals were shunted aside and largely left to their own devices. Labradoreans' travel patterns and export industries are oriented to Quebec and the North American mainland rather than to Newfoundland.

The small size of Newfoundland's population would seem to militate against treating the island as a region separate from the Maritime provinces. However, there are good historical cultural reasons for doing so. Modern scholars of eighteenth-century English visit it to study its unique dialect.[24] Furthermore, because Newfoundland joined Canada much later than did the other provinces, its British and Old World links were more intimate and enduring than theirs. Indeed, during the Great Depression, Newfoundland reverted to direct British rule, surrendering its status as a self-governing do-minion. Soon after, during the Second World War, it served as a major stag-ing area for the American military. Stephenville, the location of the largest American air base on the island, has streets named "Wyoming Drive," "Caro-lina Avenue," "Georgia Loop," "Ohio Circle," and so on, streets on which American military personnel lived and worked. Newfoundland's proximity to Europe made for lingering British and Irish influences, but its exposure to American culture in the 1940s, and the steadily improving communications links to the Maritimes and Canada, contributed to reorienting its outlook toward the North American mainland.

Is Maritime or Atlantic political culture a chimera?[25] Paradoxically, the intense sense of localism and parochialism associated with the Atlantic re-gion counters thinking of identity in cross-provincial regional terms. At the heart of questions regarding Prince Edward Islanders' identity lies a "garden myth": locals think in terms of an "Island way of life" in an unspoiled pasto-ral setting.[26] Even within the province, however, sub-provincial localism thrives. It long kept politicians from reapportioning the number of seats of its three counties, as cries of territorial equality trumped the egalitarian claim to representation by population. Localism implies close association of citi-zens with their neighbours, familiarity with political figures, and a shared history. Atlantic Canadians are more likely to be born, live, and die in their province than are Ontarians or westerners. They are more apt to stay put. For Maritimers, accustomed to long-established family farms and orchards that tend to be small, mixed, and unmechanized, moving from one Maritime farm to another is a more daunting cultural transition than that experienced by, say, rural Ontarians or Manitobans who relocate to rural Alberta or BC.

Rootedness helps to explain why: in 2003 PEI and Ontario held provin-cial elections just four days apart; 83 percent of Prince Edward Islanders du-tifully trooped off to the polls in the midst of a hurricane that left half the island's households without electricity, while only 57 percent of Ontarians voted.[27] Notwithstanding the palpable desire in those elections for regime change in Ontario and regime continuity in PEI, residents of the former were less likely than those of the latter to vote. This is because the Ontario voters were less likely than the islanders to know their neighbours, have per-sonal contact with the candidates, and be subjected by peer pressure to con-sider voting as a civic obligation. In contrast, in the small Atlantic provinces and especially in PEI, voting tends to be perceived as a virtuous act rein-forced by the intimacies of neighbourliness. An example of Atlantic Canad-ians' relative familiarity with each other in matters political exists in the links between "friends and neighbours" in the leadership selection processes in the parties.[28]

Institutional evidence indicates that a distinct Maritime/Atlantic politic-al culture is no mere idle fantasy: various forms of conscious regional inte-gration are more advanced there than elsewhere. The Council of Maritime Premiers and the Atlantic Provinces Economic Council, with their regional groupings of premiers, are matched by non-governmental organizations such as the Maritime Board of Trade and the Atlantic Institute for Market Studies. The region has been subjected to unparalleled detailed thinking about polit-ical integration: a 1970 Maritime Union Study projected improvements in both living standards and the quality of government services in a regional union, one with the aggregated power of redrawn boundaries.[29] Political union in the region is less touted now than it was some decades ago. Nevertheless, there is more evidence here than elsewhere of cross-provincial efforts in public policy and administration: witness the workings of the Atlantic Insurance Harmonization Task Force (created in 2003 by the four premiers) and vehicles such as the Maritime Provinces Higher Education Commission, the Maritime Provinces Harness Racing Commission, and the Atlantic Energy Ministers Forum.

Cultural Imagery

The Hartzian "fragment" theory's bold, creative, comparative-historical approach, as outlined in Chapter 1, may be modified to summon up metaphorical images of provincial/regional political cultures. They serve as insightful heuristic devices – however exaggerated, caricatured, stereotyped, limited, and imperfect they may be – for the purpose of discerning, comparing, and contrasting regional political cultures. This inventive rather than literal technique helps to illuminate the exceptionality of each region's political culture. Hartz stressed the role of *ideological* fragmentation in New World societies: only a fragment of Europe's full ideological spectrum was present in settings such as the US and French Canada; thus, the conservative and liberal seeds respectively, which were necessary prerequisites for the later sprouting of socialist ideas, were left behind or not yet experienced by founding settlers.[30]

The formulation posited in Table 6.1 is nuanced more to the cultural and demographic and less to the ideological in one vital respect. The two approaches are closely connected, but the thrust pursued here emphasizes the interplay of immigrants and their political ideas rather than, in the first

TABLE 6.1

Provincial metaphorical images

Province(s)	Metaphorical images
Newfoundland	Canada's Ireland and West Country England
Maritime	Canada's New England
Quebec	New (Old) France
Ontario	America's Counter-Revolution
Manitoba	The Prairies' Ontario
Saskatchewan	The Prairies' Britain
Alberta	The Prairies' America
British Columbia	Canada's Australia

instance, the dialectical interaction of ideologies. My approach is metaphorical, in that it also imagines Canadian regional/provincial politics as conjuring up, like mirrors or reflectors, the political dynamics of other societies. Although BC, for example, has had few Australian immigrants, BC politics took on a character – more so than the politics of any other Canadian province – of Australian politics. Both drew on a common pool of British immigrant workers at the turn of the twentieth century. Similarly, the tone and temper of Alberta politics feature an American Midwestern sensibility more than do those of the other provinces. More than any other province, Alberta attracted American immigrant farmers at the beginning of the twentieth century. These themes in Canada's Far West are pursued in Chapter 10. To follow through in this vein, Newfoundland may be viewed as an ideological-cultural-historical offshoot of Ireland and West Country England, whereas the Maritimes may be depicted as Canada's New England.

Newfoundland: Canada's Ireland and West Country England

To portray Newfoundland as Canada's Ireland and West Country England is simultaneously false and insightful. The contention here is merely that Newfoundland politics have appeared – more so than the politics of any other province – to resemble eighteenth- and nineteenth-century Irish and west English politics. This is the primary comparative point; nothing more is hinted. The collapse of Newfoundland's fishery in the 1990s may be seen as the New World equivalent of the Irish potato famine. After the Napoleonic wars, the fishery beckoned settlers to Newfoundland. Organized around a semi-feudal relationship between outport fishermen and St. John's fish merchants, the "truck" system virtually discarded money. For his catch, the fisherman received credit and goods in exchange. Settlers "came predominantly, and in about equal number, from Ireland and the west of England, and it is from them that the present population of the island is largely descended." Newfoundland "society was largely determined by the cultural norms and patterns of social organization and behaviour of the two founding groups, the Irish and the English," writes Sid Noel. His description is consistent with that of the fragment theory and the notion of transplanted cultural genes: "For the Irish brought with them a national heritage of poverty, Roman Catholicism, and hatred of their English oppressors; while the English brought with them from the west country a heritage of puritanical Protestantism, social deference, and semi-feudal economic relationships. Thus the constituent elements of the new community from the very beginning contained in their respective traditions and memories from the old world the seeds of social conflict in the new."[31]

Newfoundland's cultural duality, like Quebec's, was reinforced by residential segregation, unwritten law, and custom. The Irish Catholics gravitated to St. John's and the Avalon Peninsula, the English to the outports. In the Protestant north of the island, the Orange Lodge was particularly strong. Not one constituency beyond the peninsula had a Catholic majority.[32] Political divisions mirrored the economy and society: the urban centre of St. John's versus the isolated outports was Newfoundland's version of the metropolis-hinterland paradigm. The outport fishers derisively labelled natives of St. John's as "townies"; they, in turn, looked down on the rural "baymen." Irish Catholic voters sustained the early Liberal Party; the early Conservatives represented the English merchant class and adopted "Protestant Unity" as their rallying cry.

Old World politics drove the colony's first Constitution of 1832. It suggested an uncongealed and still evolving political culture. The Constitution was the product of British liberalism's ascendancy. Proclaimed in the same year as Britain's Great Reform Act, it went beyond it in providing for manhood suffrage and eligibility for office unfettered by property, rent, income, or literacy requirements.[33] Newfoundland was partly of Ireland but also unlike it. It did not become simply a colonial microcosm of Ireland, for, unlike in Ireland, political oppression did not serve the economic interests of the ruling Protestant elite. The English Protestant oligarchy opposed Confederation in the 1860s, but the heart of the opposition was among the Liberal Irish Catholics. Their "bitter folk memories were stirred by such effective propaganda as the comparison of confederation to the 1801 Act of Union between Britain and Ireland." Nearly a century later, Newfoundland in the 1940s was still "poorer than its North American neighbours but also different from them, holding to more conservative values, and preserving a culture historically rooted in the pre-industrial societies of Ireland and the west of England."[34]

In the 1860s, sectarianism became safely institutionalized. As in the Maritimes, elections, public appointments, and pork-barrelling reflected religious considerations. Newfoundland adopted a religious denominational basis of electoral representation,[35] which disappeared only in the 1970s. In Newfoundland, denominational segregation, established by compromise in the 1860s, became an unwritten law of social organization. David Bellamy described the province in the 1970s as dominated by a "rural fundamentalism" and as "only partially a secularized society."[36] As in conservative Quebec but somewhat less than in the Maritimes, the virtues of rural society were idealized and the impact of urban civilization derided in conservative Newfoundland beyond St. John's.

More than any other province, Newfoundland has been like Ireland *and* closer to Britain, known as "Britain's Oldest Colony." Until 1980, the Union Jack served as the provincial flag. In the 1990s, a leading student of Newfoundland economic development policy pointed to Ireland's "Celtic Tiger" economy as a template for the province.[37] Like Canada in the First World War, Newfoundland was automatically part of Britain's war. Unlike Canada in the Second World War, however, it was again automatically at Britain's side. Canadians had a parliamentary debate and vote on the war. Newfoundlanders, in contrast, had asked for a return of direct British rule in 1934, in the midst of financial distress. They surrendered the self-governing dominion status they had only recently gained in the Statute of Westminster. Though intimately and institutionally connected to Britain, Newfoundland was to be generationally isolated from it in a way that Canada was not. The fourth Canadian immigrant wave referred to in Chapter 1 – those urban Britons, continental Europeans, and American farmers arriving between the 1890s and 1920s – bypassed it, even more so than they did the Maritimes. Thus, Newfoundland's flirtation with labour-socialism was abstract and stunted, whereas in the West it was real and potent. In Newfoundland, "The activities of the British Labour party were avidly reported" in the 1910s;[38] in the West, they were avidly lived and replicated. Newfoundland's fishermen's union of 1913, organized by native farmer William Coaker, drew on a self-reliant, archetypically individualistic, and largely self-employed class "more closely akin to an agrarian peasantry than to an industrial proletariat."[39] Newfoundlanders' self-image was congruent with the colony's settlement: prohibited by Britain until the nineteenth century, the outports emerged as isolated outlaw communities tucked away in remote coves that were entered by neither the Royal Navy nor outside fishing boats.

This fostered a type of class solidarity quite unlike that of the British-born Western Canadian unionists. They voted for a general strike in Calgary in 1918, imposed one on Winnipeg a year later, dabbled in the syndicalism of the One Big Union, and initially applauded the Russian Revolution. Newfoundland's fishers and their leaders did not preach "workers of the world unite," as did many Western Canadian labour leaders. Joey Smallwood's socialist phase is noteworthy for its brevity, one quite different from the transplanted and sustained socialism of, for example, John Queen and M.J. Coldwell, the Manitoba and Saskatchewan Independent Labour Party (ILP) leaders. There was never much popular ideological support for socialism in Newfoundland. Although Smallwood, who saw himself as a working-class activist, headed the Federation of Labour and believed that the difference between the Liberals and the Tories was the "same difference between a to-ma-to and a to-mah-to," his commitment was to reviving the Liberal Party, not to dislodging it. "Liberalism," he wrote, "was as close as it is reasonable or practical to think the Island could get to Socialism."[40]

Voting patterns in two 1948 referenda that led to Confederation forcefully exhibited the cleavage between St. John's and the outports. Catholics and Protestants were generally identified with the anti- and pro-confederate forces respectively: the Catholic archbishop of St. John's was one of Confederation's most vociferous critics. In the aftermath, the Confederate Association was converted into the Liberal Party, and the anti-confederate Responsible Government League became the core of the new Conservatives.[41] Danny Williams, elected Newfoundland's Conservative premier in 2003, is the son of Conservative parents who opposed Confederation in 1949. Newfoundland's relative preference for oligarchic, hierarchical, personal, and deferential politics survived through the Smallwood era. In the 1960s, as in the nineteenth century, virtually all members of the House of Assembly lived in St. John's, and many had tenuous links with the ridings they represented. Smallwood treated many constituencies as if they were like the rotten boroughs of pre-Reform Britain, parachuting into them candidates who were the sons of cabinet ministers and prominent personal supporters.

In recent decades, Newfoundland has moved nearer to mainstream Canadian norms and conditions. The personalized, gladiatorial politics of the Smallwood era gave way to policy and administrative reforms typical of those in the other provinces. The political parties – long held together by loose networks of personal relationships and the bestowing of multifarious rewards and deprivations – have adopted constitutions and processes similar to those of parties in the rest of Canada. Electoral boundaries have been redrawn to reflect urbanization, and political leadership has become more fluid; in 1989, the province had three premiers over the course of forty-four days. The vexed issue of denominational schooling has been resolved.[42] A flowering of Newfoundland culture and nationalist spirit led to the pursuit of more autonomy from foreign investors in economic development.[43] The province, no longer going "cap in hand" to Ottawa, has challenged federal power more than its Maritime neighbours: Brian Peckford, zealously pursuing control of offshore resources, served as "the bad boy of Confederation" in the 1980s. At that decade's end, Clyde Wells – with substantial support making him the most popular leader in English Canada – undid the Meech Lake Accord. And in a 2004 reprise of the battle over offshore revenues, Newfoundland's government ordered the removal of Canadian flags from provincial buildings, something inconceivable in any other of the English-speaking provinces.

THE MARITIMES: CANADA'S NEW ENGLAND

Shane O'Dea once remarked that "Newfoundland's history is Newfoundland's culture."[44] The same formula could be applied to the history and culture of the Maritimes, though not to those of the more westerly provinces. As it did in Newfoundland, Britain ruled the Maritimes in the eighteenth century. In PEI, Anglo-Irish Protestants, well established before the Great Famine, dominated business and politics in the late eighteenth and early nineteenth centuries.[45] It was British New England, however, that helped shape Maritime political culture. Even before 1712, New Englanders were a power on the scene, "a strong formative influence in the making of the Atlantic Provinces," providing them with their "surplus population."[46] Today, many Maritimers continue the connection through relatives in the "Boston States." British pre-Loyalist and Loyalist colonists share common New England origins; the former laid the foundations of permanence for the region, the latter reorganized it. In many respects, the Maritimes were the northern social extension and economic partner of New England. Although a political colony of Britain, the Maritimes were an economic and cultural satellite of pre- and post-revolutionary America. Massachusetts settlers and their system of courts took root there in the 1750s and 1760s, under justices striving to enforce New England precedents. Britain actively encouraged migration to the Maritimes from New England but discouraged it from the British Isles. Nova Scotia offered New Englanders in the mid-eighteenth century what Alberta offered Midwestern Americans in the early twentieth century: free land.

Kenneth McRae, the first to apply Hartz's ideological fragment theory to Canada, described Nova Scotia as "a new New England whose failure to join the other [American] colonies in revolt was the result of economic, geographic, and military factors rather than of any significant difference in outlook."[47] A pre-revolutionary contingent of seven thousand settlers from New England "imparted to the province the character of a northern segment of New England and appeared as the logical completion of the process by which New Englanders had, for generations, come to regard Nova Scotia as their own."[48] The Maritimes' less numerous early German and Swiss settlers had a subordinate status: the first such group of fifteen hundred huddled in segregated, guarded barracks, denied access to either land or employment. Some Maritime immigrants came directly from Britain – Irish Ulstermen, some Yorkshire farmers, and a mass movement of Highland Scots – but the region was culturally more akin to New England than to old Scotland. In terms of political style too, the Maritimes lay within the New England sphere of influence: "The political patricians of the Atlantic Provinces bore little resemblance to those of the mother country and appeared to be in the grip of the demeaning influences of the pork-barrel that flowed in from the United States."[49]

Despite the formative presence of New Englanders, nascent democratic and liberal impulses were relatively subdued in the Maritimes, both before and after the American Revolution. The Loyalist influx overwhelmed but also fused with the pre-Loyalist order. In Upper Canada, in contrast, Loyalism by itself was formative. The two Loyalist segments flanking French Canada differed in that one represented the seaboard, the other the frontier. Nova Scotian Loyalists contained among their ranks a sprinkling of gentlemen, esquires, physicians, clergymen, and graduates of Harvard, Yale, and King's (Columbia). Barely a handful of Upper Canadian Loyalists belonged to the professions. Rather, in Upper Canada, "we scent at once the atmosphere of the American frontier,"[50] a scent unlike that of Nova Scotia or PEI. Liberalism reigned in both regions, but the Maritime variant was more tory-tinged than its Upper Canada equivalent. According to George Rawlyk, Maritime political culture probably congealed in about 1850 against the backdrop of a stagnant population whose prevailing attitudes persisted in a context of little inmigration.[51] Much of Canada's nineteenth-century immigrant wave, that consisting largely of British liberals (and, in 1820, including John A. Macdonald and his family), had bypassed the Maritimes and settled in Upper Canada. This wave's politics barely influenced Maritime society. As a result, Maritime reformers were few in number when the struggle for responsible government began. Maritime Loyalists played a more important role in attaining it than did their Upper Canada counterparts, whose contribution was overshadowed by that of the immigrants. Contrast Joseph Howe's liberalism with George

Brown's. Both men favoured the move to responsible government: however, the former, a Nova Scotian, looked eastward to Britain; the latter, of Upper Canada, looked westward to the backwoods of Canada. Howe was the son of a Loyalist, a group with an identity of collective persecution. "Howe's loyalty for his native province may have approached fanaticism, but it in no wise exceeded his loyalty for the mother country." He was "the loyalist *par excellence*," whose "highest ambition"[52] was to secure Nova Scotian representation in the British House of Commons, an idea not common among Upper Canadians, and certainly not the aspiration of a William Lyon Mackenzie or a Robert Baldwin. Howe's political evolution from "mild tory to reforming assemblyman"[53] reflected the Maritimes' cautious ideological evolution.

Nova Scotia's rugged frontier, out of which New Brunswick was carved, imposed a measure of equality on those settling in its isolated rural areas. The governmental institutions that arose, however, were more aristocratic and exclusive than liberal and egalitarian. "The Loyalists were inclined to fear liberal reforms involving popular control of government after their experiences in the former colonies." Nevertheless, government evolved, and after 1837 it "came to resemble the American rather than the British pattern"[54] in extending the powers of the elected Assembly. A lingering tory institution in the three Maritime colonies was their unelected upper houses; Nova Scotia's survived until 1928. Parochialism and social immobilism prevailed, rather than liberal acquisitiveness, enterprise, and materialism. America's civil war simultaneously frightened Maritimers and stimulated their economy. The 1866 termination of free trade and America's Fenian menace made Confederation appealing for conservative reasons in the Maritimes, whereas the expansionary possibilities excited Upper Canada's market liberals, its economic and political elites.

In many respects, Maritime politics did not change significantly between the late eighteenth and mid-twentieth centuries. The touchstones of conservatism – localism, tradition, caution, stability, social order, hierarchical religions, and elitism in the economic and political realms – took root, survived, and indeed thrived. Cementing them were a pervasive system of patronage, a climate of deference to authority, and cross-generational, familial, cradle-to-grave partisan loyalties that were more pronounced in the region than anywhere else in English Canada. As in Newfoundland, partisan sectarianism in the Maritimes proved more symbolic than substantive. Parties differed by virtue of the personalities and puffery of their leaders, not their principles or policies. Religion and patronage reinforced partisanship, structuring political inputs and outputs. For decades, one could not foretell which party would win in PEI elections, but one could be certain that twenty-one Protestants and nine Catholics would be elected. Customs and multi-member ridings arose in all three provinces to accommodate and dampen religious cleavage. Religious cleavage in much of the Maritimes resembled the future class cleavage in the urban West, the hub around which politics revolved. To be a non-partisan in the Maritimes was akin to being a heathen; to switch partisan affiliation was akin to renouncing one's religion and converting. What was remarkable was not the early sway of conservative liberalism (or liberal conservatism) but its lasting power. "Provincial politics in New Brunswick," begins one account in the 1970s, "might best be described as parochial, stagnant, and anachronistic – reminiscent, in some ways, of politics in nineteenth century Britain before the reform movement."[55] -

The Acadians who returned and re-emerged after their deportation from the region were culturally distinct but ideologically compatible with Maritime Loyalism and conservatism. The "Acadian Renaissance" of the late nineteenth century fed the growth of national symbols as it did elsewhere in the Western world. As in the case of the Québécois, however, Acadian national symbols were designed to inspire ethnic solidarity, to "act as a substitute for material advancement through acceptance of the capitalist assimilationist structure of English Canada."[56] Despite their solidarity and growth – by the 1950s, they made up about two-fifths of New Brunswick – the Acadians were geographically clustered as a secondary fragment, one less privileged than other New Brunswickers. They held barely a sixth of the legislature's seats in nearly a century of elections.[57] Franco-Manitobans, in contrast, came to be overrepresented in their legislature, despite their alleged linguistic and cultural oppression.[58] Acadians attained in the Charter of Rights an entrenched status for themselves and their language that exceeds that for Franco-Manitobans or anglophone Quebecers. New Brunswick's legislature and government are now constitutionally charged with preserving and promoting the francophone community, members of which are entitled to communicate and receive provincial government services in French. Moreover, Acadians gained an elevated status as "they have become political power-brokers within New Brunswick's ultra-conservative political system."[59] In 2003, the once outcast Acadians were acknowledged in a royal proclamation that designated an annual "Day of Commemoration of the Great Upheaval" of 1755. That

Acadian gains were achieved under the Conservatives, whose base was the Loyalist southwest rather than the Acadian northeast, reflected only a partial eclipse, as we have seen, of the politics of ethnicity as evidenced by the meteoric rise of the CoR Party.

The simultaneous weakness of agrarian radicalism and the isolated, concentrated presence of socialism in the Maritimes are indicative of the region's relative conservatism. Socialism languished in Atlantic Canada, unlike in Ontario and especially the West, because the carriers of labour-socialism in the fourth wave of immigration at the turn of the twentieth century bypassed the region. The sole and revealing exception to this pattern, the one that confirms the rule, was Cape Breton, where the Maritime coal and steel industries were located. They attracted working-class Britons who formed a Cape Breton ILP in 1917; three years later, this became the heart of Nova Scotia's ILP.[60] Indeed, of the fewer than fifteen thousand Canadian unionists affiliated with the CCF through their union locals in the 1950s, ten thousand were from the miners' union in Nova Scotia.[61]

Although agricultural and rural interests could drive politics in the Maritimes, as they did on the prairies, they did so in quite different ways. Subsistence rather than commercial farming was the Maritime order: a way of life rather than a business. It was diverse (fruit, dairy, potatoes, poultry) rather than specialized and mechanized. Having no wheat, Maritime agriculture had no king. Maritime agriculture did not foster and could not sustain large numbers of co-operatives, as on the prairies. Thus, the agrarian revolt in the Maritimes, as compared to its Prairie and Ontario counterparts, who elected farmers' parties to government, was no more than a whisper to a roar. The conservatism of Maritime farmers and the radicalism of westerly farmers were reinforced by their respective relationships to the land. The Maritime farmer inherited or divided long-held family farms, often on marginal land. In the west, pioneers cleared prime, virgin lands. Many of western Ontario's nineteenth-century farmers were of the third wave of immigration, those who brought British liberal ideas and an expansionary outlook driven by entrepreneurial ambition and notions of progress. As in the Maritimes, mixed agriculture prevailed in Ontario, but it was prosperous, not subsistent. Further west, on the prairies, the fourth immigrant wave brought American physiocratic, Jeffersonian notions, as well as British socialist schemes for land nationalization. Such influences, evident and powerful in the West, were feeble when existent in the East.

Staples and Formative Events

The economistic-communications frame of Harold Innis' "staples" approach and S.M. Lipset's "formative events" construct, both outlined in Chapter 1, fit with, rather than run counter to, Hartz's ideological "fragment" theory. This is the case in Atlantic Canada and in the other regions as well. Hartz acknowledged the limitations of his "single factor [analysis that] cannot illuminate all situations, [but nevertheless] can illuminate many."[62] When Gad Horowitz set out to apply the fragment theory to Canada, Hartz reminded him that other factors – he specifically cited urbanization, class, and the availability of capital[63] – must be appreciated in conjunction with the transplantation and interaction of the ideological genes of founding settlers.

Innis' meticulous monumental studies of the Atlantic cod fisheries, as well as of the lumber and fur industries and the CPR, demonstrated the interaction of geography and culture. Innis linked the "aggressive commercialism of the West County based on the fishing industry" with the restrictions on settlement growth in Newfoundland. The Atlantic fishery in the Maritimes and Newfoundland was oriented outwardly and easterly[64] – toward Europe primarily but to the American colonies and the British West Indies as well. A quadrangular trading arrangement arose, with Maritime fish and then lumber circulating in exchange for manufactured goods from Britain, wheat from America, and sugar and rum from the West Indies. These patterns reinforced Atlantic Canada's British ties and identity. The Atlantic fishery emanating from the St. Lawrence River, in contrast, oriented itself inward, along the river and its tributaries. This meant contributing to the eventual westerly and southerly push of the fur, forestry, and wheat sectors. With New Brunswick settled by Loyalists at the end of the eighteenth century, forests soon became the staple that fired that colony's growth. Ships were constructed of and loaded with Maritime lumber, which, upon arrival in Britain, was exchanged for British, especially Irish, immigrants coming to the British North American colonies in the very same ships.

After Maritimers were cajoled, manipulated, and bribed by the British and Canadians to enter Confederation, their economic hopes lay in the possibility that their coal, iron, steel, and other manufacturing industries would capture Canadian markets via their bargained-for Intercolonial railroad. The opposite, however, occurred: most new Maritime industries and markets were captured by central Canadian entrepreneurs and corporations. Among Maritimers, this fed "colonial attitudes and the ingrained insecurities of their society."[65] Such attitudes reinforced resignation and deferential inclinations. As Ontarians, Britons, Americans, and continental Europeans streamed onto the prairies in the early years of the twentieth century, at least 300,000 Maritimers abandoned their region, largely for the US, amid Maritime deindustrialization.[66] A symbolic expression of this was the eventual relocation of the general office of the Bank of Nova Scotia – Canada's second-oldest bank (founded in the 1830s, with operations in the Caribbean beginning in the 1880s) – to central Canada.

One thrust of neo-Innisian thinking led to an economic dependency theory with cultural implications.[67] We may adapt it for our purposes: just as Canada has been on the periphery of Western capitalism, the Atlantic region has been on the edges of Canadian capitalism. Just as this school of thought has depicted Canada as a victim of national oppression by American corporations, we may present Atlantic Canada as a victim of an overbearing central Canadian corporate class – a region neglected by self-anointed Canadian cultural "guardians" in central Canada, one treated insensitively by the federal government. From this perspective, Atlantic regional development has been economically crushed and culturally marginalized. The feelings of some Canadians that, in the universe of mass popular culture, they are second-class Americans are paralleled by Atlantic Canadian feelings – stemming from relative dependence and powerlessness – that they are second-class Canadians. Neo-Innisian thought fostered economic nationalism out of a fear of American political and cultural assimilation,[68] but here the parallelism for Atlantic Canada ends. Advocates for state assistance for Canada's national, cultural industries are not paralleled by any equivalent influential claimants pushing their provincial states in the East. Canada's regional cultural intelligentsias see themselves as Canadians first; like their Ontarian counterparts, they define themselves primarily as "non-American" rather than "non–central Canadian."

Seymour Lipset's "formative events" paradigm fixes a "founding moment" as a historical cultural marker. A single momentous event produces an enveloping ethos that informs and constrains future political discourse and behaviour. In the context of Atlantic Canada, there are three such moments for three distinct Atlantic cultures. Newfoundland had two of them: its rebuff of Canada in the 1860s and its entry in the 1940s. Anglo-Maritimers and Acadians share the same formative event: the expulsion of the latter in 1755. The Acadians, unlike the Québécois, were not so much subjugated as they were uprooted and dispersed. Those who escaped to northeastern New Brunswick were "fugitives."[69] Later, many in the Acadian diaspora returned. However, the British cast for the region was set with their expulsion. Indeed, New Brunswick's courts came to rule that, even earlier, 1660 – the year of the Restoration of Charles II and long before British colonization – marked the point of reception of English law.[70]

These defining formative events were complemented by what we might call three subsequent cultural "quakes." Newfoundland's quake was the reimposition of direct British rule in the 1930s. In the Maritimes, it was the American Revolution and then the attainment of responsible government (Nova Scotia was the first British colony to achieve this) in the 1840s. Newfoundland's economic bankruptcy demonstrated its non-viability as an independent state. Fiscal scandals rattled confidence in its parties and government. The political system collapsed in a way that it did not elsewhere in Canada, for Newfoundland had no Ottawa to turn to in the dirty thirties to alleviate its financial predicament. Commission Government under the British marked a considerable move away from the booty and boondoggle of Newfoundland public administration. It also helped set the stage for union with Canada after the war.

In the Maritimes, the decamped Loyalists and their values melded smoothly with Nova Scotia's pre-revolutionary colonials. New Brunswick's Loyalists differed somewhat from the rest: they were a founding fragment in the region's western reaches. Saint John received a royal charter in 1785 and became known as "the Loyalist city." New Brunswick came to exhibit some commonality with Ontario and Manitoba in its anti-Catholic, anti-French prejudices. Orange Lodges were incorporated by its legislature in 1875, and Protestant clergymen "seemed to be praying for their own New Brunswick version of the Manitoba [Schools Question]."[71]

The American Revolution helped populate the Maritimes, but neither the Maritimes nor Newfoundland – which the Loyalists avoided and which was thus even less liberal than the Maritimes – had a liberal or nationalist rebellion, no equivalent of those in Upper and Lower Canada. Like them, however, the Maritimes had their Family Compacts and Reformers, a tension between the ensconced and aspiring classes. The Maritimes were not as liberal as Upper Canada because the region had fewer early nineteenth-century British liberal immigrants. Nevertheless, the clamour for responsible government became irresistible. One battle fought by Maritimers, which had no Ontario parallel, was for "better terms" in Confederation's early years. Whereas

Ontario's relative wealth fuelled that province's determination to lessen federal power in the late nineteenth century, the relative disadvantaging of the Maritimes contributed to that region's eventual embrace of strong central government. The theme of improving local conditions through federal power, through equalization grants and regionally designated programs, thus came to characterize the Maritimes' constitutional position.[72]

Atlantic Canada and the "Fragment" Theory

At first blush, the Achilles heel of Hartz's "fragment" theory seems exposed when the theory is applied to Atlantic Canada. There are tenuous connections in the region between its substantial tory traditions and a relatively insubstantial historical socialist presence. Hartz brilliantly highlighted the corporate-organic-collectivist component common to both tory and socialist *Weltanschauungen* of society's nature and man's place in it. Following Hartz's theoretical path, Horowitz argued that "the relative strength of socialism in Canada is related to the relative strength of toryism."[73] The theory might seem to founder, however, on shaky empirical moorings in Atlantic Canada. If socialism is the ideological offspring of a pre-existing competitive mating of tory communitarian and liberal rationalist-egalitarian constellations of thinking, why has socialism been so historically weak in the region? No region in Canada received as many Loyalists, and no region was as reticent to embrace or sustain socialist ideas.

Atlantic Canadian political culture – moulded by British as well as British American colonists and guided by British governors – developed quite unlike that of Britain. The lack of parallelism in the ideological development of Britain and Atlantic Canada is expressed in the contrasts between their party systems. Britain's Liberals came to be squeezed and undermined by labour-socialists on their left and tories on their right, in an era of collectivist politics.[74] They lost ground to and were displaced by Labour in a left-right two-party system in which a new left party – drawing on a substantial urban labouring class – replaced an older, bourgeois party. In Atlantic Canada, in contrast, the older British-style two-party system and the very same party names persisted, but a socialist party did not emerge. Moreover, the ideological fissures between toryism and liberalism – evident in British policy struggles over trade, the franchise, and the conflicting interests of established agricultural-aristocratic wealth on the one hand and entrepreneurial-financial-industrial classes on the other – were not present in Atlantic Canada. The region's Liberals and Conservatives have always been less ideologically distinct than in the other Canadian regions. One must note, however, that Atlantic Canada was never the heavily industrialized urban society that Britain was. It had no enclosure movement and no large critical mass of marginalized working-class city folk. It was always a relative backwater rather than a centre for finance capital. There has always been a consciousness of established wealthy families (the Irvings, the Stanfields, the McCains) in the region, but never much class-consciousness or class conflict.

To attribute Atlantic Canada's relatively recent and tentative flirtations with the social democratic NDP as connected to the region's tory legacy is to imagine a remarkably long ideological gestation period. There is no need, however, to attribute to Hartz's theory an abstraction it does not have. Hartz appreciated that the rise of socialism requires large cities, a substantial class of wage labourers, and capitalism. Historically, these were lacking in the Atlantic region. A neater, more direct but less theoretically elegant explanation for socialism's historical weakness and its provisional advances and foothold of late does go back, in part, to the transplantation of ideological-cultural genes, as Hartz would have it. It makes no claim, however, that the combustible interaction of tory and liberal ideas in the political culture produced socialist ones. Rather, the proposition here is simple and more modest than that of Hartz, though not inconsistent with his framework: that Canada's fourth wave of immigrants – the radical English, Scots, Americans, and continental Europeans who arrived at the turn of the twentieth century – avoided Atlantic Canada because it had already been settled and because it offered relatively bleak economic prospects.

This suggests, in reverse, that whatever receptivity exists in contemporary Atlantic Canada to social democratic ideas is a product of the region's increasing integration – year by year and decade by decade – into a broader, modern, and more national Canadian ideological mainstream. There, social democratic parties and ideas have been in currency for nearly a century. On a material rather than ideological superstructural plane, the Atlantic provinces, as the weak sisters of Confederation, have an objective interest in social democratic formulations that address the region's inequalities in terms of the living standards and welfare conditions of its residents. Thus, Michael Ornstein's findings,[75] that Atlantic Canadians are more "left-wing" than other English Canadians in their policy preferences, are consistent with the low class status of the former as compared with that of the latter. In this respect, Atlantic Canadian political culture is modernizing.

In support of Hartz's tory-cum-socialist thesis, one might cite the cases of Atlantic Canada's red tories. There are more of them in this region than in any other. A partial list might include Eugene Forsey, Robert Stanfield, Dalton Camp, and David MacDonald. Yet another latter-day self-described "Red Tory" is Newfoundland premier Danny Williams. Eugene Forsey's academic interests revolved around the mechanics of Canada's monarchical tory-structured parliamentary system, but his professional career was in the service of workers in the trade union movement, the core of the CCF-NDP's constituency.[76] That Forsey ended his distinguished career as a Liberal senator spoke to the iterative integrative character of Canada's evolving political culture. It is one in which tories, liberals, and socialists began, as they had in Europe and as Hartz had observed, to interact as parents and children – sometimes quarrelling, sometimes accommodating – rather than as aliens whose political ideas were unfathomable to one another. Robert Stanfield, as leader of the Conservative Party, never rejected but did not worship at the altar of market liberal principles. He combined a tory view of man's imperfectibility with concerns about poverty and the well-being of the less fortunate. He did so in terms of his definition of the national interest – that social order rather than private enterprise ought to be his party's cardinal principle.[77] Stanfield's "guru," Dalton Camp, "regarded himself as a Red Tory" according to his biographer, "as accurate a label as any."[78] He railed against the "Real Right" – the Republicans in Washington and the Reform and Canadian Alliance Parties in Ottawa. Lastly, David MacDonald, who served as a federal Conservative backbencher and cabinet minister in the 1970s and 1980s, was another self-described red tory. In his later, redder stage he ran for the NDP in the 1990s. The politics of these Atlantic Canadian Conservatives had much in common with the world views of Canada's social democrats, and may be contrasted with those of the West's conservatives – the Mannings, Stockwell Day, Ralph Klein, Stephen Harper, and the Saskatchewan Party – which shared much with that region's populist Social Credit, Progressive, and Midwestern American agrarian traditions.

Although Hartz's ideological fragmentation thesis is limited in its ability to account for Atlantic Canadian political culture, and must be stretched in order to do so, it is brilliantly luminescent when applied to the case of Quebec. There, the dialectical ideological path to which Hartz pointed – before the onset of the Quiet Revolution – proved remarkably prescient. And it is to Quebec, the most culturally distinct of Canada's regions, to which we now turn.

7
Quebec: Political Culture of a Distinct Society

History is an inseparable, critical element of national identity. A group's discourse defines its shared traits, tribulations, achievements, and aspirations. Journalists consider newspapers a first draft of history. Their content and tone communicate the prevailing values of their day. So may their names. *Le Devoir* (Duty) and the *London Free Press* assert contrasting ideological messages. In classical conservative or feudal thinking, duty comes before freedom, obligations precede rights. *Le Devoir,* founded by Henri Bourassa, came to be edited as well by André Laurendeau and Claude Ryan, eminent Quebec Liberals. Both were Catholic nationalists with strong collectivist orientations. Ryan once hailed Lionel Groulx – the conservative priest who long served as the province's foremost historian and most prominent nationalist – as the founder of modern Quebec. The *Free Press* of both London and Winnipeg communicate in their names something of the liberal frontier spirit that bore them. Both were voices, at different times, of the expanding western edge of Canada. They were launched in places and times of relatively few constraints, where individual ambition was encouraged and when the obligations of individuals to their nascent societies were less firm or established than in Quebec.

Professional historians and university departments of history appeared later in French Quebec, after the Second World War, than elsewhere in Canada. Quebec's intellectuals, however, have been more engaged in and influential in public debates than their Anglo-Canadian counterparts.[1] Their writings have coloured the way in which Quebecers see themselves and address contemporary challenges. Quebec's historians, like historians everywhere, have contributed to the construction of Quebecers' identity by fashioning images that point to a particular future direction for their society. François-Xavier Garneau – Quebec's pioneer of historical writing – offered a sturdy amateurish history that held sway in the nineteenth century. It depicted racial antagonism as history's driving force, a series of battles between *les canadiens* and their Indian, British, American, and Anglo-Canadian foes. In the twentieth century, Groulx synthesized Catholic ideology with the nationalist ideals that had been cultivated and celebrated. The pivot in his narrative was the Conquest. French Canadians were presented as a conquered but not spiritually defeated people who persevered through their relative goodness and the superiority of their religion and rural lifestyle. New France was idealized, and those who fought for *survivance* within Confederation were glorified. A Montreal school of historians, developed after the Second World War, depicted the Conquest and the British occupation as having destroyed a viable colony, one with a vibrant French Canadian bourgeoisie. French Quebec had been mauled by the cumulative catastrophic impact of subordination. This made independence a vital necessity, a vehicle for breaking the chains of national oppression. The Parti Québécois (PQ) drew in part on this narrative in making the case for sovereignty in the 1980 referendum.[2]

A Laval school of history, most notably reflected in Fernand Ouellette's *Economic and Social History of Quebec, 1760-1850*, absolved the English of responsibility for retarded economic development, attributing it instead to the *mentalité collective* of French Canadians. In this interpretation, the French had mismanaged agriculture, chosen to remove themselves from economic development, and preferred to complain about imagined wrongs imposed by the English.[3] Soon after, a new school of revisionist neo-nationalist history arose that proposed that French Canada had been a "normal" society rather than a distinctive one, as both the Montreal and Laval schools had contended. Quebec required independence, as Lucien Bouchard put it, for it was a normal society and not a "normal" country, quite unlike Canada, with its forced and strained bilingual, bicultural façade. This new generation of historians – enveloped and socialized by the Quiet Revolution – declericalized Quebec's history and redefined Quebec as a modernized society, one in which, notwithstanding the Conquest's calamitous consequences, a denouement of progressive independent statehood awaited. For many of them, the issue of whether the Conquest and British rule retarded French Canadian development was a non-issue. What the different schools of Quebec historiography have in common is their mixture of social scientific rigour with ideological purpose. If nothing else, the failure of the referenda on sovereignty – against a backdrop of the Quiet Revolution's success – demonstrated that independence was not indispensable to the democratization and modernization of Quebec's culture.[4]

Quebec sociologist Gérard Bouchard, Lucien's brother, has rejected the old historical schools that saw French Canadians, English Canadians, Aboriginals, and others in terms of their differences.[5] He has also parted with the modernists' paradigm of Quebecers as a "normal" people in the mainstream of Western socio-economic development, for – unlike Australians, Latin Americans, English Canadians, and Americans – they have not achieved political independence. Bouchard sees Quebec as a *société neuve*, a new society that includes diverse French speakers welcomed by Quebec's current society. He appears to begin and end with a Quebec-centric narrative. His orientation assumes a cohesive Quebec society and culture that the historical record – the struggles between the English and the French, and the quite separate experiences of Quebec's Aboriginals – betrays.

Since the 1980s, Quebec intellectuals and the Quebec government have moved away – in tandem with Canada and other Western liberal states – from the old ethnic conceptualization of nationalism. They have redefined *la nation québécoise* by turning somewhat from the common historical cultural experience of French Canadians to presenting Quebec as a modern, pluralistic, heterogeneous community bonded by a common territory, democratic institutions, and the French language. This turns the old notion of *la nation québécoise* on its head by celebrating diversity, promoting the integration of minority cultural communities, and positing a common civic culture, a *culture publique commune*.[6] It is based on universal values – democracy, participation, equality, free expression, and socio-economic solidarity – rather than on an exclusive ethnic history. In every society, however, including those of English Canada and the US, there is some resistance to a pure civic nationalism with no historic cultural lineage. In every civic state, there is a dominant ethnic charter group, and almost every ethnic state makes some room for minorities. Quebec's political culture is moving on a continuum from ethnic to civic nationalism. It is not wholly one or the other.

The flight, economic humbling, and linguistic reorientation of anglophones have facilitated a redefinition of Québécois identity. Quebec City's anglophones once made up 40 percent of the city; today they account for 4 percent. By the 1990s, the use of French had expanded dramatically. Many anglophones – about a quarter million between the 1970s and 1990 – left the province. Those remaining were more likely than their forebears to become bilingual. Those with English as a mother tongue became more likely to adopt French as their home language than the reverse, the opposite of what was occurring in the rest of Canada. Quebec's unilingual anglophones declined as a force in Quebec society; English-language school enrolments dropped by over half between the 1970s and 1990s.[7] Anglophones, now outnumbered by allophones, shrank from a quarter of the population at Confederation to a twelfth; they account for less than 1 percent of provincial government employees. Today, fewer than one in twenty Quebecers cannot speak French; their incomes trail those of bilingual workers. The 1970s best-selling *White Niggers of America*, its title a characterization of francophone Quebecers, quickly dated.[8]

Notions of Anglo-Canadian oppression have dulled, but the new conceptualization of Quebec's transcultural civic nationalism dilutes – though does not by any means eliminate – French Quebecers' old sense of a collective ethnocultural identity. If civic nationalism is indeed a feature of Quebec's modern political culture, as official and intellectual discourse purports, the paradoxical upshot may be to weaken Quebec's claim to distinctiveness and the pursuit of separation. A dilemma facing nationalists and nationalist historians is the depressed birth rate among "old stock" or *pure laine* Québécois. The province recruits francophone and allophone immigrants from diverse backgrounds to offset the decline. As they meld with the original French Canadians, a new breed of francophone is emerging, one for whom Quebec's history and old institutions, such as the St. Jean Baptiste Society, are unfamiliar and less relevant. "New stock" Quebecers are oriented to the future, not the past.

The narratives of Quebec's history contrast with Anglo-Canadian accounts of Canadian development; Quebec's literary histories also contrast with those published in France. Quebec's literary history summons up the province as a *"pays incertain"* (uncertain country), a place of memories that must be retained.[9] This is quite unlike anything that could be said of continental French literature. Early English Canadian historical tracts differ too, in that they were promotional of material progress and western expansion. They extolled Canada's imperial connection to Britain. For English Canadian historians, mainly Ontarians, Lord Durham's Report proposing assimilation of the French and responsible government had welcome implications: commercial expansion and colonial self-government in a British parliamentary context. They presented Ontario as the harbinger and guardian of such virtues and Quebec as an impediment to them. Whiggish progressivism rather than religious traditionalism imbued this English Canadian recital of history through the turn of the twentieth century. First World War battlefields then contributed to a psychological distancing from Britain. Simultaneously, conscription reinforced French Canadian distancing from English Canada. English Canadian political-historical studies became fixated on Canada's international status, as well as on the relationship of empire to colony and then to nation-state. This was something quite removed from French Canadian concerns. In short order, American progressive historians and environmental determinism influenced English Canadian historians like Frank Underhill and political economists like Harold Innis. The former looked to the US for political modelling; the latter drew attention to a transatlantic economic order.

In common, English and French Canadian historians cannot agree among themselves about how to periodize their histories, both of which are challenged by the "new social history," whose practice emphasizes economic change and social relations rather than political and constitutional developments.[10] After the 1960s, English Canadian popular historians such as Pierre Berton and Peter Newman pursued national themes through English Canadian perspectives and emphases. Meanwhile, English Canada's academic historians turned to cellular studies of "limited identities" such as ethnicity, gender, region, class, and urbanism. In this context, Quebec and the Québécois appeared largely as one of many Canadian places and groups. Although English Canadian storytelling did accord them a crucial role during the country's creation and early evolution, it relegated them to such a diminished place in subsequent history that ultimately they became but one strand in a growing and complex mosaic of cultures.

In Quebec, historians consciously integrated the identities of their "others" into Quebec's national history. Although English Canadian scholars have written about gender in a way that disrupts the traditional historical narratives, Quebec historians have used the subject to reinforce theirs.[11] Their sociologists and intellectuals in the 1960s and 1970s engaged in studies of Quebec's culture that helped shift political debate in Quebec from "cultural sovereignty" to "sovereignty." They helped move political discourse from "fragmented, limited demands" such as bilingualism and separate schools to "global" decrees making French the language of work, commerce, and immigrants' education.[12]

Quebec historiography from the time of Durham's assimilationist report until the Quiet Revolution was one of "tradition-direction." It fostered collective societal reverence for the past and its institutions. French Quebecers were "inner-directed," to use David Riesman's model of social character development. Successive generations internalized and perpetuated adult and institutional authority.[13] Ontarian and Western Canadian societies collectively were outer-directed, in the sense of being driven by ideas and models emanating principally from Britain and the US. English Canadians as individuals, like the compliant middle-class Americans of whom Riesman wrote, also became "other-directed" – shaped more by their peers and the market than by their families – as they adopted new technologies and became urbanized.

From Subjugation to Sovereignty

Two critical landmarks in the development of Quebec's political culture fall exactly two hundred years apart: 1759 and 1959. The first, a battle on the Plains of Abraham in Quebec City, effectively transferred New France to English suzerainty. The second, the death of Maurice Duplessis, provided the opening for the Quiet Revolution. The province's "sovereignty" referenda in 1980 and 1995 were symbolic attempts to undo at the ballot box what Wolfe's muskets had accomplished two centuries earlier. The national struggle has always been at the heart of Quebec politics and in the soul of its culture. Omnipresent, it expresses itself in alternating bouts of calmness and agitated engagement. English Canadians – perplexed by a culture they do not share – take note of events in the province when they reverberate on the pan-Canadian stage: the rebellions of 1837-38, the conscription crises, the Front de libération du Québec's terrorism, the PQ election in 1976, the sovereignty referenda, and the sudden and surprising elevation of the Bloc Québécois as Her Majesty's Loyal Opposition in 1993. Nationalism, like populism, is an ideology that cuts across the fissure of "left" and "right." It may be married to conservative, socialist, or even liberal constellations of thought. It oscillates like a pendulum; it does not pass like a fever.

The cultural contrasts between Quebec and the other regions of Canada are much more striking than the contrasts between English Canada's regions. Quebecers have more progressive social attitudes and are less supportive of American foreign policies than are other Canadians. Quebec's premier is more than a first minister at the apex of the political system. He is a societal leader too, unlike the other premiers, by virtue of heading the only francophone jurisdiction in North America. Institutionally, Quebec has its Code civil, which is rooted in the Napoleonic Code and Roman law; the rest of Canada operates with the uncodified English-based common law. A historical difference between English and French Canadians was their attitude to Canada's expansion. French Canadians were not magnetized by the frontier. They did not share the optimistic, expansive, fearless, and independent mentality of the Ontarians who flooded the prairies. They expressed, according to A.I. Silver, "a strain of pessimism, defeatism, or demoralization"[14] about western settlement, and they disbelieved in the material value of prairie land. This characterization presupposes that French Canadians should have wanted to "expand" side by side with an inevitably much larger contingent of English Protestants. French Quebecers, as Silver appreciated, feared that a move to the west meant expatriation and a loss of national identity.

Temperamentally, Quebecers' view of democracy is less plebiscitarian and pan-Canadian than that of the rest of Canada. In the West, a populist tradition exists of stressing the pursuit of "the common sense of the common people" – as the Reform Party and some before and after it argued – in the form of popular initiatives, referenda, recall, and elected senators. The only issue in Quebec for which a referendum has been deemed imperative is sovereignty. Consider the manner in which Quebec, as opposed to Newfoundland, abolished its public denominational schools in the 1990s: the latter employed two referenda; Quebec did not consider such a route. Quebecers' experience in the conscription referendum in the 1940s was negative; their collective will was swamped by the collective will of other Canadians. In the 1992 referendum on the Charlottetown Accord, Quebec conducted its own referendum independently of the one in the rest of Canada, one with quite distinct rules for funding and eligibility. Only Quebec barred Canadians from voting if they had not resided in the province for the previous six months.

Quebecers' attitudes regarding their place in Canada stand apart from those of Canadians in other regions. When asked which level of government – federal, provincial, or municipal – they trusted to spend their money most wisely, Quebecers, more so than Canadians in any other province and twice as often as Ontarians, chose their provincial government.[15] They and their academics think about regions and regionalism differently than do Anglo-Canadians. When asked what region they live in, Quebecers are the least likely to name their province and the most likely to refer to a specific region within it. When Anglo-Canadian scholars ponder the challenges of regionalism, they generally refer to a province or group of provinces, but Franco-Québécois academics focus on geographic areas of Quebec. Their discourses differ too: since the late 1980s, while Anglo-Canadian sociology has become less interested in regional inequalities, their Québécois counterparts have become more engaged with it, but in the Quebec context.[16]

In no region outside Quebec has the possibility of separation been as seductive or real. In comparison with those of Quebec, other Canadians and their provincial governments have been relatively quiescent, content to ne-gotiate better conditions for themselves or acknowledgments of their status. Atlantic Canadians have long been fixated on equalization, on gaining ac-cess to resources through which to improve conditions and public services to levels like those enjoyed in other regions. British Columbians have pursued recognition for their province as one of five Canadian regions. Albertans have clamoured for the principle of equality of all the provinces. Westerners have generally taken positions of perceived exclusion: "The West Wants In" was the Reform Party's campaign slogan in the 1988 federal election. Ontarians have stood by the federal government on constitutional issues, generally iden-tifying their interests with the policies of Ottawa. Only Quebec has the dis-tinction of unilaterally trying to alter its status in Canada. That posture has been driven by more than allegations of unfairness, grist for the political mill in all provinces. It has been rooted in cultural distinctiveness. This tran-scends issues of fiscal imbalances, demographic weight, and status in federal institutions. Quebecers' position is grounded in a feeling of nationhood, even among the province's federalists. Among all the regions, that is some-thing exclusive to Quebec alone.

A troika of feelings feeds Quebec's secessionist impulses.[17] Two are anti-thetical: fear and confidence. The former is concern for the future of the French language, the latter an assertion of ability engendered by an economic cultural revolution: "we can do it." A third feeling, rejection, swings back and forth. It was heightened dramatically during the Meech Lake process. Two social-psychological forces powered the surge of the independence move-ment between the 1970s and 1990s.[18] One was the growth, led by the intelli-gentsia and militants, in the numbers of those who see themselves as "Québécois" (with a corresponding decline in those who call themselves "French Canadian"). By 2005, more than six in ten of Quebec's francophones defined themselves as "Quebecer only" or "Quebecer first but also a Canad-ian." This sentiment now has a viceregal voice at Rideau Hall: "We are both Quebecers," intoned the governor general's spouse. "We are Quebecers be-fore being Canadians."[19] The second social-psychological force was the rising belief that the economic consequences of Quebec sovereignty would not be as adverse as originally predicted; indeed, such a belief is now well entrenched. Attitudinal differences between Canada's francophones and anglophones are particularly striking on the language issue.[20] Most Quebec francophones feel that too little is done to promote French in the rest of Canada, but many anglophone Canadians outside Quebec see the existing measures as excessive. However, all regions share an emergent consensus, one which did not exist in the past, that bilingualism is "an essential characteristic of Canada." In addition, the majority of Canadians, wherever they live, believe that its elimination would have negative consequences.[21]

Quebec is the only place in Canada where there is substantial zest for sovereignty. Ten years after the 1995 referendum, Quebecers were divided in equal numbers on whether yet another referendum ought to be held and on how they would vote. Only a minority of them, however, supports seceding from Canada to become an independent country. Thus, since the 1970s, the more ambiguous terms "sovereignty" and "sovereignty-association," rather than "separation" and "independence," have been proposed by most advocates seeking a popular mandate for altering the constitutional status of the province. Unchanged since the 1960s is the relative affinity of youth for sovereignty and the relative leeriness of older Québécois regarding it. What has changed is that the youthful 1960s and 1970s partisans of independence have themselves aged. Most PQ members are now over fifty. Aiding the push toward sovereignty is the Quebec state's capacities; in Stéphane Dion's estimation, Quebec's is the most powerful sub-national government in the Organisation for Economic Co-operation and Development.[22]

Quebec and the Fragment Theory

The wellspring of a feeling of nationhood lies in the ideological and ethnic origins of Quebec society. From the perspective of Hartz's "fragment" theory, Quebec's ideological development best demonstrates – among all of Canada's regions – how conservative seeds (quasi-feudal in the case of Quebec, tory in the case of English Canada) may produce socialist fruit after the rain of liberal thought enters the ideological atmosphere. For Hartz, socialist radicalism was retarded in Quebec because its feudal origin had no liberalism to challenge it. "The French Canadian, having escaped the Enlightenment, escapes also Jacobinism and Marxism, since these later radicalisms are fed by the Enlightenment spirit."[23] Hartz wrote just as liberalism was revolutionizing Quebec's society, opening the way for socialist notions to enter French Quebec's political discourse. His paradigm had anticipated as much. Hartz used the generic term "feudal" intentionally to describe French Canadian political culture because the term was nebulous and could be used in the rather idiosyncratic way that Tocqueville employed it. Hartz was not referring to the actual institutions of the medieval world: he used the term "feudal" for purposes of analytic convenience and generalization, to denote an outlook, an orientation to politics, an ideological disposition that was pre-liberal.

In the United States, according to Hartz, liberal ideology became the national religion, around which a unifying spirit evolved. The American Constitution, for example, is worshipped as a sacred document; oaths of allegiance are sworn to it. In Quebec, a quasi-feudal ideology became the national religion, with the Roman Catholic Church serving as the object of collective allegiance. The Quiet Revolution transferred national devotion from the church to the state of Quebec. The American and Quebec experiences part company in that a globalizing messianism propelled America, as was evident in its treatment of ideological dissidents at home and its behaviour on the world stage. In Quebec, a thoroughly non-messianic resignation to English dominance, combined with pride in the genius of its religion and culture, prevailed. They were the ramparts thwarting external influences. After 1960, Quebec's collectivist communitarianism – now welded with liberalism – persisted in a transmuted, sublimated, semi-socialist form. In English Canada, in further contrast to both the United States and Quebec, a muted version of liberalism took hold, one tempered by tory and, later, social democratic streaks in its political culture.

To be a French Canadian before the Quiet Revolution was to be a pre-Enlightenment, pre-liberal Catholic in a collectivist, organic, hierarchical, and co-operative society. This outlook contrasts starkly with a liberal society's ideological stress on the primacy of competing, atomistic, free individuals – the dominant orientation in the cases of the English Canadian and American fragments since their beginnings. In a European context, this contrast exists between the ideological underpinnings of the ancien régime and the Declaration of the Rights of Man and Citizen. The former view is one of government designed for humans by God and passed on by the wisdom of the ages. It is not government as a contract between free and equal individuals. It is the difference between the coin stamped with "liberté, égalité, fraternité" and the coin – that of France's Vichy regime – that read "travail, famille, patrie." Québécois speak of "social solidarity," a phrase absent from and somewhat foreign to English Canadian thought.

There was, to be sure, a streak of *rouge*, or liberalism, in nineteenth-century Quebec. It was reflected in the rebellion of the *patriotes*, the attainment of responsible government, the broadening of the franchise, the growth of political parties, the establishment of public schools, and the Institut Canadien – a group of young radical liberal intellectuals. However, the liberalism of nineteenth-century French Quebec pales when placed next to the liberalism of English Canada or the US. Responsible government was achieved in the old Province of Canada due to English Upper Canadian pressure rather than French Lower Canadian ferment. "In Upper Canada the movement aims at responsible government," reads one autopsy of the 1837 rebellion, "but in Lower Canada the goal is national independence."[24] Quebec's publicly funded schools were organized under the exclusive aegis of Catholic and Protestant school boards, unlike those in the other provinces (except Newfoundland). The relatively brief life of the Institut Canadien – born in the 1850s, gone by the 1880s – revealed the feebleness of French Canada's liberalism. Quebec was the last province to make schooling compulsory, the last to give women the vote (1940), and the last to establish a Civil Service Commission (1943).

Hartz, who revelled in cross-cultural comparisons of personalities and events, noted, "There is a democratic movement in [nineteenth-century] French Canada, but when we abstract the nationalist elements from it, it shrinks in power."[25] Read, for example, two reports published at about the same time: compare the first, Tocqueville's account of "democracy" (liberalism) in America, with the second, Durham's scathing assessment of French Canada as a people with no literature or history. Quebec had no equivalent of Ontario's Egerton Ryerson, America's John Dewey, or France's Saint-Simon, the progressives of their day. Through the first half of the twentieth century, Quebec had no one to challenge Groulx, who approvingly cited the conservative dicta and assumed the Christian resignation of de Maistre rather than the rationalist and liberal dispositions of Voltaire and Rousseau.

Feudal ideology served as the conscious nationalist ideology of the French Canadian fragment. The values that Groulx, and Garneau before him, sought to discover in the past were those that would confront, not accommodate or extend, the moderate liberalism imported by the British after the Conquest. When the British conquerors were lauded, as they were in Thomas Chapais' *Cours d'histoire du Canada*, it was for their pre-liberalism, which "providentially" saved French Canada "from the horrors of the French revolution, the anti-clericalism, and materialism of modern France,"[26] the infidel. French Canada's clergy, the leading political class, opposed the 1837-38 rebellions. "Certainly one can hardly imagine a popular movement, a Jacksonian drive, for example, being crushed by the clergy as the Rougists were crushed,"[27] noted Hartz in one of his cross-cultural juxtapositions. Modernity was rejected in the boast that French Canada's language was closer to that of the Golden Age under Louis XIV than anything spoken in Europe.

Let us push the comparative perspective. As in English Canada and the United States until recent times, a myth of agrarian virtue held sway in French Canada, but there was nothing "grit" about it, as in Ontario, and nothing "populist" about it, as in the US. Where is any French Canadian equivalent of the variety of "Progressives" who appeared in Congress and the House of Commons, and who swept to power in a number of states and provinces? It was certainly not Réal Caouette's Créditistes. Like English Canada's Progressives, they were largely from rural areas, but unlike the Progressives, they were galvanized from the top down by a singular leader and they faded with him. In contrast, the Progressives were organized from the bottom up by notions of grassroots governance. Nor is André Laurendeau's Bloc Populaire, which fared poorly at the polls, the Quebec equivalent of the Progressives. His nationalism was more influenced by the ethnocentric, conservative Groulx than by the cosmopolitan, liberal Laurier.[28] Nowhere in Anglo-America was there an equivalent of seigneurialism. Although the institution was phased out eventually in French Canada as a concession to liberalism, the Quebec legislature was still dealing with the remaining rights of the seigneurs in 1935.[29] Quebec's clergy cited the corporatist and feudalist ideals of Salazar's Portugal as a model for dealing with the modern world.[30] There were no French Canadian counterparts of English Canadian social gospellers such as J.S. Woodsworth and Salem Bland, who reached out to new immigrants in the city via "labour" churches and "people's missions." Quebec's Catholic hierarchy, in contrast, reached in – to consolidate and shield an established homogeneous community and its faith.

Quebec's faint liberalism was not so much indigenous as it was a by-product of British rule and the Loyalist influx. It was one of the "benefits" of occupation; it did not spring up from the French Canadian nation. "The whole structure of the feudal order," wrote Ramsay Cook, paraphrasing Fernand Ouellette, "was hostile to the emergence" of a developing bourgeoisie before the Conquest. There was a pervasive "atmosphere of feudal paternalism."[31] Certainly, Quebec increasingly took on an industrial capitalistic appearance as the nineteenth century wore on, but its society did not live "by the socio-economic dictates of a capitalistic universe."[32] The liberal sentiments expressed by Henri Bourassa, the grandson of *patriote* leader Louis-Joseph Papineau, came from "a loyal son of the Church and a temperamental conservative," one who "tried to reconcile liberalism with Ultramontanism."[33] Pierre Trudeau cited the lack of liberalism in the French Canadian experience as the impediment to democracy in Quebec. The *canadiens* had been neither "psychologically nor politically prepared"[34] for representative government in the nineteenth century.

The story did not change much in the first half of the twentieth century. "In 1958," lamented Trudeau, "French Canadians must begin to learn democracy from scratch."[35] Duplessis' modus operandi was to conduct himself like a "prince" who rewarded friends, punished opponents, and exacted payoffs from contractors; "these methods had many features of a preindustrial society, which agreed perfectly with the conservative dogma, which in turn had been created expressly to assure the continuation of the traditional society that Quebec had been in the middle of the nineteenth century."[36] Although corruption has been typical of both liberal and conservative societies, patronage is an accepted, routine norm in patriarchal or feudal ones. Under Duplessis, state capacity and structures were skeletal. When the Union Nationale was defeated in 1960, the government of Quebec had fewer than a dozen economists and no Department of Education, a comment on how "public" its public schools were.

The French Canadian experience until 1960 was one of reaction, an excellent example of what Hartz termed "the impulse of the fragment to flee in the face of new experience."[37] That Hartz's theory applied to French Canada is corroborated by the independent analysis of Marcel Rioux, a Quebec sociologist. Neither man cited nor was apparently aware of the other's work, yet both employed a similar dialectical model. Just as Hartz thought of Europe's history as a succession of three ideological eras, so too did Rioux of Quebec's. Duplessisme, according to Rioux, tallied with "the ideology of conservation," or conservatism. A second ideology, "the ideology of contestation and recoupment," emerged in the late 1940s, came to power in the Quiet Revolution, and was, according to Rioux, in "the liberal tradition." The third ideology, "the ideology of development and participation," emerged as he wrote in the 1960s.[38] It identified with worldwide socialist movements for decolonization and national liberation. Recall that 1960 was no less a revolutionary year in West Africa than in Quebec, as France's colonial empire was formally dismantled. The outside world crashed in ("bombardment," as Hartz put it) on the French Canadian fragment.

Rioux, writing before René Lévesque's social democratic PQ had contested an election, described in a Hegelian dialectical manner similar to Hartz's how this third ideology drew on some aspects and rejected others of the two antecedent eras. This socialist ideology agreed with liberals on Quebec's need for modernization but did not hold that the model for emulation was necessarily liberal North America. Yet this ideology reached back to the past ("Je me souviens" was stamped on licence plates), as did the ideology of conservatism. Socialist and conservative Quebecers depicted Quebec's history as one of an exploited and dominated society, but the former rejected the old elites and the old ways as hopelessly reactionary, whereas the latter exalted them.

The PQ synthesized conservatism's *la survivance* with liberalism's *rattrapage* and came up with socialism's *dépassage* and *épanouissement*. It wanted to retrieve the pre-liberal notion of organic community in the face of growing liberalism. Socialism required the liberalism of the Quiet Revolution to set the stage. Because the PQ was both appealing to tradition and promising change, and because it was not English as was the CCF-NDP, it could not be dismissed as heretically foreign, as the CCF had been in Quebec. By the 1970s, the social democratic PQ was an acceptable, moderate alternative to the more radical and sectarian groupings such as the Front de libération du Québec (FLQ), the Rassemblement pour l'indépendance nationale (RIN), the Communist Party, the Trotskyists, and the Parti socialiste du Québec (PSQ). They had sprung up, suddenly, swiftly, with the demise of Duplessis and the diminished but continuing presence of the pre-liberal outlook. The link between conservatism and socialism is reflected, among other places, in Fernand Dumont's *The Vigil of Quebec*, in which the qualities and values of French Canadian union leaders were characterized as anti-capitalist, Catholic, and collectivist.[39] This is precisely what English Canadian socialists liked about them. The linkages and interaction between feudalism, liberalism, and socialism in Quebec were reflected in the very creation of the PQ. It drew on the former Liberal minister Lévesque to be its leader and amalgamated Pierre Bourgault's left-wing and socialist RIN with the right-wing and conservative Ralliement national, which was led by a Créditiste.

Gad Horowitz, building on Hartz, observed this phenomenon in the 1960s. Before the Quiet Revolution, he noted, Quebec's Catholic unions rejected joining the international unions and denounced them as too radical and socialist; after the Quiet Revolution, they denounced them as not social-ist enough. There was no contradiction because, before the Quiet Revolu-tion, these unions were Catholic; after it, they were national. Quebec's union movement went from attacking the American Federation of Labor for its dis-cussion of the public ownership of railways to attacking it for its declaration of allegiance to private enterprise.[40] The church had organized the union and *caisse populaire* movements as Catholic corporatist institutions. The Quiet Revolution transformed both of them but did not abolish them. Rather, they became radicalized, labour extremely so. Precisely because of the dialectical transformation of Quebec politics, Horowitz, in his role as a socialist politic-al activist, preferred that English and French Canada stay together. He did so, he said to red tory Canadian nationalist George Grant, "because French Can-ada may now be advancing farther along the road to social democracy than English Canada [so] that if we stick with the French we can learn something from them in that regard."[41]

Like "social solidarity," "corporatism" is a related notion that marks Que-bec's political culture as distinct from English Canada's. Hartz considered using "corporatism" rather than "feudalism" in his conceptual framework, but he settled on the Marxist triad of feudal (for the French Canadian and Latin American fragments), liberal or bourgeois (for the English Canadian, American, and Dutch South African fragments), and socialist or radical (for the Australian fragment). He did so because the term "corporatism" is not as clearly understood or prevalent as "feudalism."[42] It is precisely in Quebec, however, that "corporatism" has resonance in political discourse.[43] Champi-oned by the Roman Catholic Church and by the regimes of Mussolini, Franco, and Salazar, corporatism sees state policy as emerging from the co-ordinated, consensual, and co-operative efforts of elite decision makers who represent officially sanctioned constituencies of interests such as finance capital, indus-trialists, and the trade union movement. In the conservative version of corpo-ratism, these groups subordinate their special interests to the common good, under the guidance of either the church or a totalitarian party or both. Que-bec's clergy sympathetically embraced this model in the 1930s as an alterna-tive to communism, as a way to mollify an increasingly urban and restive working class. In that decade, fascist sympathies had more traction in Quebec than in the rest of Canada. This played a role in Canadian neutrality vis-à-vis the Spanish Civil War, something English Canadian leftists tried to change.

During the Lévesque PQ's term in office, ministers spoke proudly of Quebec as a "corporate state" to differentiate it from other provincial regimes and Ottawa. During the PQ's first seven years in office, nearly thirty tripartite economic summits – uniting the principal economic peak associations at one table – were held.[44] In 1983, under the auspices of the PQ, the Quebec Federation of Labour launched a capital development fund that called on the solidarity and savings of Quebecers. By 2003, with nearly five billion dollars in investments, it was a major player in the Quebec economy, one that touted its singular culture and ties to both the worlds of finance and labour. Under Lucien Bouchard's PQ, tripartite summits brought together the provincial state and peak associations of employers and employees to iron out a societal consensus regarding the direction of public policy; such an approach is atypical in Anglo-America, where the outlook is one of competing, not co-operating, economic and sectoral interests. Two such conferences in 1996, in which community and social groups participated as full partners alongside industry, labour, and government, eventually led to the National Assembly's unanimous adoption of a unique North American statute to "combat poverty and social exclusion."[45]

Nationalism and its various manifestations in Quebec came full circle as Hartz suggested: a feudal tradition, when combined with a sudden influx of liberal ideas in the mid-twentieth century, produced an environment in which socialist impulses could thrive. Quebec's socialists since the 1960s have drawn on both the collectivist and organic principles of French Canada's feudal legacy and the egalitarian and rationalist components of its liberal Quiet Revolution. Conversely, they have rejected the hierarchical authoritarianism of the feudal outlook and the competitive individualistic outlook of liberalism. The new nationalism of Quebec was built around the state rather than the church, with the French language as the thread common to both. The very term "province" fell into disrepute as Quebec's government became a "national" government. Symbolically, the long-standing postal abbreviation for Quebec (PQ for Province of Quebec) was discarded too.

Does the PQ qualify as a socialist or social democratic force? Lévesque's and Parizeau's PQ, as well as Bouchard's BQ, proclaimed themselves "social democratic," a term no other governing party in Canada, besides the CCF-NDP, has ever used to describe itself. Indeed, the PQ applied to join the Socialist International (SI). Its application, sympathetically received, was rejected only because the NDP was already a member – SI rules allowed for only one socialist member party per country. Present at Lévesque's funeral in 1987, former French prime minister Pierre Mauroy pointedly noted that "he was attending the funeral as a representative of the French Socialist Party."[46]

The NDP saw the PQ as an ideological ally; thus, Dave Barrett, BC's NDP premier, forayed into the province to build links. English Canada's social democrats admired the PQ's socialist policy orientation: legislating the most progressive income tax regime and the highest minimum wage in the country, waiving fines against thousands of strikers, and establishing the most severe anti-strikebreaking laws of any province. The national question, however, finally trumped socialist camaraderie. The PQ presided over the largest stable of publicly owned Crown corporations in the country – from the monster Caisse de dépôt et placement pension fund and Hydro Québec to interests in the broadcasting, automobile insurance, forestry, mining, petroleum, agrifoods, housing, cultural, and financial sectors. The PQ won elections with solid support in the organized labour movement and declared "itself social democratic on the German and Swedish model."[47] Unlike the Quebec Liberal and other provincial regimes, even those of the NDP, the PQ regime attempted to achieve a form of partnership with public-service unions.[48] The PQ's social democratic agenda, from which it has not wavered, was outlined in Lévesque's *My Quebec:* reducing income disparities, ensuring equality of opportunity, and increasing participation in political life and enterprise.[49] After Lévesque's departure, Parizeau reaffirmed the PQ's social democratic objectives, but under Bouchard, the former Conservative, such talk was left to party militants.

The fragment theory does not claim that the rise of social democratic ideas and parties in Quebec in the 1960s and 1970s was exclusively the result of the interaction of feudal and liberal ideas in the political culture. Hartz and those who applied his theory understood that Quebec, progressing from a rural, agrarian, Catholic identity, was becoming urban, industrial, and secular. The Québécois were moving from the farms and parishes to factories, tenements, and new government offices. In brief, some of the material conditions necessary for the rise of socialist ideology were being met. But so had they been in the United States, Hartz would quickly have noted. Unlike its American equivalent, however, social democracy of the PQ variety was viable because the feudal tradition in Quebec had been confronted, shattered, and transfigured by its antithesis: liberalism. Significantly, the liberal tradition in America had not undergone a similar experience. Because liberalism emerges as a major force in Quebec as late as it does – only in the 1960s – the rise of socialism is retarded, occurring much later and perhaps more vigorously than in English Canada. There, in contrast, socialism's appearance had much to do with the direct transplantation of British socialists.

Canada's New (Old) France

Atlantic Canada, as we saw, is the oldest part of English Canada, but it is Quebec that is the oldest part of Canada. Its founding settlers were the first of the five broad immigrant waves identified in Chapter 1. Under Parisian control, New France accepted Catholic immigrants only. What developed in civil society before and after the Conquest was a rural, quasi-feudal seigneurial system.[50] The formal evacuation and decapitation of New France's political and economic elites with the Treaty of Paris in 1763 shifted societal leadership to the colony's Catholic clergy. Economic leadership fell to a small new Anglo business class of merchants, many of whom came from the New England colonies. Constitutionally, Britain's Quebec Act in 1774 recognized and protected Catholic expression and the French language. Inevitably, this fed a festering tension in the polity: a French Catholic society ruled by a British governor.

The image of Quebec as Canada's New France is neither historically contentious nor problematic. Spun off from the monarchial, aristocratic, absolutist, and clerical ancien régime, this fragment escaped the liberal French Revolution but not the Seven Years' War. It was thus cut off, as well as thrown off, from the new Europe in a way that the British North American colonies were not. New France was in tune ideologically with Old France rather than the new France of the Age of Reason. Whereas British developments – the rise of Whig liberalism and the repeal of the Corn Laws and colonial trade preference – materially affected the Canadian colonies, French developments were impious and dangerous and hence irrelevant to Quebec. To its societal leaders, the Catholic clergy, mother France had been monstrously violated and ideologically disfigured. It was natural that the church served as guardian and agent of French Canadian identity and nationalism, for although the British had taken political command, they guaranteed New France's religious and linguistic continuity. The hierarchical and authoritarian British political order was more consistent with French Canada's heritage than was the rival American model of 1776. The habitants were less keen, however, to see the emergence of representative government than were their British masters. Whereas the American colonists had insisted on no taxation without representation, many French Canadians resisted elected assemblies precisely because, to them, such assemblies implied inevitable taxation.[51] Into the 1950s, Quebec's French political class purposefully and repeatedly professed loyalty to the British Crown, to the principle of hereditary monarchy.

In Europe's national societies, more homogeneous than those of Quebec and English Canada, conservatism and liberalism collided; by contrast, cultural separation in Quebec facilitated the collusion of the tory-touched liberal English and the conservative French elites. As Hartz noted, the illiterate *habitants* identified with Papineau's nationalism but could not fathom his liberalism.[52] Thus, the rebellions of 1837-38, a cultural quake in Quebec's political history, proved essentially an ethnic struggle with a secondary national claim for responsible government. In this respect, it was unlike the political battle in Upper Canada at the same time. Although the fight for self-governance was eventually won in Quebec, a new liberal society was not forthcoming. The clergy supported the British Crown, condemned the Enlightenment, and assaulted change. Confederation merely offered Quebec a consolidation of its traditions. These were entrenched in sections 92, 93, and 133 of the BNA Act. These powers permitted Quebec to keep political modernization at bay.[53]

Life and work within separate but complementary solitudes meant that social policy for the French was decreed by the church but that economic policy beyond agriculture was dictated by English Montreal and a few American corporations in the resource sector. The respective strength and weakness of liberal thinking in English and French Quebec were mirrored institutionally in higher education: in 1911, over 1,300 of the province's 200,000 English were at universities versus just over 700 of some 1,300,000 French.[54] Anglophone students were ten times as numerous in the sciences as francophones. French Canadians largely absented themselves from secular schooling, the escalator upon which one ascends to economic and social power. Their low wages made Montreal a city of tenants, a contrast to other Canadian cities.[55] The conjunction of little capital and little technical expertise relegated most French Quebecers to the lower rungs of the labour force. Everett Hughes' classic study of Quebec's industrial transformation in the 1940s documented the structure of a typical industrial plant's hierarchy: unilingual francophones held the jobs below the position of foreman, unilingual anglophones held the jobs above, and a bilingual foreman served as go-between in the two worlds of labour and management. Hughes presciently foresaw the possibility that, as the French Canadian experience in industry deepened in the context of growing urbanization, French Canadian society would become distinctly less familial and more impersonal. In the professional realm, Montreal's anglophone doctors and lawyers were concentrated in a small downtown district of a dozen square blocks, but their francophone counterparts were less likely to be specialists and more likely to be scattered across the city and the province.[56]

Laurier's liberalism, like Trudeau's later, was self-taught, not derived from the Quebec majority culture. At the level of political elites, important consociational linkages transcended the English Canada–Quebec divide. Duplessis, for example, endorsed George Drew and John Diefenbaker but spurned Louis St. Laurent, in part because of their ideologies. At the mass level, it did not matter much: in every federal election where a Quebecer was a party leader (Laurier, St. Laurent, Trudeau, Brian Mulroney, Bouchard), Quebecers have voted for him. In lamenting Quebec's antipathy to democratic liberalism before the Quiet Revolution, Trudeau cited the unlikely intermeshing of the church and public broadcasting, Radio-Canada. On the morning of Duplessis' last electoral hurrah in 1956, the following conservative and stridently anti-Enlightenment prayer was aired:

> Sovereign authority, by whatever government it is exercised, is derived solely from God, the supreme and eternal principle of all power ... It is therefore an absolute error to believe that authority comes from the multitudes, from the masses, from the people, to pretend that authority does not properly belong to those who exercise it, but that they have only a simple mandate revocable at any time by the people. This error, which dates from the Reformation, rests on the false principle that man has no other master than his own reason ... All this explanation about the origin, the basis, and the composition of this alleged sovereignty of the people is purely arbitrary. Moreover, if it is admitted, it will have as a consequence the weakening of authority, making it a myth, giving it an unstable and changeable basis, stimulating popular passions and encouraging sedition.[57]

The New Quebec

The triumphant breakthrough of liberalism in the 1960s had dual political expressions. Those exerting their energy at the provincial level (Jean Lesage, Lévesque, Pierre Laporte) turned to the provincial state to modernize society. Those who entered the federal arena (Maurice Lamontagne, Trudeau, Jean Marchand) sought modernization and *rattrapage* via equal access with liberal English Canada at the centre. Alternative visions emerged in the conflicting language laws of 1977 and 1982: Quebec's Charter of the French Language versus Ottawa's Charter of Rights. Within Quebec society, the events of the late 1980s demonstrated that many francophones considered anything less than unilingual French commercial signage as the Conquest's continuing legacy, and that anglophones saw bilingual signs as "a symbol that Quebec is a 'social contract' between two linguistic communities."[58] Within the Quebec state, divisions arose too between business liberals (à la Robert Bourassa and Jean Charest) and welfare liberals and social democrats (à la Lévesque and Parizeau). The PQ created ministers of social solidarity and income security as well as a minister of state for planning; the Liberals created a minister responsible for privatization. This fissure was expressed by a bipartisan group, headed by Lucien Bouchard in 2005, that criticized "the unhealthy suspicion of private business" in some sectors of Quebec society and called on the government "to ensure that all Quebecers speak and write English as well as a third language."[59]

In the new Quebec after 1960, a new middle class – la nouvelle bourgeoisie – arose. Members of this new class were linked to the burgeoning public sector fostered by the Quebec state's activism. In this environment, as in other modernized societies, the role of religion and family as agents of political socialization was increasingly taken over by peers and schooling. An example was the wholesale transformation of Quebecers' attitudes to the idea of family itself. They went from having one of the highest birth rates in the Western world to having its lowest. Alarm over the demographic implications led the government to pay a bébé-bonus to parents, one with an escalating incentive to procreate. In the religious sphere, churches were largely abandoned. Here, as elsewhere, the national question could impinge: in the 1995 referendum, a group called "Nuns for the Yes" (to sovereignty) appeared, only to be quickly followed by the Hells Angels declaring for the "No" side. It was a comical throwback to the nineteenth-century partisan maxim that "Heaven is Blue and Hell is Red."[60] As for liberalism's expression in social values, the new Quebec, as in the Maritimes, has a higher than average proportion of "extroverted traditionalists." Their essential values include historical tradition, family, and duty. Quite unlike Atlantic Canada, however, the new Quebec also features a disproportionate number of "connected enthusiasts" and "social hedonists"[61] who tolerate sexual permissiveness and pursue immediate gratification.

In spurning Jean Chrétien in 1993, French Quebec revealed how disillusioned it had become with the Trudeauiste image of Canada. Chrétien was the first native son and leader of a major party in a federal election to be rejected by Quebec. On the other hand, Québécois were true to their traditional nationalism in flocking to another native son, Bouchard. Trudeau's successive victories in Quebec (his last, in 1980, captured all but one of its seventy-five seats) simply disguised the divisions between sovereigntists and federalists. That dynamic forcefully expressed itself only in contests between the PQ and the Liberals in the provincial arena because many sovereigntists abstained from federal participation, to Trudeau's advantage. He came to be electorally successful but vilified in his own province, and electorally unsuccessful but extolled outside it. Ironically, it was his caucus – more than half were Québécois – that rode roughshod over Quebec's objections to unilateral changes to the Constitution in 1981.

Modernization was reflected in the political parties. The PQ became the leading Canadian example of a classic mass party, turning to rank-and-file members to determine policy and leadership. In the 1980s, it became the first Canadian party to elect its leader by a direct vote of party members. It and the BQ relied on a large number of small financial contributions by individuals rather than on a small number of large contributions by corporations, as did the federal Liberals and Conservatives before 2004. In this populist respect, the PQ and BQ shared much in common with the Western Progressives of the 1920s, Alberta Social Credit in the 1930s, the Saskatchewan CCF in the 1940s, and the federal Reform Party in the 1990s.

The interaction and development of ideologies in Quebec appear more muddled than in English Canada because Quebec's ideological discourse – in terms of left and right, conservative, liberal, and socialist – has been more fluid than English Canada's. All is mediated and shaped by an ethnic nationalism that is more coherent than its diluted English Canadian counterpart. The fact that a single nationalist family, the Johnsons, as we noted in Chapter 2, produced premiers for three ideologically competitive parties (the conservative Union Nationale, the social democratic PQ, and the liberal Liberals) demonstrates this. Meanwhile, British Canadians were demoting themselves from charter group to just another "ethnic group," one of increasingly many in Canada. In part, this new self-characterization was a way to counter Quebec's fight for nationhood. Conversely, Quebec's nationalists recast their struggle in territorial rather than ethnic terms to strengthen their claims to nation-statehood. The salience of Quebec nationalism, relative to the left-right distinction in its political culture, was revealed in a 1980s cross-cultural survey of university students in Britain, Australia, New Zealand, the United

States, and Canada. Respondents were asked to categorize themselves as left-ists or rightists. For every national grouping, this self-location overshadowed their nationality in predicting their attitudes to equality, the role of govern-ment, women, and minorities. Notably, this finding was significantly and especially weakest among French Quebecers.[62] This indirectly points to the depth of the nationalist question in Quebec. In the other states, the issue of statehood is taken for granted, but in Quebec it is subject to fierce debate and political engagement.

The story of conservative, quasi-feudal Quebec revolutionizing itself dem-onstrates that ideological fragments may escape their pasts as well as be trapped by them. Ideological evolution in English Canada was fed by successive im-migrant waves. In Quebec, as in the United States, ideological development was internal, feeding on itself. Liberalism's appearance in Quebec is a case of spontaneous combustion, a product of and a reaction to lengthy immobilism against a backdrop of socio-economic change. Conservatism, liberalism, and socialism have been so moulded by Quebec's nationalist context that their links to English Canadian conservatism, liberalism, and socialism have been temporary and tenuous. Thus Mulroney captured Alberta and Quebec, but their alliance was so improbable that it died with his departure; thus Pearson and Trudeau promoted the equality and universality of two languages, even while Quebec's provincial Liberals insisted on linguistic particularism, on the sanctity of Montreal's French *visage*; thus the NDP built a coherent and genuinely national party in English Canada, but its Quebec connection was so flimsy that it was captured by FLQist Paul Rose, the rehabilitated mur-derer of Laporte; thus Social Credit won easy-money adherents in Quebec and Alberta but fragmented into nationally exclusive parties.

The Quiet Revolution, manifested on a number of fronts, was complete by the 1980s, and Quebecers began to look beyond it.[63] Modernization is irreversible. The division of labour in which English served as the sole lan-guage of industry and commerce is long gone. In the 1960s, when francophone Quebecers earned two-thirds of what their anglophone counterparts did, the Quebec state became the *moteur principal* of the economy. The nationalist baton of state building was then passed on to the private sector in the 1980s and 1990s, to a homegrown corporate francophone haute bourgeoisie, loosely labelled Quebec Inc. Where once the best and the brightest had entered the seminary and then, after 1960, the government, they were more likely by the 1980s to go into business. "Less cultural and romantic in tone," noted Claude Jean Galipeau, Quebec nationalism became "more forthrightly economic and pragmatic ... The emerging ideological option is to move away from the welfare state *(l'état providence)* and state capitalism *(l'état entrepreneur)* and towards a strategic state."[64] Compare, for example, two 1978 Ontario and Quebec laws respecting the protection of agricultural land: Ontario's decidedly decentralist approach reflected a reluctant interventionist attitude; Quebec opted for a direct, centralized regime expressing greater concern with ensuring provincial agricultural self-sufficiency.[65]

Quebec and Alberta became the leading proponents of free trade for Canada, but they did so for differing reasons: Alberta's neo-conservative (market liberal) political culture is more in tune with American political culture than is that of any other province. In Quebec, language offers a shield against Americanization. Among Canadians, Quebecers are the most likely to think of closer ties with the US as positive.[66] American trade and investment flows are not perceived as cultural threats, unlike in Ontario, where public opinion was most opposed to the Free Trade Agreement with the US. Quebec's free trade posture, however, did not mean extracting the provincial state from activism in economic development. Between 1998 and 2002, the Quebec government injected nearly four billion dollars in risk capital to finance businesses. In 2002 alone, government corporations provided about 70 percent of venture capital investments, some through tax measures, while in Ontario the rate was nearer 30 percent.[67]

Economic change in Quebec was facilitated and paralleled by changes on the educational front. In the early 1950s, only 30 percent of fifteen- to nineteen-year-old francophones were in school. In the early 1960s, for every 100 children who entered grade one, only 23 went on to college or university. By 1983, 87 of each 100 went on to post-secondary education.[68] In 1970, 90 percent of the graduates of the École des hautes études commerciales went into government positions; by 1985, a mere 5 percent did.[69] The consequence of these developments has been convergence in economic structures, patterns of work, technological developments, and material conditions between francophones and anglophones within and outside Quebec. Quebec as a province and Quebecers as a whole went from a relatively poor to a middling economic status. Per capita incomes continued to lag behind those of Ontario, Alberta, and BC, but they came to exceed those of the other six provinces.[70] Notwithstanding the narrowing of the economic welfare gaps, the two cultures – those of Quebec and English Canada – came closer to political rupture than ever before.

Cultural convergence is not the same as cultural identity. Divergent national ambitions were products of language and history as well as finance and incomes. Elevated economic status powers nationalist aspirations. A challenge to the future of Quebec's culture lies in projections regarding its growth: by mid-century, its population is expected to increase by only 300,000, to fewer than 8 million, at a time when the first language of well over a billion North Americans will be English or Spanish. Many of Quebec's future immigrants will be visible minorities. Although an overwhelming majority of Quebecers (81 percent) are amenable to having a premier drawn from this group, it is systemically underrepresented in public institutions: in 2005, about a fifth of the Island of Montreal was composed of visible minorities, yet they accounted for only 1 of its 105 municipal councillors, none of its twenty-six municipal judges, and fewer than 6 percent of its municipal employees.[71]

Only after the advances and growing self-confidence of the Quiet Revolution could neo-conservative or market liberal ideas, like socialist ideas earlier, circulate and take hold. Ideological influence from abroad occurred more easily in the context of a materially transformed society. By the 1950s, the contradictions between the changing realities of French Quebecers' lives – urban, industrial, technologically advanced – and the old ideology that resisted and denigrated these forces proved too strong to sustain. Quebecers became secure enough about their collective cultural survival to open to other forms of conformist North American behaviour. These are expressed in Quebec in the rise of home ownership, suburbanization, the demise of the traditional extended family, high rates of abortion, low rates of marriage and fertility, and relative tolerance for the sins of old, such as homosexuality and teen sex. Quebecers collectively are now more socially liberal than English Canadians and Americans.[72] Paradoxically and dialectically, the feudal fragment became more socially liberal than the liberal fragments. It did so because it is now more social democratic than it was and because of the intensity of the reaction against the values of the old regime. Quebec has gone through some of the same debates and experiments with cultural emancipation, identity politics, economic restructuring, and state intervention as other Western societies. It is in this context that neo-conservative thinking found some reflection in Charest's government and Mario Dumont's Action démocratique du Québec.

In moving from the debate regarding Quebec's history and political culture to a consideration of Ontario, one is struck by the fact that until relatively recently scant attention has been accorded to Ontario qua Ontario. The province is not a microcosm of Canada; nor is Canada Ontario writ large, but the province's centrality, prominence, and pre-eminence in Canada – in contrast to Quebec's distinctiveness and declining relative weight – feed a conflation of Ontario and English Canada. We now turn to that lack of distinction.

8
Ontario: Archetypal English Canadian Political Culture

No region or province is a perfectly typical specimen of English Canada, let alone Canada itself. Similarly, no single person presents an original pattern or is an exact model for a larger group. Non-Ontarians are justifiably resentful of any assumption that Ontario – which many see as Canada's vain imperial centre in matters political, economic, and cultural – represents, speaks for, or projects a larger English Canada. They are right. Ontarians do not suffer from other Canadians' sense of distance from the levers of national economic and political decision making. Despite mutterings by some of its premiers, Ontario is not known for regional grievances, for feeling ignored, taken for granted, shunted aside, or shortchanged. Such sentiments and conditions are identified with Quebecers and Western and Atlantic Canadians. Ontarians have touted grandness rather than victimization. Only here is the legislature a "parliament" and its members MPPs. Only here has a city claimed "world class" status. Ontario's demographic weight, wealth, and power buttress its pre-eminence. So, naturally, the Ontarian is often depicted as the quintessential English Canadian.

One political scientist describes Ontario as "Canada writ small."[1] Another notes that Ontario's secession from Canada – unlike Quebec's, Newfoundland's, or the West's – is inconceivable: "Ontario *is Canada* to a degree no other region can claim."[2] Ontarians have a particularly weak sense of provincial identity or distinctiveness vis-à-vis other Canadians. Native-born Ontarians are less likely to value or bask in their provincial roots than are Atlantic Canadians or Québécois. The subtitle of a journalist's account of Ontario's relations with Ottawa is *Ontario's Struggle for a Separate Identity*,[3] but this conflates a fleeting bureaucratic battle with common Ontarians' struggles. They do not strive for a separate identity, something other Canadians possess. Ontarians are more likely than Canadians elsewhere to articulate a pan-Canadian position, less likely to think of their own province as a region or part of a region, or to think of Canada as a composite of quite different regions whose residents have regionally diverse outlooks and interests. One example will suffice: a stable of mainly Ontario writers (twenty of twenty-two) produced the assertively titled book *Close the 49th Parallel Etc*,[4] yet that line of latitude has nothing to do with their own province's boundary. Like most Ontarians, the contributors live south of that parallel, so to "close" it would exclude them from Canada. They staked the western Canadian international boundary to make their case regarding the Americanization of Canada, but the West has been more sympathetic to American intercourse and interests than has Ontario.

Ontario's dominance makes the extrapolation to English Canada convenient and tempting. Ontarians skew national public opinion surveys because they account for almost four in ten Canadians, making up approximately half the population of the nine so-called English Canadian provinces. Ontario's population share in Canada is much larger than the combined California and New York shares in the US. Moreover, unlike them, Ontario has a claim to centrality, in that it is located in the heart of the country and the continent. Southern Ontario is Canada's geographic centre – the area from which the distance to every other Canadian is minimized. America's largest states are on its coasts, far from the middle American mainstream in both their makeup and political temperaments. New York's automobile licence plates call it the "Empire State," but Ontario would have a stronger claim as Canada's "Empire Province," oxymoronic though that phrase may be. Neither New York nor California has equivalent national political, communications, transportation, or cultural hubs. Greater Toronto alone accounts for about one-fifth of Canada's gross domestic product. Ontario is central Canada par excellence, although westerners may refer to it as "the East," and Atlantic Canadians may think of it as Upper Canada.

We may discern Ontario's political culture both from a wholly interior understanding and comparatively. Socio-economic development has been much more dramatic in Ontario than in Atlantic Canada but less so than in the West. In Atlantic Canada, regime changes exhibit the predictable comings and goings of a traditional two-party system, with the protagonists barely distinguishable on ideological and policy grounds. They feature the politics of "ins versus outs." In the West, political life began and exploded in the context of a remote and largely unoccupied hinterland that became the engine of national economic growth, the main magnet for immigrants at the turn of the twentieth century. In short order, this threw up unorthodox (to central and Eastern Canadians) ideas, movements, and parties such as the Non-Partisan League and the Progressives, then the CCF and Social Credit, and later still, the Western Canada Concept and the Reform Party. Ontario partisan politics and political culture have fallen between Eastern and Western poles: not as staid as in the Atlantic region but not as ideologically pungent as in the West. In contrast to Quebec, Ontario does not require its own nationalist party; nor can Ontarians conceive of launching one. In contrast to the West, Ontario has no sense of regional alienation. Ontarians feel no need for a federal party with a regional agenda or appeal. Like Atlantic Canadians, Ontarians are content to use established parties as vehicles to communicate their political preferences, though Ontarians have exhibited more receptivity to agrarian radicalism and social democracy.

Ontarians' identification with Canada and their insouciance about their own province are expressed in political participation. Ontarians always have higher turnouts in federal elections than in provincial ones. Their federal turnouts are above the national average, but their provincial turnouts are well below it.[5] This contrasts with all the provinces east of Ontario, where turnouts are highest at the provincial level or roughly equal at both levels. Ontarians, after Albertans, have the lowest provincial turnouts in Canada. (The low Alberta turnout may be related to the province's quasi-party system. Albertans know that regime change is not in the offing – there has been only one since 1935 – but Ontarians have a competitive party system, more competitive in terms of the popular vote spread than in any other province.) Compared to other Canadians, Ontarians are the least interested in and knowledgeable about provincial politics; only a fifth could identify either David Peterson or Bob Rae just weeks before their election as premiers. Toward the end of his term, only seven in ten could identify Rae as leader of his party, and only three knew the identity of the opposition leader.[6]

For much of the twentieth century, Ontario-based historians and political scientists were preoccupied with the story of nation building. Academic luminaries such as Donald Creighton, Harold Innis, and R. MacGregor Dawson were busy describing and analyzing the personalities, economic forces, and political structures driving the growth and workings of Canada's development. One could say that, except insofar as it related to the broader Canadian story they were telling, their provincial turf was neglected. No history of Ontario was in the league of W.L. Morton's magisterial *Manitoba: A History*.[7] There was no Ontario equivalent of the University of Toronto Press' ten-volume series *Social Credit in Alberta: Its Background and Development*, in the 1950s. A similarly pallid literary image of Ontario long existed: "Neither urban nor rural Ontario has been adequately represented in modern Canadian poetry or fiction, in sharp contrast to the rest of Canada," read an assessment in the late 1960s.[8] Quebec political studies, in contrast to Ontario's, entered and enjoy a world of their own, one as deep, wide, and contentious as that of any nation-state. Rich veins of Maritime and Newfoundland political-historical studies have also flowed. Until fairly recently, Ontario politics have been noteworthy for their relative neglect.

Why, in the past quarter century, has a more steady stream of Ontariana appeared? Quick and easy answers point to the growth of academic specialization, the emergence and output of public interest research groups, and the appearance of a more aggressive and critical journalistic culture. A more sophisticated explanation points to the fragmentation of the Canadian story. The tale of nation building is old history; the contemporary challenge is to keep cemented what has been constructed. Ironically, as Canadian identity has been branded and more heralded than it once was – with the creation of Canadian citizenship in the 1940s and universal social programs and a flag in the 1960s – the provinces have partly eclipsed the Canadian state. Collectively, with Ontario in the lead, they raise and spend more revenues, engage more employees, and have more contact with and day-to-day effect on the lives of Canadians than does Ottawa.

There is no single reason for the swelling interest in things Ontarian; there are many, corresponding to the increasing complexity of Ontario. Ontario's recent governments, assertively active against a backdrop of substantial but strained fiscal resources amid above-average population growth, have purposely fed consciousness of Ontario by Ontarians. This has contributed to the rise and vigour of a wider range of interest groups than in the past. Many of them court the publicity that accompanies confrontations with government. In 1995, for example, demonstrators burst through police lines and into the legislature. They wreaked tens of thousands of dollars in damage, even before their newly elected government could set out its agenda in the Speech from the Throne. Ontarians, like Canadians generally, have become more litigious, feisty, cynical, and critical of governmental institutions and their office holders.

At the end of the Second World War, there were 400,000 more Ontarians than there were Quebecers; half a century later, the margin was nearer to 5 million and widening. Today there are more Ontarians than there were Canadians in the 1940s. In contrast, the populations of a number of provinces –

Newfoundland, Saskatchewan, New Brunswick, Manitoba – have stabilized and at times declined. Despite dynamic growth, Ontario politics were characterized by long periods of apparent inertia. A Liberal regime ruled uninterrupted for more than a third of a century, from 1871 to 1905. A single premier, Oliver Mowat, was in command for two-thirds of that time. No other administration in Canada matched such longevity in the nineteenth century. In the twentieth century, another Ontario regime set the national record for durability: the Conservatives governed continuously for forty-two years, from 1943 to 1985. In their case, the successful ingredient was not a long-lasting leader but periodic bouts of leadership regeneration, approximately once each decade. With this formula, the Conservatives projected an image of experience, predictability, and stolidity to those in search of such assurances. For others, they assumed a new and fresh, if not compelling, persona.

In accounting for his personal success and that of his party, Premier Bill Davis once observed that in Ontario "bland works."[9] The Tories, during their dynasty, successfully bridged Old Ontario – agrarian, rural, small-town, white, Protestant, and conservative – with the increasingly urban, cosmopolitan, polyethnic, and multiracial liberal society of New Ontario. This led John Wilson to characterize the provincial political culture as "progressive conservative," to see the Conservatives as masters of such a fusion. "The fact that power has changed hands so infrequently at Queen's Park lends support to the idea that those values which have been assigned to the whole of English Canada – 'ascriptive,' 'elitist,' 'hierarchical,' 'stable,' 'cautious,' and 'restrained' – belong only to Ontario."[10] Stability, moderation, and continuity seemed Ontario's natural political order.

Then, suddenly, in the course of three elections over eight short years between 1987 and 1995, Ontarians exhibited a volatility that belied blandness and political somnolence: they elected three successive majority governments of three different partisan stripes. The Conservatives' hold on power proved flimsier, their dominance less hegemonic, than had appeared. They stumbled from being a perpetual first to being a third party that garnered no more than a quarter of the vote in two successive elections. In regaining office in 1995 on a neo-conservative platform, the Conservatives challenged any prior understanding of the moderate character of the provincial political culture. They revealed their own as well as Ontario's ideological transformation. Their long reign, when it began in 1943, had also featured a radical platform, one promising "economic and social security from the cradle to the grave," pensions, mothers' allowances, and "the fairest and most advanced labour laws."[11] In 1995, they won on program promises to shrink welfare rates and rolls, cut taxes, and downsize government.[12]

Ontario's politics of constancy, sobriety, and predictability between the 1940s and 1980s were actually a mixture of reality and chimera. The province's seemingly calm political waters were surface phenomena. Down below much swirled. Notwithstanding their long uninterrupted tenure, the Conservatives last won a majority of Ontarians' votes in 1929 (although they came reasonably close on three occasions since). The key to their triumphs lay in being the principal beneficiaries of the first-past-the-post electoral system in a remarkably resilient three-party system, the most competitive of its kind in the provinces since the 1940s. The Conservatives seemed safely and semi-permanently ensconced in office, with the Liberals (usually) and the CCF-NDP (occasionally) alternating as the official opposition. Minority governments were formed in the 1940s, 1970s, and 1980s. This is something rare in Atlantic Canada and Quebec. It leads to the question of the origins of Ontario's parties, the ideological configuration of the party system, and the bases of party support.

Immigrant Waves and Ideological Fragmentation

The ideological-cultural clefts of Ontario politics are rooted in the province's settlement patterns. Immigrants, their ideological baggage and aspirations, and the creation and fortunes of political parties are all related. Ontario's political culture has been shaped by four of the five significant immigrant waves to Canada. These are, in order, the late eighteenth-century conservative Loyalists; a large, mainly rural and reform liberal, British tide in the first half of the nineteenth century; a smaller, predominantly British urban labourist stream at the turn of the twentieth century; and a multi-rippled wave from diverse international sources since the Second World War. The varied influences of these groups have been expressed in Ontario's party system through leadership and in voting behaviour. Immigrants and their ideas have also left their mark in the agenda of public policy and the conduct and face of public administration.

Three of Canada's five immigrant waves – the second through the fourth – anchored and culturally sustained the forces that evolved into Ontario's three political parties. The first, the French wave of Canadian immigration – the key to fathoming Quebec's political culture – predated Ontario but was not wholly irrelevant to it. This wave's eventual offshoot, Franco-Ontarians, had their educational and linguistic interests play out in some of the policy dramas of Ontario politics. Franco-Ontarians in eastern and northeastern districts also became a consistently reliable base of support for the federal Liberals and the provincial NDP. The second wave, the formative charter group of Loyalists, established what became Ontario and furnished the ideological nucleus and early personnel for what eventually became the Conservative Party. The third wave, that of nineteenth-century British along with some post-revolutionary American farmers in western Ontario, informed the causes and provided the leaders for the Reform-cum-Liberal Party. The fourth wave, of British urban labourists, in conjunction with an infusion of reformist ideas from south of the border, nourished a multiplicity of sectarian labour-socialist factions and reform movements that eventually crystallized as the CCF-NDP. The motley fifth wave, more accurately wavelets, that has landed since the Second World War did not generate any political party, but it compelled the established parties to reorient their messages and open their ranks to newcomers.

The roots of the Conservatives lie in the Loyalists of Ontario (which was then western Quebec), who numbered about ten thousand by 1790. Fewer in number than those of the Atlantic region, these Loyalists were of greater import, for they were a founding political fragment. At the turn of the nineteenth century, Aboriginals still outnumbered settlers in all regions of what is now Ontario. Like the French Canadians, the Loyalists were a defeated ideological fragment, but unlike them, they were not cut off from Europe. The Constitutional Act of 1791 separated Upper Canada from Quebec to accommodate each side's preferred legal and land tenure systems. British political and religious institutions served as models for the Loyalists, even in their very un-British frontier environment. Social and economic development proceeded quite differently from that of Britain. While Britain was urbanizing and industrializing, Ontario was in the throes of agricultural colonization. Land, which served as the basis for aristocratic status in the Old World and was hard to come by there, was plentiful in Upper Canada. It was granted to Loyalists in gratitude and acknowledgment of their fealty; many of them, in turn, sold parts of their land grants to post-revolutionary American settlers. Crown land was sufficiently plentiful to serve as pay to the colony's early public servants.

Designated with the honorific and inheritable name of United Empire Loyalist (UE or UEL), the Loyalists proved vital in the War of 1812, which helped to embellish and mythologize their self-perceived status as the British Empire's foremost colonists. Some had now fought twice in its defence. The Loyalist "elite, especially, tended to identify themselves as an 'imperial' rather than a 'colonial' people."[13] John Beverley Robinson is a good example of a leading Loyalist with a developed sense of empire.[14] Born in Quebec in 1791 to a distinguished Virginia Loyalist family, he served as Upper Canada's chief justice. Along with tories such as William Allan and D'Arcy Boulton, who came directly from Britain in the 1790s, Loyalists became the backbone of the oligarchic Family Compact, a powerful grouping of colonial administrators, judges and lawyers, ranking clergymen, and local captains of finance and commerce. Some in the Compact, unlike their counterparts in Quebec's Chateau Clique, "may even have held [like tories of old] a quasi-aristocratic contempt for business and mere money-making ... The Compact came out of the war [of 1812] with a finely-developed sense of loyalty and an awareness that they had led in the battle to keep out the Americans, their institutions, and their ideas." The French Revolution and the War of 1812 were pivotal in shaping the elite's world view: "The first imparted to them a 'tory' attitude towards change and reform, the second gave them an acute sense of leadership, loyalty to Britain and a strong anti-Americanism."[15] Like Britain's Tories, they denounced reformers as wild, dangerous "Jacobins."

The Loyalists' toryism was certainly infused with whiggism. It had to be: the purer British toryism of Elizabeth I, Hooker, and the Stuarts had been swept away more than a century earlier in the Glorious Revolution of 1688. Thus it could be said that a heavily tory-streaked liberalism initially prevailed in Upper Canada but that reform challenges to it were not long in coming. Like Quebec's clergy, the Loyalists of the Family Compact served as societal leaders, but unlike them, they held positions of political power under the British governor. Lord Durham, the radical British Whig who canvassed the state of Canadian politics, described the Compact as a corrupt and insolent clique of tories.

The second ideological-cultural fragment in Ontario is the immigrant wave that swelled the population from 77,000 to 952,000 in the forty years between 1811 and 1851.[16] These immigrants came overwhelmingly from the British Isles and provided the core of what eventually became the Liberal Party. The largest group (about 60 percent) among them, but lowest in status, was Irish. The Ulstermen among them were Anglican, tory, and fiercely anti-Catholic. Their Orange Order arose in the 1830s, its members' votes powerful enough to induce John A. Macdonald to become an Orangeman in the 1840s. From the mid-nineteenth to the mid-twentieth century, Toronto's mayoralty seemed to pass from one Orange Masonic Protestant to another. Victorian Ontario's urban parades reflected this political cultural force: in Hamilton in the 1870s, the Orange Order organized more parades than any other national-religious community.[17] The Irish provided the raw labour for canal and railroad construction, a preview of what the Chinese were later called upon to do in the west. Roughly equivalent numbers of English and Scots made up the other British settlers. Many were in the forefront of opposition to the Loyalist high tory right of the Family Compact. Their cultural and political legitimacy lay in their Britishness. Scottish-born Robert Gourlay, William Lyon Mackenzie, and George Brown all immigrated to Upper Canada between 1817 and 1843. W.W. Baldwin, father of future premier Robert, was an Old Country Whig. To be sure, they were not all cut from identical ideological cloth, but collectively they had much in common as critics of the established order. Gourlay, the most radical, was banished from the colony for sedition; the more conservative Baldwin supported aristocracy and primogeniture. What they shared was British birth and the then radical Reform struggle for "responsible government" along British lines. Mackenzie's Canadian Alliance Society had agents in England who tapped the resources of British Reformers. Baldwin's Political Union was modelled "after the manner of our fellow subjects in England," his "whole scheme squarely in the British political tradition – from the form of organization to the principles that the Union was formed to promote. American influence and republican or ultra-democratic ideas were minimized."[18] The ideological flavour and ferment of liberal reform is expressed in some of the newspaper titles of that day: the *Kingston Whig* (formerly the *British Whig*), the *Galt Reformer*, the *St. Thomas Liberal*, and the *Chatham Freeman*.

Upper Canadian liberalism, as expressed by some Reformers, drew on the voting support of post-revolutionary, non-Loyalist American farmers who came to the then western reaches of the province. It also drew on American examples. Whether the subject was education, primogeniture, canal building, the ballot, the structure of government, or its costs, Mackenzie and his radical allies pointed to American, more often than British, practice. In 1826, he noted that the province's liberalism was "owing chiefly to our neighbourhood to the United States, and the independent principles brought into the colony with them by settlers from thence."[19] The Clear Grits, composed of old radicals keen on free trade with the US, attempted after the failed 1837 rebellion to revive some of the agrarian republicanism expressed in the 1820s and 1830s.

Although the heavy British tide of immigrants in the 1830s "carried radical and democratic ideas with them to the colonies ... [m]ost of the contemporary evidence points in the other direction, however, and suggests that the British immigration contributed a distinctly conservative influence to Upper Canada." English radicals often became Upper Canadian Tories once they became landowners. The conservatism of the nineteenth-century British wave, suggested Gerald Craig, "appears to have been much stronger than that of the old Loyalist population, who were accused by some contemporaries of being strongly tinged with 'republican principles.'"[20] Thus, although British and American liberal influences moderated the Loyalists' conservatism, the Loyalist legacy in turn tempered Upper Canadian liberalism: "Upper Canadian conservatism was a major formative influence upon the nature of the reform tradition in the province."[21] The mainstream of reform came to be represented by moderates such as the Baldwins and Brown rather than the democratic radicalism of Gourlay and Mackenzie. Macdonald's first Dominion government was aptly titled Liberal-Conservative; that is what it was ideologically.

As immigration receded in the second half of the nineteenth century, and as more native Ontarians appeared, the province developed an identity and outlook separate from both Britain and America. "Grit" is a distinctly Ontarian term that arose at mid-century. The Grits presented themselves as politically courageous, enduring agriculturalists; Tories depicted them as disruptive of continuity and order. With time, the Grits expunged their republican tinges with British liberalism. Watchwords of the dawning era were "progress" and "liberty" in the context of "loyalty" to British imperial institutions.[22] "Progress" was expressed in the drive for western expansion and the building of canals and railroads to facilitate commerce and industry. "Liberty" was expressed in the undoing of the old Family Compact and the high tory right through the achievement of responsible government.

Geographically, conservatism was strongest in the eastern counties, where Loyalists had settled; liberalism was robust in the southwest, where British and American liberals gravitated. This serviceable generalization was expressed electorally well through the twentieth century. "If the rule were reduced to a township-to-township basis," wrote Robert Bothwell, "it becomes clearer and truer: some towns and townships never voted anything but Grit, and some never anything but Tory."[23] Noteworthy are the farm organizations that surfaced after the 1870s, the Grange and the Patrons of Industry, which were branches of American organizations. They inserted a further tinge of rural populism into the provincial political culture. Some writers have pointed to a palpable conservatism among Ontario's late nineteenth-century farmers – a retreat into a classical economic liberalism. Others have depicted organizations like the Patrons as heralds of collectivist alternatives to capitalism's ills. Still others have seen them as links to the radical agrarian impulses of earlier in the century.[24] Whatever perspective characterizes the ideological identity of this complex community,[25] agrarianism waned, urbanization waxed, and rural liberalism came under stress. Its fading bellow, if not last gasp, was the election of the United Farmers of Ontario (UFO) in 1919, a lashing out at the irreversible, inexorable decline of agriculture. Mitch Hepburn's Liberals drew on this rural liberalism in the 1930s.

A third, minoritarian, ideological-cultural fragment arrived at the turn of the twentieth century. Many artisan and working-class Britons, largely English, were pushed out of Britain by a stagnant economy generating static real incomes. They were pulled into Canada by the promise of opportunity, better living standards, and upward mobility. Most headed for the West, where free and cheap land was still to be had, and the demand for cheap labour was high. Some settled in Ontario's rising and expanding industrial centres: Toronto, Hamilton, Ottawa, and London. In Toronto, the percentages of the British-born increased as those of Canadian birth decreased. Some Britons went to Montreal; still others, as we have seen, went into Cape Breton's coal mines. Their appearance in Ontario tipped the urban-rural balance of a now mature agricultural society. By 1911, a majority of Ontarians lived in cities. Between 1891 and that year, the population of Toronto more than doubled as rural areas sustained an absolute population loss. Those of English "ethnic" origins became the province's largest group, and noticeable but still small numbers of Eastern Europeans appeared. Jews came to outnumber the Irish in Toronto. The longer-standing German and French Canadians were marginal political players, though in northwestern Ontario Finns became the backbone of the Communist Party. That party, like the Finnish villages and urban foreign "enclaves" that sustained it, faded with ethnic assimilation and broader participation in mainstream politics.[26] As Ontario moved from a rural to an urban identity, new issues – sanitation, education, labour laws – emerged on the political agenda.

The British immigrants came from a Britain politically and ideologically quite different from the one that the earlier wave – that of the Macdonalds, Mackenzies, and Browns – had left in the first half of the nineteenth century. The British artisan helped sate Ontario's appetite for skilled, disciplined labour, but he brought more than that, as Martin Robin points out: "He imported his skill in union organization and labour politics accumulated over decades in Britain." British developments "had a profound effect on the political activities of the Canadian commonwealth comrades."[27] A flavour of the labourist sensibility appears in the new Ontario newspaper titles thrown up: the *Labor News, Labour Advocate*, the *Ontario Workman, Trade Unions Advocate, Industrial Banner*, and the *Palladiums of Labor*. In Britain, the radicalization of the labour movement in the 1880s, the formation of its Independent Labour Party in the 1890s, and the cumulative influences of earlier ideological groups like the Social Democratic Federation melded vibrantly with socialist notions growing in British intellectual circles. These tendencies appeared full-blown on the British political stage in the form of the Labour Party, which took power in 1924 as the Liberal Party, inheritors of the Whig tradition, frayed. Canada's labour-socialists hoped this model of political development would be emulated in their new society.

The new urban, industrial, artisan, and working-class British Ontarians – like their earlier nineteenth-century liberal, rural predecessors – were culturally and therefore politically legitimate in their new society. Their veritable Britishness, in a British North America celebratory of Britain's global reach and imperial dominance, countered potential assaults on their political biases as being foreign or otherworldly. In Canada, these new British Canadians were simply importing, replicating, and propounding the New Britain's working-class consciousness. "Carried by British trade unionists and drawing on the British Socialist tradition, Canadian socialism could claim to be an indigenous rather than 'alien' ideology."[28] Keir Hardie, British Labour's founder, and Ramsay MacDonald, its future prime minister, appeared in Ontario's cities to rally labour and socialist forces to political action. British Canadians, in turn, reinforced "imperialism and its hierarchies of race and class," as southwestern Ontario's petroleum workers did when they went abroad – to Dutch West Java, the West Indies, Galicia, and India among other places – as "an imperial overclass by virtue of their 'whiteness,' 'Britishness,' and technical expertise."[29]

Most of Ontario's early labour leaders were British immigrants – well over half of Toronto's most prominent ones between the 1860s and 1890s[30]

– but there were critical American sources too of labour activism and progressive currents of thought in late Victorian Ontario. Labour leaders moved easily back and forth across the border; the altruistically utopian Knights of Labor as well as craft unions like the Coopers' International spread their organizational tentacles northward. American writers like Henry George, movements like the Single Tax Association, and American religious thinkers and progressive social scientists helped reshape English Canadian social criticism, pushing it from the sacred and spiritual to the secular and material.[31] The labourist ideological fragment, and the union sub-culture it engendered in parts of Ontario, was a minoritarian force. Unlike Loyalism, it was not a formative influence. It was less profound too than the earlier British liberal wave, for it was numerically smaller. And Ontario, by the time of its arrival, was long settled, its arable lands occupied. Nevertheless, it had political expression in 1919 when a dozen Labour candidates were elected as MPPs. It also found political voice in Toronto as the torch of civic leadership was passed on. In the 1930s, James Simpson – an English-born artisan immigrant, earnest social gospeller, and one-time leader of the Typographical Union and the Toronto Labour Council – was elected the city's mayor, a post held in earlier decades by the Loyalist Robinson and the Reformer Mackenzie.

The labour-socialists struck roots, but their political vehicle – the ILP, one of the forebears of the CCF-NDP – served as the youngest, weakest sister in Ontario's three-party system. Its mere presence as a significant political force, however, set Ontario apart from the pattern of party politics in both Atlantic Canada and Quebec. The co-operative efforts of farmer and labour forces in the 1919 election, and their subsequent coalition government, proved short-lived because their underlying interests, backgrounds, and ideological outlooks differed so strongly. They shared contempt for the "old line parties" and were critical of the factory system, but they were divided on issues such as tariffs, prohibition, compulsory education, the eight-hour day, and a minimum wage.

The rise of the ILP, and then the CCF, came with the growth of the city. What encouraged the growth of social democracy was the Second World War: the efficacy of massive wartime planning and wage and price controls confirmed the CCF's prescriptive analysis favouring a planned, centralized economy over a collapsed, exploitative capitalist one.[32] After the war, Keynesianism won over both the old-style liberals and the social democrats. Although the CCF-NDP, Liberals, and Conservatives appeared to be converging ideologically, the NDP was unmistakably on the left (the other two alternated as centre and centre-right parties) and still is. The Cold War and capitalism's success halted and retarded the advance of the CCF, but it survived.[33] Its crowning glory eventually came in the NDP's election in 1990.

Ontario's fourth immigrant wave, beginning in the late 1940s and continuing today, has been its most diverse – a kaleidoscope of peoples from many states. What these non-British ethnocultural groups – first, Eastern and Southern Europeans, then Caribbeans, Latin Americans, Middle Easterners, and Asians – have in common is that they appeared in the context of an already congealed political party system. Unlike the earlier waves, this wave begat no new political party; its ripples are too varied, its numbers too small. The votes of these immigrants, however, are vital to the fortunes of the existing parties. Thus, they have influenced party policies, recruitment, and public administration. Initially, non-British immigrants were limited in the political and public administration arenas by conventions excluding their participation at senior leadership levels. Unlike the earlier and later British and American immigrants, they were culturally suspect. Italians and others, including Jews fleeing Nazism, were interned during the war as suspect "enemy aliens." Aboriginals were still disenfranchised, and the few visible minorities were beyond the political pale. Only in 1957 did a Slav – an Ontarian – first appear in a federal cabinet; only in 1969 did a Jew, another Ontarian.

Against the backdrop of revulsion at the Holocaust, the Universal Declaration of Human Rights (1948), and an increase in immigration from nontraditional sources that was facilitated by the elimination of racial criteria in 1960s immigration policy, the face of Ontario, particularly that of metropolitan Ontario, changed. As it did, the political culture slowly changed too. In 1962, Ontario became the first province to adopt a Human Rights Act. Still, in the 1970s, 97 percent of Canadians were of European ancestry, with the balance mainly Aboriginal. By the 1990s, about a quarter of Ontarians – a percentage highest among the provinces – were foreign-born. Members of the older, more established European communities, such as Toronto's Portuguese, who in that decade accounted for more than two-thirds of Canada's Portuguese churches and businesses, became increasingly more dispersed and less segregated as they suburbanized.[34] As non-Europeans increased in number, and issues of ethnic, racial, and religious discrimination gained prominence, Ontario's new visible minorities – small but growing in a still largely white, European sea – had a critical stake in their equality rights. They and others long in the political shadows – women, Franco-Ontarians, Aboriginals, gays and lesbians, and the disabled – forced their concerns onto the political agenda. Fundamental and profound constitutional change (the Charter) reinforced their efforts.

Political parties were compelled to react and cater to the new demography. The Liberals and the NDP responded to the egalitarian and sometimes collectivist concerns of ethnocultural organizations that used the language of systemic discrimination. They embraced affirmative action programs in the public sector. The Conservatives appealed to the entrepreneurial instincts of members of visible minorities. Over time, the Conservatives shed any vestige of their classical tory view that the good society was natural, ascriptive, and hierarchical. They adopted a neo-conservative focus on the individual's skills, effort, and ambition. All the parties were obliged and motivated by changing values to open up to and recruit minority candidates and cabinet ministers, turning the old convention of exclusion into one of required inclusion. In this context, the non-British European minorities – Slavs, Scandinavians, Germans, Jews, Greeks, Italians – began to appear as "non-ethnic," increasingly perceived as part of the old ensconced white establishment, once the preserve of the Anglo-Celtic group. Some fraternal groups of Indo-Canadians and others turned directly to political action by buying party memberships and capturing local nominations in areas where they were concentrated and were becoming players in leadership races. At the political apex, the once race-proud Conservatives elected a Jewish leader in the 1980s (inconceivable just a decade or two earlier); in 2002, they elected a premier who was half Ukrainian. The parties themselves, however, like most Canadian parties, are empty shells in cold storage between election campaigns; their memberships fluctuate wildly, driven by the organizational imperatives of the one-member-one-vote regimes they have adopted. The Conservatives, for example, had a membership of 100,000 in 2002; it plummeted to 3,000 the following year and then ballooned to 66,000 in 2004 when they again chose a leader.[35]

Ontario as America's Counter-Revolution

Ontario has been both of America and against America. The America and Americans that Ontario embraced are its anti-Americanist and un-American elements such as its Loyalists and draft resisters. Seymour Lipset saw two countries coming out of the American Revolution: the United States and Canada.[36] The "Canada" he had in mind was Ontario, for the areas to its east were established colonies, and those to its west had barely been explored. An immediate by-product of the American Revolution, Ontario has also been inextricably connected to America's evolution. Ideologically, Ontario is different from America in both its Loyalist genesis and recent politics. In the late twentieth century, it elected a social democratic government. How un-American! In electing a social democratic government – indeed, in electing any social democrats – Ontario confirmed again, in a manner that reminds us of its origins, how unlike America it is. Ideologically influenced by the American colossus, it has also repelled and been repulsed by it. From the 1860s until the Diefenbaker era a century later, Ontario's Conservatives were the pioneers and standard-bearers of Canadian economic nationalism. Under both Liberal and NDP regimes in the 1980s and 1990s, Ontario opposed continental economic integration via free trade. English Canadian nationalism – largely defined by what it is not: American – has always been centred in Ontario, in its historically shielded manufacturing and cultural industries.

Ontario's founding conservatives, or, more precisely, conservative liberals, were American counter-revolutionaries. Terms identifying the conservative values of Ontario's founders – "elitism, ascription, hierarchy, continuity, stability, and social order"[37] – are often used to distinguish Canada from the United States. Loyalism began with loyalty to the British Crown and rejected a strong popularly elected legislature in favour of a concentrated, robust, and non-representative executive government. Authority was understood to come, properly, from on high rather than from the deliberations and consent of the masses below. Ontario created a bond between religion and the state, but the revolutionary French and Americans severed one. The Constitutional Act designated a quarter of Upper Canadian Crown lands as reserved for "a Protestant clergy," referring to the Church of England. These lands were later shared with the Church of Scotland. Eventually, Reformers succeeded in secularizing the reserves, arguing, like the Americans, that awarding Crown land to certain denominations at the expense of others was inconsistent with the New World's religious heterogeneity. The Reformers also led the fight for non-sectarian public education, as in the US. One cannot, however, write of the rise of national democracy in Upper Canada, as one can of the US, for it was a dependent, beseeching colony, neither nation nor democracy. In the US, Jacksonian forces had no need to challenge a religious establishment, as did the Reformers. In Lower Canada, in further contrast, the *rougistes* had little interest in such a challenge because their leaders were loyal sons of the church, and French Quebec was monolithically Catholic.

There is an ambivalent, contradictory element in Ontario's anti-Americanism, for the province has been deeply touched by American reform liberalism, arguably as much as by that of Britain itself. Therefore, it has been possible for a revisionist historical account to challenge Upper Canada's alleged founding as anti-American, anti-revolutionary, tory, inegalitarian, and hierarchical.[38] In this view, the Loyalists were completely liberal, driven by the same intellectual currents that influenced the fledgling United States. In this understanding of Upper Canadian identity, colonial politics were a struggle between two liberal visions. The first, a reactionary one – traditional or constitutional liberalism – extolled parliamentary institutions and the restraints imposed on the political executive by responsible government, judicial independence, free speech, the rule of law, and competing political parties. These liberals saw such institutional devices as necessary checks on political man's innate greed and ambition. The second rendition of liberalism – labelled civic republicanism – strove for a communitarian, participatory, democratic order with little or minimal economic inequality: it championed the virtuous citizen, the individual who places public welfare before private profit. This version of liberalism posited a view of the "community" as based on a shared sense of spirited patriotism. In Upper Canada, however, the political order was obviously based on more than institutional liberal restraint, for it included an established church, a Family Compact, and a monarchy, as well as opposition to republicanism. Oddly, Janet Ajzenstat and Peter J. Smith's description of civic republicanism resembles much of Robert Stanfield's rendition of toryism,[39] yet they deny that toryism ever breathed in Canada.[40] Their Canadian version of two battling liberal visions parallels the intellectual underpinnings of the struggles between America's Hamiltonians and Jeffersonians.

In this interpretation of Upper Canada's political culture, civic republicans in the nineteenth century elevated the interests of the petite bourgeoisie – small-property owners, particularly farmers and craftsmen – over those of the haute bourgeoisie, the economic elite with a vested interest in state-supported commercial development. The defeat of the 1837 rebels, in this view, led to a decline of civic republicanism in the colony's political culture but not to its death. From this perspective, quarrels about Canadian identity and nationality – as reflected in modern Canada's Meech Lake and Charlottetown Accord imbroglios – have their origins in and may be linked to the competing liberal strands of constitutionalism and civic republicanism of nineteenth-century Upper Canada. From the civic republican vantage point, Ontario and English Canada's broad political culture, like America's, revolves around issues of morality and virtue. Civic republicans dwell on the struggle between wealth and virtue as if one precludes the other and renders them mutually exclusive.

The challenge to this interpretation is to account for the tory and social democratic impulses, however secondary, embedded in Ontarian and English Canadian political culture. If Ontario's and America's historical struggles and political values are variations of the same constitutional liberal versus civic republican theme, what explains Canadian-American ideological differences as manifested in their party systems? Denying Ontario's toryism and socialism tells those who have described themselves as "tories" or "socialists" that they do not know of what they speak, that they do not know who they truly are. It tells Ontario's Conservatives that they were always only a mere version of America's Republicans, although Upper Canada's Tories, from which the Conservatives emerged, fought American republicanism in the War of 1812. Conservatives resisted America's lure with the National Policy of 1879 and decried it in the free trade election of 1911. Ignoring the social democratic strain in Ontario's political culture tells socialists, like Ed Broadbent, who served as a vice-president of the Socialist International, that he is a liberal Democrat, even though it is inconceivable that liberal Democrats would aspire to such a position. Ironically, this interpretation is similar to Hartz's fragment analysis of the United States – which Ajzenstat and Smith dismiss for Canada – in that he demonstrated that those who are wrapped up in a fragment culture misrecognize themselves.[41]

Another ambivalence in Ontario's historical anti-Americanism appears in its economic posture. Sheltered from American trade, Ontario became Canada's economic powerhouse by virtue of the protective National Policy. Today, however, over 60 percent of American investment in Canada is in Ontario, and 85 percent of Canadian exports are destined for the US. In the 1990s, Ontario-manufactured autos and auto parts were the largest component of that trade. Ontario was the major Canadian beneficiary of the Defence Production Sharing Agreement of the 1940s, the Auto Pact of the 1960s, and the Free Trade Agreement of the 1980s. An acclaimed interpretive book on Ontario, *From Heartland to North American Region State*, depicts the province as now tied positively to the American economic behemoth. In this story, Ontario is not America's counter-revolution or antithesis but, possibly, the "premier" regional cog in a continental industrial machine. The book's front cover features a map of North America in which Ontario's borders are delineated, but that separating the US from the rest of Canada is omitted. The economic and public finance evidence marshalled between the covers tells a story of fiscal evolution and policy transformation. The growth of Ontario's welfare state is detailed against a backdrop of federal cuts in provincial transfer payments in the 1990s, the free trade regime with the US, and lessened reliance on other provinces for what Ontario exports and consumes.

In this scenario, Ontario is being simultaneously "pushed" away by Ottawa and "pulled" toward the US. "Economic determinism" has shifted the province from its historical interest in an east-west axis to a north-south one, so that, as Tom Courchene puts it, "Ontario as a region state is more than a state of mind of private sector agents: it is also a 'mind of state.'"[42] He deftly traces Ontario's ongoing policy shifts as exemplified in Bill Davis' entente with Ottawa, David Peterson's diversion of resources from the private to the public sector, Bob Rae's subsequent struggle with "fiscalamity," and Mike Harris' "Common Sense Revolution" and the "struggle to restore fiscal sanity."[43] In a later reflection on his thesis, Courchene called for North American currency integration, or "dollarization,"[44] and the termination of yet another Canadian-American distinction.

There is a striking acultural quality to this analysis. Nowhere does it give space to the thoughts, beliefs, values, or traditions of Ontarians. In fact, it was left to a journalistic version of Courchene's thesis to assert its cultural dimension. John Ibbitson writes of an alienated Ontario on "a road that may end in a fork with Ottawa going one way and the rest of Canada another." In this surrealistic scenario, Quebec stays but Ontario exits, as it "will become the greatest and most intractable challenge to Confederation." For Ibbitson, as for Courchene, "Ontario's economy is the essence of its culture."[45] This assumes that "rational choice" – the basis of neo-liberal economics – is cultural choice. But economic determinism is not the only determinism. If it were, neither Upper Canada nor the modern state of Canada would have been created. Both represented triumphs of politics over economics, of cultural affinity over market logic. There is no evidence in either Courchene's or Ibbitson's books that Ontarians feel any closer to the US than in the past or that they are supportive of more economic or cultural integration with it. Indeed, Ontarians were more opposed to free trade with the US than were Canadians in any other province.[46]

Nor is there evidence that Ontarians are supportive of their provincial government's criticisms of Ottawa. In this respect, they are quite unlike other Canadians. Survey research points up Ontarians' distinctive attitudes to federal and provincial politics. In a massive academic survey in the 1970s, Ontarians – by a yawning margin – were the only Canadians who said they felt closer to their federal than to their provincial government. Only in Ontario did a majority think the federal government was the "most important" government. Ontarians' images of federal parties were stronger and their images of provincial parties weaker than the images of parties held by those in the other provinces. Ontarians also expressed more "affection" for Canada than did Canadians elsewhere. Ontarians' engagement with federal politics – measured by indicators such as voting, reading habits, political discussions, contacting officials, and campaign activity – was stronger than the national mean. Conversely, they engaged with provincial politics at a level below the national mean. The gap between federal and provincial political participation rates was greater in Ontario than in any other province.[47] A CBC survey reinforced these findings: among Canadians, Ontarians were the most likely to identify the term "government" with Canada and the least likely to identify it with their province.[48] All this makes fed-bashing in Ontario less effective politically than elsewhere.

In the 1990s, and into the first decade of this century, Ontarians continued to reveal weaker provincial identity and stronger national identity than did other Canadians. In 2000, less than a quarter of Ontarians expressed more trust in their provincial government than in the Ottawa government. A multi-year survey in 2002 showed that only in Ontario did a majority – a substantial majority – feel that their province was treated with the respect it deserved in Canada. And in 2005, the percentage of Ontarians who identified with their province first was also substantially less than what it was for Canadians in the other English-speaking provinces identifying with their province.[49] Ontarians expressed such sentiments just as Ottawa was constructing, and Ontario's premiers were lambasting, serious distributional inequities in fiscal transfers to the province for welfare and immigration programs.

A disjunction developed in the 1990s between Ontario's premiers – one a social democrat, the other a neo-conservative (suggesting that ideology mattered not on this issue) – and its people. As Ontario's leaders weakened in their belief that the interests of the province and Ottawa were the same, Ontarians did not. Their attachment or "sense of belonging" to their province plummeted during the decade, and their attachment to Canada remained higher and stable.[50] More Ontarians participated in federal than provincial politics and voted in higher percentages for the Chrétien Liberals, the authors of the federal cutbacks, than for the provincial Conservatives, who loudly protested the province's shabby treatment. Ontarians, unlike other English

Canadians, are relatively oblivious to appeals to provincialism or regionalism; they are also more suspicious of Americanization than are English Canadians elsewhere.

Ontarians, particularly in Toronto, are the main purveyors of English Canada's "national" cultural industries. Canada's self-styled "national" newspapers, the *Globe and Mail* and the *National Post,* are published in the city. So too is "Canada's weekly newsmagazine," *Maclean's.* Toronto is home to English Canada's public national broadcaster, the CBC, and to its largest private sector counterpart, CTV. Their "national" newscasts emanate from there. Ontario is home to the National Ballet, the National Film Board, Library and Archives Canada, and to the overwhelming majority of national associations and interest groups. Ontario anchors English Canadian publishing and dominates its theatre, television, and film production. It is Canada's financial, industrial, and political capital. It is where national policy is articulated and debated in parliament. It is from Ontario that Canadian Press, a co-operative of regional and local papers, disseminates Canada's news. Ontario's dominance of and centrality to the English Canadian cultural world reinforces English Canada's non- and anti-Americanism, its self-identity.

The New Ontario

There is little awareness in today's Ontario of who the Loyalists and Reformers were and what they stood for. Loyalist descendants no longer put UE after their names; if they did, few Ontarians would know its significance. Aristocratic status is not as glorious as it once was. British governors and organizations like the Imperial Order Daughters of the Empire (unlike the Daughters of the American Revolution) are long gone. The backgrounds of recent lieutenant-governors speak to an Ontario that the Loyalists and Reformers of old might not recognize or sanction. Since the 1990s, one has been black, another a woman, and a third an Aboriginal. This contrasts starkly with Ontario's beginnings, when settlers arrived with black slaves, women lacked property and civil rights, and Aboriginals were deemed outcastes beyond the pale of civilization. Change in Ontario's political culture was evolutionary but with revolutionary upshots. Incremental changes produced in their totality transformative qualitative change. Yet, Loyalist residue still clings to provincial emblems: the Union Jack on the flag, the crown on automobile licence plates, Queen's Park, and the province's motto: *Ut incepit fidelis sic permanet* (Loyal she began, loyal she remains). Upper Canadian pedigreed institutions, such as Upper Canada College and the Law Society of Upper Canada, survive.

Ontario politics, like Canadian politics more broadly, have historically revolved around three axes: religion, language, and the rural-urban cleavage.[51] Enmity between Protestants and Catholics has faded, but religion's head still rears occasionally. Only in Ontario are Catholic schools constitutionally entitled to public funding. The extension of that funding in the 1980s – endorsed by all three political parties – provoked the ire of many, including the Anglican bishop of Toronto. This tempest contributed to undoing the Tory dynasty. A decade later, the United Nations' Human Rights Commission lambasted Ontario for its discriminatory treatment of non-Catholic faiths. Some of their adherents sued but failed to gain equivalent support or to strip Catholics of theirs. Religion no longer charges politics as it once did because fewer Ontarians, like Canadians generally, are affiliated with the traditional major denominations. The 2001 census revealed that in Greater Toronto – once a bastion of Anglican toryism – the numbers of Anglicans and United Church followers had shrunk to a mere 7 percent each of the population. Each group is well outnumbered by Muslims and Sikhs combined. There are twice as many Hindus as Baptists, and Buddhists outnumber Presbyterians in the city. Those professing "No Religion" are among the province's fastest-growing denominations. Increased religious diversity and abstention is reinforced by the Charter's prohibition against discrimination. This may contribute to the increasingly easy neutralization of religious cleavages as political flashpoints.

A half century ago, the provincial political culture would not have tolerated a non-Christian, non-white, or non-male cabinet minister, but today their presence in cabinets is *de rigueur*. Compared to those of the past, few Ontarians today know or care about their politicians' ethnicity, gender, or religious affiliations. Half of Bob Rae's deputy and assistant deputy ministers were women and visible minorities. Ombudsmen, as well as employment equity and race relations officers, have become part of the bureaucratic class in government and the broader public sector. Language issues – once complicated by religion and ethnicity (with Irish Catholics battling French Catholics for supremacy on separate school boards, and the Orange Order fighting the claims of Franco-Ontarians)[52] – have dimmed. In the 1960s, Ontarians began to demonstrate nonchalance about voting for prime ministers from Quebec. Less than two decades earlier, in 1949, the *Toronto Star* had emblazoned its front page with the now inconceivable headline "Keep Canada British ... God Save the King" when Conservative leader George Drew courted Montreal's anti-conscriptionist mayor in a federal election.[53] An example of the muffling of the language issue was the extension of governmental French-language services, again with all party support, in the 1980s. Linguistic pluralism, like religious pluralism, has dampened the political cleavages of old. Now only one in twenty Ontarians report French as a mother tongue, but nearly four times as many report a non-official language.

Urban-rural tensions still resonate in the new Ontario but in new as well as old ways. Of the twenty-four premiers since Confederation, only Rae came from and represented Toronto. Conservative victories in the 1990s, constructed on the party's historic rural and small-town base, were complemented with the support of upwardly aspiring suburbanites and comfortable exurbanites. The Conservatives owed their victory, in part, to catering to the fears and prejudices of older, white Ontarians, as in their pejorative characterization of government affirmative action programs as "quotas" that discriminated against them. The Conservatives could win and govern with little support in Toronto. In the 2003 election, they were shut out completely in the city. The NDP's base, as always, is in working-class industrial centres and the poor, disaffected North. Although urban issues – transit, gridlock, smog, waste disposal, housing, and homelessness – increasingly drive the public policy agenda in all provinces, this is especially true of Ontario, the most urbanized and industrialized among them. Its "golden horseshoe" – running westward from Oshawa around Lake Ontario to Niagara Falls – has more manufacturing jobs than do eight provinces combined.

More than one in three Ontarians were not born in the province. Of these, three-quarters were born abroad. A majority of Canada's immigrants settle in the province and a majority of these in Greater Toronto. The complexion of these immigrants makes the city possibly the most culturally diverse pluralistic metropolis on the globe. Its peaceable, tolerant character makes it an enviable model for others. Immigrants know they are coming to Canada and to a specific city, but their awareness of Ontario is vague at best before their arrival and probably does not increase much afterward. In contrast, immigrants to other parts of Canada more easily develop a regional consciousness; in short order, they learn experientially and by cultural osmosis that they reside and labour on the periphery rather than in the political and economic heartland of their new country. Peripheral status breeds

regional discontent; imperial status does not. Cosmopolitan centres like Toronto and dominant provinces like Ontario project their cultures and foist
their values onto those in their hinterlands, rather than vice versa.

Just beyond northwestern Ontario, the hard frontier of the Canadian Shield
gives way to the soft frontier of the Prairies. The cultural centre of English
Canada is in Ontario, but its longitudinal dividing line lies just west of it, in
eastern Manitoba, where rock disappears and plains stretch to the horizon.
Social scientists and historians, struck by the sameness of the vast, flat agricultural grasslands that extended to the Rocky Mountains and by the
commonality of farmers' interests, long thought of the Prairies as one of five
distinct, coherent Canadian regions. When we probe the Prairie political cultural landscape and take note of the eclipse of the farm economy, a new
dividing line comes into view. Since the Second World War, and especially
since the 1960s, Manitoba and Saskatchewan have shown more affinity with
each other than they each have with Alberta. This is the case with respect to
their levels of economic welfare, resource endowments, and – more critically
here – in ideological and partisan predispositions. Manitoba and Saskatchewan have been receptive to social democracy; Alberta has been hostile to it,
exhibiting a marked preference for neo-conservatism. Manitoba, established
in 1870, was an ideological fragment of a fragment, an offshoot of Ontario.
Saskatchewan was established in 1905, as the fourth wave of Canadian immigration – turn-of-the-twentieth-century Britons, along with continental
Europeans – flooded the prairies and bolstered the wheat economy. It is the
political cultural development of a new region of the mind, the Midwest, to
which we now turn.

9
The Midwest: Social Democratic Political Culture?

Canadian social scientists and historians have focused much attention on the Prairie region's reaction to Ottawa's impositions: tariffs, bilingualism and multiculturalism, discriminatory transportation and purchasing policies, the control of natural resources, a gun registry, and so on. Grievance has long been part of the language of east-west relations, although the phrase "Western alienation" entered the lexicon of Canadian politics only in the 1970s. This frame of inquiry cannot account for the political diversity *on* the prairies. There have always been striking dissimilarities between the three Prairie provinces. In Manitoba, for example, but not in the other Western provinces, the provincial Conservatives – like their partisan kin in Ontario – have won seats in every election running back to the nineteenth century. For a longer period than anywhere else in Canada, Manitoba had a coalition government that at various times consisted of Liberals, Conservatives, Progressives, Social Crediters, and the CCF, or some combination of these. In Saskatchewan, liberalism was stronger than in any other English Canadian province until the 1940s. That province then spawned English North America's first and most successful social democratic regime, one that came to power in 1944 and was still in power more than six decades later, with but two interregnums. Alberta, in further contrast, has had a quasi-party, or one party dominant, system since the province's creation, a party that, whatever its label, has been at perpetual loggerheads with Ottawa.

Diverse political patterns have expressed themselves on the prairies in both federal and provincial arenas. Consider the results of the last three federal elections of the twentieth century. The Reform/Alliance Party captured twenty-two, twenty-four, and twenty-three of Alberta's twenty-six seats, its best performance in any province. In Manitoba, the Liberals snared more votes and seats than their competitors in all three campaigns. In Saskatchewan, in these same elections collectively, the NDP won more seats and garnered a higher share of the popular vote than in any other province. Although the NDP was shut out in Saskatchewan in the 2004 election, its popular vote in the Midwest (Manitoba and Saskatchewan) was higher than in any other region.[1] To come to terms with these contrasts at both the federal and provincial levels, we must pierce the inner texture of Prairie politics; the tug-of-war between the West and Ottawa is beside the point as an explanation.

From a political culture perspective linked to a regional analysis, an unmistakable fissure has emerged and widened, one that separates the eastern Prairies, or the Midwest, from the Far West – Alberta and British Columbia. The CCF-NDP has held office in every decade in Saskatchewan since the 1940s and, in Manitoba, since the 1960s. It is misleading to baldly label Midwestern political culture as social democratic, for that conveys a hegemonic overtone. In a comparative light, however, it is in this region that social democracy has gained its greatest acceptance and enjoyed its most sustained success. At first blush, this seems counterintuitive: why would social democracy take hold in an agrarian hinterland region where self-employed, independent, small farmers dominated? In such a setting, individualist values, petit bourgeois entrepreneurial instincts, and right-wing ideas may be expected to prevail, as they have in Alberta. In contrast, social democracy, with its emphasis on collectivist values, government planning, and the welfare state, is traditionally the clarion of urban groups – industrial wage labourers and those without property. The key to this puzzle lies in unpacking the ideological baggage of the Midwest's charter or founding settlers.

Manitoba, metaphorically, might be best understood as the Ontario of the prairies. This accounts for the persistently strong Conservative and Liberal traditions in the province. It helps to explain why the Liberals, the dominant party in Ontario in recent federal elections, have also been more successful in Manitoba than in any other Western province in those same elections. Although Saskatchewan initially was also an Ontario offshoot, its political discourse and partisan configuration came to resemble the politics of early twentieth-century Britain, with labour-socialist ideas – in an unlikely rural setting – gaining ascendancy. In Alberta, the ideas of homesteading American farmers had a determining influence on the curvature of politics.

In pursuit of the differences *between* the Prairie provinces, one also encounters striking political divisions *within* them. In Manitoba, Winnipeg exhibited a level of class-consciousness and conflict before and after the 1919 General Strike that was more in the European than the North American scheme of politics. In Saskatchewan, farmers once identified with radical, collectivist causes, but by the 1960s they turned away from them, with the result that the NDP found itself governing in spite of overwhelming rural opposition. In Alberta, the astonishing durability of governing regimes has been accompanied by the idiosyncratic inconstancy of their partisan stripes: no governing party, once defeated, has avoided fading almost immediately, never to regain office.

The analysis here employs concepts of ideology, ethnicity, political geography, and religion. Elements of toryism, liberalism, and socialism all came to be planted on the Prairies but in varying proportions in the different regions of each province. Early representatives of these ideological currents included men as diverse as Sir Rodmond Roblin, Thomas A. Crerar, John Diefenbaker, Henry Wise Wood, William Aberhart, J.S. Woodsworth, and Tommy Douglas, none of whom were born on the prairies. This is not surprising, because Prairie provincial societies were shaped in the late nineteenth and early twentieth centuries. Ideas and ideologies first appeared on the Prairies as imports from older societies. Their leading spokesmen and standard-bearers must be appreciated in terms that transcend quirks of personality and circumstance. Rather, the ideas and behaviour of Prairie political leaders – like those of leaders everywhere – are better understood as reflecting the popular and ideological-cultural bases of their support. Notwithstanding his charisma and oratorical skills, Douglas could not have been elected as Alberta's premier; nor could Aberhart, despite his comparable inspirational abilities, have succeeded in Saskatchewan. The societies of Saskatchewan and Alberta, and the geographic configuration of their residents' dominant ideological orientations, were too dissimilar to embrace each other's leaders. In his heyday, Douglas perhaps could have swayed Manitoba because it and Saskatchewan have been more similar to each other than either has been to Alberta. This is another way of seeing the Midwest – rather than the three Prairie provinces – as a distinctly coherent political region.

The fourth wave of Canadian immigration, between the 1890s and the 1920s, had three ripples: Britons, Americans, and continental Europeans. Their collective impact was greatest on the prairies, where they arrived on the heels of the region's charter group of Ontarians. These four groups and their ideas helped shape the future contours of Prairie politics. Between 1881 and 1921, the Prairie population exploded from 100,000 to 2 million; during a shorter period – from 1896 to 1913 – occupied land expanded from 10 to 70 million acres. In 1913 alone, one immigrant arrived in Canada for every eighteen in the Canadian population, and most of them immediately boarded trains and headed west. In the United States, in contrast, only one immigrant per eighty of the population arrived in 1914, the year of greatest immigration in that decade. The largest and most important founding charter group in the Midwest, however, consisted of internal migrants: land-hungry Ontarians. As they broke its virgin soil, they established and led the region's skeletal political and cultural institutions. The soon hyperventilated wheat economy flourished, and the prairies came to be "the breadbasket of the British Empire." Central Canada's political class carved two provinces out of the North-West Territories in 1905 because it feared that a single province might come to rival and overtake Ontario or Quebec in wealth and power. Saskatchewan began with a Liberal regime because the Laurier government had its lieutenant-governor appoint one.[2]

Transplanted Ontarians, bringing their tory-touched and liberal Grit biases with them, launched Conservative and Liberal Parties. Immigrant Britons led and provided the causes sustaining nascent labour-socialist parties and fledgling trade unions. American homesteaders were more important in Saskatchewan than in Manitoba, but in both they were much less influential than in Alberta. Americans had little interest in Manitoba, as it had been created in 1870, two decades before their own "last best West" had been fully occupied. Americans made up no more of Manitoba's population than they did of the national average, whereas they well exceeded the national average in Saskatchewan and Alberta. Britons, along with Ontarians, were the most eagerly sought immigrants: both had cachet as British subjects in British North America.

The continental European ripple – Slavs, Germans, Scandinavians, Dutch, and others – had significant demographic weight, but it was on the periphery of the political system. Europeans were recruited by the federal government because of economic pressures on the railroad companies, which bemoaned, as late as 1922, that 34 million acres of land were still unoccupied within fifteen miles of their tracks.[3] The Midwest's flood of pioneers even included some exotic elements of European nobility – titled aristocrats known as the "French Counts" founded what became Whitewood, Saskatchewan[4] – but they left little trace. Most of the Europeans were dirt poor; most of the Poles were illiterate.[5] The votes of Europeans were keenly sought, but they themselves were informally excluded from governing. They practised a politics of deference. Discriminated against, suspected as culturally foreign, and fearful of provoking assaults on themselves, they voted for and yielded to the Anglo-Saxon-led parties, usually the Liberals, who had opened the gates to the continental Europeans' entry and were perceived as more tolerant than

Conservatives. In Winnipeg, the Dominion's third-largest city, some – especially Ukrainians and Jews – were sufficiently concentrated and enthralled with the Russian Revolution to provide the country's strongest base for the Communist Party. It is a comment on the advance of the once marginalized minorities that, in the 1990s and for the first time, Slavs (Gary Filmon and Roy Romanow) served as the Midwest's premiers. It is a comment on the change in the region's cultural values that this went unnoticed, that the "ethnic" label, when applied to those of European descent, no longer evokes stigma or proffers benefit.

Aboriginals stand out as a systemically disadvantaged group. They contribute to delimiting the Midwest as a region. Louis Riel's 1869 and 1885 Métis rebellions in what became Manitoba and Saskatchewan respectively were formative events in the region. The rout of the Métis, somewhat like the expulsion of the Maritimes' Acadians more than a century earlier, determined that the region would have an English and white, rather than a bilingual and Native, cast. Indians and Métis were excluded from politics, although John Norquay, Manitoba's premier in the 1870s and 1880s, may be considered Canada's only Aboriginal provincial premier, as one of his forbears was Indian. In the 1950s, the CCF was the first party to seek out an Indian candidate to contest Rupertsland, a sprawling northern riding that contains many reserves and Métis.[6] In contrast, the other parties were late in recognizing and championing Aboriginal causes: Ross Thatcher's Liberals, for example, favoured assimilation and dispensing with Aboriginal group rights.[7] Aboriginals, who have appeared in every Manitoba NDP cabinet, have brought forth an assortment of programs and grants benefiting Natives. Nevertheless, as a group, Aboriginals remain low on the socio-economic ladder: they account for the vast majority of the Midwest's prison inmates, and their personal income levels are a mere 60 percent of the Western provinces' average.[8]

Aboriginals make up about 3 percent of Canadians but 14 percent of Manitobans and Saskatchewanians, by far the highest provincial percentage. Saskatchewan's First Nations project they will make up 32 percent of the provincial population by 2045.[9] Their weight and voting preferences have become increasingly important in shaping the outcome of elections and public policy, as well as in defining the Midwest's political culture. In both urban cores and northern rural areas, Aboriginals have come to flock to the social democratic NDP. In the 1981, 1990, and 2003 Manitoba elections, between 72 and 83 percent of those voting on reserves voted NDP.[10] In the 1990s, the preference of Aboriginals for the NDP led Manitoba's Conservatives to illegally fund counterfeit "independent" candidates who were Aboriginals, in an attempt to split the NDP vote. The ensuing scandal contributed to defeating the Conservative government.

Prairie politics are associated with protest parties, populism, and progressivism. These forces have many faces, some complementary, others conflicting. Prairie left populism sprang from rural co-operatives, pursued labour-farmer alliances, critiqued corporate capitalism, and prescribed activist government to circumscribe it. Prairie right populism mobilized along regional rather than class lines, played down leftist notions of participatory democracy in favour of direct democracy via referenda, and never extended its critique of corporate power beyond the banks, big government, and the credit system.[11] David Laycock's dissection of populist and democratic thought on the Prairies in the first half of the twentieth century serves up four distinct philosophical strains: crypto-Liberalism, radical democracy, social democracy, and plebiscitarian populism.[12] Crypto-Liberalism drew its cues from Ontario's nineteenth-century Clear Grit reform tradition and combined it with opposition to central Canadian dominance. This strain was strongest in Manitoba. Its followers, the Progressives, saw the Liberals as having strayed from their liberal principles. However, most of the Progressives and their national leaders, who were Manitobans, were eventually co-opted back into their original fold, the parliamentary liberalism of the Liberal Party. The second strain, radical democracy, proved temporarily vibrant only in Alberta. Breaking decisively with partyism and parliamentarism, it drew on some co-operative and syndicalist notions, propounding a system of "group government" in which delegates representing differing socio-economic classes or interests would collectively fashion public policy. The social democratic populist tendency had its most widespread success in Saskatchewan, where an urban labour party, a farmers' union, and socialist intellectuals forged a winning alliance. This tendency expressed popular power in the economic and political spheres by creating the welfare state and extending both it and economic planning beyond anything imagined by liberal democracy. Plebiscitarian democracy, as espoused by Alberta Social Credit, began with the logic of technocratic expertise and claimed Christian moral justification as well as class transcendence.

Long before these dissections of Prairie populist thought were made, W.L. Morton characterized the biases of Prairie politics.[13] He drew attention to the initial exceptional condition of the Prairie provinces as colonial, subordinate creatures of Ottawa that lacked constitutional control of their natural resources until 1930. Over time, this colonial bias and the political struggle against it did not end but came to be complemented by a radical agrarian phase: the economically booming region threw up farmers' movements that burst onto the national political stage (in 1921 the Progressives displaced the Conservatives as the second-largest party) as well as into provincial politics. The United Farmers of Alberta (UFA) and the United Farmers of Manitoba (UFM) swept into office in 1921 and 1922 respectively. Then, in the 1930s, with Social Credit's Alberta triumph, the Prairies embarked on a utopian quest, reflected in a readiness to adopt untried methods to achieve ideal ends. That utopian sortie may be stretched to include Saskatchewan's turn to social democracy in the 1940s. Its leaders, such as Baptist preacher Douglas, used old-fashioned British labour rhetoric but spoke of socialism as paving the path to the New Jerusalem.

A significant change since the era of which Morton wrote is the shift in economic and demographic weight among the Prairie provinces. Winnipeg, as "the gateway to the West" and its transportation and distribution centre – one that attracted and retained skilled immigrant labourers – lost its advantage over time to other cities.[14] In the 1930s, Saskatchewan's population was the third-largest among Canada's provinces; Alberta's was the smallest outside the Maritimes. At the end of the Second World War, the three Prairie provinces had approximately equal numbers. After oil was discovered, Alberta vaulted ahead. By the early twenty-first century, there were almost three Albertans for every Manitoban and more than three for every Saskatchewanian. Saskatchewan is the sole province to have exceeded 1 million in population, only to fall back below that mark.

Attitudes articulated and policies pursued by weighty, wealthy, and correspondingly louder Albertans and their government are easily, but often mistakenly, attributed to the Prairie region as a whole. As Alberta has grown more powerful than the other two provinces – so much, indeed, that it alone now stands for a mythical "West" – the political outlooks of Manitoba and Saskatchewan, amid challenging economic conditions, have moved increasingly closer together and away from those of Alberta. Over time, Alberta has exhibited more in common with BC than with the Midwest, from its "have" status (in counterpoint to the Midwest's "have-not" standing) to its vigorous disputes with Ottawa and its embrace with BC of Social Credit and the Reform/Alliance Party. Albertans have become fixated on capturing the economic benefits of their province's growth, but Saskatchewanians, as is reflected in their distinct academic school of political economy, have historically been more concerned with the regional distribution of the benefits and costs of national growth.[15] In contrast to the Far West, the Midwest has exhibited a proclivity for social democracy, the NDP, provincial Crown corporations, a strong federal government, and redistributionist fiscal policies. A 2002 survey revealed that a majority in the Midwest, unlike the majority in the Far West, had more trust and confidence in the federal government than in their provincial governments.[16]

The society of the Midwest is both younger and older than that of any other region. It has the highest percentages of those under eighteen (largely because of the Aboriginal birth rate) and those over sixty-five (largely because of economic lag). Both age groups have heightened interest in state-driven social programs, such as education and health, which are social democracy's priorities. Thus, another way of highlighting the political cultural partition between the Midwest and the Far West relates to their respective weights in the right-wing Reform Party, which favoured downsizing the state's social programs. Although the incident that launched the party in 1987 (a federal defence contract at Manitoba's expense and to Quebec's benefit) did not materially affect it, the Far West accounted for 90 percent and the Midwest for only 10 percent of delegates to the party's 1989 assembly.[17]

Manitoba: The Ontario of the Prairies

Federal Liberal success in Manitoba in the 1993 through 2004 elections suggests that this is the Western province most synchronous with Ontario. Manitoba also began as the province most true to the values of Ontario. Its early tory-touched liberal farmers, mostly pioneering transplanted Ontarians, patterned their flag on Ontario's, with its Union Jack. In the 1880s, Manitoba's farmers rejected all suggestions of secession from Canada and annexation by the US. That decade represented "the triumph of Ontario democracy"[18] as Ontarians flooded in, carried by the newly constructed Canadian Pacific Railroad. They remoulded the province's original bilingual and bicultural Métis character and imported the Ontarian municipal county system before conceding its inadequacy in the new environment. In the language rights or Schools Question debate, Manitoba proved more Orange than Ontario. American-inspired farm organizations such as the Grange and the Patrons of Industry arrived in the province only after their establishment in Ontario. Four of Winnipeg's six mayors between 1901 and 1914 were Ontarians.[19] Indeed, with the exception of Ed Schreyer, every Manitoba premier between the 1880s and 1988 was born in Ontario or was of Ontarian parentage. It seemed both fitting and telling that as the twentieth century dawned, the premier was Hugh John Macdonald, the son of Ontario's John A. Well through the First World War, a majority of cabinet ministers and MLAs were Ontarians. Manitoba and Canada's then most influential journalist, J.W. Dafoe, was a Loyalist descendant from Ontario. So was J.S. Woodsworth, the social gospeller, General Strike hero, and founding leader of the CCF. Another link between the two provinces was national Progressive leader Thomas Crerar, who was offered the premiership of both between 1919 and 1922.[20] The affinity in public opinion in the two provinces expressed itself in the free trade elections of 1911 and 1988: Manitobans, like Ontarians and unlike Albertans, spurned the option both times.

Rodmond Roblin, premier from 1900 to 1915, was a good representative of Manitoba's tory-touched liberalism. Toryism found voice in Roblin's castigation of direct legislation, an American idea – the initiative, referendum, and recall – that every Prairie political party, except Manitoba's Conservatives, endorsed. It was "A Socialistic and Un-British Plan," he asserted, "a form of degenerate republicanism."[21] His critique was marketable in Ontarianized, tory-touched, rural Manitoba but not in Americanized, populist, rural Alberta. Manitoba's fundamentally liberal farmers had little interest in Henry Wise Wood's class appeal to farmers and occupational representation because their liberalism, as expressed by Crerar, was closer to that of central Canada and Britain, in that it denied any connection with class politics. Thus, Manitoba's provincial crypto-Liberals, the governing Progressives, merged with the Liberals by the 1930s to become Liberal-Progressives, but the rank and file of the provincial UFA turned to Social Credit, going from one impractical notion to another. Federally, Crerar and his deputy leader Robert Forke, another Manitoban, entered Mackenzie King's cabinet, but many of Alberta's Progressive MPs, including some of the UFA elite, became part of parliament's Ginger Group and went into the CCF. Whereas Roblin as a proud tory accepted a knighthood, Wood declined one on the grounds of his American birth and background.[22]

Privileged Ontarians reflected Manitoba's early tory-touched liberalism. Winnipeg's business elites from the 1870s to the 1930s were not so much Horatio Alger figures operating in an uncultured environment reminiscent of the one further west, since they were moneyed and well connected. Segregating themselves in the city's south end, they enjoyed privileged lives that differed from those of the less affluent labouring classes in the north, east, and west ends.[23] Eventually, the Ontarians were challenged by new arrivals on the scene – the urbanized Britons who brought Old World labour-socialist predilections with them. Between 1901 and 1915, Winnipeg quadrupled in size. The city became the home of Canada's first Independent Labour Party (ILP); by 1899, twenty-seven separate unions marched in its May Day parade. A year later, Arthur Puttee, editor of the city's labour newspaper, the *Voice*, was elected to parliament. Europe's labour-socialist sectarianism was reproduced in Winnipeg: social democrats, labourists, communists, anarchists, Fabians, syndicalists – all had organizations, however fleeting. Every 1919 General Strike leader except Woodsworth had emigrated from Britain to the city between 1896 and 1912. The two coherent and lasting parties that emerged in the strike's aftermath were a new British-led and -inspired ILP and the continental-based Communist Party. In 1923, when Ontario's ILP was falling apart, the Manitoba ILP boasted that it held more than two dozen municipal council seats, Winnipeg's mayoralty, and representation in both the provincial legislature and parliament. However, antipathy existed between Manitoba's organized farmers and its organized workers. Every rural newspaper in the province condemned the strike, and issues such as the eight-hour workday were ridiculed in the countryside. Labour's attitude to farmers was similarly antagonistic; UFM members were ineligible to join the ILP. Farmers demonstrated radicalism in breaking with the "old line" parties, but as the CCF party secretary put it, "It was not that old country Scotch socialism that the farmers were talking about."[24]

The Britishness of the ILP was reflected in its twenty aldermen who were elected in polyglot, multi-ethnic Winnipeg between 1920 and 1945, none of whom was of German, Polish, or Ukrainian descent. In the 1920s, 85 percent of them were British-born; in the 1930s, 70 percent. Of the four Jews, three were Britons, although the Jewish community hailed overwhelmingly from Eastern Europe. Not one of the ILP aldermen was born in Winnipeg. In contrast, the Citizens' League – a municipal coalition of Liberals and Conservatives – was composed mainly of Canadian natives, its largest group of aldermen coming from southern Ontario.[25] Clifford Sifton, Wilfrid Laurier's powerful minister for the West, was obviously referring to strike leader and future ILP Winnipeg mayor John Queen when he spoke of "Scotch mechanics from the Clyde – turbulent, riotous, spoiling for trouble."[26] In Canada, the modern, turn-of-the-twentieth-century British labour-socialist wave of immigration had its greatest urban impact in Winnipeg and Vancouver. (Its most profound rural influence, as we shall see, was in Saskatchewan.) This accounts for the historical strength of the CCF-NDP in those cities. Voting

patterns in Winnipeg through the first half of the twentieth century and beyond demonstrated that CCF support correlated positively and dramatically
with British birth.[27] Social democracy became rooted, institutionalized, and
cross-generationally transmitted in the provincial political culture.

Manitoba's early Conservative, Liberal, and Farmers' governments relied
on the votes of continental-born farmers but denied them access to the higher
echelons of those parties. Nor were many to be found in the UFM and its
successor farm organizations. The continental Europeans in Winnipeg were
branded as subversives during the strike, although the strike leadership itself
was British. Anglo-Canadians conflated the war in Europe with a war against
a presumed enemy at home, interpreting the strike as a conflict between Britons and the subversive European immigrants in their midst.[28] Journalist J.W.
Dafoe demanded that Ottawa "clear the aliens out of this community and ship
them back to their happy homes in Europe which vomited them forth," and
ex-premier and Judge Hugh John Macdonald urged a wholesale deportation
of Ukrainians, Russians, Poles, and Jews.[29] Intimidated and cast as undermining authority, the continentals generally deferred politically. "Canadian
Ukrainians do not have influence," intoned one of their Manitoba newspapers in 1932, the year of the CCF's birth. Another lamented: "We are poor
and need political help. Ukrainian farmers and workers depend for their
livelihood on the more powerful. This forces us to support a politically influential party. Affiliation with small radical parties brings Ukrainians only
discredit and ruin."[30] Such sentiments were important because in the 1940s
Ukrainians and Germans together counted for a quarter of the population.

As second and third generations of continental Europeans appeared,
acculturation, assimilation, intermarriage, and ethnic mingling proceeded.
Rural ethnic bloc settlements frayed, foreign mother tongues faded, and Europeans' social and economic security improved. A "prairie compact" or social
contract was forged among the diverse European minorities who progressively adopted English as their common language of co-operative work.[31]
Concomitantly, their political submission began to give way. At mid-century,
the Manitoba Farmers Union emerged as a rival to the established Anglo-
Saxon farm organization, the Manitoba Federation of Agriculture (the UFM's
successor). Its leader, an Eastern European and future CCF MP, was the
father-in-law of future NDP premier Ed Schreyer. The union was a rural link
for the Winnipeg-based, British-led CCF, which touted the success of New
Zealand's "labour-farmer" coalition government.[32]

The CCF's substantial Winnipeg base suffered chronic underrepresent-ation in the legislature, making it appear less formidable than it really was. This helps to explain why the social democratic tendency in the provincial political culture could not prevail until the 1960s. In 1922, for example, the votes for the six Labour MLAs equalled those for twenty-seven non-Labour MLAs. In 1945, the CCF captured as many votes as the triumphant Liberal-Progressives; however, in terms of numbers of ridings, the CCF ran a distant third behind the much less popular Conservatives because Winnipeg, the CCF's stronghold, was allotted only ten of the legislature's fifty-five seats between the 1920s and the late 1940s. In the 1950s, a new redistribution law required that seven urban electors equal the weight of four rural ones, a "pro-gressive reform" that underlined how much more the CCF had been system-atically hobbled previously.

A number of vital elements came together in the 1969 election to further social democracy's fortunes. A more equitable electoral system apportioned nearly half the seats to Greater Winnipeg. Simultaneously, the ethnic minor-ities in both rural and urban areas moved away from the Liberals and Con-servatives and toward the NDP in what one historian characterized as an "ethnic revolt."[33] The politics of deference and the biases of Old World pol-itics gave way. Referring to such changes among Manitoba Ukrainians, David Orlikow observed that they "take their politics from work and not from the church or the fraternal organizations ... nor had their politics [been] deter-mined by the Russian Revolution."[34] Orlikow spoke from experience, having represented the CCF-NDP at four levels of government for half a century between the 1940s and 1990s. Other ingredients in the NDP's rise to power were the selection of Schreyer – the party's first non-Anglo-Saxon, first Catho-lic, and first non-Winnipeg leader – and the ideological repositioning of the other parties. The ethnic minorities' swing to the NDP was facilitated by the fact that its new leader's background was akin to theirs. He modified the party's image as one of Protestant preachers and urban unionists.

Meanwhile, in the late 1950s and early 1960s, Manitoba's Conservatives and Liberals, under the urban, progressive conservative Duff Roblin and a Franco-Manitoban leader respectively, had both crept toward the centre of the political spectrum. Now they dramatically changed tacks. As Winnipeg and its more left-wing influence were expanding, they chose new leaders who represented the old, rural, and conservative traditions of the province, just as those were in decline. That many party members responded negatively to the shift reveals how great a departure it was. For example, the president of the

Young Liberals left his party for the NDP on grounds that it best represented small-l liberalism. The sentiment was confirmed by a post-election survey of 100 Liberals that showed that 30 deserted their party, "and of these twenty six voted NDP – the consensus being 'that party was doing what the Liberal party ought to be doing.'"[35] As an MP, Schreyer also had mused favourably about Liberal-NDP fusion at the federal level.[36] He exhibited his ideological dexterity and popularity in enticing a Liberal Franco-Manitoban into his cabinet to sit as a Liberal-Democrat. Schreyer and the party then won two by-elections in districts the party had never held, converting a minority government into a majority one.

Exactly fifty years to the day after the end of the General Strike, the 1969 election recast provincial politics for the rest of the century and beyond. The Liberals became the marginalized weak sister in Manitoba's two-and-a-half party system, playing a role similar to that of the NDP in Ontario. Social democracy's advance from peripheral player to main holder of office since 1969 embedded it further and wider in the provincial political culture. The NDP inserted itself into the mainstream of Manitoba politics, establishing itself as experienced in governing and a permanent contender for power. It changed the provincial political culture, just as the province's socio-cultural composition contributed to changing it. A third of Schreyer's cabinet were Unitarians; a quarter were Jews. A third of Howard Pawley's cabinet in the 1980s were Slavs. What has not changed is the historical cleavage between rural, Ontarianized, southwestern Manitoba – which has never elected a CCF-NDPer – and the multicultural traditional social democratic bastions of working-class Winnipeg; they have rarely elected Conservatives (the Diefenbaker landslide of 1958 was the sole exception).

Saskatchewan: A British Labourist "Touch" on the Prairies

Saskatchewan is the province that has most supported social democratic values. This bias in its political culture is traceable, as in Manitoba, to settlement patterns. Social democracy took hold despite the province's geography: once, it had a labour force made up largely of farmers; it has never had a top-tier regional centre like Vancouver, Calgary, or Halifax. Regina and Saskatoon, roughly equivalent in size, are quite unlike Winnipeg, which contains more than half of Manitoba's population and dominates the province. Saskatchewan is Canada's most agrarian province (with the exception of PEI), but specifically agrarian values and forces have been less determinative in its politics than might have been expected.

As in Manitoba, transplanted Ontarians manned the formative economic and political institutions.[37] Unlike in rural Manitoba, however, a powerful British labourist presence existed in Saskatchewan's farm districts and small towns. British labourism, making common cause with some indigenous North American influences, eventually rivalled the Ontarians' grafted liberalism. Importantly, Saskatchewan harboured more continental Europeans and Catholics than either Manitoba or Alberta. They proved indispensable to social democracy's prospects because their votes represented the determining swing factor in elections fought between the Liberals, with their roots in Ontarian-settled districts, and the CCF, with its strength in British-settled ones. In the 1920s, continentals outnumbered Anglo-Saxons in eight of Saskatchewan's sixteen federal constituencies; in contrast, Alberta had only two such constituencies. As in Manitoba, authorities perforce shunted the Europeans, particularly Eastern Europeans, onto the marginal farm districts, as the prime land was already occupied by the Ontarians who had arrived before them. Initially, the Eastern Europeans cowered politically, confronted by ethnic prejudice and 125 Saskatchewan locals of the anti-Catholic Ku Klux Klan, who backed the Conservatives. Only six non-Anglo-Saxon, non-Scandinavian candidates bravely came forward in the 1925 provincial election.[38] Between 1929 and 1933, fourteen thousand immigrant Europeans on the prairies were deported for turning to social welfare relief. Gradually, through the late 1930s and the 1940s, their subservience to the Liberals subsided. The ideological direction and leadership of the British labour-socialists was combined with the voting support of no-longer-deferential continental Europeans to catapult the CCF into office in 1944.

Unlike in the other Prairie provinces, no Farmers' government swept to power in Saskatchewan because the province's dominant farm organization – the Saskatchewan Grain Growers Association (SGGA) – and the governing Liberals had overlapping leadership, most of it Ontarian. Saskatchewan's Progressives and Conservatives were partly undone in the inter-war years by the national trend to media consolidation, the rise of one-newspaper cities and their control by press chains. The traditional partnership of press and party was undermined except in the case of the Liberals, whose allies controlled the remaining provincial papers.[39] While the federal, Manitoba, and Alberta Liberal Parties were rejected in the Progressive revolt of the 1920s, Saskatchewan's Liberals carried on, endorsed by all six of the province's daily newspapers and buttressed by the votes of the continentals and those of Ontarian origins. Although the continentals were vital to the Liberals' hold

on power, that party's Anglo-Saxon leadership and the province's establishment held them in contempt. In a 1923 letter to Clifford Sifton, Dafoe re-
counted a conversation between himself and Premier Charles Dunning,
Mackenzie King's future finance minister, in which Dunning voiced his scorn
for the continentals: "He [Dunning] says the country doesn't want any Poles
at all. Ruthenians [Ukrainians] are a good deal better but he seems to think
that they deteriorate in this country particularly if they are educated. He says
they can be educated all right but that they cannot be civilized, at least not in
one generation; and that the educated Ruthenian is a menace to his own
countrymen and to the community."[40]

Prairie dissatisfaction with the status quo in the 1920s fuelled the creation of a rival Saskatchewan farm organization, the Farmers' Union of Canada, founded and led by former British railway worker and trade unionist
Louis McNamee. Dunning saw the union as "eating up" the SGGA; it was "an
out and out radical deadbeat organization, appealing directly to the impecu-
nious."[41] The difference between the SGGA's largely Ontarian and the Farmers' Union's largely British leadership broadly represented the differences
between Ontario liberal and British socialist tendencies in the provincial political culture. The Farmers' Union favoured not only a national but also an
international farmers' union.[42] Saskatchewan attracted fewer Britons than
either Manitoba or Alberta, but, more critically, it had as many British *farmers* as the other two provinces combined. In the other provinces, Britons generally settled in the cities; in Saskatchewan, given its rural character, they
were to be found disproportionately in small towns and on farms. The success of the Farmers' Union led to the eclipse and takeover of the rival SGGA
and the formation of the UFC (SS) – the United Farmers of Canada (Saskatchewan Section). In less than a decade, that led directly to the creation of
the Farmer-Labour Party in the early 1930s. The UFC (SS) was unique among
Canadian farm organizations in its socialist bent. The motto of its founding
branch, "Farmers and workers of the world unite," contrasted with the UFA's
motto, "Equity."[43] Unlike the UFA, which insisted on voluntarism, the UFC
(SS) deemed a compulsory wheat pool an essential transitional vehicle to socialism. Its two most important officials were former members of the British
Labour Party and the Socialist Party of the United States. The socialist, British,
labourist, and agrarian hues of the UFC (SS) were visible in two planks in its
1930 platform: the first called for "abolition of the competitive system and
substitution of a co-operative system of manufacturing, transportation, and
distribution"; the second favoured "free trade with the mother country."[44] It

also endorsed a land nationalization scheme patterned on the British Labour Party's rural platform.

In addition to the pivotal role of Britons and British socialist ideas, other vital influences helped shape Saskatchewan's version of social democracy, rendering it much more than a mere offshoot of British labourism. These forces included indigenous co-operatives, a home-grown agrarian radicalism, American left populist and Rooseveltian ideas, and the activities and writings of the CCF's brain trust (which included figures such as David Lewis and Frank Scott, as well as the League for Social Reconstruction).[45] Out of such diverse sentiments, a Saskatchewan ILP emerged in the larger centres, modelled on the successful neighbouring Manitoba ILP. As in Manitoba, it was largely composed of British socialists, unionists, and teachers, including M.J. Coldwell, a British-born Fabian. When the UFC (SS) and the Saskatchewan ILP united to form the Farmer-Labour Party, Coldwell became its leader. Advancing the socialist outlook in Saskatchewan political culture was the strongest provincial co-operative movement in the country. It became an integral component of the CCF, the Farmer-Labour Party's successor in the 1930s. In the 1940s, after Woodsworth's death, Coldwell took on the reins of the national CCF. It seemed both fitting and telling that Coldwell's successor and Saskatchewan's future premier was Tommy Douglas, a Scottish-born immigrant politically socialized as a youth in working-class, class-conscious Winnipeg.

Continentals could switch allegiance from the Liberals to the CCF because it, like its agrarian forerunner the UFC (SS), was open to their participation in a way that the UFM, the UFA, the Liberals, and the Conservatives were not. Reprints of the CCF's Regina Manifesto appeared in German, Ukrainian, French, and Hungarian. In the 1930s and 1940s, a majority of provincial CCF convention delegates were non-Anglo-Saxons. In contrast, 85 percent of Liberal and 96 percent of Conservative leaders (defined as MLAs, candidates, and constituency officials) were Anglo-Saxons.[46] Furthermore, a major bar that prevented continental Catholics from voting for social democrats was lowered in the 1940s. In the 1930s, a papal encyclical and the archbishop of Regina had attacked socialism as contrary to the Catholic faith, but in the 1940s the church declared concern for social welfare, endorsed the co-operative movement, and told its adherents they were free to vote for any party that was not communist. This contributed to stripping away a vital base of Liberal support. As evidence, between the 1934 and 1944 elections CCF support rose by 218 percent in the most European part of Regina.

American influence in Saskatchewan, though substantial, was secondary to Ontarian and British influences. Moreover, the Americans that Saskatchewan did have – the 1911 census recorded 13 percent, compared to only 3 percent in Manitoba and 22 percent in Alberta – were more supportive of social democracy than those in Alberta. Alberta's Americans embraced the UFA and then Social Credit. In Saskatchewan, in contrast, four of the CCF's eleven caucus members in the early 1940s were Americans, some of whom had supported socialist Eugene Debs' presidential bid. The explanation for this is that in Saskatchewan, unlike in Alberta, the majority of Americans were non-Anglo-Saxons and fewer of them had English as a mother tongue. They had much in common with their continental European kin, especially in their outlooks. Saskatchewan had a substantial number – larger than in Alberta – of Scandinavians, both European and American. Saskatchewan's Scandinavians proved more receptive, as did Scandinavians in Europe, to socialist entreaties than did American Anglo-Saxons, Alberta's dominant rural group. Saskatchewan thus featured more robust British, European, and European-American socialist rural influences than did Alberta.

In the 1950s, Saskatchewan produced another political phenomenon, John Diefenbaker. He made it possible for the Conservatives to become a national party because, unlike other Conservative leaders, he was neither wholly Anglo-Saxon – he championed "unhyphenated Canadians" – nor identified with central Canadian interests. For the first time, European Canadians gravitated to the Conservative banner. Ethnic interaction and the easing of prejudices now occurred within the Conservative Party, with the result that the Conservatives were no longer crippled in Saskatchewan's European-origin areas. At the same time, Diefenbaker's red toryism, his populism, and his commitment to agricultural interests made him equally acceptable to rural Anglo-Saxon farmers, who recognized him as an established Ontario-born Canadian, not as a naturalized European one. The Prairies could finally rally to the federal Conservatives because, under Diefenbaker, the party differed qualitatively from what it had been under Robert Borden, Arthur Meighen, R.B. Bennett, and Colonel George Drew.

Although Seymour Lipset's *Agrarian Socialism* dealt with Saskatchewan, its title is a misnomer in reference to the province. The Saskatchewan CCF-NDP has always fared better in cities and towns than in the countryside. More precisely, it was a case of British-style labourist socialism succeeding in an unlikely agricultural setting. None of the CCF-NDP premiers – Tommy Douglas, Woodrow Lloyd, Allan Blakeney, Roy Romanow, or Lorne Calvert –

were farmers. Saskatchewan did produce one British-born non-socialist premier, Dunning. However, he represented an older part of the British and
Canadian heritage. Thus, he went on to win a federal seat in PEI. The only
part of the Maritimes that would have sent a Douglas to Ottawa was Cape
Breton, for it was subject to the same type of new British working-class influx
as Saskatchewan. The connection between British birth and socialist inclinations was revealed in the 1970s, when Douglas represented Nanaimo, BC, as
an MP. In the 1920s, with almost half its population born in the British Isles,
it was the most British city in Canada, but the British labourist-socialist imprint on a provincial political culture became, paradoxically, most profound
in Canada's most agrarian province.

As was the case in BC, social democracy became the pivot around which
Saskatchewan politics aligned; opposition to the CCF-NDP coalesced, adopting whatever partisan mantle was convenient and unsullied. Thus, by the
late 1970s, the Liberals disappeared from the legislature for the first time.
Their supporters defected in droves to the long-dormant Conservative Party,
whose popular vote skyrocketed from 2 to 54 percent between 1971 and
1982. This represented no ideological realignment but rather a regrouping
of right-wing business liberals, with the Conservatives, playing the role of
unabashed free enterprisers indistinguishable from the Liberals, replacing
them as the preferred anti-socialist standard-bearer. The Conservatives – once
the party of prejudiced, race-proud Anglo-Saxons – recast and remade themselves. They projected a populist image, opening themselves to full participation of the now long-acculturated ethnic minorities. Although officially
committed to privatization,[47] the new Conservative government maintained
the stable of Crown corporations created by the CCF-NDP and, unlike governing Conservatives in other provinces, designated a minister and a legislative committee to oversee the province's portfolio of Crowns. They did so
because social democracy in Saskatchewan had successfully produced an
"embedded state ... where decades of aggressive, entrepreneurial government
activity have extended the state into almost every sphere of daily life."[48] The
criminal conviction of fourteen Conservative MLAs – including the former
deputy premier – and two caucus workers on charges of fraud and breach of
trust in the 1990s led to the dissolution of the party. The rightist, anti-socialist
reflex in the political culture simply regrouped and arose from the Conservatives' ashes under a new, untarnished label in 1997: the Saskatchewan Party,
led by a former federal Reform MP.

Social democracy in Saskatchewan revealed its essential urban character after the 1970s. The NDP lost power in the 1980s precisely because it lacked a rural constituency. In 1986, it led in votes but trailed in seats because of the lingering rural bias in the electoral map. In both the 1999 and 2003 elections, the party won office without capturing a single farm constituency. Its triumph was one of city over country: in both contests, the NDP won all eleven of Regina's seats. In Saskatoon, it prevailed in ten of eleven seats in 1999 and then in nine of twelve in 2003. Saskatchewan thus replicated – as in Britain and Manitoba – a left-right, urban-rural political dynamic, the Liberals becoming the "half" in a two-and-a-half party system. The election of four Liberals in 1999 in the context of a minority legislature led to a phenomenon that suggested that Saskatchewan, as with its early turn to social democracy, could again become a Canadian trendsetter: a coalition government of NDPers and left-leaning Liberals. In Saskatchewan, as in Canada, Britain, and the Western world generally, social democracy and welfare liberalism (the credo of what remained of Saskatchewan's Liberals) were ideologically converging.

The Social Democratic Tradition

In the early 1890s, there were no social democrats in any Canadian legislature; in the early 1990s, parties calling themselves social democratic came to govern more than three-quarters of Canadians in five provinces and one territory. Social democracy's influence expanded from the streets and the periphery of Canadian political life into its mainstream. In the 1990s as well, the federal NDP sustained an electoral setback more severe than it or its CCF predecessor had previously experienced, but social democratic values had become too ingrained in the Canadian political culture – and particularly in the Midwest – to disappear, whatever the party's electoral fortunes might be.

The Midwest's social democratic tradition is integrally linked to a broader national and international social democratic movement in a way that the region's conservative and liberal traditions, as exemplified by their Conservative and Liberal Parties, are not. Although the latter are best seen as confederal parties, the NDP has always been an integrated one.[49] That is, the NDP is the most tightly knit, ideologically, organizationally, and cross-governmentally, of Canada's parties. Once, the Midwest's Liberals and Conservatives were also more intimately linked with their federal counterparts, never as tightly as in the Maritimes but more so than in Ontario and Quebec. Jimmy Gardiner,

Charles Dunning, and Stewart Garson served as federal Liberal ministers after serving as Midwestern Liberal premiers. Gardiner believed in one liberal
ideology and one Liberal Party; he saw his provincial party and government
as subordinates to federal administrations. Although he is considered a regional figure on the national scene, he did not think of himself in such terms.[50]

The affiliation and philosophy of the NDP transcend provincial boundaries. In this, the party is unlike the modern-day federal Liberal and Conservative Parties, whose provincial counterparts tend to be functionally and legally
separate organizations with discrete membership lists. The federal NDP is
but a federation of provincial parties; it has no members as such. Federal and
provincial NDP election efforts are run out of the same provincial offices,
unlike those of the other parties. The NDP shuns cross-partisans – those who
belong to one party provincially and another party federally – but the other
parties often pursue them. The NDP is part of a global union of fraternal
social democratic parties whose membership of approximately 100 million
in 140 states makes it the world's largest coalition of political forces.[51] As
evidence of this internationalism, the Manitoba NDP in the 1960s and 1970s
invited Sweden's Social Democratic premier and Germany's Social Democratic chancellor to address its annual convention. At the same time, and as a
sign of its ideological mellowing and comfort with left liberalism, it invited
a member of the US Democratic National Committee.[52]

The distinctive philosophical disposition of the NDP was reflected in
the appearance of a national cadre of social democratic planners and public
administrators. In the 1940s, the Douglas government recruited Andy Brewin,
a future Ontario NDP MP, to draft its "showpiece" labour legislation. A future Ontario MLA, Ken Bryden, served as a Saskatchewan deputy minister. In
the 1960s, after the Saskatchewan NDP's defeat, some of its bureaucrats, most
notably A.W. Johnson, were recruited by Ottawa to aid in the construction of
the national welfare state. In the 1970s, the Schreyer government in Manitoba turned to others with experience in Saskatchewan's CCF government to
formulate policy in the energy, economic development, auto insurance, and
municipal reorganization fields, as well as to advise in the creation of new
Crown corporations. By the 1990s, some in this social democratic bureaucratic cadre had served as deputy ministers in three different provinces, all in
NDP administrations. One did so in four provinces.[53] No other party has
experienced such a cross-provincial phenomenon. It speaks to a national as
well as ideological consciousness that transcends provincial parochialism.

In theory, the NDP is a mass party driven and built around its members rather than a top-down party that revolves around and is controlled by its leaders and their prerogatives. In practice, the institutionalization of the NDP helped make it look increasingly like its opponents as they themselves moved toward adopting the NDP's mass membership model. As the governing party in the 1990s, the Saskatchewan NDP had fewer members – twenty-seven thousand, or less than 4 percent of the electorate – than it did in the 1940s: thirty-eight thousand, or 6 percent of the electorate.[54] The right-wing populist Reform Party, as well as the Liberals and Conservatives – in opening up their leadership selection processes in the form of closed primaries and by dramatically expanding their memberships – had arguably equal if not stronger claims to being mass grassroots parties.

To be sure, the Midwest's social democratic ideology, as more broadly in Canada and Europe, was diluted with the passage of time. It has certainly not been extinguished. Social democracy's original principles – equality, freedom, the elimination of discrimination, and the establishment of a co-operative economic and social system that trumps pursuit of individual interest for the common good – remain. But the message has been softened; the messengers have been mellowed by the hard knocks of neo-liberal "reality." Social democracy in the Midwest, as elsewhere, has gone from some fellow-travelling with socialism and communism, its radical sisters, to an increased fellow-travelling with liberalism. Even this generalization is shaky, however, in that numerous early twentieth-century social democrats – such as many in the ranks of the Midwest's Social Gospel tradition – had been liberals and tories who had been radicalized by witnessing economic dislocation, the ills of urbanization and industrialization, and war. Similarly, some mid- and late twentieth-century liberals who had been socialists were conservatized by economic growth, capitalist accommodation of the welfare state, and an inexorable ongoing technological revolution. Social democratic thought in the Midwest, and Canada generally, like virtually all political thought, has not been monolithic and has been swayed by setting and context.

The face of social democracy turned in each quarter of the twentieth century, although the shifts in thinking were neither sharp nor exclusive. Each quarter featured a dominant and some parallel themes in social democratic thought. The themes, in chronological order not sharply bounded, are the Social Gospel, social planning, social security, and social movements. In the first quarter's Social Gospel period, the message of clergymen such as

Woodsworth, Wesley College's Salem Bland, and A.E. Smith of Brandon[55] effectively bridged fissures between city and country, between wage labourers and independent farmers. Social gospellers were associated with many causes: the single tax, prohibition, free trade, working conditions, pacifism, deficit reduction, and urban reform. Social gospellers deprecated theological complexities and dedicated themselves to helping man, unlike evangelical Christians such as Alberta's Wood, Aberhart, and Ernest Manning, who were driven to saving man. Woodsworth and Smith left the established church because it was insufficiently worldly; the evangelicals left because it was too worldly. The president of the Selkirk CCF Association summed up the link between Christianity and socialism in a pamphlet: "Socialism means a system of cooperative effort, whereby we all work for the common good of all and ... [for] Christianity ... such a system is in keeping with the principles of Nazareth."[56] Both Tommy Douglas and Lorne Calvert had been ministers in churches (Baptist and United) once associated with or growing out of the Social Gospel tradition.

In the second quarter's social planning phase, urban intellectuals – mainly from Montreal and Toronto but also at Winnipeg's United College and the city's League for Social Reconstruction branch – became the movement's "brain trust." The league published *Pioneers in Poverty*, the thread of their analysis being "capitalism versus planning" rather than "capitalism versus socialism" (a word eschewed in the book).[57] Manitoba's long-time CCF leader and former mayor of Winnipeg authored *Social Credit or Social Ownership?*,[58] highlighting their ideological differences. Less sustained by preachers than Social Credit was, the movement's evolving culture was inspired by the rising industrial unions and flavoured with notions of nationalized industries. Meanwhile, agrarian radicalism and the family farm eased their way into agribusiness and more corporatist endeavours with conservative outlooks. The socialist creed of social and economic planning proved indispensably efficacious during the Second World War. This lifted the CCF to unprecedented popularity nationally, in Manitoba, and in Saskatchewan, where it swept into office. Soon thereafter, the drawing of the Cold War's Iron Curtain helped discredit state-driven central planning. Economic recovery undermined the party's analysis that, without socialist measures, depression was inevitable[59] and compelled social democratic rethinking.

In the third quarter's social security period, Keynesianism held out the promise of repairing rather than replacing capitalism. The new paradigm did not require public ownership: instead, it meant moving in a socialist direction by dramatically expanding the ken and scope of government, using its instrumentality to construct and solidify the welfare state. Social democrats postulated that the social and developmental objectives that motivate public enterprise could be attained through government's regulatory powers, through indirect management, through "functional socialism."[60] Crown corporations were to be maintained and defended, but the appetite for new ones flagged. In other Western countries, the growth of the welfare state meant that power gravitated to the central government, but in Canada's decentralized federal system it meant the dramatic expansion of the provincial state. Pierre Trudeau, in one of his redder moments, wrote of social democracy being built from the provinces up rather than raining down from the national centre.[61] Saskatchewan's pioneering social legislation in the health, welfare, and labour fields, which demonstrated as much, provided models for Ottawa and other provinces to follow. This was also the time when the vociferously anti-capitalist Regina Manifesto gave way to the milder Winnipeg Declaration of 1956, and the "old party" CCF transformed itself into the "new party" NDP.[62]

In the fourth quarter, the Keynesian consensus unravelled. As the fiscal crisis of the state intensified, social democracy became identified with defending and preserving social security programs in the face of retrenchment. Saskatchewan succeeded in maintaining its social safety net despite federal cutbacks in transfer payments, and the NDP became the champion of a Social Charter – entrenching rights to welfare programs – in the Constitution. Socialists also began to look more favourably on deconcentrated, decentralized power structures. The major new thrust in social democratic thinking, however, was its embrace of new social movements associated with an emergent post-materialist ethos against a backdrop of globalization. Long-standing peace movements, fraternal ethnic associations, and traditional women's groups were augmented by new politically determined and sophisticated arrivals: feminists, Aboriginal associations, visible minorities, gays and lesbians, animal rights activists, the disabled, environmentalists, and above all, the anti-globalization movement. Social democratic thinking and the NDP had earlier made special allowances for co-operatives and union representation in party organs, but now the movement and party embarked on the purposeful pursuit and accommodation of other interests, especially women, visible minorities, gays and lesbians, and Aboriginals. Women, who were guaranteed seats on the party's senior councils, were aggressively recruited as candidates and potential leaders, more so than by the other parties. The interests of visible minorities were championed by support for employment equity and

affirmative action programs. Aboriginals in particular became a vital component of the NDP's electoral constituency in the Midwest. Although social
democratic ideology does not stress "identity" politics per se, it came to recast class as lived in part through race, gender, ethnicity, and so on. Social
democracy held out the promise that exploitation and discrimination based
on such distinctions would be eliminated. Another shift in the thinking of
some social democrats, one in the direction of neo-conservatism, was a growing deprecation and critique of public managers, now seen as not necessarily
more responsive to the public interest than were private managers.

Early British Fabianism influenced the CCF, but the NDP was not as
keen to tilt toward latter-day Fabian thinking. The federal NDP did not asso-
ciate itself readily with Tony Blair's "Third Way," which merged the essential
values of the centre and centre-left.[63] Neither party, however, jettisoned the
centre-left's traditional values of social justice, solidarity, and progress. Long-
standing concerns – poverty, the conditions of the work world, social disor-
der, the need for deeper democratic reform, environmental degradation, and
the evolving roles of women and technology – remained. What changed were
some of the established social democratic approaches, such as public ownership, comparatively high taxation regimes, and the privileging of producers'
interests at the expense of consumers. Social democracy's orientation maintained its Keynesian concern with macro-economic stability. What fell away
was the insistence on state interference as preferable to laissez-faire. The new
trend was to lessen rather than increase people's dependence on the state.
Support for funding educational infrastructure was justified in the pursuit of
"higher" educational standards. Social democrats became increasingly open
to forming partnerships with the private and voluntary sectors, and to reconciling social compassion with individual ambition and enterprise.[64]

A certain convergence of neo-conservative and social democratic thinking is exemplified in the work of John Richards, who exited the Saskatchewan NDP caucus to sit as an independent socialist in the 1970s. By the
1990s, he was a business professor associated with the right-wing C.D. Howe
Institute. He remained in the social democratic fold but lamented what he
saw as the irresponsibility and growing incredibility of the federal NDP's
economic analysis and policy prescriptions. In his significantly titled *Retooling
the Welfare State*, he argued for reconciling the continuing importance of
welfare with fiscal conservatism.[65] His defence of the collective public role of
the state was combined with an insistence that social democrats face up to
government failures as well as the market failures they dwell on. Unwavering

in his social democratic commitment to greater equality of condition, Richards depicted the welfare state as a flawed work-in-progress but one with continu- ing relevance. Its social programs, in this view, are vital because a circum-scribed neo-conservative state and capitalism cannot deliver a decent life for most people. Romanow lauded Richards' thinking as contributing to sharp-ening and clarifying social democratic analyses and values – and doing so without illusions.[66]

There is a collectivist ideology and culture in the social democratic NDP that fits well with the co-operative tradition in the Midwest. Structurally, the NDP is now more than ever a conventional party, but its members and sup-porters are more likely than opposing partisans to think alike on issues[67] and to see themselves as part of a movement. Like a co-operative, the NDP is organized around members and their ideas. The federal Liberals and Con-servatives, despite appearances as mass parties, are driven more by their lead-ers and their leaders' agendas. The federal NDP's performance in the Midwest suggests that, for social democrats, a party leader's geographic origins are of less importance than they are for Canadians of other political stripes, yet another demonstration that this region's social democratic culture transcends regionalism.

10
The Far West: Parvenu Political Culture

The "Far West" is an improbable regional category because, to begin with, its component provinces of Alberta and British Columbia are separated by North America's most prominent and challenging topographical feature, the Continental Divide. One province is of the prairies, the other of mountains and the sea. Political studies of the two provinces have accentuated the particular characteristics of each rather than providing a comparative perspective that would seek out their similarities to and differences from other provinces. Treated as silos, Alberta and British Columbia have appeared as political islands unto themselves. Two edited academic collections, devoted to the governments and politics of Alberta and BC respectively, are thus devoid of references to each other's province, even though the two provinces are neighbours.[1] If one pursues a comparative regional political cultural analysis, however, the apparently whimsical pairing of Alberta and BC makes some sense despite glaring differences in their political landscapes. The logic for harnessing together the provinces of the Far West lies in their common upstart character. These provinces brim with the promise of advancement for their residents. This region, more than any other, has beckoned migrants from other parts of Canada with its prospect of entry to a charmed circle.

North America's western reaches have always been associated with opportunity and fresh beginnings, with potential wealth and upward mobility. "Go west young man" communicates that, in a frontier environment, a lack of qualifications and status is a surmountable barrier in one's quest for riches or power. New Brunswick served as the Maritimes' western frontier in the eighteenth century. Then, western Upper Canada represented the retreating wilderness in the first half of the nineteenth century. The prairies of Rupert's Land and the North-Western Territory, as well as BC's coast, were Canada's borderland edges after that. The Panama Canal's completion in 1914 furnished BC with an efficient opening to the world for its natural resources, particularly to markets on the American eastern seaboard and in Europe. The discovery of oil in Alberta in the mid-twentieth century propelled human and financial resources there. Spiking commodity prices and the rise of Asia's "tiger" economies in the last quarter of the century brought increased power and influence to the Far West. Alberta and Saskatchewan were once defined by some as the "New West,"[2] but Saskatchewan's economic muscularity proved short-lived and erratic as that of BC and Alberta proceeded from strength to strength.

The West's centre of gravity has noticeably tilted westward. In 1931, more than half of all westerners lived in the Midwest; today, about four of five of them live in the Far West. The evolution of Lloydminster, an amalgamated municipality since 1930, reflects the shift: its Alberta side overtook its once more populous Saskatchewan side. In 2000, its city hall relocated to Alberta as well. The Calgary-Edmonton corridor alone now has more people than the Midwest. Once, Albertans, Saskatchewanians, and Manitobans shared a common link as prairie folk. Subsequently, however, the ties between the two westernmost provinces tightened, with the result that Albertans now have more in common with British Columbians than with their Prairie neighbours. The interaction between them is evident in interprovincial migration: in the last quarter of the twentieth century, more than four of five Albertans and British Columbians who relocated did so to each other's province. In contrast, Manitobans who migrated interprovincially overwhelmingly chose Ontario as their destination; Ontarians, in turn, were the largest migrant group in Manitoba.[3] Stockwell Day is an example of a political figure who has crossed between Alberta and BC. Comfortable in both political milieux, he served as Alberta's finance minister and then easily relocated to represent a BC riding as federal leader of the opposition.

The shared politics of many in the Far West expressed themselves in the embrace of the Reform/Alliance and then Conservative Parties between the 1993 and 2004 federal elections. Provincially, they expressed themselves earlier, in their election of Social Credit governments, which, in both provinces, transmuted themselves into an anti-socialist force. Only in these two provinces was the party ever a player. During its life, the Reform Party reimagined Canada. Its populist discourse challenged the country's "politics of cultural recognition" with the principle of "universal citizenship"; it denigrated special status for Quebec, bilingualism, multiculturalism, Aboriginal self-government, and increased levels of immigration.[4] In the first decade of the current century, both provinces sported right-wing regimes – BC's Liberals and Alberta's Conservatives. Their shared neo-liberalism drove their public policies. Both governments pursued private sector solutions to public policy challenges in a way that the Midwest's social democratic governments certainly have not. The Far West provinces, however, were once liberal leaders on women's issues, the first to end the disqualification of women from entering civil professions and to facilitate their admittance into incorporated companies.[5]

Conservative ideas emanate from and are well received in the Far West. The Vancouver-based Fraser Institute, the country's most prominent right-wing think-tank, has had its greatest influence in shaping public policy in this region. The Far West produced the neo-conservative *Western Standard* and the right-of-centre *Alberta Report* and *BC Report*. It is where the conservative *National Post* attracts a disproportionate share of its subscribers. The *Post*'s conservative broadcast-news partner, *Global National*, is produced in Vancouver and draws a disproportionate share of its viewers in the Far West. The newscast attracts more Conservative voters across the country than either its CBC or CTV counterparts, although each of them has many more viewers overall.[6] A difference within the Far West is that BC's political culture, one that pits leftists against rightists, is riven and conflicted. In Alberta, where the left is marginalized, there is more of a societal consensus about political values. In the Far West, individualism is vaunted; in Saskatchewan and Quebec, by contrast, there is noticeable pride in overarching communal values, social solidarity, and collectivist approaches. Residents in the Far West are more oriented to the future than are Atlantic Canadians or the Québécois, who have a stronger historical consciousness and more of a common past. The Far West's recent governments, especially Alberta's, have become keen to privatize their stables of Crown corporations, unlike the Saskatchewan and Quebec governments. In creating BC Hydro in the 1960s, BC's Social Credit government engaged in "province building," using the instrumentality of the provincial state in the form of a Crown corporation to foster private corporate economic development and avoid federal taxation.

Consistent with the Far West's parvenu political culture is the brash, rude, and ostentatious quality of many of its political figures, especially but not solely in BC. Inebriated Alberta premier Ralph Klein appeared at a homeless shelter to scold its occupants as habitually unpleasant loafers. Yet, he suffered no loss in public respect. BC premier Gordon Campbell's conviction for drunk driving was similarly shrugged off. The atmosphere of provincial politics in BC has been filled with colourful personalities, character assassination, emotional intensity, dirty tricks, and a level of ideological polarizatiòn that has generated hateful characterizations of opponents. One BC premier, W.A.C. Bennett, was known as "Wacky"; he characterized his NDP opponents as "barbarians at the gates." There have been persistent elements of charisma, fancy, fantasy, and scandal to leadership in the Far West. An Alberta premier in the 1930s was undone by his sex life. Another, William Aberhart, was a magnetic figure, compared by his followers to Abraham Lincoln. One of BC's first premiers renamed himself Amor de Cosmos (né William Smith), a zany name that hints of a vision consistent with BC's image in popular culture as an escapist's lotusland. One of its more recent premiers (Bill Vander Zalm) lost office because of a transaction related to Fantasy Gardens, his biblical theme park. The premier before him, Bill Bennett, was charged with illegal insider trading on the stock market, and the premier after him, Mike Harcourt, was brought down over a bingo scandal. BC had seven premiers between 1991 and 2001, but Alberta, as a sign of its relative political stability, had only six over the seventy-year span from 1935 to 2005.

In contrast to BC's history of polarized politics, Alberta's century-long history speaks to a socially shared political understanding. Only in connection with this province have political scientists framed studies of political parties and leadership selection in terms of a "quasi-party system" and "quasi-democracy."[7] Charismatic and populist leaders have fared well in Alberta. Here, more than elsewhere in English Canada, the premier is viewed as far-sighted, trustworthy, and indomitable, one whose followers are grateful for that leadership, reminding us of Carlyle's "great man" theory of politics. Only here have the premierial and the provincial been so conjoined, as in "Ralph's world." After Quebec, it is in Alberta that the premier comes nearest to being the societal spokesperson for his province. Unlike Quebec, however, Alberta has appeared as *la belle province sans merci*.

Attitudes to federal power have been more stridently critical in the Far West than in the Midwest. The Far West's governments have for decades posed common fronts in resisting what they consider to be federal assaults on provincial autonomy: they stood together in opposition to the centralizing recommendations of the 1930s Royal Commission on Dominion-Provincial Relations; the Midwest's governments did not. An example of perceived common interests is that, since 2003, the two provinces' cabinets have held annual joint meetings, something neither has done with any other province. Albertans have mused about building a provincial "firewall" as a rampart against federal intrusions. The posture of BC's leaders regarding Ottawa, however, "bespeaks something of a love-hate relationship."[8] Residents of both provinces have shared common rage against Ottawa when they have felt collectively wronged. Those in the Far West have the least "trust and confidence" in the federal government; Albertans have, by far, the most "trust and confidence" in their provincial government. In contrast, midwesterners have greater faith in Ottawa than in their provincial administrations.[9] British Columbians' political passions have been more directed toward each other than have those of Albertans, who have been relatively detached from provincial politics. They have the lowest Canadian turnouts in provincial elections[10] because there is little polarization in that arena.

Albertans have consistently "wanted in" on the setting of the national agenda, on having their views count. Over the decades, British Columbia's governments have been more fixated on ensuring that their province is recognized as a region, one of five in the country. Among Canadians, British Columbians are the most likely to think of their province as the region of the country they live in.[11] A howl went up from BC in 1995 when it was not designated as a "region" in Ottawa's Regional Veto Statute respecting the constitutional amendment formula. BC pursued a similar tack in the 1960s. Alberta's governments, in contrast, have doggedly insisted on the principle of provincial rather than regional equality and had that enshrined in the Constitution Act's amending formula. The Midwest's governments have not invested much in pursuit of either principle. Their overriding concern, as chronic laggard provinces, has been to ensure greater equality of conditions for their residents and to reduce fiscal imbalances between themselves and wealthier provinces such as those of the Far West in the ability to deliver social services. In this respect, the Midwest has resembled the Atlantic region. Both Western regions have vociferously opposed "special status" for any region or province. They share antipathy to Quebec's exceptionalist aspirations, an aversion that is stronger than that of Ontarians and Maritimers and was so expressed in their response to the Meech Lake and Charlottetown Accords. On the other hand, BC and Alberta have gone along with Quebec's decentralist proposals on the condition that all provinces have access to them.

Contemporary attitudes are rooted in historical experience. The arrival of the railway was a formative event in all four Western provinces; however, what it represented to British Columbia differed from what it represented to the Prairie provinces. As was the case for the Maritimes, the promise of a railroad was a precondition for BC's entry into Confederation. On the prairies, the coming of the CPR was a precondition for settlement; the Prairies, unlike BC, were a territorial colony of Canada. As on the prairies, the population of BC exploded at the turn of the twentieth century. Unlike the prairies, however, BC had an industrial and corporate rather than an agrarian frontier.[12]

Alberta and BC were set apart politically and culturally by their differing settlement patterns. British immigrants were the most important group in the political making of BC. In Alberta, after initial Ontarian dominance, Americans played a more pivotal role than in any other province. Large numbers of them, especially Nebraskans and Dakotans expert in dry-farming techniques, moved up into the western prairies and became the backbone of the UFA, the province's most powerful organization. As a bizarre but instructive example of the lingering American presence throughout the century, one may note the Dakotan who arrived on a horse-drawn wagon in 1910, and who, seven decades later, appeared at a meeting of the province's separatist Western Canada Concept.[13] In contrast to provincial farm organizations elsewhere, the UFA's board of directors contained more American-born than either Canadian- or British-born members.[14] The UFA grew out of the American Society of Equity, to which many of its members had belonged. Direct democracy proposals, championed by the UFA, and inflationary monetary reform ideas – the essence of Social Credit – were notions that swept the American plains in the late nineteenth century. American UFAers, such as former Kansas governor J.W. Leedy and credit expert George Bevington, popularized such ideas after immigrating to Alberta. These ideas were co-opted by Social Credit just as the UFA was saddled with the Depression, which engulfed it in the 1930s. This opened the way for a change in government and ideological direction, in that Social Credit had no interest in the UFA's notion of co-operative "group government" and was based on a leader-oriented type of democracy. The post-war division of Europe and the reorientation of Alberta's economy around oil eased Social Credit's transformation from enemy of the banks to conventional right-wing movement. Ernest Manning went from serving as the treasurer and premier of a government that attacked the "Fifty Big Shots of Canada" and speculative finance capital (not big capital per se) to serving as a director of the Canadian Imperial Bank of Commerce. Like the American government, Alberta's government became an implacable foe of socialism. As in America, agrarian radicalism eventually gave way to corporate agribusiness.

BC socialism was more radical than Prairie socialism because the province's hinterland economy differed so strongly from that of the Prairies: more coal and hardrock mining and much less farming.[15] The conditions in the isolated, remote company towns of the forestry and mining sectors incubated a vigorous class-consciousness. Some of it was imported full-blown from the mother country, as many of the workers in these one-industry company towns hailed from industrialized, urban, distressed, and status-divided Britain during the fourth wave of Canadian immigration. The radical ideological makeup of this group fed talk of class warfare in its new setting. Many workers and their organizations in the resource hinterland were pugnaciously syndicalist, located where young men were concentrated, families were few, industrial accidents many, and living and working situations rough. Such conditions stoked radicalism, whereas Vancouver's more mixed social composition and setting dampened it and fed reformist working-class politics.[16] Vancouver's amenities and its workers' conditions were better. Here, workers' outlooks were tempered with those of intellectual socialists and urbane Fabians, who preached a parliamentary and evolutionary path to socialism. Vancouver lacked significant non-British immigrant ghettos, so its working class was more socially homogeneous than Winnipeg's or Toronto's.

The early American influence in BC was less potent than in Alberta, for it was concentrated in the mining and logging sectors rather than being widespread on farms and ranches. Nevertheless, it is noteworthy. It was a highly unusual kind of American influence; one might say a distinctly un-American, American influence. On its formation, the Socialist Party of BC (which still exists) adopted the platform of the US Socialist Party. When the radical American Miners' Union crossed into Canada in the 1890s, it came first to BC, and only from there did it spread into Alberta. When Vancouver's logger employers banded together as an association, they modelled their rules and regulations on those of a Seattle group in the same industry. Just as Saskatchewan labour politics were influenced by developments in Manitoba, Alberta's early labour politics fell partly under the spell of their BC brethren, who helped capture an Alberta labour convention to establish a provincial labour party. Socialist Americans contributed to mobilizing radical miners, and the Canadian tour of American socialist presidential candidate Eugene Debs had more purchase in BC than in Ontario. Nevertheless, British workers in BC's communities were familiar with unionism and were much more numerous than Americans. Whereas Alberta's American farm leaders took cues from American agrarian politics, the successful political efforts of BC's miners offered cues to America's workers: the political action of the British Columbians "generated shock waves throughout North American labour circles."[17]

The population growth of BC – it went from second-smallest to third-largest province in less than a half century – made it a magnet for aggressive entrepreneurs as well as wage labourers. The left-right dynamic in the provincial political culture became more ingrained there than in any other province. As in Manitoba, BC's electoral system and its coalition governments frustrated social democrats and socialists. The CCF, for example, led the popular vote in the 1952 election, but the overnight emergence (as sudden as in Alberta) of Social Credit consolidated the left-right dialectic in provincial politics in short order. Social Credit, winning power on a paltry 30 percent of the first-choice ballots in an alternative-vote system (engineered by the outgoing Liberal-Conservative coalition government to keep the CCF from power), soon changed the rules again. Dual member constituencies were gerrymandered so that Social Credit could win more of them with narrow margins. Much of the CCF-NDP vote was hived off so that the party won fewer seats with massively concentrated but wasted majorities.

Alberta as Canada's Great Plains America

Alberta has come closer than any Canadian province to imitating the politics of the American Great Plains states. "Alberta," declared one of its MPs in 1907, "from the border northward to Edmonton, might be regarded as a typical American state."[18] Alberta was North America's last agricultural frontier. From the 1890s, Americans poured over its border and into western Saskatchewan as well. Wilfrid Laurier's immigration minister, Albertan Frank Oliver, assigned them high status, describing them as "desirable in every way. They are people of intelligence, of energy, of enterprise, of the highest aspirations." In contrast, "we resent the idea of having the millstone of this Slav population hung around our necks."[19] In 1911, American-born Albertans (22 percent of the population) outnumbered the British-born, Ontario-born, and European-born. Almost certainly, this was the largest concentration of Americans in any jurisdiction outside the US. Canadian-born Albertans were a minority in their own province. Ontario liberalism, which earlier held sway, was fused with the more dynamic liberal populism of the Americans. Americans and their ideas helped shape provincial politics because they settled in the politically determinative rural areas. Their influence was particularly pronounced in the south: Lethbridge adopted "American style"[20] civic commission government before the First World War. In contrast, Alberta's immigrant working-class Britons gravitated toward the politically underrepresented cities.

Alberta's populist liberalism, like that of America's, was unalloyed by toryism; it was more radical and plebiscitarian than that of the Midwest's Progressives, who became a "dilapidated annex"[21] of the Liberals and were amenable to working within the confines of a strong, centralizing parliamentary executive. Some Albertan MLAs spoke of parliamentary responsible government as a form of state dictatorship. By the late 1920s, the federal Progressives were a spent force in every province except Alberta. There, the UFA federal Progressives gained votes and seats because the ideological cloth from which their constituents were cut differed from that of the more timid Progressives elsewhere. It seemed fitting and telling that UFA president Henry Wise Wood, the "Uncrowned King of Alberta" according to his biographer,[22] was a forty-five-year-old veteran Missouri populist when he emigrated. He refused the premiership because he felt it inconsistent with his American background; he turned down a knighthood because of his values. Alberta's maverick provincial government once refused to appear before a Royal Commission, insistent instead on addressing its brief to "the Sovereign People of Canada,"[23] an expression of the American rather than British notion of sovereignty. One Social Credit MLA complained that too much time was being spent on the coronation festivities of 1937 rather than on monetary reform, a sentiment that could not have been uttered, without political cost, at Queen's Park or in the very British province of British Columbia.

American ideas were potent in the UFA, but there were also significant British Canadian influences in it. William Irvine, Calgary's Labour MP, and Robert Gardiner, the British-born UFA president after Wood and leader of parliament's Ginger Group, were clergy trained in the Social Gospel tradition. So too was Norman Priestly, the CCF's national secretary and Aberhart's leading critic during his heyday. This influence, however, was insufficient to offset the American populist-liberal-evangelical sway in the rural areas. The leftist current in Alberta was a minoritarian one. To be sure, one-third of Calgarians were British-born; their city, which tottered on the edge of a general strike in 1918, served as the site of the founding meetings of both the syndicalist One Big Union and socialist CCF. Calgary, however, was also a relatively small city in the largely rural setting of Alberta and not immune to the rural influence: the city also served as the headquarters for the Society of Equity, the Non-Partisan League, the UFA, and Prairie evangelism, all of which had American roots. Concentrated in the cities, the British labour-socialist influence was overwhelmed and overpowered in rurally tilted Alberta. Alberta

Social Credit also had urban origins, but its popularity was to prove greater in the countryside because its social values resonated there.[24]

Monetary reform, all the rage at UFA conventions, was rarely broached at UFM, UFO, or UFC (SS) conventions. Americans, as newly minted Albertans, contributed to spreading the gospel of inflationary monetarism and agitated for populist democracy. Many of them had fundamentalist theological predilections, the faith of a "quite exceptional" 20 percent of the province's Protestants.[25] Wood was one of them, a member of the Disciples of Christ; his sole, unfinished book was titled *Social Aspects of the Life of Christ.* Wood's gospel, however, had more in common with the Social Gospel than with Aberhart's, which said nothing of social justice. Aberhart's gospel focused on Jesus, the Apocalypse, church attendance, and the infusion of morality into politics. Nevertheless, Wood looked benignly at Aberhart's rise to power. Eminent sociologist S.D. Clark, an Albertan, noted that "the religious-political experiment in Alberta resembled very closely that tried much earlier in Utah; in both cases, religious separatism sought support in political separatism, and encroachments of the federal authority were viewed as encroachments of the worldly society."[26] Aberhart effectively merged the prophetic and messianic Christian gospel with Social Credit. Although the latter was a British theory, its Albertan incarnation arguably owed more to nineteenth-century American agrarianism (the Greenback and Free Silver movements) than to its British parent. Alberta Social Credit was liveliest in evangelical, parochial, and rural districts and most suspect among Catholics and in the cities, but Social Credit in Britain was most robust in Catholic, urban, and cosmopolitan circles.[27] Major Douglas, the Scottish founder of Social Credit, came to disown his Albertan acolytes,[28] demonstrating the tenuous links between Canadian and British Social Credit.

The American and religious influences in Alberta are noteworthy but ought not to be exaggerated. The UFA's "group government" idea, for example, had no traction on the American Great Plains or among its populists. And Social Credit's religious appeal was not as critical to its victory as its critique of the discredited UFA and the use of underconsumption theory. Although British Columbia's social democrats looked to the programs of the successful British, Australian, and New Zealand Labour Parties and lauded Britain's welfarist Beveridge Report, Alberta's Social Crediters depicted it as a plan to redistribute poverty. Relatively few Americans came to Alberta in the fifth wave of immigration after the Second World War. Nevertheless, the initial

radical liberal American influence (which mutated as contemporary conservatism or neo-liberalism) sunk roots. Some of the Americans who did come
after mid-century were vital players in the province's development as oil company executives and managers. Between 1955 and 1970, nine of the fifteen
presidents of Calgary's exclusive and influential Petroleum Club were Americans.[29] In no other province were Americans so prominent as captains of
industry. Calgary logically became the first Canadian city to have a direct air
link to Houston, the Texan oil capital. The Reform/Alliance proposals for
parliamentary and constitutional reform – free votes for MPs, referenda, a
Triple-E Senate, recall of MPs, legislative hearings for judicial appointments,
and the addition of property rights to the Charter – all pointed to models
from south of the border.

The border between Alberta and Saskatchewan may be an artificial line
of longitude, but the differing settlement patterns on its opposite sides produced starkly diverse ideological traditions. Saskatchewan threw up a powerful co-operative movement and the country's most successful socialist party.
Alberta also proved hospitable to co-operatives but looked more kindly than
Saskatchewan on private competitive ventures. The fissure between the two
provinces ran right through the twentieth century, reflected in their approaches
to grain marketing. In the 1920s, Saskatchewan's socialist farm leaders, like
E.A. Partridge, insisted on a compulsory wheat pool, describing it as a transitional vehicle to socialism. Albertans, in contrast, agitated for a voluntary
pool, depicting the compulsory scheme, in Wood's words, as "a denial of
freedom."[30] In the 1990s, that ideological fight was re-engaged: as Alberta's
right-wing Conservative government supported and its farmers voted for an
open competitive marketing regime, Saskatchewan's left-wing NDP government supported and its farmers voted for maintaining the Canadian Wheat
Board's monopoly.[31] Albertans, unlike Saskatchewanians, had regarded the
CCF as "a repudiation of the rugged individualism which had always characterized the farmers of Alberta." It was "inevitable," according to philosopher
John Irving, "that a Social Credit rather than a socialist movement would
prevail" there.[32] Political scientists were making the same observation when
the twenty-first century began: "the ideology of the NDP appears to be somewhat antithetical to the political culture of Alberta, with its greater emphasis
on individualism."[33]

Like socialism, Social Credit was certainly a radical philosophy, and it
did appeal to some socialists, including William Irvine. However, by the 1940s,

Social Credit had defined socialism rather than the banks as its enemy. Social Credit successfully welded the votes of agrarian Albertans with those of
the urban small-business classes and some blue-collar workers. The same
formula worked for the party in BC. However, though UFA meetings featured debates and exchange, Social Credit assemblies were akin to revival
meetings, with participants adopting "O God, Our Help in Ages Past" as their
theme song. Aberhart was on occasion referred to as "Our Saviour," and the
party's logo was·a green Christian cross on a white background.[34] At the Reform Party's national assembly in 1992, the elder Manning lauded the party's efforts as a "crusade," an allusion to religious purpose. Similarly, the
Canadian Alliance's Stockwell Day was the only party leader in the 2000
federal election unhesitant to affirm his religious beliefs, something that led
to ridicule. In Alberta, professions of faith by political leaders have a long
history. The moral and social views of southern Albertans have at times seemed
more in tune with those in America's southern states and Bible belt regions
than with those of the rest of Canada.

The UFA pursued giving life and form to direct democracy in government, but Social Credit's democracy was more plebiscitary. In its view, governmental policy making, a matter of technical skill and special qualification,
was best left to experts. The public was to weigh in on their proposals by
voting "yes" or "no." Both Aberhart and Major Douglas believed that one
need not understand Social Credit to vote for it. Alberta's long periods of
single-party hegemony contributed to the notion of provincial public administration as properly "business government." In this view, good government
is minimal, designed to serve as "the interpreter and steward of the general
community will ... to keep control out of the rabble's hands."[35] In contrast,
the same observer noted, public administration in BC has been a matter of
"weathering ideological storms,"[36] a product of incessant struggle between
left and right parties with competing, divergent ideas of government's proper
place and administrators' appropriate role.

Again, as with the American influence, it is important to note but not to
exaggerate Alberta's redneck image and its history of right-wing agrarian populist hegemony. The provincial political culture has never been monolithic.
None is. The electoral system contributed a great deal to making it appear as
such. The Conservatives have repeatedly swept the rural ridings, but northern and mining districts, as well as Edmonton, have exhibited substantial left
liberal and social democratic sympathies. So too did Calgary at one time. Alberta's miners were radical socialists, but as the mines closed, that radicalism

was shut down too. In the rural northeast, settled by continental Europeans, a Ukrainian CCF MLA was elected in the 1950s, replicating the party's success among the same culturally marginalized groups in the Midwest. In recent decades, Edmonton, cooler to the Conservatives than is the rest of Alberta, has become known as "Redmonton." It is where the NDP twice won most of its sixteen seats in the 1980s; the party served as Official Opposition after three successive elections in that decade. Edmonton is where the generally unpopular federal Liberals held seats during the Jean Chrétien and Paul Martin years. It is where eight of nine opposition MLAs were elected in 2001 and where the governing Conservatives won only three of nineteen seats in 1997 and only two of eighteen in 2004.

Provincial anti-Conservative sentiment has shifted in recent years from the NDP to the more ideologically fickle Liberals, who tried to outflank the Conservatives on the right in one election in the 1990s.[37] They captured the votes of four in ten Albertans in the effort, their best performance since the First World War. This is further testimony to the drawing power of right-wing appeals in Alberta, compared to other Western provinces. The strength of the Conservatives and the emergent Alberta Alliance in 2004 (for a combined 57 percent of the vote) speaks to the continuing vitality of Alberta's right-wing political culture. The Conservatives, the most successful party dynasty in recent Canadian history, have now prevailed in ten consecutive elections. The anti-socialist, anti-Liberal baton was passed on by Social Credit to the provincial Conservatives in the 1970s but not in the same way that the UFA's penchant for populist monetary reform had been passed on to Social Credit in the 1930s. Conservative Peter Lougheed was a modernizing technocrat rather than a "people versus elites" populist promoter. At the federal level, Alberta's populist flame was ignited in 1993 by the Reform Party and then passed on to the Canadian Alliance. The reconstituted, Alberta-led Conservative Party then represented it in 2004.

Populism is a more elusive idea than socialism or liberalism. In the Far West, populist discourse has both reproduced itself from its earlier manifestations and been transformed. Albertan populism has differed from the Midwest version but not only in its more strident "Ottawa bashing." Common to both populist versions has been the notion of "the people" – defined by cultural, geographic, or historic roots – and the perception of a looming threat or crisis represented by an external force or power bloc. For the Midwest's social democratic and liberal populists, the foe has been "big business" or corporate capitalists; for the Far West's rightist populists, it has been

THE FAR WEST

"big government." Continuity is evident in Alberta's early and later populists' characterization of the people: Social Credit depicted them as "consumers," Reform/Alliance saw them as middle-class taxpayers, and Ralph Klein viewed them as "ordinary Albertans" or "stakeholders." All three conceptions contrast with the more prevalent conception of social citizenship in the Midwest. Discontinuity in Alberta populism appears in the identification of the people's villains: although to Social Credit it was "big government" and "big banks," Reform/Alliance was largely silent on corporate power, and Klein's government came to be the voice of both "big government" and "big corporations."[38]

For a long time, Alberta's electoral map heavily favoured rural ridings, so that farmers' votes trumped those garnered in urban districts. As late as the 1950s, Calgary and Edmonton accounted for only ten of the legislature's fifty-seven seats. These cities had significant labour movements, but they counted for less than the countryside in shaping provincial politics and in defining the provincial political culture. A largely rural populist political culture infused and captured even the cities. Today, in contrast, Calgary and Edmonton account for half the seats. The steadily growing power of these cities was evident even before the spike in energy prices during and after the 2003 war in Iraq. In the 1990s, the Calgary-Edmonton corridor generated a GDP that was 40 percent higher than the average for Canada's large cities. Experiencing one of North America's strongest advances in economic output and population growth, it became "Canada's western tiger."[39] Since then, massive capital investments in the oil sands and bounteous economic surpluses have created a new balance of economic power in Canada as well as Alberta. Alberta's urbanization leads the rural districts to look increasingly to the cities, where political direction is concentrated and from which largesse is dispensed, for signals of political change. In 2004, the ruling Conservative Party won all but three of Calgary's twenty-three seats; however, should the large urban centres turn away from the party, the rural areas will follow suit, just as they did in 1971 when every constituency in both Calgary and Edmonton abandoned Social Credit in favour of the Conservatives.

British Columbia as Canada's Australia

More than any other province, British Columbia and its politics have resembled Australia and its politics. Both BC and Australia were first settled in the nineteenth century on the edges of the world's pre-eminent empire: both represented greater Britain on the Pacific. Both had gold rushes in the 1850s;

the licensing mechanisms for BC's prospectors were based on those of Australia.[40] The societal equivalents closest to BC's first work camps were probably those of Australia, New Zealand, and the American west coast.[41] Both BC and Australia have resource-based economies, with staples located and extracted in the far-flung nooks and crannies of their hinterlands. Both originated from and largely remain urban societies. Both were made more accessible by the opening of canals (Panama, Suez) on other continents that linked them to metropolitan economies and cultures. Both developed distinguishing myths – the Australian Bush Myth and British Columbians' self-image of splendid isolation in a paradise environment. Both Australia and BC offered opportunity, a new beginning, and the prospect of indolence. Settlers in both thought of their new Eden as the location in which to pursue utopian ends. Radicals in both societies saw them as a potential "workingman's paradise."[42] Both Australia and BC require referenda for constitutional change, and BC modelled its electoral system in 1952-53 after the Australian alternative-vote system.

Both BC and Australia were leftist ideological offshoots of Britain. Settled earlier than BC in the nineteenth century, Australia inherited the then radical liberal progressive ideology of Bentham's utilitarianism. Settled later, at the turn of the twentieth century, BC acquired the then radical ideology of labour-socialism. In both societies, the formative settlers were working-class immigrants from industrial Britain, who carried with them the strong class awareness of their mother country.[43] Both BC and Australia developed left-right, urban-rural, and class-driven political cleavages, and both spawned major political parties competing around the rhetoric of class struggle. Both continue to be parvenu societies that hold out the prospect of quick rags-to-riches success. Both offer the prospect of personal liberation and the promise of individual and social advancement and fulfillment. Both have become preferred destinations for Asian immigrants.

Throughout its history, BC has attracted migrants; as the twenty-first century began, it was the only province in which those born outside it still outnumbered natives. BC has been depicted as an ideological fragment of Edwardian Britain at the turn of the twentieth century.[44] In the critical first two decades of that century, the cast of British Columbia politics was set. Transplanted Britons were the single-largest group in the population, larger in number than those born in the province or those coming from the rest of Canada. Of the 175,000 Britons taking up residence in the province between

1891 and 1911, fewer than one in seven was middle or upper class by occupation. Many in this smaller group came in pursuit of status, "to retrieve a life-style denied them at home, that of a 'gentleman.'"[45] The more numerous Britons of modest backgrounds helped fuel class-consciousness from the bottom up, through active participation in the labour movement; their middle-class counterparts did so from the top down. The political clout of the newly arrived Britons overwhelmed that of those who had come earlier. Especially marked was the British working-class' residential segregation. Vancouver's Main Street served as a rough geopolitical boundary between the "haves," the white-collar and entrepreneurial classes to its west, and the "have-nots," the blue-collar wage labourers to its east.

As on the prairies, Britain's labour leaders and causes had strong followings in this very British society, British Columbia. Late Victorian and Edwardian Britain was a time of flux and uncertainty: stagnating real wages, emigration, growing class tensions, the rise of the trade union movement, and the establishment of the Labour Party. As late as 1941, nine of BC's fourteen CCF MLAs were British-born. British-accented BC labour leaders were prominent throughout the century. The common cultural bond that united BC's upper-, middle-, and working-class Britons was their imperial link and colonial consciousness. The title of the capital's newspaper, the *Daily Colonist*, conveyed that bond.

BC's late railway connection with Canada in the 1880s meant that the national political parties, the Liberals and Conservatives, appeared no sooner there than they did in Alberta or Saskatchewan. After an initial period of non-partisan politics, the impetus for the development of parties came more from the political strength of the labour movement than from central Canada. Labour and socialist parties had been active long before the CCF appeared in the 1930s. Only in BC have there been labour and socialist MLAs in every decade since the 1890s. In 1898, six pro-labour MLAs held the balance of power in the legislature. Farmers' parties were less viable as political instruments than on the prairies because the agricultural sector was smaller and more diverse (fruit, cattle, dairy, vegetables, as well as grains). Farmers were isolated in distant and difficult-to-access valleys and plateaus, and on Vancouver Island. In 1921, only 16 percent of the workforce was engaged in agriculture; a decade later, it was less than 6 percent. The United Farmers of British Columbia therefore proved to be a political joke compared to its potent UFO, UFM, UFC (SS), and UFA counterparts. Organized labour was the much more robust political force in BC, in the mining, lumbering, and fishing industries of the remote one-industry towns of the Interior and on the coast. Organized labourers such as longshoremen (J.S. Woodsworth was one) helped to transform Vancouver, Canada's premier western entrepot, into the West's largest city.

BC's discordant, bipolar political culture crystallized in the 1930s. In its first outing, the CCF attained major party status, winning about one-third of the vote. The Liberal-Conservative coalition governments in the 1940s were driven by this challenge. Working-class spokesmen denounced what they depicted as the avaricious privileged classes represented by the government. When Social Credit appeared as a force in the 1950s, it simply served as the new anti-socialist, coalitionist standard-bearer. Until then, BC Social Credit had been a fractious, minuscule group whose thinking, as in Alberta originally, was technocratic. Under W.A.C. Bennett, it turned away from the "science" of monetary reform and toward "embracing individualism, Christianity, and free enterprise," as it had in Alberta, and became "more sensual than cerebral."[46] With assistance from its Alberta namesake, BC Social Credit came to represent fiscal frugality and moral responsibility rather than easy money. It depicted the coalition government as interventionist and subversive of freedom. The Social Credit label in BC became one of convenience for CCF opponents, a name familiar due to Alberta's proximity and the label's success there. The coalition character of Social Credit was reflected in its cabinet in the 1970s and 1980s: no fewer than eight of Bill Bennett's fourteen ministers were former Liberals or Conservatives. The Social Credit caucus included a former Trudeau cabinet minister (Jack Davis) and a future Conservative prime minister (Kim Campbell); it came to be led by a former Liberal and future provincial Reform Party leader (Bill Vander Zalm). Only in British Columbia could the ideological gulf between such allies, joined in a political marriage improbable anywhere else in Canada, seem narrower than the space between Social Credit and the NDP. The alliance on the right – that began in the 1940s and continues to this day – had been foreseen in 1936 by a student of BC politics: "If the C.C.F. lives and grows, the two old parties will have to unite to save the social and economic institutions with which they are so intimately related."[47]

Socialism and labourism have been potent, radical, and consistent forces in BC politics. In this, the province's politics are quite unlike those of Alberta and markedly similar to those of Australia. In 1987, for example, BC witnessed a one-day strike of 300,000 unionists (part of a movement known as Solidarity) hostile to the government. Unions boycotted the provincial labour relations council for four years. Popular consciousness of BC's ideological divide has been striking. A 1980s survey revealed that about two-thirds of the electorate agreed with the statement that provincial elections "are contests between free enterprise and socialism"; over four-fifths of Social Credit's former Liberals and Conservatives felt so.[48] The radicalism of BC socialism also made it unlike the Midwest's socialism. BC boasts "a sharper left-right focus than any other part of English-speaking North America."[49]

What puzzled outsiders was the sudden swing of the electorate from the leftist bias of the late 1980s to the rightist bent of the 1990s. In 1988, for example, the NDP captured nineteen of the province's thirty-two federal ridings, but in 1993, Reform prevailed in twenty-four of them (and the NDP in only three). The explanation for this incongruity lies only partly in the vagaries of the electoral system, in which a slight shift in votes may trigger a tipping point in seats. A fuller explanation lies in the sense of distance, deep-seated feelings of regional alienation and marginalization, and the populist spirit of many British Columbians, especially those beyond the Lower Mainland. From this perspective, the NDP's embrace of the Meech Lake and Charlottetown Accords made the party look like an old, co-opted, establishment party. British Columbians, like other westerners, perceive the accommodation of Quebec as a project of the Liberals and Conservatives who serve central Canadian interests anchored in the Toronto-Ottawa-Montreal triangle. Historically, the NDP has been the party most sympathetic to Quebec's self-determination, and this has hurt it. As a signal of social democratic camaraderie, NDP premier Dave Barrett once ventured there to make common cause with René Lévesque's Parti Québécois, but nothing came of it.

More so than in Alberta, the notion of a single homogeneous provincial political culture in BC is problematic. This was evidenced in the 2000 federal election: about half the electorate (living mainly in the Interior and the suburbs) opted for the Alliance Party; the other half (concentrated in Vancouver and Victoria) voted for the Liberals, NDP, Progressive Conservatives, and Greens. BC's rugged geography, with its pockets of settlement here and there, once yielded a variety of localized political outlooks that only in their totality produced the ideologically driven bipolarity of the provincial party system. The geographic insularity of BC's remote communities diminished their susceptibility to province-wide shifts. When communications technology was less advanced, with news and information less instantaneous, BC's distant and secluded communities were "more likely to escape or deflect the prevailing electoral winds"[50] of the day. The spread of province-wide media helped change that: when in 1991 broadcasters included the Liberal leader in a televised leaders' debate, this, more than any other development, contributed to catapulting that party into Official Opposition (after it had been wholly absent from the legislature since the 1970s). It also sank Social Credit. By the late 1990s, the Liberals replaced Social Credit on the political spectrum as the anti-NDP coalition party, an amalgam of Liberals, Conservatives, Reformers, and ex–Social Crediters.

Religion, Socialism, and Social Movements

Early Canadian voting studies demonstrated that religion was a strong determinant of political choice.[51] Catholics were disproportionately sympathetic to the Liberals; Protestants, particularly those with negative attitudes regarding Catholics, were disproportionately inclined to favour the Conservatives. As the dominant religious umbrella in English Canada, Protestantism includes Anglicans, Presbyterians, Methodists, Baptists, members of the distinctively Canadian United Church, and many others. Over time, Canadian society has become simultaneously more diverse in its religious composition (with Muslims, Hindus, Sikhs, Buddhists, and others complementing an older Jewish element) and more secular. Religious diversity and especially secularism are particularly striking in BC, where the established Christian denominations have steadily lost ground to non-believers and Eastern religions. BC is home to about three in ten of Canada's Buddhists and half its Sikhs. The province has by far the highest provincial percentage (36) of atheists and agnostics in the land. They now outnumber BC's Catholics by a ratio of two to one and are more numerous than its Protestants.[52] Statistics Canada reports that BC is the only province with not a single pocket of high religious attendance.

Secularism in BC fits with the province's historic socialist predilections, and Christian fundamentalism fits with Alberta's historical antipathy to socialist causes. Alberta has been the province most receptive to Christian evangelicalism. As early as 1908, the *Calgary Daily Herald* reported that American and central Canadian "evangelists seem to have a grip on the city."[53] With respect to religion, BC is somewhat similar to Australia.[54] In that evangelical Christians have played leading political roles there, Alberta resembles the US. Alberta has many more Protestants than those professing no religion. Atheistic socialism appeals to reason and to the exclusion of organized religion from public life; evangelicalism appeals to emotion and faith. The Social Gospel – that wellspring for early twentieth-century Canadian socialism – was not as vibrant in the Far West as in the Midwest.[55] A survey of BC NDP activists in the 1980s revealed that 56 percent of them labelled themselves atheists, triple the percentage for their Social Credit counterparts.[56] Although evangelicals have not been as prominent in BC politics as in those of Alberta, the connection between evangelicals and BC Social Credit was evident in the latter's heyday. A 1950s survey showed that over 70 percent of BC's fundamentalist ministers supported Social Credit, whereas over 60 percent of United Church ministers preferred the CCF.[57] Only in 1990 did Social Credit remove from its constitution a clause that referred to fostering Christian principles as one of its objectives. Fundamentalist Bill Vander Zalm, as Social Credit premier, terminated medicare funding of abortion but was overruled by the BC Supreme Court. More than a decade later, that Court sanctioned same-sex marriages, but Alberta's did not.

The American influence in Alberta in the twentieth century's early years "favoured a steady invasion of unorthodox social and religious leaders and associations."[58] Cardston, in southern Alberta, was begotten by ten families led by the son-in-law of Mormon leader Brigham Young who travelled north from Utah in 1887. Political and religious tendencies became interrelated and mutually reinforcing. Albertan Solon Low, Social Credit's national leader in the 1950s, was the son of Mormon Utahans; Preston Manning, the Reform leader in the 1990s, was Aberhart's godson. Aberhart's immensely popular weekly radio broadcasts – listened to by nearly half of Albertans – proclaimed that "the principles of the old line politicians and their henchmen are like those of the men who betrayed the Christ."[59] No clergyman or politician outside of Alberta attracted much of an audience for that sentiment. The main casualty of Aberhart's – and later Ernest Manning's – religious broadcasts was the United Church, with its Social Gospel antecedents, highly trained pastorate, substantial lay participation, and humanitarian ethic.[60] Anti-Semitic conspiracy theories were at the heart of Major Douglas' economic analysis. Aberhart fostered them inadvertently in his use of Douglas' Social Credit jargon. Despite Manning's purge of the party's anti-Semites, anti-Semitic incidents were never fully expunged: the Keegstra affair of the 1980s – he a Social Credit politician convicted of promoting hatred against Jews – may be depicted as part of his party's legacy of religious intolerance.[61]

That conservative religious influence lingers in Alberta can be seen in the federal party leaders recently produced by the province: Preston Manning,

Stockwell Day, and Stephen Harper are all evangelical Christians. By contrast, Joe Clark, a Catholic, proved more popular outside his province than in it. The links between evangelical Christianity and neo-liberal conservatism on the one hand, and between secularism and social democracy on the other, are also revealed by the national electorate's preferences. The 2004 Canadian Election Study showed that, outside Quebec, the federal Conservative Party, led by Harper and rejected by the old Progressive Conservative Clark, captured more than half of self-identified "fundamentalist" voters. The Conservatives were more popular among this religious group than among any other (Catholic, Protestant, Non-Christian, and No Religion). In contrast, the NDP fared much better among the "No Religion" respondents than among those professing a religion; its weakest level of support was among fundamentalists.[62] As a sign of Alberta's fundamentalist bias, its government was the only one to argue, alongside several religious groups, against same-sex marriage at the Supreme Court in 2004. Causes such as gay rights, abortion, assisted suicide, and the decriminalization and public provision of illegal drugs have had a much higher and more positive profile in BC than in Alberta. On the issue of gay marriage, age affects attitudes more than does province of residence; nonetheless, among English Canadians, British Columbians have been the most supportive of gay marriage, and Albertans have been the most opposed.[63] Only Alberta's government broached the possibility of invoking the Charter's "notwithstanding" clause to override the Supreme Court ruling that prohibits hiring discrimination against gays, something Alberta's Human Rights Act ignores.

The connection between ethno-religious identification and politics has waned over time but varies by group. Old ethnic groups – Eastern and Southern Europeans in the Midwest and Ontario – have become established, assimilated, and less susceptible to bloc appeals. Meanwhile, the new Asian groups have become politically prominent, even as their acculturation and integration are still in their early stages. Their particular clout is noticeable in Greater Vancouver: Indo- and Chinese Canadians have been recruited by party organizers and have mobilized among themselves to buttress the campaigns of aspiring party leaders and local candidates. In the Punjabi community, Canada's sponsored immigration program facilitated such mobilization as "it created quasi-feudal networks" that concentrated power in the hands of a few families.[64] In 2003, Indo-Canadians constituted 40 percent of the BC wing of the federal Liberal Party. A year later, the first married couple simultaneously elected to parliament were foreign-born Indo-Canadian

Conservatives. Leadership also reflects demographic change and perceptions of ethnicity. About the same time that BC's Liberal government used a referendum to curtail Aboriginal aspirations, the NDP chose a Métis woman as its leader to replace the party's defeated Indo-Canadian premier (Ujjal Dosanjh), the country's first. In the 1970s, the BC NDP's selection of Barrett represented the party's symbolic break with its long history of continuous Anglo-Saxon leadership and its British ethnic base. He served as Canada's first and only Jewish premier.

BC and Alberta also differ as regards the strength of their social movements and their relationship to the emerging divide between materialists and post-materialists. Materialists talk of promoting economic growth, fighting inflation and crime, maintaining social order, and boosting military capacity. Post-materialists place a premium on protecting nature and free speech, on moving toward a more humane, less impersonal, less money-driven society, one with more participatory decision making and deliberation in governmental affairs. Social movements – environmental, peace, feminist, anti-globalization, gay and lesbian, the disabled, and the post-materialist counterculture generally – that are reflected in the alternative media, new age religions, communal lifestyles, and the drug culture (a mainstay in BC's economy) resonate in BC in a way that they do not in Alberta. BC gave birth to the *Georgia Straight,* Canada's first alternative newspaper, and to Greenpeace, some of whose founders and leading lights were radical expatriate Americans repelled by America's role in the world.[65] Although the social democratic NDP has come to embrace the social movements associated with post-materialism, BC's shifting ethnic composition poses problems for the party's prospects. A 1990s survey in the province showed that 30 percent of those of European ancestry were post-materialists, as opposed to only a tenth of BC's Asians.[66]

BC sports a disproportionate share of Canada's "cosmopolitan modernists" – those with a global world view, respect for education, and a desire for innovation. Vancouver has a higher than average proportion of "autonomous rebels" – those with a strong belief in human rights. Suspicious of authority, they express skepticism regarding traditional institutions. British Columbians may be contrasted with the "anxious communitarians" disproportionately clustered on the Midwest prairies, whose values include community – "we are our brother's keeper." Midwesterners also fear the future more than do British Columbians.[67] Environmental networks have been particularly robust in BC, where environmental debates have been especially heated and where

Canada's best-known environmentalist, David Suzuki, lives. Environmentalism finds supporters across the political spectrum everywhere in the world,
but environmental activists have been most assiduously courted by and attracted to leftist parties. For evidence that in BC environmentalism's roots
are older and its base broader than elsewhere in Canada, consider that the
Sierra Club's BC chapter dates back to the 1960s, whereas the Prairie chapter
was formed only in 1995. The club has almost as many members in BC as in
the rest of Canada, excluding Ontario. Similarly, a disproportionate number
of donors to the World Wildlife Federation reside in BC.[68]

BC's "new left" environmentalists and "old left" labour unions forged
an alliance against corporate business interests, but it was strained by the
nature of the provincial economy. Environmentalists are intent on conservation, on fighting pollution and ecological despoliation; unionists seek to
maintain their jobs in the profit-driven, efficiency maximizing, resource-
extraction industries.[69] In opposition in the 1980s, the NDP capitalized on
popular environmental concerns by attacking Social Credit's "hypercapitalist
ideology."[70] In the 1990s, when the NDP was in power, its relationship with
environmentalists soured as wilderness battles invariably produced conflicts
between the party's environmental and labour constituencies. The forest sector's corporations exploited this schism by funding an anti-environmental
opposition whose leading spokesperson was the long-time president of the
woodworkers union.[71] The resulting tumult provided ferment for a rising
Green Party, which won over 12 percent of the vote in the 2001 election.
Together with the Marijuana Party, the Greens garnered just 6 percent fewer
votes than the long-established NDP. In Alberta, in contrast, environmental
issues and counterculture causes are not nearly so contentious or prominent.
There, the Greens could muster only 3 percent of the vote in the 2004 provincial election. Economic development interests, such as those in the high-
polluting oil sands projects, have always had the ear of Alberta's government.
No surprise: it led the assault on Canadian ratification of the Kyoto Protocol.

Another striking but unnoticed difference between Albertan and British
Columbian orientations relates to the national question. The Council of
Canadians, the largest politically active non-corporate interest group of citizens in the country, has six times as many chapters in BC as in Alberta, more
in BC than in all the provinces stretching from Quebec to the Rocky Mountains combined.[72] Although there is little variation between Albertan and
British Columbian opinions regarding the Quebec question, yawning differences appear on the issue of continental economic integration. Among

Canadians, Albertans were the most supportive of the Canada-US Free Trade Agreement. British Columbians, along with Ontarians, were the most opposed.[73] In the free trade elections of 1911 and 1988, a majority of Albertans voted for the party of free trade, but a majority of British Columbians voted against it.

Albertans and their governments are not disposed to American annexation but are less fearful and less critical of the American behemoth than are British Columbians. It is hardly conceivable that an Albertan premier would refuse the US access to a long-used military test site – as BC NDP premier Glen Clark threatened to do – in response to an economic irritant (management of the west coast fishery). Indeed, America's controversial testing of cruise missiles in Alberta proceeded with relatively little outcry within the province and much more outside it, particularly among peace activists who are, like environmentalists, most prominent in BC. Many British Columbians loosely identify with the transnational Pacific Northwest region – terms such as "Cascadia" and "Ecotopia" have been used to describe it[74] – but Cascadia is a plastic notion, quite fluid and "capable of morphing into different shapes and sizes."[75] BC has little public appetite for any political linkage with the US. It is home to a vibrant anti-globalization movement; Alberta is not. Vancouver was the site of a controversial confrontation between human rights activists and police during the APEC summit there.[76] Albertans are not known for such activism or such causes.

Of the regions composed of more than a single province – Atlantic Canada, the Midwest, and the Far West – the Far West exhibits by far the greatest internal differences between provinces in traditions and values. Both BC and Alberta share exposure to the dramatic boom and bust cycles of international commodity markets, yet their politics differ greatly. Nevertheless, the consistent demographic and economic growth of the Far West means that this region, more than any other, will increasingly influence the future contours of Canadian political culture – if we may speak of it in the singular. So long as the Far West is blessed with bountiful resources, the panegyrical promise of prosperity and comfort in a setting of natural scenic beauty will lure migration. The upstart and parvenu qualities shared by Albertans and British Columbians contribute to the region's steadily growing incremental power in Canada. By 2004, the Far West, once the country's most sparsely populated region, accounted for 24 percent of Canadians, as did Quebec. In the creation and redistribution of seven additional seats for parliament that year, the Far West accounted for five.

Going forward, the Far West will easily overtake Quebec and will possibly come to challenge Ontario's pre-eminence in defining English Canada's values. If growth in the Far West maintains its pace, and if Quebec secedes, Canadian political debates may come to pivot more around the cultural divides between Alberta's materialists and British Columbia's post-materialists and less around those separating westerners and easterners. Following global economic trends, Canada will become more of a Pacific nation, one whose compass is tugged further in a westerly direction to the Far East and pulled less across the Atlantic to the Old East.

Conclusion

The pursuit of Canadian political culture is akin to the pursuit of a mirage. It is constantly shifting, dependent on the seeker's imagination and what she is looking for. This does not make the subject unreal but points to its elusiveness, its ever-changing character. However historically anchored a country's political culture may be, there will always be a dynamic quality to it. To insist on definitively pinpointing its essence is to miss seeing it as a work in perpetual process. Civic nationalists suspect any definition of political culture that dwells on the past because they seek to transcend it with the values held in common by society's contemporary citizens. Such conceptions of the nation unabashedly champion whatever the political culture of the here and now may be. Obviously then, civic nationalists have no interest in projecting their version of today's political culture into the future. The bias of this study differs greatly from theirs: it sees the country's political culture as shaped by its past and impelled by some notion of the future or hoped-for future. However, this effort has been driven more by curiosity than by clairvoyance or creed. It is constructed largely from past to present rather than from present to past, from considering Canadians' current values and issues and then tracing them back into the past.

The past influences what is to come, but that future is not absolutely bound by or obligated to that past. Violent clashes have occurred, but the Canadian political tradition has been primarily one of evolutionary and incremental change. That is why a grounding in political history and established institutional principles is a vital prerequisite for understanding Canada, how Canadians think and behave, and where they may be headed. Institutions such as parliaments, political parties, and legal principles change as the political culture that envelops them changes. It is within existing inherited political institutional structures, however, that cultural values accommodate and express themselves; those institutions are in turn modified and trans-formed, usually gradually, by the changing cultural values.

Can we find a single unifying thread in contemporary Canadian politic-al culture? The country is too complex, its regions and peoples too varied, and its history too contentious to unequivocally assert the existence of *a* singular Canadian identity or value system. Canadians are varied, their val-ues variegated. Every Canadian has multiple identities. Specific contexts me-diate the particular identity – gender, class, religion, region of residence, and so on – that is summoned up. Canadian political culture is no less resistant to specification. It is this, but it is also that. It is more than the sum of its parts, however defined, and it is not bound by any Canadian's lifetime. The question "what is Canada's political culture?" is therefore simple to put but not obviously answerable. Every state's political culture draws on its history, institutions, and the symbols shared by its people. In the United States, the question of the country's national political culture is also perplexing, given that the Union and Confederate states, which fought a bloody civil war, are part of the same "national" political culture. National political culture is in good measure defined by such conflicts. In Canada, no conflict has been as acute as the Conquest.

Recurring and enduring existential debates about Canadian identity are part of Canada's identity, its way of life. They are an integral component of its political culture. National traumas and regional tensions will persist. They are a definitive and, paradoxically, stable part of the Canadian condition and community. Their form, expression, intensity, and context will vary. Simi-larly, the issue of Canadian identity will probably never be satisfactorily de-cided or resolved for all. The quest to permanently resolve issues of identity is as quixotic as the notion of permanence itself. Canadians demonstrated that they could become a sovereign people without adopting the declaratory proclamations once urged upon them by their leaders in the form of megaconstitutional reform.[1] To define a singular, all-embracing, and mono-lithic Canadian identity denies the heterogeneity that has always character-ized Canada. Perhaps Canadians' common identity does not extend beyond their passports, which, not long ago, also pronounced them to be British subjects.

The treatment of Canadian political culture in this study has been mul-tinational, intra-national, and territorial. A Québécois or a Métis who ad-dressed the subject, informed by a different sensibility, would almost certainly fashion it differently, and possibly in a different language. This book draws heavily on the past. It chronicles changes in Canadian political culture, but unlike some, such as Charles Taylor and Alan Cairns, it does not contend that because Canada allows for multiple identities and allegiances to exist and flourish it is the product of some new synthesis – post-national and post-modern.[2] I have focused on political practice and historical outlooks rather than on reconciling contemporary Canadians' competing rights claims or grappling with the reconfiguration of Canadian citizenship or federalism.

Talking about Canada's "national" political culture posits a questionable assumption regarding Quebec. This book has primarily explored English Canada. The consideration of Quebec's political culture herein appears as something of an exotic sidebar. Quebec's language, temperament, legacy, and discourse render it so different from the other regions that it stands apart from them collectively as an outlier. Quebecers exhibit an unmistakable territorial possessiveness and distinctive internal strife that are absent elsewhere in Canada. Certainly, every region has unique features, but Quebec's are of a qualitatively different order whether or not one deems it a nation. English and French Canadians struggled separately to survive and maintain their distinct identities next to a large, more culturally homogeneous, and sometimes menacing neighbour. What changed is that though "English Canada" continues to speak English, it is no longer so obviously British but multicultural. And though more Quebecers than ever speak French, they no longer see their province as the beating heart of a pan-Canadian francophone nation but as a nation in its own right.

If we insist on looking for a singular national political culture, we will find and define it. We may even, as social scientists are wont to do, measure and quantify it. If we like what we find, we may extol the values we identify as virtues. On the other hand, if we look for regional political cultures, we will detect those too. It is a matter of perspective, of where the telescope or microscope is directed. Long-established regional loyalties – colonial and then provincial, as in Atlantic Canada – have never been wholly supplanted by national ones despite the efforts of the Canadian state to develop a sense of nationalism, albeit of a moderate tone.[3]

Most analyses of Canadian political culture presuppose a unified underlying reality. The account in this study opted for significant selection, contrast, combination, and comparative impressions. This entailed some expansiveness and variety rather than the simplicity and intensity of a single thesis-driven analysis. This book has tried to counter the vertigo of placelessness that characterizes much of the writing on Canadian political culture. A question it raises is not so much why a regional approach is needed, but how it can be neglected. My treatment points to the utility of thinking about Canadian political culture as an amalgam of regional political cultures. Some think that the very framework of regional analysis is passé. "As a tool of analysis, 'regionalism' is a concept whose time is gone,"[4] asserted Ramsay Cook less than a decade before the Reform Party and the Bloc Québécois tapped and unveiled the palpable regional animosities unleashed by the Meech Lake and Charlottetown Accords. To be sure, a regionally based analysis is always in danger of overshadowing the "national experience."[5] This study has endeavoured to place and account for distinctive regional forces in a national context without pursuing the theme of an overarching unity in Canadian political culture. That any political culture can be designated as the expression of some fixed national or regional culture is questionable.

It is a truism that much about Canada is contested, polarized, and centrifugal. In this, Canada is not unique. A reader of this book might ask questions of it that are of a pragmatic and policy-oriented nature. Has the Canadian experiment been successful? Are there too many unbridgeable differences among its peoples and regions? Are the limitations and failures of Canada's political institutions fatal? These have not been the subjects of my eclectic contemplation. Differences regarding national purpose and political direction are common to all polities. So are complaints regarding institutional limitations and failings. Formulating and reconciling differences of identity and citizenship in the modern world are the subjects of "high" politics and the purview of political philosophy. These are beyond the scope of this study. "Success" or "failure" of the Canadian political community is absent from the lexicon of Canadian politics deployed in the foregoing pages.

The kinds of differences pursued in this book largely address a lower order of politics. They cast light on such things as the making and breaking of regional partisan alliances, the configurations of social and ideological forces, and the political economies and formative events that have informed them. It is old hat to proclaim or herald the end of long-established ideological categorizations such as left and right, conservative, liberal, and socialist. However popular and repeatedly expressed such a sentiment may be, experience and practice give the lie to it. To dismiss terms such as conservatism, liberalism, and socialism neglects the reality that they continue to reverberate in Canadians' political discourse, as evidenced by the very names of Canada's political parties, the principles and policies they wrangle over, and the manner in which they characterize one another's outlooks.

Like Philip Resnick, this book has pointed to Canada's European roots,[6] but its primary focus has been on how those ideological origins played out politically rather than on how they informed identity. Canadian parallels with European developments are evident, as but one example, in the first half of the nineteenth century.[7] Mass politics, by then well established in the United States, were inhibited in Britain until the 1820s by anti-Jacobin hysteria, a frenzy that resonated in the British North American colonies. The waves of revolutionary fervour that swayed throughout continental Europe in the 1830s had their echoes in the Upper and Lower Canadian rebellions. The Canadian equivalent of Europe's conservative recoveries in the early 1840s was Lord Durham's design to temper ethnic unrest through the cultural assimilation of the French in a united Province of Canada. Soon after, Europe's widespread revolutions of 1848 coincided with Canada's revolution in its governing institutions – the attainment of responsible government.

Canada's New World setting offered opportunities for a greater political and economic equality than was possible in the Old World. Its proximity to the American liberal experiment – a consciously designed and triumphantly declaimed venture – and the rise of the United Nations and its Universal Declaration of Human Rights helped guide Canadians in pushing the institutional frontiers of individual freedom. It has been Canada's unique social composition that has informed its recognition and accommodation of group rights.

Canada, like other societies and the international community as a whole, is driven and divided by ideological disagreements about who and what ought to prevail politically. These differences infuse debates over how to define democracy, oppression, justice, equality, good leadership and government, and so on. The strongly diverse directions of Canada's regional politics, played out against the backdrop of a – to date – stable Canadian polity, suggest that the Canadian experiment has indeed been a success. More precisely, we may observe that Canada is a resounding success by international standards and experience.

Evaluating "the Canadian experiment" might imply the existence of experimenters with some conscious plan. The constitutional designs of John A. Macdonald and Georges-Étienne Cartier have not completely fallen by the wayside, but they are now only barely recognizable because their Canada and its political culture faded long ago. It is perhaps part of Canada's British political cultural heritage to muddle through political crises, and part of its French conservative heritage to have done so cautiously and defensively in the context of perceived cultural vulnerability. English and French Canadians demonstrated their ability to stumble along successfully by providing for constitutionally protected language groups and provinces. They continue to stumble along *ensemble* and as others – Aboriginals and visible minorities – have joined them. This speaks to an "experiment" in which no conclusive definitive observations are tenable. Signposts may be identified along the way, but Canadians' collective path has no predetermined destination. The future of Canadian political culture and Canadian identity is perforce contingent rather than determined. It never has been, and never will be, permanently fixed.

The idea that Canada has created, must create, or will create a new sense of nationality or national spirit in order to survive is as old as the country itself. Edward Blake, the only Liberal leader who failed to serve as prime minister, insisted soon after Confederation that "the future of Canada depends very much upon the cultivation of a national spirit."[8] The impetus to define and cultivate that spirit continues to haunt many Canadians, their public intellectuals, politicians, and media. Canada's intelligentsia and chattering classes have exhibited periodic compulsive bouts of trying to divine Canadians' collective identity and the essence of Canadian nationhood. Their consensus on the question has not extended far beyond the common denominator of their own nationalism. "Canada's historians," Carl Berger astutely observed, "have all been nationalists of various hues, and sometimes their judgments about what was central to the past and what was peripheral arose as much from divergent conceptions of nationality as from disagreements about interpretations of the same evidence."[9] Like those historians, this study has been content to reflect on past behaviour rather than to venture onto the even more uncertain terrain of dissecting the present and the *terra incognita* of the future. Canada has more than survived: it has thrived, the envy of many. Canadian identity on the world stage is distinct. To define that identity, however, is to enter the muddied, swirling waters of competing visions of the collective self.

National symbols, like myths, may be seen as visible expressions of political culture. They may be wielded to stir loyalties, to distinguish one nation from another. Symbols provide ways for nationals to define themselves; symbols of national self-image include flags, anthems, and constitutions.[10] Heraldic and other colonial symbols of mother Britain and pre- and post-revolutionary France (the fleur-de-lys and the Napoleonic Code) merged over time with native ones. Many gave way. The Union Jack, the Red Ensign, the British Empire, the BNA Act, the Imperial Order Daughters of the Empire, "God Save the Queen," and the principle of parliamentary supremacy have been more complemented than displaced. New indigenous symbols of identity appeared: the Mountie, the Maple Leaf flag, the totem pole, the Constitution Act, the Order of Canada, the principle of constitutional supremacy, bilingual signage, and a bilingual version of "O, Canada." Peter Newman's *The Distemper of Our Times* described the passionate flag debate of the mid-1960s as marking "the symbolic passing of attitudes of a generation, a triumph of the Canadian present over the Canadian past."[11] That "present," however, has passed too. It is the distemper that persists.

A nation is an imagined community. Its people are bound together by their common symbols and their media, which give them a sense of who "we" are. The "we," however – the ethnically Ukrainian farmer from Canora, Saskatchewan, the Loyalist housewife from Bathurst, New Brunswick, and the Haitian-born governor general from Montreal – have never and may never meet each other. Yet, they are all Canadians who think of themselves as part of the "we." Political culture, then, cannot be dissociated from how the "we" is defined. If New Brunswick had not been carved out of Nova Scotia, or Nunavut out of the Northwest Territories, the very question of New Brunswick's or Nunavut's political culture could not emerge. Newfoundland was not a part of Canada until 1949, yet its pre-Confederation history is now part of what we consider Canadian political history.

The symbolic universes of English Canadians and Québécois and the identities they nourish are informed by their familiarity with quite diverse historical figures and epochs. For example, anglophones are more likely to think in terms of Macdonald and Confederation than are francophones, who tend to focus on Jacques Cartier and the period predating the Conquest.[12] Such perceptions feed differing loyalties and identities. So too does historical revisionism. Louis Riel, branded and hanged as a traitor by English Canadians, was hailed by parliamentarians a century later as a heroic figure and Father of Confederation. Pierre Trudeau, once overwhelmingly embraced by the Québécois electorate and largely unpopular in that of English Canada, now commands respect in the latter but has fallen into political disrepute in the former. Death often redeems leadership in the service of myth making, and the past is rewritten to suit contemporary agendas. The Maple Leaf flag, originally derided by some conservative English Canadians as a capitulatory sop to Quebec and as an insulting rejection of Canada's British heritage, came to be booed in Quebec and cherished by those same English Canadians in less than a generation.

In *Reflections of a Siamese Twin*, John Ralston Saul has lauded the Canadian version of democratic evolution as based neither on the American notion of unchecked individualism nor the European experience of class strife. For him, Canada's political culture is moored in the balancing of personal freedom and public good. As the centrepiece of his book, he offers up the 1848 handshake of Robert Baldwin and Louis-Hippolyte LaFontaine and their collaborative formation of the Province of Canada's first responsible government, marking the beginning of the Canadian form of parliamentary democracy. However, *Reflections of a Siamese Twin* betrays the limitations of the bi-nationalist view of Canada that is enshrined in its title: shoehorned into its midst, a chapter regarding the role of Aboriginals and their nationalism is tellingly titled "A Triangular Reality."[13] Further evidence of Canadian pluralism is highlighted in the discourse of multiculturalism proffered by Will Kymlicka, who salutes the Charter of Rights for its recognition of multiculturalism in the form of polyethnic rights. For him, a multinational federation like Canada's, one that includes Aboriginal nations and French Canadians, can successfully combine a weak sense of national unity with a strong level of resilience and stability.[14] Differing perspectives and approaches confirm that there is no sole universal, coherent, and stable Canadian "identity" subscribed to by Canadians. They have always had multiple identifications and loyalties, even when Canada was less culturally pluralistic. Nevertheless, they have to date managed to live peaceably, both together and apart.

Some describe and defend what they see as Canada's "discursive" political culture. Simone Chambers and Jeremy Webber refer to a Canadian "conversation."[15] Webber is a passionately irrepressible patriotic booster: "What makes up the soul of our identity as Canadians – is the conversation we have had in this rich and magnificent land."[16] Chambers, citing the highly charged language issue in Quebec, writes of how continuous dialogue in a context of mutual respect among participants led to reasonably legitimate outcomes and social peace.[17] Her account, which appeared in the mid-1990s, was undercut by the deeply divisive referendum on Quebec's sovereignty. Her presumption was of an existing sense of common community. It may be, however, that the development of a strengthened sense of English Canadian nationhood and partnership or genuine conversation with French Quebec requires divorce. "In order to create a real sense of community between Canada and Québec," write Louis Imbeau and Guy Laforest, "Canada will have to think of itself without Quebec."[18]

When he was prime minister, Paul Martin mused about "exporting" Canadian values, and commented that "the world needs more Canada."[19] Many Canadians think their values serve as a lodestar or exemplar for others. Intellectuals such as Saul and Kymlicka depict Canada as a model of a tolerant, democratic, and egalitarian society in a cosmopolitan, peaceable, and multicultural setting. From this perspective, Canada projects "soft power" – the power of its values and practices – as opposed to the "hard" power of economic sanctions and military might. Many Canadians, who style themselves as peacekeepers and honest, impartial brokers on the world stage, are attracted to this idea. This attitude has elements of national-centric pretense and sermonizing. It hints at conceit and hubris, which are not virtues associated with paragons. Canada commands some respect abroad because it lacks both an imperial history (save as a colony itself) and imperial ambitions, and because its institutions deliver and sustain a high quality of life in an open and relatively egalitarian political society. Canada is a country settled and built by immigrants, one finding its footing in today's rapidly changing environment of globalized communications networks and liberalized trade in goods and services. Thus, the rhetoric of exporting values begs a question: What values are Canadians prepared to import from other cultures? Can Canadians make so bold as to be critical of others – whether Americans or Iranians – who may wish to export their values too, also thinking them a gift to others? The political culture of Canadians lies only partly in what they say or the values they preach: more importantly, it encompasses and expresses what they do and how their country works.

The point of a book is defeated, and any conclusion is a failure, unless it strives to learn from the history it presents and the method it deploys. My crafted excavation of Canadian political culture suggests two countervailing tendencies or thrusts. From today's vantage point, notwithstanding my peering through a historical lens at the diverse ideological baggage and aspirations of distinct waves of immigration, modern Canadians seem more alike in their tastes. They share more in common as they intermarry, often relocate for employment, travel more frequently across the country, watch the same television programs, and appear more fickle in their federal partisan preferences than in the past. From the perspective of politics in Canada's regions, however, the opposite appears to be happening. Long-established ideological and partisan fissures have taken hold. Atlantic Canadian political culture, for example, despite its steadily proceeding transformation, continues to exhibit more traditional and staid features than that of the Far West. Within the politically propulsive Far West, however, Alberta's politics of consensus and suspicion of federal power hold as much sway today as they did almost a century ago. In British Columbia, ideological polarization is no less muted than in the past. Ontario, as English Canada's cultural hegemon, is no less moderate in its political sensibilities – compared to East and West – than in the past. Nor are its politics and people any less preoccupied with English Canada's relationship to the United States. It is only in Quebec that a political cultural revolution, however quiet, took hold.

This book has traced the unfolding of Canadian political culture through the prism of ideologically identifiable and distinct immigrant waves, and has highlighted them in their regional settings. This book's story suggests that current debates regarding national identity and purpose are best understood through an appreciation of what informs the dramatic variations in regional traditions and the competing visions they engender. The upshot of normative philosophical and institutional debates regarding the parameters of individual and group rights and the transformation of governmental structures is never wholly predictable. However, such debates become more manageable in the context of knowing and being sensitive to, to use the vernacular, "where people are coming from." On one level, this phrase refers to the abstract formulations that respond to contemporary conditions and concerns. Equally important to its meaning are the experiential legacies that Canadians derive from their places of origin, as well as from those of their forebears and the conditions of their departure. This meaning vitally informs their abstractions and aspirations. In many respects, Canadians and the regions they live in have grown increasingly alike; in other respects, they have moved further apart. The dualistic paradox that revisits Canada's periodic debates regarding national unity is that seeking to foster a heightened sense of togetherness unleashes the forces of further dissension.

Notes

INTRODUCTION

1 Michael Adams, *Sex in the Snow: Canadian Social Values at the End of the Millennium* (Toronto: Viking, 1997), and *Fire and Ice: The United States, Canada and the Myth of Converging Values* (Toronto: Penguin, 2003).

2 See, for example, the debate between Paul Nesbitt-Larking, "Canadian Political Culture: The Problem of Americanization," and Anthony A. Peacock, "Socialism and Nationalism: Why the Alleged Americanization of Canadian Political Culture Is a Fraud," in Mark Charlton and Paul Barker, eds., *Crosscurrents: Contemporary Political Issues*, 5th ed. (Toronto: Thomson Nelson, 2006), 4-22 and 23-35.

3 Christopher Dunn, "Comparative Provincial Politics: A Review," in Keith Brownsey and Michael Howlett, eds., *The Provincial State in Canada* (Peterborough: Broadview, 2001), 441.

4 Most notably David J. Elkins and Richard Simeon, eds., *Small Worlds: Provinces and Parties in Canadian Political Life* (Toronto: Methuen, 1980).

5 Ailsa Henderson, "Regional Political Cultures in Canada," *Canadian Journal of Political Science* 37, 3 (September 2004): 595-615.

6 William M. Reisinger, "The Renaissance of a Rubric: Political Culture as Concept and Theory," *International Journal of Public Opinion Research* 7, 4 (1995): 328-52.

7 Alan Cairns, "The Electoral System and the Party System in Canada, 1921-1965," *Canadian Journal of Political Science* 1, 1 (March 1968): 55-80.

8 Nelson Wiseman, "Cairns Revisited – The Electoral System and the Party System in Canada," in Paul W. Fox and Graham White, eds., *Politics: Canada*, 7th ed. (Toronto: McGraw-Hill Ryerson, 1991), 265-74.

9 Nelson Wiseman, "The Pattern of Prairie Politics," in Hugh G. Thorburn and Alan Whitehorn, eds., *Party Politics in Canada*, 8th ed. (Toronto: Prentice-Hall, 2001), 351-68; "Provincial Political Cultures," in Christopher Dunn, ed., *Provinces: Canadian Provincial Politics* (Peterborough: Broadview, 1996), 21-62; and "A Note on Hartz-Horowitz at Twenty: The Case of French Canada," *Canadian Journal of Political Science* 21, 4 (December 1988): 795-806.

10　Alain-G. Gagnon and James P. Bickerton, eds., *Canadian Politics*, 1st ed. (Peterborough: Broadview, 1990), Bickerton and Gagnon, 2nd and 4th eds. (1994, 2004).

11　Louis Hartz et al., *The Founding of New Societies* (New York: Harcourt, Brace, and World, 1964).

12　Gad Horowitz, "Conservatism, Liberalism, and Socialism in Canada: An Interpretation," *Canadian Journal of Economics and Political Science* 32, 1 (1966): 143-71.

13　Louis Hartz, *The Liberal Tradition in America* (New York: Harcourt Brace, 1955).

14　Alan C. Cairns, "Political Science, Ethnicity and the Canadian Constitution," in David P. Shugarman and Reg Whitaker, eds., *Federalism and Political Community* (Peterborough: Broadview, 1989), 117.

15　Nelson Wiseman, "The Folly of Constitutional Reform," in J.L. Granatstein and Kenneth McNaught, eds., *"English Canada" Speaks Out* (Toronto: Doubleday, 1991), 54-66.

16　Gerald Friesen, *The Canadian Prairies: A History* (Toronto: University of Toronto Press, 1984).

17　Nelson Wiseman, *Social Democracy in Manitoba: A Political History of the CCF-NDP* (Winnipeg: University of Manitoba Press, 1983).

18　John Porter, *The Vertical Mosaic* (Toronto: University of Toronto Press, 1965), 382.

CHAPTER 1: PATHWAYS TO CANADIAN POLITICAL CULTURE

1　Gabriel A. Almond, "Comparative Political Systems," *Journal of Politics* 18 (1956): 391-409.

2　Alexis de Tocqueville, *Democracy in America*, 2 vols. (1835 and 1840; repr., New York: Vantage Books, 1990).

3　André Siegfried, *The Race Question in Canada* (orig. pub. 1906, 1st English trans. 1907; repr., Toronto: McClelland and Stewart, 1966).

4　Colin Campbell and William Christian, *Parties, Leaders, and Ideologies in Canada* (Toronto: McGraw-Hill Ryerson, 1996), 12-13.

5　Seymour Martin Lipset, *Agrarian Socialism: The Co-operative Commonwealth Federation in Saskatchewan* (1950; repr., Garden City, NY: Doubleday, 1968), 64, 84-90, 90-103; "Producer Vote Supports Single-Desk Sale of Barley," *Agrivision* (Ottawa: Agriculture and Agri-Food Canada, April 1997); "One Vote Could Decide Barley Marketing," *Agriweek*, 11 November 1997, 1; William Kirby Rolph, *Henry Wise Wood of Alberta* (Toronto: University of Toronto Press, 1950), 195.

6　Carl Berger, *The Writing of Canadian History: Aspects of English-Canadian Historical Writing 1900-1970* (Toronto: Oxford University Press, 1976), and Edward Hallett Carr, *What Is History?* (New York: Vintage Books, 1961).

7　Seymour Martin Lipset, *Political Man: The Social Bases of Politics* (Baltimore: Johns Hopkins University Press, 1981), 282-86.

8　David V.J. Bell, *The Roots of Disunity: A Study of Canadian Political Culture* (Toronto: Oxford University Press, 1992), 16-20.

9 Louis Hartz, *The Liberal Tradition in America* (New York: Harcourt Brace, 1955).

10 Louis Hartz et al., *The Founding of New Societies* (New York: Harcourt, Brace, and World, 1964).

11 Hartz, *The Liberal Tradition*, 3.

12 Robert L. Stanfield, "Conservative Principles and Philosophy," in Paul Fox and Graham White, eds., *Politics: Canada*, 8th ed. (Toronto: McGraw-Hill Primus, 1995), 307-11.

13 Karl Marx and Friedrich Engels, *Selected Correspondence* (New York: International Publishers, 1942), 466-68.

14 Samuel H. Beer, *British Politics in the Collectivist Age* (New York: Alfred A. Knopf, 1965).

15 Kenneth D. McRae, "The Structure of Canadian History," in Hartz et al., *The Founding of New Societies*, chap. 7.

16 Gad Horowitz, "Conservatism, Liberalism, and Socialism in Canada: An Interpretation," *Canadian Journal of Economics and Political Science* 32, 1 (1966): 143-71.

17 Rod Preece, "The Myth of the Red Tory," *Canadian Journal of Social and Political Theory* 1 (1977): 3-28.

18 Tom Truman, "A Scale for Measuring a Tory Streak in Canada and the United States," *Canadian Journal of Political Science* 10 (1977): 597-614.

19 Richard J. Van Loon and Michael S. Whittington, *The Canadian Political System: Environment, Structure and Process* (Toronto: McGraw-Hill, 1971), 275-76.

20 H.D. Forbes, "Hartz-Horowitz at Twenty: Nationalism, Toryism, and Socialism in Canada and the United States," *Canadian Journal of Political Science* 20 (1987): 287-315.

21 Janet Ajzenstat and Peter J. Smith, "The 'Tory Touch' Thesis: Poor History, Bad Political Science," in Mark Charlton and Paul Barker, eds., *Crosscurrents: Contemporary Political Issues*, 3rd ed. (Toronto: ITP Nelson, 1998), 84-91. The book is Janet Ajzenstat and Peter J. Smith, eds., *Canada's Origins: Liberal, Tory, or Republican?* (Ottawa: Carleton University Press, 1995).

22 Elizabeth Mancke, "Early Modern Imperial Governance and the Origins of Canadian Political Culture," *Canadian Journal of Political Science* 32 (1999): 3-20.

23 John McMenemy, *The Language of Canadian Politics: A Guide to Important Terms and Concepts*, rev. ed. (Waterloo: Wilfrid Laurier University Press, 1995), 249.

24 George Grant, *Lament for a Nation: The Defeat of Canadian Nationalism* (Toronto: McClelland and Stewart, 1965), and W.L. Morton, *The Canadian Identity* (Toronto: University of Toronto Press, 1961).

25 Gad Horowitz, *Canadian Labour in Politics* (Toronto: University of Toronto Press, 1968). See Frank Milligan, *Eugene A. Forsey: An Intellectual Biography* (Calgary: University of Calgary Press, 2004).

26 Gad Horowitz, "Tories, Socialists, and the Demise of Canada," *Canadian Dimension* 2, 4 (May-June 1965): 12-15.

27   Hugh G. Thorburn, ed. *Party Politics in Canada*, 4th ed. (Scarborough: Prentice-Hall, 1979).

28   Lipset, *Agrarian Socialism*, xi, xxv.

29   Seymour Martin Lipset, *Revolution and Counterrevolution* (New York: Basic Books, 1968).

30   Seymour Martin Lipset, "Value Differences, Absolute or Relative: the English Speaking Democracies," in *The First New Nation: The United States in Historical Comparative Perspective* (Garden City, NY: Basic Books, 1967), 240-42, 284-85.

31   Edgar Z. Friedenberg, *Deference to Authority* (White Plains, NY: M.E. Sharpe, 1980).

32   Seymour Martin Lipset, *Continental Divide: Values and Institutions in Canada and the United States* (New York: Routledge, 1990).

33   Seymour Martin Lipset, "Historical Traditions and National Characteristics: A Comparative Analysis of Canada and the United States," *Canadian Journal of Sociology* 11 (1986): 113.

34   David J. Elkins and Richard Simeon, *Small Worlds: Provinces and Parties in Canadian Political Life* (Toronto: Methuen, 1980).

35   Norman Frohlich and Joe A. Oppenheimer, *Modern Political Economy* (Englewood Cliffs, NJ: Prentice-Hall, 1978).

36   Kenneth J. Arrow, *Social Change and Individual Values* (New York: John Wiley and Sons, 1951).

37   Arthur K. Davis, "Canadian Society and History as Hinterland versus Metropolis," in Richard J. Ossenberg ed., *Canadian Society: Pluralism, Change and Conflict* (Scarborough: Prentice Hall, 1971), and Ralph Matthews, *The Creation of Regional Dependency* (Toronto: University of Toronto Press, 1983).

38   M.H. Watkins, "A Staple Theory of Economic Growth," *Canadian Journal of Economics and Political Science* 29 (May 1963): 141-58.

39   Statistics Canada, *Farm Cash Receipts from Farming Operations – 1993*, cat. no. 21-603E (May 1994), reproduced in Rand Dyck, *Provincial Politics in Canada: Towards the Turn of the Century*, 3rd ed. (Scarborough: Prentice-Hall, 1996), table 13.6, 660-61; table 13.15, 668.

40   Harold A. Innis, *The Fur Trade in Canada: An Introduction to Canadian Economic History*, rev. ed. (Toronto: University of Toronto Press, 1999).

41   Quoted in Ian Parker, "Harold Innis, Karl Marx and Canadian Political Economy," in J. Paul Grayson, ed., *Class, State, Ideology and Change: Marxist Perspectives on Canada* (Toronto: Holt, Rinehart and Winston, 1980), 362.

42   Robert J. Brym, "Political Conservatism in Atlantic Canada," in Robert J. Brym and R. James Sacouman, eds., *Underdevelopment and Social Movements in Atlantic Canada* (Toronto: New Hogtown Press, 1979), 65-66.

43   H.C. Pentland, "The Development of a Capitalistic Labour Market in Canada," *Canadian Journal of Economics and Political Science* 25, 4 (November 1959): 450-61.

44 Margaret Ells, "Loyalist Attitudes," in G.A. Rawlyk, ed., *Historical Essays on the Atlantic Provinces* (Toronto: McClelland and Stewart, 1967).
45 McRae, "The Structure of Canadian History," 245.

CHAPTER 2: SURVEYING AND COMPARING POLITICAL CULTURES
1 Heinz Eulau, *The Behavioral Persuasion in Politics* (New York: Random House, 1963).
2 Martin Goldfarb, "Polls and Pollsters in Canadian Politics," in Hugh G. Thorburn, ed., *Party Politics in Canada*, 6th ed. (Scarborough: Prentice-Hall, 1991), chap. 4.
3 Burns W. Roper, "Are Polls Accurate?" *Annals of the American Academy* 472 (March 1984): 24-34.
4 William Mishler, *Political Participation in Canada* (Toronto: Macmillan, 1979), table 3.4, 57.
5 Gabriel A. Almond, "Foreword," in Richard J. Ellis and Michael Thompson, eds., *Culture Matters: Essays in Honor of Aaron Wildavsky* (Boulder: Westview Press, 1997), ix.
6 Alan C. Cairns, "Alternative Styles in the Study of Canadian Politics," *Canadian Journal of Political Science* 7, 1 (March 1974): 126.
7 Angus Campbell et al., *The American Voter* (1960; repr., Chicago: University of Chicago Press, 1976).
8 Gabriel A. Almond and Sidney Verba, *The Civic Culture: Political Attitudes and Democracy in Five Nations* (Princeton: Princeton University Press, 1963).
9 Edgar Z. Friedenberg, *Deference to Authority: The Case of Canada* (White Plains, NY: M.E. Sharpe, 1980).
10 Neil Nevitte, *The Decline of Deference: Canadian Value Change in Cross-National Perspective* (Peterborough: Broadview, 1996).
11 John Bartlett Brebner, *North Atlantic Triangle: The Interplay of Canada, the United States and Great Britain* (Toronto: McClelland and Stewart, 1966).
12 Frank H. Underhill, *Canadian Political Parties* (Ottawa: Canadian Historical Association, 1970).
13 National Geographic Society, *Atlas of the World*, 5th ed. (Washington, DC: National Geographic Society, 1981), 310.
14 George Lichtheim, *The Concept of Ideology and Other Essays* (New York: Vintage Books, 1967), 4-7.
15 J.A. Laponce, *Left and Right: The Topography of Political Perceptions* (Toronto: University of Toronto Press, 1981), 47.
16 John Meisel, *Working Papers on Canadian Politics* (Montreal and London: McGill-Queen's University Press, 1972), 83.
17 Neil Nevitte and Roger Gibbins, *New Elites in Old States: Ideologies in the Anglo-American Democracies* (Toronto: Oxford University Press, 1990).
18 Nevitte, *The Decline of Deference*.

19   Ronald Inglehart, "The Silent Revolution in Europe: Intergenerational Change in Post-industrial Societies," *American Political Science Review* 65 (1971): 991-1017, and *Culture Shift in Advanced Industrial Society* (Princeton: Princeton University Press, 1990).

20   Nevitte, *The Decline of Deference,* table 2-3, 34; 71.

21   Ibid., figure 2-7, 38.

22   Ibid., figure 2-4, 40.

23   Ibid., 41.

24   Ibid., 20. Emphasis in original.

25   Ibid., 42.

26   Giacomi Sani, "The Political Culture of Italy: Continuity and Change," in Gabriel A. Almond and Sidney Verba, eds., *The Civic Culture Revisited* (Boston: Little, Brown, 1980), 274.

27   Ibid., 288.

28   Ann L. Craig and Wayne A. Cornelius, "Political Culture in Mexico: Continuities and Revisionist Interpretations," in Almond and Verba, *The Civic Culture Revisited,* 331.

29   Richard Simeon and David J. Elkins, "Provincial Political Cultures in Canada," in David J. Elkins and Richard Simeon, eds., *Small Worlds: Provinces and Parties in Canadian Political Life* (Toronto: Methuen, 1980), 31-76.

30   Canada Council, *Seventeenth Annual Report, 1973-74* (Ottawa: Canada Council, 1974), 114, 116.

31   John C. Courtney, Karman B. Kawchuk, and Duff Spafford, "Life in Print: Citation of Articles Published in Volumes 1-10 of the *Canadian Journal of Political Science/Revue canadienne de science politique,*" *Canadian Journal of Political Science* 20, 3 (September 1987): table 8, 634, and Richard Simeon and David J. Elkins, "Regional Political Cultures in Canada," *Canadian Journal of Political Science* 7, 3 (September 1974): 397-437.

32   Rand Dyck, *Provincial Politics in Canada,* 2nd ed. (Scarborough: Prentice-Hall, 1991).

33   Simeon and Elkins, "Provincial Political Cultures in Canada," 40.

34   Seymour Martin Lipset and William Schneider, *The Confidence Gap* (New York: Free Press, 1983), figure 1-1, 17.

35   Ian Stewart, *Roasting Chestnuts: The Mythology of Maritime Political Culture* (Vancouver: UBC Press, 1994), chap. 2.

36   Simeon and Elkins, "Provincial Political Cultures in Canada," table 3, 41.

37   Allan Kornberg, William Mishler, and Harold D. Clarke, *Representative Democracy in the Canadian Provinces* (Scarborough: Prentice-Hall, 1982), 88.

38   Michael D. Ornstein, "Regional Politics and Ideologies," in Robert J. Brym, ed., *Regionalism in Canada* (Toronto: Irwin, 1986), 47-87.

39 Michael D. Ornstein and H. Michael Stevenson, *Politics and Ideology in Canada* (Montreal and Kingston: McGill-Queen's University Press, 1999), 184.

40 Statistics Canada, *Provincial Economic Accounts* (Ottawa: Minister of Industry, Science and Technology, 1992), xii.

41 Ornstein, "Regional Politics and Ideologies," table 2, 67.

42 Simeon and Elkins, "Provincial Political Cultures in Canada," table 11, 53.

43 Stewart, *Roasting Chestnuts*, figures 1, 2, and 3, 17-18.

44 Ornstein, "Regional Politics and Ideologies," 78.

45 Ibid., 79.

46 Mishler, *Political Participation in Canada*, chap. 5, and Lester W. Milbrath, *Political Participation: How and Why Do People Get Involved in Politics?* (Chicago: Rand McNally, 1965), chap. 5.

47 Paul Howe and David Northrup, *Strengthening Canadian Democracy: The Views of Canadians*, Policy Matters 1, 5 (Montreal: Institute for Research on Public Policy, July 2000), tables 1, 2, and 3, 57-59.

48 Ian Stewart, "More than Just a Line on the Map: The Political Culture of the Nova Scotia – New Brunswick Boundary," *Publius* 20 (Winter 1990): 99.

CHAPTER 3: CONSTITUTIONS AND INSTITUTIONS AS CULTURE

1 William E. Conklin, *Images of a Constitution* (Toronto: University of Toronto Press, 1989), 3.

2 Brian Barry, *Sociologists, Economists, and Democracy* (London: Collier-Macmillan, 1970).

3 Vincent Ostrom and Elinor Ostrom, "Cultures: Frameworks, Theories, and Models," in Richard J. Ellis and Michael Thompson, eds., *Culture Matters: Essays in Honor of Aaron Wildavsky* (Boulder: Westview Press, 1997), 83.

4 James Eayers, *In Defence of Canada: From the Great War to the Great Depression* (Toronto: University of Toronto Press, 1964), 71.

5 A.E. Safarian, *Foreign Ownership of Canadian Industry* (Toronto: University of Toronto Press, 1973), 71.

6 Quoted in Edgar McInnis, *The Commonwealth Today* (Sackville, NB: Mount Allison University Publications, 1959), 7.

7 Constitution Act, 1867.

8 Peter H. Russell, Rainer Knopff, and Ted Morton, *Federalism and the Charter: Leading Constitutional Decisions* (Ottawa: Carleton University Press, 1989), 4.

9 *Singh v. Minister of Employment and Immigration* (1985), 17 D.L.R. (4th) 422, and *Hunter v. Southam Inc.* (1984), 11 D.L.R. (4th) 641.

10 Constitution Act, 1982, s. 2(a).

11 Ibid., ss. 8, 10(b), and 12.

12   *Reference re Secession of Quebec,* [1998] 2 S.C.R. 217. See http://132.204.132.231/
      quebec/en/renvoi.en.html.
13   Constitution Act, 1982, s. 52.
14   Andrew Heard, *Canadian Constitutional Conventions: The Marriage of Law and Pol-
      itics* (Toronto: Oxford University Press, 1991).
15   Supreme Court of Canada, *Re Constitution of Canada* (1981), 125 D.L.R. (3rd) 1.
16   *Debates of the House of Commons* (6 April 1989), 153. Mulroney was referring to
      the power of governments to invoke s. 33 of the Charter to override certain rights.
17   Peter H. Russell, *Constitutional Odyssey: Can Canadians Become a Sovereign People?*
      3rd ed. (Toronto: University of Toronto Press, 2004).
18   Quebec, *Rapport de la Commission royale d'enquête sur les problèmes constitutionnels*
      (Quebec: Province du Québec, 1956).
19   Constitution Act, 1982, s. 59.
20   *Constitution Amendment Proclamation, 1983,* SI/84-102. The Constitutional Accord
      on Aboriginal Rights is in David Milne, *The Canadian Constitution: The Players and
      the Issues in the Process that Has Led from Patriation to Meech Lake to an Uncertain
      Future* (Toronto: James Lorimer, 1991), 333-38.
21   Alan C. Cairns, *Citizens Plus: Aboriginal Peoples and the Canadian State* (Vancouver:
      UBC Press, 2000).
22   J.R. Mallory, *The Structure of Canadian Government* (Toronto: Gage, 1984), 4-6.
23   John Ralston Saul, *Reflections of a Siamese Twin: Canada at the End of the Twentieth
      Century* (Toronto: Viking, 1997), 130, 137, 175, 177, 182-83.
24   David Docherty, *Legislatures* (Vancouver: UBC Press, 2004), and Graham White,
      Cabinets and First Ministers (Vancouver: UBC Press, 2005).
25   Donald J. Savoie, *Governing from the Centre: The Concentration of Power in Canadian
      Politics* (Toronto: University of Toronto Press, 1999).
26   Charlottetown Accord, Draft Legal Text, 9 October 1992, http://www.solon.org/
      Constitutions/Canada/English/Proposals/CharlottetownLegalDraft.html.
27   David E. Smith, *The Invisible Crown: The First Principle of Canadian Government*
      (Toronto: University of Toronto Press, 1995).
28   Graham Fraser, "We Want to Keep Monarchy," *Toronto Star,* 31 May 2002, A16.
29   Ibid.
30   W.L. Morton, *The Canadian Identity* (Toronto: University of Toronto Press, 1962),
      84-85.
31   *Liquidators of the Maritime Bank v. Receiver General of N.B.* (1892), A.C. 437, and
      Attorney General for Ontario v. Attorney General for Canada (1896), A.C. 348.
32   J.E. Hodgetts, "Implicit Values in the Administration of Public Affairs," in Kenneth
      Kernaghan, ed., *Canadian Public Administration: Administration and Profession* (To-
      ronto: Butterworth's, 1983), 472.
33   Ronald I. Cheffins and Patricia A. Johnson, *The Revised Canadian Constitution:
      Politics as Law* (Toronto: McGraw-Hill Ryerson, 1986), 36.

34   Garth Stevenson, *Unfulfilled Union: Canadian Federalism and National Unity*, 4th ed. (Montreal and Kingston: McGill-Queen's University Press, 2004).

35   Alan Cairns, "The Living Canadian Constitution," *Queen's Quarterly* 77, 4 (Winter 1970): 483-98.

36   Jennifer Smith, *Federalism* (Vancouver: UBC Press, 2004).

37   Gary Levy and Graham White, eds., *Provincial and Territorial Legislatures in Canada* (Toronto: University of Toronto Press, 1989).

38   Graham White, "Big Is Different from Little: On Taking Size Seriously in the Analysis of Canadian Governmental Institutions," *Canadian Public Administration* 33 (1990): 527-34.

39   Michael Ignatieff, *The Rights Revolution* (Toronto: Anansi, 2000).

40   Peter W. Hogg and Allison A. Bushell, "The *Charter* Dialogue between Courts and Legislatures (Or Perhaps the *Charter of Rights* Isn't Such a Bad Thing After All)," *Osgoode Hall Law Journal* 35 (1997): 75-123.

41   Kent Roach, *The Supreme Court on Trial: Judicial Activism or Democratic Dialogue?* (Toronto: Irwin Law, 2001), 13.

42   Constitution Act, 1867, s. 92(13) and (16).

43   Avigail I. Eisenberg, "Justice and Human Rights in the Provinces," in Christopher Dunn, ed., *Provinces: Canadian Provincial Politics* (Peterborough: Broadview, 1996), chap. 18.

44   *Vriend v. Alberta (A.G.)*, [1998] 1 S.C.R. 493.

45   F.L. Morton and Rainer Knopff, *The Charter Revolution and the Court Party* (Peterborough: Broadview, 2000).

46   Joseph F. Fletcher and Paul Howe, "Canadian Attitudes toward the Charter and the Courts in Comparative Perspective," *Choices* 3, 3 (May 2002): 4-29, and "Support for Charter Runs Strong: Survey," *Toronto Star*, 12 April 2002.

47   "Support for Charter," and Fletcher and Howe, "Canadian Attitudes," figure 13, 18.

48   Peter H. Russell, "The Political Purposes of the Canadian Charter of Rights and Freedoms," *Canadian Bar Review* 61, 1 (March 1983): 30-54.

49   Richard Vengroff and F.L. Morton, "Regional Perspectives on Canada's Charter of Rights and Freedoms: A Re-examination of Democratic Elitism," *Canadian Journal of Political Science* 33, 2 (June 2000): 380.

50   Kenneth McRoberts, "Separate Agendas: English Canada and Quebec," *Quebec Studies* 13 (Fall 1991-Spring 1992): 4.

51   Peter H. Russell, *The Judiciary in Canada: The Third Branch of Government* (Toronto: McGraw-Hill Ryerson, 1987), 304.

52   F.L. Morton and Michael J. Withey, "Charting the Charter, 1982-1985: A Statistical Analysis" (paper presented at the annual meeting of the Canadian Political Science Association, Winnipeg, 6-8 June 1986), 11.

53   Philip G. Lister, "Criminal Trends in Appellate Courts of Canada," *Chitty's Law Journal* 23 (1975): 84.

54   *Singh v. Minister of Employment and Immigration* (1985), 17 D.L.R. (4th) 469.

55   *R. v. Askov* (1990), 2 S.C.R. 1199.

56   *Auton v. British Columbia* (9 October 2002), CA027600 (B.C.C.A.), and *Chaoulli v. Quebec (Attorney General)*, [2005] 1 S.C.R. 791.

57   *Federal-Provincial Conference of First Ministers on the Constitution, Verbatim Transcript*, Ottawa, 8-13 September 1980 (Ottawa: Canadian Intergovernmental Conference Secretariat, n.d.), and Roy Romanow, "Shortcomings and Dangers in the Charter," in Paul W. Fox and Graham White, eds., *Politics: Canada*, 7th ed. (Toronto: McGraw-Hill Ryerson, 1991), 79-83.

58   Raymond Bazowski and Robert MacDermid, "Constitutional Imaginings and the Nation-State," *American Review of Canadian Studies* 27, 2 (Summer 1997): 221-52.

59   Peter McCormick, *Supreme at Last: The Evolution of the Supreme Court of Canada* (Toronto: James Lorimer, 2000), 116, 139.

60   Pierre Elliott Trudeau, *A Mess That Deserves a Big "No"* (Toronto: Robert Davies, 1993), 11-12.

61   David Milne, *The Canadian Constitution* (Toronto: James Lorimer, 1991), chap. 5, and Roy Romanow, John Whyte, and Howard Leeson, *Canada ... Notwithstanding* (Toronto: Carswell/Methuen, 1984).

62   Tsvi Kahana, "The Notwithstanding Mechanism and Public Discussion: Lessons from the Ignored Practice of Section 33 of the Charter," *Canadian Public Administration* 44, 3 (2001): 255-91.

63   "Manley Dismisses Monarchy as Queen Begins 12-day Trip," *Toronto Globe and Mail*, 5 October 2002.

64   Strategic Counsel, "Polling Results," *Toronto Globe and Mail*, 27 September 2005.

65   Donald V. Smiley, *Canada in Question: Federalism in the Eighties*, 3rd ed. (Toronto: McGraw-Hill Ryerson, 1980), 17; *Manitoba (Attorney General) v. Canada (Attorney General)*, [1981] 1 S.C.R. 876; *Dixon v. British Columbia (Attorney General)* (1986), 7 B.C.L.R. (2nd) 186.

66   John C. Courtney, *Elections* (Vancouver: UBC Press, 2004), 56.

67   Canada, *Report of the Committee on Election Expenses* (Ottawa: Queen's Printer, 1966), and the Royal Commission on Electoral Reform and Party Financing, *Reforming Electoral Democracy: Final Report* (Toronto: Dundurn Press, 1991).

68   Strategic Counsel, *A Report to the Globe and Mail and CTV: 2005 BC Election Polling Program – Wave 2* (Toronto: Strategic Counsel, May 2005), 5.

69   As an example, see most of the chapters in Paul Howe, Richard Johnston, and André Blais, eds., *Strengthening Canadian Democracy* (Montreal: Institute for Research on Public Policy, 2005).

70   Neil Nevitte et al., *Unsteady State: The 1997 Canadian Federal Election* (Toronto: Oxford University Press, 2000), figure 4.4, 55.

71   André Blais et al., *Anatomy of a Liberal Victory: Making Sense of the Vote in the 2000 Canadian Election* (Peterborough: Broadview, 2002), 46, 52-53.

72 Frank H. Underhill, *Canadian Political Parties* (Ottawa: Canadian Historical Association, 1957).

73 *Re The Initiative and Referendum Act,* [1919] A.C. 935.

74 George Grant, *Lament for a Nation* (Toronto: McClelland and Stewart, 1965).

75 Martin Robin, ed., *Canadian Provincial Politics: The Party Systems of the Ten Provinces,* 2nd ed. (Scarborough: Prentice-Hall, 1978).

76 Luc Bernier, Keith Brownsey, and Michael Howlett, eds., *Executive Styles in Canada: Cabinet Structures and Leadership Practices in Canadian Government* (Toronto: University of Toronto Press, 2005), chaps. 6 and 10.

77 Harold D. Clarke et al., *Absent Mandate,* 3rd ed. (Toronto: Gage, 1996).

78 Nevitte et al., *Unsteady State,* 68.

79 Blais et al., *Anatomy of a Liberal Victory,* 117-18.

80 Ibid., table 6.1, 92, and Elisabeth Gidengil and Neil Nevitte, "Something Old, Something New: Preliminary Findings of the 2004 Canadian Election Study" (seminar presentation at the Department of Political Science, University of Toronto, 22 October 2004).

81 Lisa Young and Joanna Everitt, *Advocacy Groups* (Vancouver: UBC Press, 2004).

82 Leslie Pal, *Interests of State: The Politics of Language, Multiculturalism and Feminism in Canada* (Montreal and Kingston: McGill-Queen's University Press, 1993).

83 Benjamin Cashore, "Flights of the Phoenix: Explaining the Durability of the Canada-US Software Lumber Dispute," *Canadian-American Public Policy* 32 (December 1997): 1-63.

84 Fred Thompson and W.T. Stanbury, "The Political Economy of Interest Groups in the Legislative Process in Canada," in Richard Schultz, Orest M. Kruhlak, and John C. Terry, eds., *The Canadian Political Process,* 3rd ed. (Toronto: Holt, Rinehart and Winston, 1979), 234.

85 Robert Presthus, *Elite Accommodation in Canadian Politics* (Toronto: Macmillan, 1975).

86 John Douglas, "Court to decide bilingualism rules," *Winnipeg Free Press,* 8 December 1990, 8.

87 Ekos Research Associates, "Rethinking Government," July 1999.

CHAPTER 4: CULTURE, BICULTURE, MULTICULTURE, ABORIGINAL CULTURE

1 Canada Council, *Thirty-Fourth Annual Report, 1990-91* (Ottawa: Canada Council, 1991), 6.

2 Auguste Comte, *The Positive Philosophy* (1855; repr., New York: AMS Press, 1974).

3 Anthony Downs, *An Economic Theory of Democracy* (New York: Harper, 1965).

4 Karl W. Deutsch, *Nationalism and Social Communication* (Chicago: MIT Press, 1966).

5 Karl W. Deutsch, *Tides among Nations* (New York: Free Press, 1979), 302.

6 Louis Balthazar, "The Faces of Québec Nationalism," in Alain-G. Gagnon, ed., *Quebec: State and Society,* 2nd ed. (Scarborough: Nelson Canada, 1993), 8.

7   Frank Underhill, *In Search of Canadian Liberalism* (Toronto: Macmillan, 1960), 222.

8   S. Delbert Clark, "The Importance of Anti-Americanism in Canadian National Feeling," in H.F. Angus, ed., *Canada and Her Great Neighbor: Sociological Surveys of Opinions and Attitudes in Canada Concerning the United States* (Toronto: Ryerson Press, 1939), 243-45, and Seymour Martin Lipset, "Historical Tradition and National Characteristics: A Comparative Analysis of Canada and the United States," *Canadian Journal of Sociology* 11, 2 (Summer 1987): 113-55.

9   Margaret Atwood, *Survival* (Toronto: Anansi, 1972).

10 Murray Campbell, "What We're Really Like," *Toronto Globe and Mail*, 28 December 2002.

11 J.L. Granatstein et al., *Twentieth Century Canada*, 2nd ed. (Toronto: McGraw-Hill Ryerson, 1986), 389.

12 A.R.M. Lower, *Colony to Nation*, 5th ed. (Toronto: McClelland and Stewart, 1977).

13 Donald Smiley, "Reflections on Cultural Nationhood and Political Community in Canada," in R. Kenneth Carty and W. Peter Ward, eds., *Entering the Eighties: Canada in Crisis* (Toronto: Oxford University Press, 1980), 28.

14 Carl Berger, *The Writing of Canadian History: Aspects of English-Canadian Historical Writing 1900-1970* (Toronto: Oxford University Press, 1976), 54.

15 W.S. Wallace, "The Growth of Canadian National Feeling," *Canadian Historical Review* 1 (June 1920): 138.

16 Quoted in Berger, *The Writing of Canadian History*, 206.

17 Quoted in Chris Dafoe, "A Tale of Two Culture Ministers," *Toronto Globe and Mail*, 25 January 1992, C7.

18 Canada, *Shaping Canada's Future Together: Proposals* (Ottawa: Supply and Services Canada: 1991), 35.

19 *La Politique québécoise du développement culturel* (Quebec: Ministère d'État au développement culturel, 1978).

20 For the many areas administered by PEI's Department of Community and Cultural Affairs, see its website at http://www.gov.pe.ca/commcul/index.ph3.

21 Ontario Ministry of Culture and Communications, *Annual Report, 1988-89* (Toronto: Ministry of Culture and Communications, 1988), 13-17, and *Annual Report, 1990-91* (Toronto: Ministry of Culture and Communications, 1991), 16.

22 Quoted in "End Official Bilingualism," *Toronto Globe and Mail*, 10 January 1992, A1-A2.

23 Frank H. Underhill, introduction to André Siegfried, *The Race Question in Canada* (1st English trans. 1907; repr., Toronto: McClelland and Stewart, 1966), 1.

24 Ian Greene, *The Charter of Rights* (Toronto: James Lorimer, 1989), 198.

25 W.L. Morton, *Manitoba: A History*, 2nd ed. (Toronto: University of Toronto Press, 1967), 160, 177, 192, and Gerald Friesen, *The Canadian Prairies: A History* (Toronto: University of Toronto Press, 1984), 196.

26   A.I. Silver, *The French-Canadian Idea of Confederation, 1864-1900* (Toronto: University of Toronto Press, 1982), 84, 106, 147.

27   Nelson Wiseman, "The Questionable Relevance of the Constitution in Advancing Minority Cultural Rights in Manitoba," *Canadian Journal of Political Science* 25, 4 (December 1992): 697-721.

28   Dominion Bureau of Statistics, *Canada Year Book, 1967* (Ottawa: Minister of Trade and Commerce, 1967), tables 14, 18, and 19, 197-200.

29   Everett C. Hughes, *French Canada in Transition* (Chicago: University of Chicago Press, 1943).

30   Michael O'Keefe, *Francophone Minorities: Assimilation and Community Vitality*, New Canadian Perspectives (Ottawa: Minister of Public Works and Government Services Canada, 1997).

31   Parliamentary Debates on the Subject of Confederation (Quebec, 1865), 60, quoted in Mason Wade, *The French-Canadian Outlook* (Toronto: McClelland and Stewart, 1964), 42.

32   Royal Commission on Bilingualism and Biculturalism, general introduction to *The Official Languages*, book 1 of *Report of the Royal Commission on Bilingualism and Biculturalism* (Ottawa: Queen's Printer, 1967), xxxi.

33   "Francophone Hospital Wins Case against Cuts," *Toronto Globe and Mail*, 8 December 2001, A15, and Court of Appeal of Ontario, *Lalonde v. Commission de restructuration des services de santé*, 7 December 2001, docket c33807, http://accessjustice.ca/documents/lalonde.pdf.

34   "Montreal Suburbs Lose Megacity Case," *Toronto Globe and Mail*, 8 December 2001. The appealed decision is *Baie D'Urfe (Ville) c. Quebec*, Quebec Court of Appeal, 16 October 2001, [2001] J.Q. no. 4821.

35   Quoted in Jane Moss, "The Drama of Identity in Canada's Francohpone West," *American Review of Canadian Studies* 34, 1 (2004): 81.

36   Pierre Fournier, "The Future of Quebec Nationalism," in Keith Banting and Richard Simeon, eds., *And No One Cheered: Federalism, Democracy, and the Constitution Act* (Toronto: Methuen, 1983), 156.

37   Harry H. Hiller, "Dependence and Independence: Emergent Nationalism in Newfoundland," *Ethnic and Racial Studies* 10 (July 1987): 265.

38   Ross Laver, "How We Differ," *Maclean's*, 3 January 1994, 8-10, and Centre for Research and Information on Canada, *Portraits of Canada*, http://www.cric.ca/pdf/cric_poll/portraits_2005/eng_national_hl.pdf.

39   The Council for Canadian Unity, "Portraits of Canada 2000: An Analysis of the Results of CRIC's National Tracking Poll," http://www.cric.ca/pdf/cric_poll/portraits/portraits2000_poll.pdf.

40   Gordon O. Rothney, "The Denominational Basis of Representation in the Newfoundland Assembly, 1919-1962," *Canadian Journal of Economics and Political Science* 28, 4 (November 1962): 557-70.

41 "Ontario Refuses to End Catholic School Support," *Toronto Globe and Mail*, 6 November 1999.

42 Will Kymlicka, *Finding Our Way: Rethinking Ethnocultural Relations in Canada* (Toronto: Oxford University Press, 1998), 7.

43 Augie Fleras, "Multiculturalism as Society Building: Doing What Is Necessary, Workable, and Fair," in Mark Charlton and Paul Barker, eds., *Crosscurrents: Contemporary Political Issues*, 2nd ed. (Scarborough: Nelson Canada, 1994), 25-40.

44 J.S. Woodsworth, *Strangers within Our Gates* (1909; repr., Toronto: University of Toronto Press, 1972).

45 John Porter, *The Vertical Mosaic* (Toronto: University of Toronto Press, 1965).

46 Statistics Canada, "Census of Population: Immigration, Birthplace and Birthplace of Parents, Citizenship, Ethnic Origin, Visible Minorities and Aboriginal Peoples," *The Daily* cat. no. 11-001-XIE (21 January 2003), http://www.statcan.ca/Daily/English/030121/d0303121a.htm.

47 Kenneth McRoberts, *Misconceiving Canada: The Struggle for National Unity* (Toronto: Oxford University Press, 1997), chap. 5.

48 Elizabeth Wangenheim, "The Ukrainians: A Case Study of the 'Third Force,'" in Peter Russell, ed., *Nationalism in Canada* (Toronto: McGraw-Hill, 1965), 72-91.

49 For example, Neil Bissoondath, *Selling Illusions: The Cult of Multiculturalism in Canada* (Toronto: Penguin, 1994), and Reginald W. Bibby, *Mosaic Madness: The Poverty and Potential of Life in Canada* (Toronto: Stoddart, 1990).

50 Preston Manning, *The New Canada* (Toronto: Macmillan, 1992), 317.

51 Richard Ogmundson, "On the Right to Be a Canadian," in Stella Hryniuk, ed., *20 Years of Multiculturalism* (Winnipeg: St. John's College Press, 1992), 47.

52 Yasmeen Abu-Laban and Christina Gabriel, *Selling Diversity: Immigration, Multiculturalism, Employment Equity, and Globalization* (Peterborough: Broadview, 2002).

53 "Portrait of Two Nations," *Maclean's*, 3 July 1989, 48-49.

54 Daniel Francis, *National Dreams: Myth, Memory, and Canadian History* (Vancouver: Arsenal Pulp Press, 1997), 73-75.

55 Pierre Vallières, *White Niggers of America* (Toronto: McClelland and Stewart, 1971).

56 Quoted in William Johnson, "The Danger of Preaching Paranoia," *Toronto Globe and Mail*, 19 December 2002, A23.

57 Statistics Canada, 1996 Census, "Aboriginal Population by Mother Tongue Showing Knowledge of Aboriginal Languages," http://prod.library.utoronto.ca:8090/datalib/datar/cc96/nation/980113/n08_1301.ivt.

58 Kathy Brock, "Consensual Politics: Political Leadership in the Aboriginal Community," in Maureen Mancuso, Richard G. Price, and Ronald Wagenberg, eds., *Leaders and Leadership in Canada* (Toronto: Oxford University Press, 1994), 225-41.

59 Menno Boldt and J. Anthony Long, "Tribal Traditions and European-Western Political Ideologies: The Dilemma of Canada's Native Indians," *Canadian Journal of Political Science* 17, 3 (September 1984): 542.

60 Quoted in Royal Commission on Aboriginal Peoples, *Restructuring the Relationship*, vol. 2, part 1 of *Report of the Royal Commission on Aboriginal Peoples* (Ottawa: Supply and Services Canada, 1996), 109.

61 Royal Commission, *Restructuring the Relationship*, part 1, 136.

62 Graham White, "Westminster in the Arctic: The Adaptation of British Parliamentarianism in the Northwest Territories," *Canadian Journal of Political Science* 24, 3 (September 1991): 506.

63 "Bill C-23: First Nations Fiscal and Statistical Management Consultation Act Introduced in the House of Commons," http://www.parl.gc.ca/common/Bills_ls.asp?lang=E&ls=c238source=library_pub&Parl=37&Ses=3.

64 Constitution Act, 1982, s. 27.

65 Michael Asch, "The Judicial Conceptualization of Culture after *Delgamuukw* and *Van Der Peet*," *Review of Constitutional Studies* 5, 2 (2000): 120, 129.

66 Michael Asch and Patrick Macklem, "Aboriginal Rights and Canadian Sovereignty: An Essay on *R. v. Sparrow*," *Alberta Law Review* 29 (1991): 498.

67 Charles Taylor, *Reconciling the Solitudes: Essays on Canadian Federalism and Nationalism* (Montreal and Kingston: McGill-Queen's University Press, 1993); Kymlicka, *Finding Our Way*; Alan C. Cairns, *Reconfigurations: Canadian Citizenship and Constitutional Change* (Toronto: McClelland and Stewart, 1995).

68 Gerald Kernerman, *Multicultural Nationalism: Civilizing Difference, Constituting Community* (Vancouver: UBC Press, 2005).

CHAPTER 5: REGIONS AND POLITICAL CULTURE

1 Daniel Glenday, Hubert Guindon, and Allan Turowetz, eds., *Modernization and the Canadian State* (Toronto: Macmillan, 1978).

2 Kenichi Ohmae, *The End of the Nation State* (New York: Free Press, 1995), and Susan Strange, *The Retreat of the State: The Diffusion of Power in the World Economy* (Cambridge, UK: Cambridge University Press, 1996).

3 Gerald Hodge and Ira M. Robinson, *Planning Canadian Regions* (Vancouver: UBC Press, 2001), chap. 9.

4 "Electoral Reform," *Policy Options* 18, 9 (November 1997).

5 Alan C. Cairns, "The Electoral System and the Party System in Canada, 1921-1965," *Canadian Journal of Political Science* 1, 1 (1968): 55-80.

6 G.R. Cook, "Canadian Centennial Celebration," *International Journal* 22 (Autumn 1967): 663.

7 Richard Simeon and David J. Elkins, "Regional Political Cultures in Canada," *Canadian Journal of Political Science* 7 (September 1974): 397-437, and "Provincial Political Cultures in Canada," in David J. Elkins and Richard Simeon, eds., *Small Worlds: Provinces and Parties in Canadian Political Life* (Toronto: Methuen, 1980), chap. 2.

8 Manitoba, *Guidelines for the Seventies* (Winnipeg: Government of Manitoba, 1973), 1:14-15.

9   Stephen G. Tomblin, *Ottawa and the Outer Provinces: The Challenge of Regional Integration in Canada* (Toronto: James Lorimer, 1995), 80-81, 149.

10 R.K. Carty, "The Three Canadian Party Systems: An Interpretation of the Development of National Politics," in George Perlin, ed., *Party Democracy in Canada* (Scarborough: Prentice-Hall, 1988), 19.

11 Herman Bakvis, *Regional Ministers: Power and Influence in the Canadian Cabinet* (Toronto: University of Toronto Press, 1991).

12 Sid Noel, "The Ontario Political Culture: An Interpretation," in Graham White, ed., *The Government and Politics of Ontario*, 5th ed. (Toronto: University of Toronto Press, 1997), chap. 3.

13 Malcolm G. Taylor, *Health Insurance and Canadian Public Policy* (Montreal: McGill-Queen's University Press, 1978), 338.

14 Peter Smith, "Alberta: Experiments in Governance – From Social Credit to the Klein Revolution," in Keith Brownsey and Michael Howlett, eds., *The Provincial State in Canada* (Peterborough: Broadview, 2001), 303.

15 Government of Alberta, "Premier's Advisory Council on Health Report," (Mazankowski Report), http://www.gov.ab.ca/home/index.cfm?page=958, and Commission on the Future of Health Care in Canada, *Building on Values: The Future of Health Care in Canada* (Ottawa: Commission on Health Care in Canada, 2002).

16 Ken Rasmussen, "Saskatchewan: From Entrepreneurial State to Embedded State," in Brownsey and Howlett, *The Provincial State in Canada*, 272.

17 Rand Dyck, *Provincial Politics in Canada: Towards the Turn of the Century*, 3rd ed. (Scarborough: Prentice-Hall, 1996), table 12.1, 646.

18 Gura Bhargava, "A City Divided by Political Philosophies: Residential Development in a Bi-provincial City in Canada," *American Journal of Economics and Sociology* 60, 1 (January 2001): 319.

19 Michael Bliss, "The Fault Lines Deepen," *Toronto Globe and Mail*, 2 May 2000.

20 S.C. 1996, c. 1.

21 R. Cole Harris, "Regionalism and the Canadian Archipelago," in L.D. McCann, ed., *Heartland and Hinterland: A Geography of Canada* (Scarborough: Prentice-Hall, 1982), 466.

22 Thomas J. Courchene with Colin R. Telmer, *From Heartland to North American Region State: The Social, Fiscal, and Federal Evolution of Ontario* (Toronto: Faculty of Management, University of Toronto, 1998).

23 Geoffrey R. Weller, "Politics and Policies in the North," in Graham White, ed., *The Government and Politics of Ontario*, 5th ed. (Toronto: University of Toronto Press, 1997), 285-86.

24 Rand Dyck, "The Socio-economic Setting of Ontario Politics," in White, ed., *The Government and Politics of Ontario*, 5th ed., 20.

25 Robert Williams, "Ontario Party Politics in the 1990s: Comfort Meets Convention," in White, ed., *The Government and Politics of Ontario*, 5th ed., 233.
26 Randall White, *Ontario since 1985* (Toronto: Eastend Books, 1998), 67.
27 A.R.M. Lower, "Ontario – Does It Exist?" *Ontario History* 15, 2 (June 1968): 65-69.
28 Ibid., 68.
29 Ibid.
30 Centre for Research and Information on Canada, *Portraits of Canada*, http://www.cric.ca/pdf/cric_poll/portraits/portraits_2005/eng_national_hl.pdf.
31 Timothy L. Thomas, "An Emerging Party Cleavage: Metropolis vs. the Rest," in Hugh G. Thorburn and Alan Whitehorn, eds., *Party Politics in Canada*, 8th ed. (Toronto: Prentice-Hall, 2001), chap. 30.
32 Peter Raymont, transcript of *The Art of the Possible* (Ottawa: National Film Board of Canada, 1978), 4.
33 Quoted in Agar Adamson and Ian Stewart, "Changing Party Politics in Atlantic Canada," in Thorburn and Whitehorn, *Party Politics in Canada*, 8th ed., 309.
34 Frank MacKinnon, "Prince Edward Island: Big Engine, Little Body," in Martin Robin, ed., *Canadian Provincial Politics: The Party Systems of the Ten Provinces*, 2nd ed. (Scarborough: Prentice-Hall, 1978), 237.
35 "Religious Observance Continues to Decline," *Toronto Globe and Mail*, 19 March 2003, and Warren Clark, "Pockets of Belief: Religious Attendance Patterns in Canada," in Statistics Canada, *Canadian Social Trends* 68 (Spring), cat. no. 11-008 (Ottawa: Minister of Industry, 2003), 2-5.
36 Noel, "The Ontario Political Culture: An Interpretation," 60.
37 Ibid., 60.
38 J. Murray Beck, "Nova Scotia: Tradition and Conservatism," in Robin, *Canadian Provincial Politics*, 200.
39 Richard Johnston, *The Challenge of Direct Democracy: The 1992 Canadian Referendum* (Montreal and Kingston: McGill-Queen's University Press, 1996).
40 The data in this paragraph are from the Centre for Research and Information on Canada, *The CRIC Papers – The Charter: Dividing or Uniting Canadians* (Montreal: CRIC, 2002).
41 Sid Noel, "Leadership and Clientelism," in David J. Bellamy, Jon H. Pammett, and Donald C. Rowat, eds., *The Provincial Political Systems: Comparative Essays* (Toronto: Methuen, 1976), chap. 4.
42 John Wilson, "The Canadian Political Cultures: Towards a Redefinition of the Nature of the Canadian Political System," *Canadian Journal of Political Science* 7, 3 (September 1974): 455.
43 Ibid., 463.
44 Nelson Wiseman, "The Pattern of Prairie Politics," *Queen's Quarterly* 88, 2 (Summer 1981): 298-315.

45   John Kendle, *John Bracken: A Political Biography* (Toronto: University of Toronto Press, 1979), 248.

46   Seymour Martin Lipset, *Agrarian Socialism: The Co-operative Commonwealth Federation in Saskatchewan* (1950; repr., Garden City, NY: Doubleday, 1968), 135.

47   John A. Irving, *The Social Credit Movement in Alberta* (Toronto: University of Toronto Press, 1959), 344-46.

48   C.B. Macpherson, *Democracy in Alberta: Social Credit and the Party System* (Toronto: University of Toronto Press, 1953).

CHAPTER 6: ATLANTIC CANADA

1   Jeffrey Simpson, *Spoils of Power: The Politics of Patronage* (Toronto: Collins, 1988), chaps. 6-9, and Sharon Carstairs, *Not One of the Boys* (Toronto: Macmillan, 1993), 48-49.

2   Statistics Canada, *Provincial Economic Accounts, Annual Estimates 1993-2000, Preliminary Estimates* (Ottawa: Minister of Industry, Science, and Technology), table 8, 128ff.

3   Christopher Dunn, "The Quest for Accountability in Newfoundland and Labrador," *Canadian Public Administration* 47, 2 (Summer 2004): 185.

4   Gerhard P. Bessler, "Central Europeans in Post-Confederation St. John's, Newfoundland: Immigration and Adjustment," *Canadian Ethnic Studies* 18, 3 (1986): 37.

5   Agar Adamson and Ian Stewart, "Changing Party Politics in Atlantic Canada," in Hugh G. Thorburn and Alan Whitehorn, eds., *Party Politics in Canada*, 8th ed. (Toronto: Prentice-Hall, 2001), chap. 22.

6   "United Right Would Lose to Martin, Poll Finds," *Toronto Globe and Mail*, 6 October 2003.

7   Ian Stewart, *Roasting Chestnuts: The Mythology of Maritime Political Culture* (Vancouver: UBC Press, 1994).

8   Ian Stewart, "Friends at Court: Federalism and Provincial Elections on Prince Edward Island," *Canadian Journal of Political Science* 19, 1 (March 1986): 132.

9   Carl Berger, *The Writing of Canadian History: Aspects of English-Canadian Historical Writing 1900-1970* (Toronto: Oxford University Press, 1976).

10 E.R. Forbes, "In Search of a Post-Confederation Maritime Historiography, 1900-1967," in David Jay Bercuson and Phillip A. Buckner, eds., *Eastern and Western Perspectives: Papers from the Joint Atlantic Canada/Western Canadian Studies Conference* (Toronto: University of Toronto Press, 1981), 49.

11 Frank H. Underhill, *The Image of Confederation* (Toronto: CBC Massey Lectures, 1964), 63.

12 E.R. Forbes, *The Maritime Rights Movement, 1919-1927: A Study in Canadian Regionalism* (Montreal and Kingston: McGill-Queen's University Press, 1979).

13 Gregory Baum, *Catholics and Canadian Socialism* (Toronto: James Lorimer, 1980), 191-204.

14 Ian McKay, "Strikes in the Maritimes, 1901-1914," *Acadiensis* 13, 1 (Autumn 1983): 45.

15 Donald J. Savoie, "New Brunswick: A 'Have' Public Service in a 'Have-Less' Province," in Evert A. Lindquist, ed., *Government Restructuring and Career Public Services in Canada* (Toronto: Institute of Public Administration of Canada, 2000), chap. 10.

16 Peter Aucoin, "Nova Scotia: Government Restructuring and the Career Public Service," in Lindquist, *Government Restructuring*, 256.

17 Michael Adams, *Sex in the Snow: Canadian Social Values at the End of the Millennium* (Toronto: Viking, 1997), 204-5.

18 "MacAulay Praised as PEI 'Cash Cow,'" *Toronto Globe and Mail*, 14 October 2002.

19 Chedly Belkhodja, "Populism and Community: The Cases of Reform and the Confederation of Regions Party in New Brunswick," in William Cross, ed., *Political Parties, Representation, and Electoral Democracy in Canada* (Toronto: Oxford University Press, 2002), chap. 7.

20 "Federal Liberals Claim Record Number of Members," *Toronto Star*, 24 July 2003.

21 Centre for Research and Information on Canada, *Portraits of Canada*, http://cric.ca/pdf/cric_poll/portraits/portraits_2005/eng_national_hl.pdf.

22 Melvin Baker, "St. John's Municipal Chairmen and Mayors, 1888-1988," *Newfoundland Quarterly* 84, 1 (July 1988): 5-11.

23 Ian Stewart, "More Than Just a Line on the Map: The Political Culture of the Nova Scotia-New Brunswick Boundary," *Publius* 20 (Winter 1990): 99-111.

24 G.M. Story, W.J. Kirwin, and J.D.A. Widdowson, eds., *Dictionary of Newfoundland English* (Toronto: University of Toronto Press, 1982).

25 J. Murray Beck, "An Atlantic Region Political Culture: A Chimera," in Bercuson and Buckner, *Eastern and Western Perspectives*, 147-68.

26 David A. Milne, "Politics in the Beleaguered Garden," in Verner Smitheram, David A. Milne, and Satadal Dasgupta, eds., *The Garden Transformed: Prince Edward Island, 1945-1980* (Charlottetown: Ragweed Press, 1982), 39-72.

27 "83% Vote in PEI Despite the Storm," *Toronto Globe and Mail*, 30 September 2003.

28 David K. Stewart, "'Friends and Neighbours': Patterns of Delegate Support at Maritime Liberal and Conservative Conventions," in R. Kenneth Carty, Lynda Erickson, and Donald E. Blake, eds., *Leaders and Parties in Canadian Politics: Experiences of the Provinces* (Toronto: Harcourt Brace Jovanovich, 1992), chap. 4.

29 Nova Scotia, New Brunswick, and Prince Edward Island, *The Report on Maritime Union, Commissioned by the Governments of Nova Scotia, New Brunswick, and Prince Edward Island* (Fredericton: Maritime Union Study, 1970).

30 Louis Hartz, *The Founding of New Societies* (New York: Harcourt, Brace, and World, 1964), 25.

31 Sid Noel, *Politics in Newfoundland* (Toronto: University of Toronto Press, 1971), 4-5.

32   Gertrude E. Gunn, *The Political History of Newfoundland, 1832-1864* (Toronto: University of Toronto Press, 1966), 207.

33   Ibid., 11.

34   Noel, *Politics in Newfoundland*, 24-25, 263.

35   Gordon O. Rothney, "The Denominational Basis of Representation in the Newfoundland Assembly, 1919-1962," *Canadian Journal of Economics and Political Science* 28, 4 (November 1962): 557-70.

36   David Bellamy, "The Atlantic Provinces," in David J. Bellamy, Jon H. Pammett, and Donald C. Rowat, eds., *The Provincial Political Systems: Comparative Essays* (Toronto: Methuen, 1976), 8.

37   J.D. House, *Against the Tide: Battling for Economic Renewal in Newfoundland and Labrador* (Toronto: University of Toronto Press, 1999).

38   Noel, *Politics in Newfoundland*, 87.

39   Ibid., 77.

40   "Document: J.R. Smallwood on Liberalism in 1926," Melvin Baker and James Overton, eds., *Newfoundland Studies* 11, 1 (Spring 1995): 82, and Joseph R. Smallwood, *I Chose Canada* (Toronto: Macmillan, 1973), 164.

41   Susan McCorquodale, "Newfoundland: Plus Ça Change, Plus C'est La Même Chose," in Martin Robin, ed., *Canadian Provincial Politics: The Party Systems of the Ten Provinces*, 2nd ed. (Scarborough: Prentice-Hall, 1978), 145-46.

42   William A. McKim, ed., *The Vexed Question: Denominational Education in a Secular Age* (St. John's: Breakwater, 1988).

43   Valerie A. Summers, "Between a Rock and a Hard Place: Regime Change in Newfoundland," in Keith Brownsey and Michael Howlett, eds., *The Provincial State in Canada* (Peterborough: Broadview, 2001), 35-36.

44   Shane O'Dea, "Newfoundland: The Development of Culture on the Margin," *Newfoundland Studies* 10, 1 (1994): 73.

45   Brendan O'Grady, *Exiles and Islanders: The Irish Settlers of Prince Edward Island* (Montreal and Kingston: McGill-Queen's University Press, 2004), 12-13.

46   W.S. McNutt, *The Atlantic Provinces: The Emergence of Colonial Society, 1712-1857* (Toronto: McClelland and Stewart, 1965), 4, 29.

47   Kenneth D. McRae, "The Structure of Canadian History," in Hartz et al., *The Founding of New Societies*, 234-35.

48   McNutt, *The Atlantic Provinces*, 61.

49   Ibid., 269.

50   McRae, "The Structure of Canadian History," 236.

51   G.A. Rawlyk, "The Farmer-Labour Movement and the Failure of Socialism in Nova Scotia," in Laurier LaPierre et al., eds., *Essays on the Left* (Toronto: McClelland and Stewart, 1971), 40.

52 J. Murray Beck, "Joseph Howe: Opportunist or Empire-Builder?" in G.A. Rawlyk, ed., *Historical Essays on the Atlantic Provinces* (Toronto: McClelland and Stewart, 1967), 143, 146.

53 J. Murray Beck, *Joseph Howe: Voice of Nova Scotia* (Toronto: McClelland and Stewart, 1964), part 1.

54 Hugh G. Thorburn, *Politics in New Brunswick* (Toronto: University of Toronto Press, 1961), 5, 8.

55 P.J. Fitzpatrick, "New Brunswick: The Politics of Pragmatism," in Robin, *Canadian Provincial Politics*, 120.

56 Perry Biddiscombe, "'Le Tricolor et l'étoile': The Origin of the Acadian National Flag, 1867-1912," *Acadiensis* 20, 1 (Autumn 1990): 120.

57 Thorburn, *Politics in New Brunswick*, 201.

58 James A. McAllister, *The Government of Edward Schreyer* (Montreal and Kingston: McGill-Queen's University Press, 1984), 148.

59 Richard Wilbur, *The Rise of French New Brunswick* (Halifax: Formac, 1989), 271.

60 J. Murray Beck, "Nova Scotia: Tradition and Conservatism," in Robin, *Canadian Provincial Politics*, 181.

61 "Organization Report to National Council by National Treasurer," 1-2 March 1952, *CCF Records, Library and Archives Canada*, Ottawa.

62 Louis Hartz, *The Liberal Tradition in America* (New York: Harcourt Brace, 1955), 21.

63 Louis Hartz to Gad Horowitz, 29 October 1965. I am grateful to Gad Horowitz for access to his files and correspondence.

64 Harold A. Innis, *The Cod Fisheries: The History of an International Economy*, rev. ed. (1940; repr., Toronto: University of Toronto Press, 1954), 191, 484.

65 T.W. Acheson, "The Maritimes and 'Empire Canada,'" in David Jay Bercuson, ed., *Canada and the Burden of Unity* (Toronto: Macmillan, 1977), 101.

66 Ibid., 97.

67 John Hutcheson, *Dominance and Dependency* (Toronto: McClelland and Stewart, 1978).

68 Ian Lumsden, ed., *Close the 49th Parallel Etc: The Americanization of Canada* (Toronto: University of Toronto Press, 1970).

69 McNutt, *The Atlantic Provinces*, 46.

70 D.G. Bell, "A Note on the Reception of English Statutes in New Brunswick," *University of New Brunswick Law Journal* 28 (Spring 1979): 200.

71 Wilbur, *The Rise of French New Brunswick*, 34-35, 79.

72 Robert Finbow, "Dependents or Dissidents? The Atlantic Provinces in Canada's Constitutional Reform Process, 1967-1992," *Canadian Journal of Political Science* 27, 3 (September 1994): 465-91.

73 Gad Horowitz, *Canadian Labour in Politics* (Toronto: University of Toronto Press, 1968), 4.

74   Samuel H. Beer, *British Politics in the Collectivist Age* (New York: Vintage Books, 1969).
75   Michael D. Ornstein, "Regional Politics and Ideologies," in Robert J. Brym, ed., *Regionalism in Canada* (Toronto: Irwin, 1986), 47-87.
76   Eugene Forsey, *Freedom and Order* (Toronto: McClelland and Stewart, 1974), and Frank M. Milligan, *Eugene A. Forsey: An Intellectual Biography* (Calgary: University of Calgary Press, 2004).
77   Robert L. Stanfield, "Conservative Principles and Philosophy," in Paul W. Fox and Graham White, eds., *Politics: Canada*, 6th ed. (Toronto: McGraw-Hill Ryerson, 1987), 376-81.
78   Geoffrey Stevens, *The Player: The Life and Times of Dalton Camp* (Toronto: Key Porter, 2003), 2-3.

CHAPTER 7: QUEBEC

1   John Porter, *The Vertical Mosaic* (Toronto: University of Toronto Press, 1965), 505.
2   Conseil exécutif, Gouvernement du Québec, *La nouvelle entente Québec-Canada – Proposition du gouvernement du Québec pour une entente d'égal à égal: la souveraineté-association* (Quebec, 1979).
3   Ronald Rudin, *Making History in Twentieth-Century Quebec* (Toronto: University of Toronto Press, 1997). See Fernand Ouellette, *Economic and Social History of Québec, 1760-1850* (Toronto: Gage, 1980), trans. Robert Mandrou [orig. pub. in French, 1966].
4   Fernand Ouellette, "The Quiet Revolution: A Turning Point," in Thomas S. Axworthy and Pierre Elliott Trudeau, eds., *Towards a Just Society: The Trudeau Years* (Toronto: Penguin, 1990), 313-41.
5   Gérard Bouchard, "Construire la nation québécoise: Manifeste pour une coalition nationale," in Michel Venne, ed., *Penser la nation québécoise* (Montreal: Québec-Amerique, 2000), 49-68. The analysis here draws on Ronald Rudin, "From the Nation to the Citizen: Québec Historical Writing and the Shaping of Identity," in Robert Adamoski, Dorothy E. Chunn, and Robert Menzies, eds., *Contesting Canadian Citizenship: Historical Readings* (Peterborough: Broadview, 2002), chap. 4.
6   Daniel Salée, "Quebec's Changing Political Culture and the Future of Federal-Provincial Relations in Canada," in Hamish Telford and Harvey Lazar, eds., *Canada: The State of the Federation 2001: Canadian Political Culture(s) in Transition* (Montreal and Kingston: McGill-Queen's University Press, 2002), chap. 7.
7   Alliance Quebec, "A Brief Prepared for Presentation to the Special Joint Parliamentary Committee of the Senate and the House of Commons" (Montreal: Alliance Quebec, 1991), 2-3.
8   Pierre Vallières, *White Niggers of America* (Toronto: McClelland and Stewart, 1971).
9   Lucie Robert, "L'histoire littéraire d'un 'pays incertain': Le cas du Québec," *Journal of Canadian Studies* 38, 2 (Spring 2004): 29-43.

10   John A. Dickenson and Brian Young, "Periodization in Quebec History: A Reevaluation," *Quebec Studies* 12 (Spring-Summer 1991): 1-3.

11   Jeffery Vacante, "Writing the History of Sexuality and 'National' History in Quebec," *Journal of Canadian Studies* 39, 2 (Spring 2005): 31-55.

12   Renée B. Dandurand, "Fortunes and Misfortunes of Culture: Sociology and Anthropology of Culture in Francophone Quebec, 1965-1985," *Canadian Review of Sociology and Anthropology* 26, 3 (May 1989): 511-12.

13   David Riesman, *The Lonely Crowd: A Study of the Changing American Character* (New Haven: Yale University Press, 1950).

14   A.I. Silver, "French Canada and the Prairie Frontier, 1870-1890," *Canadian Historical Review* 50, 1 (March 1969): 27.

15   SES Research, poll, "Fair spending," *Toronto Star,* 29 March 2005, A10.

16   Harold D. Clarke et al., *Political Choice in Canada* (Toronto: McGraw-Hill Ryerson, 1979), table 2.4, 50, and Chris Southcott, "The Study of Regional Inequality in Quebec and English Canada: A Comparative Analysis of Perspectives," *Canadian Journal of Sociology* 24, 2 (1999): 457-84.

17   Stéphane Dion, "Explaining Quebec Nationalism," in R. Kent Weaver, ed., *The Collapse of Canada?* (Washington, DC: Brookings Institution, 1992), 77-121.

18   The following analysis draws on data from Maurice Pinard, "The Dramatic Reemergence of the Quebec Independence Movement," *Journal of International Affairs* 45, 2 (Winter 1992): tables 3 and 5, 493 and 495; Centre for Research and Information on Canada, *Portraits of Canada,* http://www.cric.ca/pdf/cric_poll/portraits/portraits_2005/eng_national_hl.pdf; and Strategic Counsel, *A Report to the Globe and Mail and CTV: Quebec Referendum 10 Years Later, Federal Leadership* (Toronto: Strategic Counsel, 2005).

19   Rhéal Séguin, "G-G's Husband Blasts Separatists," *Toronto Globe and Mail,* 27 October 2005, A5.

20   André Blais, "Le clevage linguistique au Canada," *Recherches sociographiques* 32, 1 (1991): 43-54.

21   Centre for Research and Information on Canada, *Portraits of Canada,* http://www.cric.ca/pdf/cric_poll/portraits/portraits_2005/eng_national_hl.pdf.

22   Dion, "Explaining Quebec Nationalism," 118.

23   Louis Hartz et al., *The Founding of New Societies* (New York: Harcourt, Brace, and World, 1964), 7.

24   Marcel Rioux, *Quebec in Question,* trans. James Boake (1969; repr., Toronto: James Lorimer, 1978), 48-49.

25   Hartz et al., *The Founding of New Societies,* 30.

26   Ramsay Cook, *The Maple Leaf Forever* (Toronto: Macmillan, 1971), 121.

27   Hartz et al., *The Founding of New Societies,* 30.

28   Ramsay Cook, *Canada and the French Canadian Question* (Toronto: Macmillan, 1967), 106.

29 Seigniorial Rent Abolition Act, R.S.Q. 1935, c. 82.

30 Mason Wade, *The French Canadians, 1760-1945* (Toronto: Macmillan, 1955), 837.

31 Cook, *The Maple Leaf Forever*, 137-38.

32 Daniel Salée, "Seigneurial Landownership and the Transition to Capitalism in Nineteenth-Century Quebec," *Quebec Studies* 12 (Spring-Summer 1991): 21.

33 Cook, *The Maple Leaf Forever*, 106, and Denis Monière, *Ideologies in Quebec* (Toronto: University of Toronto Press, 1981), 183.

34 Pierre Elliott Trudeau, *Federalism and the French Canadians* (Toronto: Macmillan, 1968), 104.

35 Ibid., 114.

36 Rioux, *Quebec in Question*, 69.

37 Hartz et al., *The Founding of New Societies*, 47.

38 Marcel Rioux, "The Development of Ideologies in Quebec," in Richard Schultz, Orest M. Kruhlak, and John C. Terry, eds., *The Canadian Political Process*, 3rd ed. (Toronto: Holt, Rinehart and Winston, 1979), 99, 105, 108.

39 Fernand Dumont, *The Vigil of Quebec* (Toronto: University of Toronto Press, 1971), 74.

40 Gad Horowitz, *Viewpoint*, CBC Radio transcript (1965).

41 Gad Horowitz in conversation with George Grant, *Ideals of Democracy and Social Reality*, CBC TV, 9 January 1966.

42 Hartz et al., *The Founding of New Societies*, 2, 192-93.

43 See, for example, Éric Montpetit, "Can Québec Neo-Corporatist Networks Withstand Canadian Federalism and Internationalization?" in Alain-G. Gagnon, ed., *Québec: State and Society*, 3rd ed. (Peterborough: Broadview, 2004), 165-81, and Clinton Archibald, "Corporatist Tendencies in Quebec," in Alain-G. Gagnon, ed., *Quebec: State and Society*, 1st ed. (Toronto: Methuen, 1984), 353-64.

44 A. Brian Tanguay, "Concerted Action in Quebec, 1976-1983: Dialogue of the Deaf," in Gagnon, ed., *Quebec: State and Society*, 1st ed., 365-85.

45 Alain Noël, *A Law against Poverty: Quebec's New Approach to Combatting Poverty and Social Exclusion*, Background Paper – Family Network (Ottawa: Canadian Policy Research Networks, December 2002), 2. http://www.cprn.com/en/doc.cfm?doc=183.

46 Bertrand Marotte, "Quebeckers give heartfelt farewell to former premier," *Toronto Globe and Mail*, 6 November 1987, A3.

47 Raymond Hudon, "Political Parties and the Polarization of Quebec Politics," in Hugh G. Thorburn, ed., *Party Politics in Canada*, 4th ed. (Scarborough: Prentice-Hall, 1979), 228-42, and Jean-Pierre Beaud, "The Parti Québécois from René Lévesque to René Lévesque," in Thorburn, *Party Politics*, 5th ed. (Scarborough: Prentice-Hall, 1985), 238.

48 James Ian Gow, "The Career Public Service in Quebec: How to Reinvigorate the Closed Shop," in Evert A. Lindquist, ed., *Government Restructuring and Career*

Public Services in Canada (Toronto: Institute of Public Administration of Canada, 2000), 304.

49   René Lévesque, *My Quebec* (Toronto: Methuen, 1979).

50   Allan Greer, *Peasant, Lord, and Merchant: Rural Society in Three Quebec Parishes, 1740-1840* (Toronto: University of Toronto Press, 1985).

51   Louis Massicote, "Quebec: The Successful Combination of French Culture and British Institutions," in Gary Levy and Graham White, eds., *Provincial and Territorial Legislatures in Canada* (Toronto: University of Toronto Press, 1989), 71-72.

52   Hartz et al., *The Founding of New Societies*, 30.

53   Kenneth McRoberts, *Quebec: Social Change and Political Crisis* (Toronto: McClelland and Stewart, 1988), chap. 4.

54   Rioux, *Quebec in Question*, 61.

55   R. Harris, "Working Class Home Ownership and Housing Affordability across Canada in 1931," *Histoire sociale/Social History* 37 (1986): 121-38.

56   Everett C. Hughes, *French Canada in Transition* (Chicago: University of Chicago Press, 1943), chaps. 14 and 18.

57   Quoted in Trudeau, *Federalism and the French Canadians*, 110-11.

58   Marc V. Levine, "Language Policy and Quebec's *visage français*: New Directions in *la question linguistique*," *Quebec Studies* 8 (Spring 1989): 4.

59   Lucien Bouchard et al., *For a Clear-Eyed Vision of Quebec*, http://www.pourunquebec lucide.com/documents/manifesto.pdf, 8-9.

60   Vincent Lemieux, "Quebec: Heaven Is Blue and Hell Is Red," in Martin Robin, ed., *Canadian Provincial Politics: The Party Systems of the Ten Provinces*, 2nd ed. (Scarborough: Prentice-Hall, 1978), 248.

61   Michael Adams, *Sex in the Snow: Canadian Social Values at the End of the Millennium* (Toronto: Viking, 1997), 205, 210, 217.

62   Neil Nevitte and Roger Gibbins, *New Elites in Old States: Ideologies in the Anglo-American Democracies* (Toronto: Oxford University Press, 1990), 127-29.

63   Alain-G. Gagnon and Mary Beth Montcalm, *Quebec: Beyond the Quiet Revolution* (Scarborough: Nelson, 1990).

64   Claude Jean Galipeau, "Quebec: Le Contre-Courant Québécois," in Keith Brownsey and Michael Howlett, eds., *The Provincial State* (Mississauga: Copp Clark Pitman, 1992), 134.

65   Jane Matthews Glen, "Approaches to the Protection of Agricultural Land in Quebec and Ontario: Highways and Byways," *Canadian Public Policy* 11, 4 (December 1985): 665-76.

66   Centre for Research and Information on Canada, *Portraits of Canada*.

67   "Quebec Urged to Revise Capital Role," *Toronto Globe and Mail*, 18 December 2003.

68   Luc Bernier, "The Beleaguered State: Québec at the End of the 1990s," in Brownsey and Howlett, *The Provincial State in Canada* (Peterborough: Broadview, 2001), 144.

69 Alain-G. Gagnon and Khayam Z. Paltiel, "Toward Maître chez nous: The Ascend-
    ancy of a Balzacian Bourgeoisie in Quebec," Queen's Quarterly 93, 4 (Winter
    1986): 740.
70 Statistics Canada, Provincial Economic Accounts, Annual Estimates 1988-1992, cat.
    no. 13-213 (Ottawa: Minister of Industry, Science and Technology, 1994).
71 Miro Cernetig, "Quebec Slow to Integrate Minorities," Toronto Star, 16 July 2005.
72 See, for example, Gary Edwards and Josephine Mazzuca, "About four-in-ten Can-
    adians accepting of same sex marriages, adoption," vol. 60, no. 18, 7 March 2000;
    Gary Edwards and Josephine Mazzuca, "Canadians want a strict Young Offenders
    Act," vol. 60, no. 28, 13 April 2000; Gary Edwards and Josephine Mazzuca, "Half
    of Canadians today accepting of marijuana possession, most favour legalization
    for medicinal purposes," vol. 60, no. 30, 18 April 2000; Josephine Mazzuca, "Four-
    in-ten Canadians accepting of same sex marriages, adoption," vol. 61, no. 17, 8
    March 2001; Josephine Mazzuca, "More Canadians today accepting of marijuana
    possession, most favour legalization for medicinal purposes," vol. 61, no. 22, 18
    April 2001; and Dr. Thomas Hartley and Dr. Josephine Mazzuca, "Fewer Canad-
    ians favour legalized abortion under any circumstances," vol. 61, no. 85, 12 De-
    cember 2001, The Gallup Poll (Toronto: Gallup Canada, 2000 and 2001).

CHAPTER 8: ONTARIO

 1 Robert M. Krause, "Ontario: Canada Writ Small," in Robert M. Krause and R.H.
    Wagenberg, eds., Introductory Readings in Canadian Government and Politics, 2nd
    ed. (Toronto: Copp Clark, 1995), chap. 6.
 2 Roger Gibbins, Conflict and Unity: An Introduction to Canadian Political Life, 3rd ed.
    (Toronto: Nelson, 1994), 186.
 3 John Ibbitson, Loyal No More: Ontario's Struggle for a Separate Identity (Toronto:
    HarperCollins, 2001).
 4 Ian Lumsden, ed., Close the 49th Parallel Etc: The Americanization of Canada (To-
    ronto: University of Toronto Press, 1970).
 5 Rand Dyck, Provincial Politics in Canada: Towards the Turn of the Century, 3rd ed.
    (Scarborough: Prentice-Hall, 1996), table 12.1, 646.
 6 Environics Research Group, Focus Ontario 1994-4 (Toronto: 1995), 8.
 7 W.L. Morton, Manitoba: A History (Toronto: University of Toronto Press, 1967).
 8 William H. Magee, "A Pallid Picture: The Image of Ontario in Modern Literature,"
    in Ontario Historical Society, Profiles of a Province (Toronto: Ontario Historical
    Society, 1967), 233.
 9 Nelson Wiseman, "Change in Ontario Politics," in Graham White, ed., The Govern-
    ment and Politics of Ontario, 5th ed. (Toronto: University of Toronto Press, 1997), 420.
10 John Wilson, "The Red Tory Province: Reflections on the Character of Ontario
    Political Culture," in Donald C. MacDonald, ed., The Government and Politics of
    Ontario, 2nd ed. (Toronto: Van Nostrand Reinhold, 1980), 214.

11 "Drew offers 50 P.C. cut in Ontario School Tax: 22-point platform proposed,"
    Toronto Globe and Mail, 9 July 1943, 1-2, and advertisement, "Drew 22-point pro-
    gram backed by House records," *Toronto Globe and Mail*, 17 July 1943, 5.

12 As detailed in the Common Sense Revolution campaign platform, unveiled 3
    May 1994.

13 Sid Noel, "The Ontario Political Culture: An Interpretation," in White, ed., *The
    Government and Politics of Ontario*, 5th ed., 58.

14 Terry Copp, "John Beverley Robinson and the Conservative Blueprint for the Upper
    Canadian Community," *Ontario History* 64 (1972): 79-94.

15 Robert E. Saunders, "What Was the Family Compact?" *Ontario History* 49 (1957):
    173, 176, 178.

16 Frederick H. Armstrong, *Handbook of Upper Canadian Chronology* (Toronto:
    Dundurn, 1985), 272.

17 Peter G. Goheen, "Symbols in the Streets: Parades in Victorian Urban Canada,"
    Urban History Review 18, 3 (February 1990): 237-43.

18 Eric Jackson, "The Organization of Upper Canadian Reformers, 1818-1867," *On-
    tario History* 53 (1961): 104.

19 Quoted in G.M. Craig, "The American Impact on the Upper Canadian Reform
    Movement before 1837," *Canadian Historical Review* 29 (1948): 334n3.

20 Craig, "The American Impact," 348.

21 S.F. Wise, "Upper Canada and the Conservative Tradition," in Ontario Historical
    Society, *Profiles of a Province*, 36.

22 Carl Berger, *The Sense of Power: Studies in the Ideas of Canadian Imperialism, 1867-
    1914* (Toronto: University of Toronto Press), chap. 4.

23 Robert Bothwell, *A Short History of Ontario* (Edmonton: Hurtig, 1986), 99.

24 See, respectively, S.E.D. Shortt, "Social Change and Political Crisis in Rural On-
    tario: The Patrons of Industry, 1889-1896," in Donald Swainson, ed., *Oliver Mowat's
    Ontario* (Toronto: Macmillan, 1972), 211-35; Ramsay Cook, "Tillers and Toilers:
    The Rise and Fall of Populism in Canada in the 1890s," *Historical Papers* 19, 1
    (1984): 1-20; and L.A. Wood, *A History of Farmers' Movements in Canada: The
    Origins and Development of Agrarian Protest, 1872-1924* (1924; repr., Toronto:
    University of Toronto Press, 1975), 109-55.

25 Darren Ferry, "'Severing the Connections in a Complex Community': The Grange,
    the Patrons of Industry and the Construction/Contestation of a Late 19th-
    Century Agrarian Identity in Ontario," *Labour/Le Travail* 54 (Fall 2004): 9-48.

26 Dallen J. Timothy, "The Decline of Finnish Ethnic Islands in Rural Thunder Bay,"
    Great Lakes Geographer 2, 2 (1995): 45-59, and Anthony W. Rasporich, "Twin City
    Ethnopolitics: Urban Rivalry, Ethnic Radicalism and Assimilation in the Lakehead,
    1900-70," *Urban History Review* 18, 3 (February 1990): 210-30.

27 Martin Robin, *Radical Politics and Canadian Labour, 1880-1930* (Kingston: Indus-
    trial Relations Centre, Queen's University, 1968), 290.

28 Ibid., 276.

29 Christina Burr, "Some Adventures of the Boys: Enniskillen Township's 'Foreign Drillers,' Imperialism, and Colonial Discourse, 1873-1923," *Labour/Le Travail* 51 (Spring 2003): 47.

30 Gregory S. Kealey, *Toronto Workers Respond to Industrial Capitalism, 1867-1892* (Toronto: University of Toronto Press, 1980), appendix 3, 323-29.

31 Gregory S. Kealey and Bryan D. Palmer, *Dreaming of What Might Be: The Knights of Labor in Ontario, 1880-1900* (Toronto: New Hogtown Press, 1987), and Ramsay Cook, *The Regenerators: Social Criticism in Late Victorian English Canada* (Toronto: University of Toronto Press, 1985).

32 David Lewis and Frank Scott, *Make This Your Canada* (Toronto: Central Canada Publishing, 1943).

33 Dan Azoulay, *Keeping the Dream Alive: The Survival of the Ontario CCF/NDP, 1950-1963* (Montreal and Kingston: McGill-Queen's University Press, 1997).

34 Carlos Teixeira, "The Suburbanization of Portuguese Canadians in Toronto," *Great Lakes Geographer* 4, 1 (1997): 25-39.

35 "Tories Take Sides," *Inside Queen's Park* 17, 12:1 (16 June 2004).

36 Seymour Martin Lipset, *Revolution and Counterrevolution* (New York: Basic Books, 1968).

37 Dyck, *Provincial Politics in Canada: Towards the Turn of the Century,* 3rd ed., 310.

38 Janet Ajzenstat and Peter J. Smith, eds., *Canada's Origins: Liberal, Tory, or Republican?* (Ottawa: Carleton University Press, 1995).

39 Robert L. Stanfield, "Conservative Principles and Philosophy," in Paul Fox and Graham White, eds., *Politics: Canada,* 8th ed. (Toronto: McGraw-Hill Ryerson, 1995), 307-11.

40 Janet Ajzenstat and Peter J. Smith, "The 'Tory Touch' Thesis: Bad History, Poor Political Science," in Mark Charlton and Paul Barker, eds., *Crosscurrents: Contemporary Political Issues,* 4th ed. (Scarborough: Nelson, 2002), 68-75.

41 Louis Hartz, *The Liberal Tradition in America* (New York: Harcourt Brace, 1955).

42 Thomas J. Courchene with Colin R. Telmer, *From Heartland to North American Region State: The Social, Fiscal, and Federal Evolution of Ontario* (Toronto: Faculty of Management, University of Toronto, 1998), 2.

43 Ibid., 7.

44 Thomas Courchene, "Reflections on the Colloquium," (paper presented at Ontario: Exploring the Region-State Hypothesis, University of Toronto, 26 March 1999), 28.

45 Ibbitson, *Loyal No More,* 3, 6, 187.

46 Robert Everett, "Parliament and Politics," 36-37, and Rand Dyck, "Ontario," 212-13, both in David Leyton-Brown, ed., *Canadian Annual Review of Politics and Public Affairs, 1988* (Toronto: University of Toronto Press, 1995).

47   Harold D. Clarke et al., *Political Choice in Canada* (Toronto: McGraw-Hill Ryerson, 1979), tables 3.1, 3.3, 3.13, 3.16, 6.2, and figure 3.1, 70, 72, 86, 89, 180, and 76.

48   Joel Smith and David K. Jackson, *Restructuring the Canadian State: Prospects for Three Political Scenarios* (Durham, NC: Duke University Center for International Studies, 1981), 17.

49   Ross Laver, "How we Differ," and Scott Steele, "A National Mirror," *Maclean's*, 3 January 1994, 8-10 and 12-15; Centre for Research and Information on Canada, "Portraits of Canada, 2000," http://www.cric.ca/pdf/cric_poll/portraits/portraits2000_poll.pdf, 23; and Strategic Counsel, *September Survey for the Globe and Mail and CTV: National Identity, Revenue Sharing, Federalism, Foreign Affairs and New Orleans* (Toronto: Strategic Counsel, September 2005), 10.

50   Frank L. Graves, with Tim Dugas and Patrick Beauchamp, "Identity and National Attachments in Contemporary Canada," in Harvey Lazar and Tim McIntosh, eds., *Canada: The State of the Federation, 1998/99: How Canadians Connect* (Montreal and Kingston: McGill-Queen's University Press, 1999), 318.

51   Desmond Morton, "*Sic Permanet*: Ontario People and Their Politics," in White, ed., *The Government and Politics of Ontario*, 5th ed., chap. 1.

52   Marilyn Barber, "The Ontario Bilingual Schools Issue: Sources of Conflict," *Canadian Historical Review* 47, 3 (September 1966): 231.

53   Norman Penner, "Ontario: The Dominant Province," in Martin Robin, ed., *Canadian Provincial Politics: The Party Systems of the Ten Provinces*, 2nd ed. (Scarborough: Prentice-Hall, 1978), 210.

CHAPTER 9: THE MIDWEST

1   In this analysis, the regions are defined as Atlantic, Quebec, Ontario, the Midwest, and the Far West.

2   David E. Smith, *Prairie Liberalism: The Liberal Party in Saskatchewan, 1905-1971* (Toronto: University of Toronto Press, 1975), chap. 1.

3   Myron G.G. Gulka-Tiechko, "Inter-war Ukrainian Immigration to Canada, 1919-1939" (master's thesis, University of Manitoba, 1983), 21, 138.

4   Ruth Humphreys, "Dr. Rudolf Meyer and the French Nobility of Assiniboia," *Beaver* 309, 1 (Summer 1978): 17-23.

5   Victor Turek, *Poles in Manitoba* (Toronto: Polish Research Institute in Canada, 1967).

6   Nelson Wiseman, *Social Democracy in Manitoba: A History of the CCF-NDP* (Winnipeg: University of Manitoba Press, 1983), 86.

7   James M. Pitsula, "The Thatcher Government in Saskatchewan and Treaty Indians, 1964-1971: The Quiet Revolution," *Saskatchewan History* 48, 1 (1986): 3-17.

8   Robert Roach and Loleen Berdahl, *State of the West: Western Canadian Demographic and Economic Trends* (Calgary: Canada West Foundation, April 2001), http://www.cwf.ca.

9   Federation of Saskatchewan Indian Nations, *Saskatchewan and Aboriginal Peoples in the 21st Century: Social, Economic and Political Changes and Challenges* (Regina: Federation of Saskatchewan Indian Nations, 1997).

10 Michael Kinnear, "Aboriginal Participation in Elections: The Effect of Expansion of the Franchise on Turnout," *Electoral Insight* 5, 3 (November 2003): table 1, 47.

11 John Richards, "Populism: A Qualified Defence," *Studies in Political Economy* 5 (1981): 5-27.

12 David Laycock, *Populism and Democratic Thought in the Canadian Prairies, 1910-1945* (Toronto: University of Toronto Press, 1990).

13 W.L. Morton, "The Bias of Prairie Politics," *Transactions of the Royal Society of Canada*, 3rd ser., 49, 2 (June 1955): 57-66.

14 Norman E. Cameron, James E. Dean, and Walter S. Good, "Western Transition in Manufacturing: A Perspective from Two Sectors in Manitoba," *Canadian Public Policy* 11, Supplement (July 1985): 332.

15 Robin Neill, "Economic Historiography in the 1950s: The Saskatchewan School," *Journal of Canadian Studies* 34, 3 (Fall 1999): 243-60.

16 Centre for Research and Information on Canada, "Canada-U.S. Federalism Survey" (April 2002), http://www.cric.ca/pdf/cric_poll/border/border_graphs_june2002.pdf.

17 Peter McCormick, "The Reform Party of Canada: New Beginning or Dead End?" in Hugh G. Thorburn and Alan Whitehorn, eds., *Party Politics in Canada*, 7th ed. (Scarborough: Prentice-Hall, 1996), table 22.3, 359.

18 W.L. Morton, *Manitoba: A History*, 2nd ed. (Toronto: University of Toronto Press, 1967), chap. 9.

19 James D. Anderson, "The Municipal Government Reform Movement in Western Canada, 1880-1920," in Alan F.J. Artibise and Gilbert A. Stelter, eds., *The Usable Urban Past: Planning and Politics in the Modern Canadian City* (Toronto: Macmillan, 1979), 82.

20 Foster J.K. Griezic, "The Honourable Thomas Alexander Crerar: The Political Career of a Western Liberal Progressive in the 1920s," in S.M. Trofimenkoff, ed., *The Twenties in Western Canada* (Ottawa: National Museum of Man, 1972), 118.

21 Rodmond Roblin, *Initiative and Referendum* (pamphlet), 27 January 1913, R.A.C. Manning Papers, Provincial Archives of Manitoba, Winnipeg.

22 William Kirby Rolph, *Henry Wise Wood of Alberta* (Toronto: University of Toronto Press, 1950), 215-16.

23 Don Nebras, "Wealth and Privilege: An Analysis of Winnipeg's Early Business Elite," *Manitoba History* 47 (2004): 42-64.

24 Beatrice Brigden, interview with author, December 1970.

25 J.E. Rae, "The Politics of Class: Winnipeg City Council, 1914-1945," in Carl Berger and Ramsay Cook, eds., *The West and the Nation* (Toronto: McClelland and Stewart, 1976), 234-35.

26 Clifford Sifton, "Immigration problems," *Manitoba Free Press*, 6 March 1922, 11.

27 Nelson Wiseman and K.W. Taylor, "Voting in Winnipeg during the Depression," *Canadian Review of Sociology and Anthropology* 19, 2 (May 1982): 215-36, and Nelson Wiseman and K.W. Taylor, "Class and Ethnic Voting in Winnipeg during the Cold War," *Canadian Review of Sociology and Anthropology* 16, 1 (1979): 60-76.

28 Art Grenke, "The German Community of Winnipeg and the English-Canadian Response to World War I," *Canadian Ethnic Studies* 30, 1 (1988): 21-44.

29 *Manitoba Free Press*, 22 May 1919, and Hugh J. Macdonald to Arthur Meighen, 3 July 1919, cited in Bohdan S. Kordan and Lubomyr Y. Luciuk, eds., *A Delicate and Difficult Question: Documents in the History of Ukrainians in Canada, 1899-1922* (Kingston: Limestone Press, 1986), 43-45.

30 Quoted in Thomas Peterson, "Manitoba: Ethnic and Class Politics," in Martin Robin, ed., *Canadian Provincial Politics: The Party Systems of the Ten Provinces*, 2nd ed. (Scarborough: Prentice-Hall, 1978), 84.

31 William Thorsell, "Has the West Been Won?" *Language and Society* 16 (1985): 21-23.

32 *A New Deal for the Manitoba Farmer*, Manitoba CCF pamphlet, 1945, CCF Papers, Provincial Archives of Manitoba.

33 Donald Swainson, "Ethnic Revolt: Manitoba's Election," *Canadian Forum* 49 (August 1969): 98-99.

34 Interview with author, April 1972.

35 Eric Wells, "Is Being Premier of Manitoba as Comfortable as Ed Schreyer Makes It Look?" *Saturday Night*, October 1969, 42.

36 Gad Horowitz, "The Future of the NDP," *Canadian Dimension* 3 (July-August 1966): 23.

37 Edmund H. Oliver, "The Settlement of Saskatchewan to 1914," *Proceedings and Transactions of the Royal Society of Canada*, 3rd ser., 20 (May 1926): 63-67.

38 Patrick Kyba, "Ballots and Burning Crosses – The Election of 1929," in Norman Ward and Duff Spafford, eds., *Politics in Saskatchewan* (Don Mills: Longmans, 1968), 123n14.

39 J.W. Brennan, "Press and Party in Saskatchewan, 1914-1929," *Saskatchewan History* 27, 3 (Autumn 1974): 81-94.

40 Dafoe to Sifton, 13 January 1923, in Ramsay Cook, ed., *The Dafoe-Sifton Correspondence, 1919-1927* (Winnipeg: Manitoba Record Society, 1966), 137.

41 Sifton to Dafoe, 28 January 1925, in Cook, *The Dafoe-Sifton Correspondence*, 196.

42 D.S. Spafford, "The Origin of the Farmers' Union of Canada," *Saskatchewan History* 18, 2 (Spring 1965): 89-96.

43 W.L. Morton, *The Progressive Party of Canada* (Toronto: University of Toronto Press, 1950), 276.

44 Seymour Martin Lipset, *Agrarian Socialism: The Co-operative Commonwealth Federation in Saskatchewan* (1950; repr., Garden City, NY: Doubleday, 1968), 106.

45   David Lewis and Frank Scott, *Make This Your Canada* (Toronto: Central Canada Publishing, 1943), and League for Social Reconstruction, *Social Planning for Canada* (Toronto: Thomas Nelson, 1935).

46   Lipset, *Agrarian Socialism*, table 36, 235.

47   James M. Pitsula and Ken Rasmussen, *Privatizing a Province: The New Right in Saskatchewan* (Vancouver: New Star, 1990).

48   Ken Rasmussen, "Saskatchewan: From Entrepreneurial State to Embedded State," in Keith Brownsey and Michael Howlett, eds., *The Provincial State in Canada* (Peterborough: Broadview, 2001), 242.

49   The distinction is in Donald V. Smiley, *Canada in Question: Federalism in the Eighties*, 3rd ed. (Toronto: McGraw-Hill Ryerson, 1980), chap. 5, and pursued in Rand Dyck, "Links between Federal and Provincial Parties," in Herman Bakvis, ed., *Representation, Integration and Political Parties in Canada* (Toronto: Dundurn, 1991), 129-77.

50   Robert A. Wardhaugh, "Region and Nation: The Politics of Jimmy Gardiner," *Saskatchewan History* 45, 2 (Fall 1993): 24-36.

51   Michel Rocard, "Does Social Democracy Have a Future?" in Peter H. Russell, ed., *The Future of Social Democracy: Views of Leaders from around the World* (Toronto: University of Toronto Press, 1999), 14-15.

52   Wiseman, *Social Democracy in Manitoba*, 136.

53   Nelson Wiseman, "The Direction of Public Enterprise in Canada," *Commonwealth and Comparative Politics* 37, 2 (July 1999): 88n47.

54   R.K. Carty and David Stewart, "Parties and Party Systems," in Christopher Dunn, ed., *Provinces: Canadian Provincial Politics* (Peterborough: Broadview, 1996), table 1, 69, and Lipset, *Agrarian Socialism*, 244.

55   Salem Goldworth Bland, *The New Christianity* (1920; repr., Toronto: University of Toronto Press, 1973), and A.E. Smith, *All My Life* (Toronto: Progress Books, 1949).

56   W.E. Gordon, *Christianity, Socialism and the CCF*, CCF Papers, Provincial Archives of Manitoba.

57   League for Social Reconstruction, Winnipeg Branch, *Pioneers in Poverty* (Winnipeg: Manitoba Cooperative Publishing, 1938).

58   S.J. Farmer, *Social Credit or Social Ownership?* (Winnipeg, 1936).

59   *Beat the Depression Now* (1949), CCF election pamphlet, CCF Papers, Provincial Archives of Manitoba.

60   Gunnar Adler-Karlson, *Reclaiming the Canadian Economy: A Swedish Approach through Functional Socialism* (Toronto: Anansi, 1970).

61   Pierre Elliott Trudeau, "The Practice and Theory of Federalism," in Michael Oliver, ed., *Social Purpose for Canada* (Toronto: University of Toronto Press, 1961), 371-93.

62   Stanley Knowles, *The New Party* (Toronto: McClelland and Stewart, 1961).

63   Tony Blair, *The Third Way: Politics for a New Century* (London: Fabian Society, 1998).

64   Bob Rae, *The Three Questions: Prosperity and the Public Good* (Toronto: Viking, 1998).

65   John Richards, *Retooling the Welfare State* (Toronto: C.D. Howe Institute, 1998).

66   Roy Romanow, in John Richards, Robert D. Cairns, and Larry Pratt, eds., *Social Democracy without Illusions: Renewal of the Canadian Left* (Toronto: McClelland and Stewart, 1991), back cover.

67   Keith Archer and Alan Whitehorn, "Opinion Structure among Party Activists: A Comparison of New Democrats, Liberals, and Conservatives," in Thorburn and Whitehorn, *Party Politics in Canada*, 8th ed., chap. 9.

CHAPTER 10: THE FAR WEST

1   Allan Tupper and Roger Gibbins, eds., *Government and Politics in Alberta* (Edmonton: University of Alberta Press, 1992), and R.K. Carty, ed., *Politics, Policy, and Government in British Columbia* (Vancouver: UBC Press, 1996).

2   John Richards and Larry Pratt, *Prairie Capitalism: Power and Influence in the New West* (Toronto: McClelland and Stewart, 1979).

3   Roger Gibbins and Loleen Berdahl, *Western Visions, Western Futures: Perspectives on the West in Canada*, 2nd ed. (Peterborough: Broadview, 2003), 17-18.

4   Steve Patten, "The Reform Party's Re-imagining of Canada," *Journal of Canadian Studies* 34, 1 (Spring 1999): 27-51.

5   Mary Eberts, "The Rights of Women," in R. St. J. Macdonald and John P. Humphrey, eds., *The Practice of Freedom: Canadian Essays on Human Rights and Fundamental Freedoms* (Toronto: Butterworths, 1979), 235.

6   http://www.carleton.ca/sjc; http://decima.ca/en/lab/election2006/, and Christopher Dornan, "It's just news, not brainwashing," *Toronto Globe and Mail*, 17 December 2005, A13.

7   C.B. Macpherson, *Democracy in Alberta: Social Credit and the Party System* (Toronto: University of Toronto Press, 1953), and David K. Stewart and Keith Archer, *Quasi-democracy? Parties and Leadership Selection in Alberta* (Vancouver: UBC Press, 2000).

8   Philip Resnick, *The Politics of Resentment: British Columbia Regionalism and Canadian Unity* (Vancouver: UBC Press, 2000), 29.

9   Centre for Research and Information on Canada, "Canada-U.S. Federalism Survey" (April 2002), http://cric.ca/pdf/cric_poll/border/border_graphs_june2002.pdf. Data reproduced in Stephen Brooks, *Canadian Democracy*, 4th ed. (Don Mills: Oxford University Press, 2004), figure 4.5, 107.

10   Rand Dyck, *Provincial Politics in Canada: Towards the Turn of the Century*, 3rd ed. (Scarborough: Prentice-Hall, 1996), table 12.1, 646.

11   Harold D. Clarke et al., *Political Choice in Canada* (Toronto: McGraw-Hill Ryerson, 1979), table 2.4, 50.

12   Martin Robin, "British Columbia: The Company Province," in Martin Robin, ed., *Canadian Provincial Politics: The Party Systems of the Ten Provinces*, 2nd ed. (Scarborough: Prentice-Hall, 1978), chap. 10.

13   Mark Lisac, *The Klein Revolution* (Edmonton: NeWest, 1995), 234-35.

14 W.L. Morton, *The Progressive Party of Canada* (Toronto: University of Toronto Press, 1950), 39.

15 A. Ross McCormick, *Reformers, Rebels, and Revolutionaries: The Western Canadian Radical Movement, 1899-1919* (Toronto: University of Toronto Press, 1977).

16 Seymour Martin Lipset, "Radicalism or Reformism: The Sources of Working-Class Politics," *American Political Science Review* 77 (1983): 1-18.

17 Robert H. Babcock, *Gompers in Canada: A Study in American Continentalism before the First World War* (Toronto: University of Toronto Press, 1974), 34-35, 57, 70, 171.

18 Quoted in Karel Denis Bicha, *The American Farmer and the Canadian West, 1896-1914* (Lawrence, KS: Coronado Press, 1968), 130.

19 *House of Commons Debates*, 12 April 1901 and 14 July 1903, quoted in Harold Troper, *Only Farmers Need Apply* (Toronto: Griffin House, 1972), 22.

20 James D. Anderson, "The Municipal Government Reform Movement in Western Canada, 1880-1920," in Alan F.J. Artibise and Gilbert A. Stelter, eds., *The Usable Urban Past: Planning and Politics in the Modern Canadian City* (Toronto: Macmillan, 1979), 82.

21 The phrase is Arthur Meighen's. See Michael Bliss, "The Prime Ministers of Canada: Arthur Meighen, Biography," http://www.primeministers.ca/meighen/bio_2.php.

22 William Kirby Rolph, *Henry Wise Wood of Alberta* (Toronto: University of Toronto Press, 1950), chap. 8.

23 J.R. Mallory, *Social Credit and the Federal Power in Canada* (Toronto: University of Toronto Press, 1954), 141-42.

24 Alvin Finkel, "Populism and the Proletariat: Social Credit and the Urban Working Class," *Studies in Political Economy* 34 (Spring 1984): 109-35, and Alvin Finkel, "Social Credit and the Cities," *Alberta History* 34, 3 (Summer 1986): 20-26.

25 W.E. Mann, *Sect, Cult, and Church in Alberta* (Toronto: University of Toronto Press, 1955), 4.

26 S.D. Clark, *The Developing Canadian Community*, 2nd ed. (Toronto: University of Toronto Press, 1968), 134-35.

27 John Finlay, *Social Credit: The English Origins* (Montreal and London: McGill-Queen's University Press, 1972).

28 Bob Hesketh, *Major Douglas and Alberta Social Credit* (Toronto: University of Toronto Press, 1997), chap. 5.

29 Howard Palmer, with Tamara Palmer, *Alberta: A New History* (Edmonton: Hurtig, 1990), 306.

30 Lipset, *Agrarian Socialism*, 64, 84-90, 99-103, and Wood, quoted in Rolph, *Henry Wise Wood*, 195.

31 "Producer Vote Supports Single-Desk Sale of Barley," *Agrivision* (Ottawa) April 1997, and "One Vote Could Decide Barley Marketing," *Agriweek* (Winnipeg), 11 November 1997.

32 John A. Irving, *The Social Credit Movement in Alberta* (Toronto: University of Toronto Press, 1959), 230, 345.

33 Stewart and Archer, *Quasi-democracy?* 172.

34 Nelson Wiseman, "An Historical Note on Religion and Parties on the Prairies," *Journal of Canadian Studies* 16, 2 (Summer 1981): 111.

35 Edward LeSage Jr., "Business Government and the Evolution of Alberta's Career Public Service," in Evert Lindquist, ed., *Government Restructuring and Career Public Services in Canada* (Toronto: Institute of Public Administration of Canada, 2000), 399.

36 Edward LeSage Jr., "British Columbia's Career Public Service: Weathering Ideological Storms," in Lindquist, *Government Restructuring*, 441.

37 David K. Stewart, "Klein's Makeover and the Conservative Party," in Trevor Harrison and Gordon Laxer, eds., *The Trojan Horse: Alberta and the Future of Canada* (Montreal: Black Rose, 1995), 44.

38 Trevor Harrison, "The Changing Face of Prairie Politics: Populism in Alberta," *Prairie Forum* 25, 1 (Spring 2000): 119.

39 TD Bank Financial Group, "The Calgary-Edmonton Corridor: Take Action Now to Ensure Tiger's Roar Doesn't Fade" (22 April 2003), 2, http://www.td.com/economics/special/alta03.pdf.

40 Jean Barman, *The West beyond the West: A History of British Columbia*, rev. ed. (Toronto: University of Toronto Press, 1991), 63.

41 R. Cole Harris, *The Resettlement of British Columbia: Essays on Colonialism and Geographic Change* (Vancouver: UBC Press, 1997), 140, 142, 160, 295.

42 Diana Brydon, "Regions and Centres: The Literary Images of Two Countries," in Bruce W. Hodgins et al., eds., *Federalism in Canada and Australia* (Peterborough: Frost Centre for Canadian Heritage and Development Studies, 1989), 491-92.

43 R.N. Rosencrance, "The Radical Tradition in Australia: An Interpretation," *Review of Politics* 22 (1960): 121, and Russell Ward, *The Australian Legend* (New York: Oxford University Press, 1959), 18.

44 Gordon S. Galbraith, "British Columbia," in David J. Bellamy, Jon H. Pammett, and Donald C. Rowat, eds., *The Provincial Political Systems: Comparative Essays* (Toronto: Methuen, 1976), chap. 5.

45 Jean Barman, "Ethnicity in the Pursuit of Status: British Middle and Upper-Class Emigration to British Columbia in the Late Nineteenth and Early Twentieth Centuries," *Canadian Ethnic Studies* 18, 1 (1986): 32.

46 Leonard B. Kuffert, "'Reckoning with the Machine': The British Columbia Social Credit Movement as Social Criticism, 1932-52," *BC Studies* 124 (Winter 1999-2000): 9, 36.

47 Edith Dobie, "Party History in British Columbia, 1903-1933" [orig. pub. 1936], in J. Friesen and H.K. Ralston, eds., *Historical Essays on British Columbia* (Toronto: McClelland and Stewart, 1976), 79.

48 Donald E. Blake, Richard Johnston, and David J. Elkins, "Sources of Change in the B.C. Party System," *BC Studies* 5 (Summer 1981): 15.

49 Donald E. Blake, "The Politics of Polarization: Parties and Elections in British Columbia," in Carty, *Politics, Policy, and Government in British Columbia*, 67.

50 R. Jeremy Wilson, "Geography, Politics and Culture: Electoral Insularity in British Columbia," *Canadian Journal of Political Science* 13, 4 (1980): 771.

51 John Meisel, "Religious Affiliation and Electoral Behaviour: A Case Study," in John C. Courtney, ed., *Voting in Canada* (Scarborough: Prentice-Hall, 1967), 152, and Lynn McDonald, "Attitude Organization and Voting Behaviour in Canada," *Canadian Review of Sociology and Anthropology* 8, 3 (August 1971): 179.

52 Statistics Canada, "Population by Religion, by Province and Territory (2001 Census): (Alberta, British Columbia, Yukon Territory)," http://www40.statcan.ca/l01/cst01/demo30c.htm.

53 Quoted in Eric Crouse, "The 'Great Revival': Evangelical Revivalism, Methodism and Bourgeois Order in Early Calgary," *Alberta History* 47, 1 (Winter 1999): 18.

54 Australian Bureau of Statistics, *Year Book Australia, 2003* (Canberra: Australian Bureau of Statistics, 2003), "Religious Affiliation," table 5.51, 145.

55 Richard Allen, *The Social Passion: Religion and Social Reform in Canada, 1914-28* (Toronto: University of Toronto Press, 1971).

56 Donald E. Blake, R.K. Carty, and Lynda Erickson, *Grassroots Politicians: Party Activists in British Columbia* (Vancouver: UBC Press, 1991), 9.

57 Barman, *The West beyond the West*, 274.

58 Mann, *Sect, Cult, and Church in Alberta*, 153.

59 Irving, *The Social Credit Movement in Alberta*, 303.

60 Donald V. Smiley, "Canada's Poujadists, A New Look at Social Credit," *Canadian Forum* 42 (September 1962): 122.

61 David R. Elliott, "Anti-Semitism and the Social Credit Movement: The Roots of the Keegstra Affair," *Canadian Ethnic Studies* 17, 1 (1985): 78-89, and Janine Stingel, "Beyond the Purge: Reviewing the Social Credit Movement's Legacy of Intolerance," *Canadian Ethnic Studies* 31, 2 (1999): 76-99.

62 Elisabeth Gidengil and Neil Nevitte, "Something Old, Something New: Preliminary Findings of the 2004 Canadian Election Study" (seminar presentation, University of Toronto, Toronto, 22 October 2004).

63 Brian Laghi, "Gay Unions Split Country, Poll Shows," *Toronto Globe and Mail*, 14 June 2003.

64 Hugh Johnston, "The Development of the Punjabi Community in Vancouver since 1961," *Canadian Ethnic Studies* 20, 2 (1988): 1.

65 Rex Wyler, *Greenpeace* (Vancouver: Raincoast, 2004).

66 Donald E. Blake, "Value Conflicts in Lotusland: British Columbia Political Culture," in Carty, ed., *Politics, Policy, and Government in British Columbia*, 11-13.

67 Michael Adams, *Sex in the Snow: Canadian Social Values at the End of the Millennium* (Toronto: Viking, 1997), 206, 208-9.

68 http://www.sierraclub.ca/national/chapters/index.html; e-mail to author from Martha Beckett, Membership Service, Sierra Club of Canada, 26 November 2004; e-mail to author from Sara Campbell Mates, Donor Services, World Wildlife Federation Canada, 29 November 2004.

69 Kathryn Harrison, "Environmental Protection in British Columbia: Postmaterial Values, Organized Interests, and Party Politics," in Carty, ed., *Politics, Policy, and Government in British Columbia,* 290-307.

70 Jeremy Wilson, "Wilderness Politics in British Columbia: The Business-Dominated State and the Containment of Environmentalism," in William D. Coleman and Grace Skogstad, eds., *Policy Communities and Public Policy in Canada* (Toronto: Copp Clark Pitman, 1990), 150.

71 William K. Carroll and R.S. Rattner, "Old Unions and New Social Movements," *Labour/Le Travail* 35 (Spring 1995): 199.

72 Jamian Logue, Development Officer, Council of Canadians. Interview with author, 23 February 2007, and http://www.canadians.org.

73 Michael Adams, Donna Dasko, and James Matsui, "Poll Says Canadians Want to Renegotiate, Not Rip Up Trade Deal," *Toronto Globe and Mail,* 11 November 1988.

74 Joel Garreau, *The Nine Nations of North America* (Boston: Houghton Mifflin, 1981), and Ernest Callenbach, *Ecotopia* (Berkeley: Banyan Tree, 1975).

75 Matthew Sparke, "Excavating the Future in Cascadia: Geoeconomics and the Imagined Geographies of a Cross-Border Region," *BC Studies* 127 (Autumn 2000): 7.

76 W. Wesley Pue, ed., *Pepper in Our Eyes: The APEC Affair* (Vancouver: UBC Press, 2000).

CONCLUSION

1 Peter H. Russell, *Constitutional Odyssey: Can Canadians Become a Sovereign People?* 3rd ed. (Toronto: University of Toronto Press, 2004).

2 Alan C. Cairns, *Reconfigurations: Canadian Citizenship and Constitutional Change* (Toronto: McClelland and Stewart, 1995), and Charles Taylor, *Reconciling the Solitudes: Essays on Canadian Federalism and Nationalism* (Montreal and Kingston: McGill-Queen's University Press, 1993).

3 Philip Resnick, *The Masks of Proteus: Canadian Reflections on the State* (Montreal and Kingston: McGill-Queen's University Press, 1990), 212-13.

4 Ramsay Cook, "Regionalism Unmasked," *Acadiensis* 13, 1 (Autumn 1983): 141.

5 Doug Owram, "Narrow Circles: The Historiography of Recent Canadian Historiography," *National History* 1, 1 (Winter 1997): 5-21.

6 Philip Resnick, *The European Roots of Canadian Identity* (Peterborough: Broadview, 2005).

7   E.J. Hobsbawm, "Revolutions," in *The Age of Revolution, 1789-1848* (New York: Mentor, 1962), chap. 6.

8   Quoted in R.D. Francis, R. Jones, and D.S. Smith, *Destinies: Canadian History since Confederation* (Toronto: Holt, Rinehart and Winston, 1988), 39.

9   Carl Berger, *The Writing of Canadian History: Aspects of English-Canadian Historical Writing 1900-1970* (Toronto: Oxford University Press, 1976), 259.

10 David I. Kertzer, *Ritual, Politics, and Power* (New Haven: Yale University Press, 1988), 7, and David V.J. Bell, *The Roots of Disunity: A Study of Canadian Political Culture* (Toronto: Oxford University Press, 1992), 4.

11 Peter C. Newman, *The Distemper of Our Times: Canadian Politics in Transition, 1963-1968* (Toronto: McClelland and Stewart, 1968), 254.

12 Jean Pierre Richert, "The Impact of Ethnicity on the Perception of Heroes and Historical Symbols," *Canadian Review of Sociology and Anthropology* 11, 2 (1974): 156-57.

13 John Ralston Saul, *Reflections of a Siamese Twin: Canada at the End of the Twentieth Century* (Toronto: Penguin, 1997), chap. 5.

14 Will Kymlicka, *Multicultural Citizenship* (Oxford: Oxford University Press, 1995), and Will Kymlicka, "Citizenship, Communities, and Identity in Canada," in James P. Bickerton and Alain-G. Gagnon, eds., *Canadian Politics*, 4th ed. (Peterborough: Broadview, 2004), 35-54.

15 Simone Chambers, "Contract or Conversation? Theoretical Lessons from the Canadian Constitutional Crisis," *Politics and Society* 26, 1 (March 1998): 143-72, and Jeremy Webber, *Reimagining Canada: Language, Culture, Community, and the Canadian Constitution* (Montreal and Kingston: McGill-Queen's University Press, 1994), chap. 9.

16 Webber, *Reimagining Canada*, 319.

17 Simone Chambers, *Reasonable Democracy: Jürgen Habermas and the Politics of Discourse* (Ithaca: Cornell University Press, 1996), chap. 15.

18 Louis M. Imbeau and Guy Laforest, "Québec's Distinct Society and the Sense of Nationhood in Canada," *Québec Studies* 13 (Fall 1991-Spring 1992): 14.

19 "Address by Prime Minister Paul Martin at CFB Gagetown, New Brunswick, April 14, 2004" (Government of Canada, Privy Council Office). See also Andrew Cohen, "Martin's First Year on Foreign Policy – The Rhetoric of Good Intentions," *Policy Options* (February 2005): 47-50.

Bibliographic Note

Sources used for this book are cited in the endnotes. The following section lists many of them and offers others related to the topics. Many are older selections; my orientation is historical. This eclectic collection is more a sampler than a systematically constructed menu. Items in this smorgasbord of offerings piqued my interest and contributed to shaping my thinking. The primary focus here is on books.

CHAPTER 1: PATHWAYS TO CANADIAN POLITICAL CULTURE

A standard reference and good starting point is David V.J. Bell, *The Roots of Disunity: A Study of Canadian Political Culture* (Toronto: Oxford University Press, 1992). See also his more recent "Political Culture in Canada," in Michael Whittington and Glen Williams, eds., *Canadian Politics in the 21st Century*, 6th ed. (Scarborough: Nelson, 2004), 317-45. An early assessment of Canada's political condition by a foreigner is André Siegfried, *The Race Question in Canada* (1907, 1st English trans.; repr., Toronto: McClelland and Stewart, 1966). A collection of articles on political socialization (now often referred to as civic education) appears in Jon H. Pammett and Michael S. Whittington, eds., *Foundations of Political Culture: Political Socialization in Canada* (Toronto: Macmillan, 1976). For an award-winning study of historical thought and literature, see Carl Berger, *The Writing of Canadian History: Aspects of English-Canadian Historical Writing 1900-1970* (Toronto: Oxford University Press, 1976).

For ideas and ideologies in Canadian politics, consult Colin Campbell and William Christian, *Parties, Leaders, and Ideologies in Canada* (Toronto: McGraw-Hill Ryerson, 1996). The first (1974) and subsequent editions that appeared under the title *Political Parties and Ideologies in Canada: Liberals, Conservatives, Socialists, Nationalists* draw on the dialectic tory-socialist framework offered by Louis Hartz and Gad Horowitz (see below). H.D. Forbes, ed., *Canadian Political Thought* (Toronto: Oxford University Press, 1985) contains an anthology of materials ranging from 1799 to 1979. Katherine Fierlbeck, ed., offers a more recent one in *The Development of Political Thought in Canada: An Anthology* (Peterborough: Broadview, 2005). She has also authored *Political Thought in Canada: An Intellectual History* (Peterborough: Broadview, 2006). Patricia M. Marchak,

Ideological Perspectives on Canada, 3rd ed. (Toronto: McGraw-Hill Ryerson, 1988) is more commonly cited by sociologists than by political scientists.

Gad Horowitz, "Conservatism, Liberalism, and Socialism in Canada: An Interpretation," *Canadian Journal of Economics and Political Science* 32, 1 (1966): 143-71, and its longer version in *Canadian Labour in Politics* (Toronto: University of Toronto Press, 1968), chap. 1, draws on Louis Hartz, *The Liberal Tradition in America* (New York: Harcourt Brace, 1955), and Hartz, with contributions by Kenneth D. McRae, Richard M. Morse, Richard N. Rosencrance, and Leonard M. Thompson, *The Founding of New Societies* (New York: Harcourt, Brace, and World, 1964), especially Kenneth McRae's underappreciated "The Structure of Canadian History," chap. 7. Horowitz's contributions to *Canadian Dimension* are also noteworthy, particularly "Tories, Socialists, and the Demise of Canada" 2, 4 (May-June 1965): 12-15. It is reproduced in Forbes, *Canadian Political Thought,* 352-59 (see above). Critiques of the Hartz-Horowitz hypothesis abound, including Rod Preece, "The Myth of the Red Tory," *Canadian Journal of Social and Political Theory* 1 (1977): 3-28; Tom Truman, "A Scale for Measuring a Tory Streak in Canada and the United States," *Canadian Journal of Political Science* 10 (1977): 597-614; H.D. Forbes, "Hartz-Horowitz at Twenty: Nationalism, Toryism, and Socialism in Canada and the United States," *Canadian Journal of Political Science* 20 (1987): 287-315; and Janet Ajzenstat and Peter J. Smith, eds., *Canada's Origins: Liberal, Tory, or Republican?* (Ottawa: Carleton University Press, 1995). Horowitz's rebuttal to his early critics is his "Notes on 'Conservatism, Liberalism and Socialism in Canada,'" *Canadian Journal of Political Science* 11, 2 (1978): 383-99.

Seymour Martin Lipset's comparative political sociological approach to Canada–United States differences includes *The First New Nation: The United States in Historical and Comparative Perspective* (Garden City, NY: Basic Books, 1967); *Revolution and Counterrevolution* (New York: Basic Books, 1968); *North American Cultures: Values and Institutions in Canada and the United States* (Orono, ME: Borderlands, 1990); and *Continental Divide: Values and Institutions in Canada and the United States* (New York: Routledge, 1990). See also his *Political Man: The Social Bases of Politics* (Baltimore: Johns Hopkins University Press, 1981). For a critique of Lipset, see Tom Truman, "A Critique of Seymour M. Lipset's Article: 'Value Differences Absolute or Relative: The English-Speaking Democracies,'" *Canadian Journal of Political Science* 4, 4 (1971): 495-525.

Some of Harold Innis' many works include *Staples, Markets, and Cultural Change: Selected Essays* (Montreal and Kingston: McGill-Queen's University Press, 1995); *The Bias of Communication* (1951; repr., Toronto: University of Toronto Press, 1995); and *The Idea File of Harold Adams Innis,* ed. William Christian (Toronto: University of Toronto Press, 1980). Some of his classics on staples are *The Cod Fisheries: The History of an International Economy,* rev. ed. (Toronto: University of Toronto Press, 1954); *A History of the Canadian Pacific Railroad* (1923; repr., Newton Abbott: David and Charles, 1972); and *The Fur Trade in Canada: An Introduction to Canadian Economic History* (Toronto: University of Toronto Press, 1999). For the connection between Innis and latter-day

Marxists, consult Ian Parker, "Harold Innis, Karl Marx and Canadian Political Economy," in J. Paul Grayson, ed., *Class, State, Ideology and Change: Marxist Perspectives on Canada* (Toronto: Holt, Rinehart and Winston, 1980), 234-51. See also William Melody, Liora Salter, and Paul Heyer, eds., *Culture, Communication, and Dependency: The Tradition of H.A. Innis* (Norwood, NJ: Ablex, 1981). For an intellectual biography of Innis, see Alexander John Watson, *Marginal Man: The Dark Vision of Harold Innis* (Toronto: University of Toronto Press, 2005).

CHAPTER 2: SURVEYING AND COMPARING POLITICAL CULTURES

A path-breaker in the psychocultural approach, which uses public opinion surveys, is Gabriel A. Almond and Sidney Verba, *The Civic Culture: Political Attitudes and Democracy in Five Nations* (Princeton: Princeton University Press, 1963). For essays on the intellectual history of the civic culture concept, including critiques and reinterpretations of it, see Gabriel A. Almond and Sidney Verba, eds., *The Civic Culture Revisited* (Boston: Little, Brown, 1980). Noteworthy is the foreword by Almond in Richard J. Ellis and Michael Thompson, eds., *Culture Matters: Essays in Honor of Aaron Wildavsky* (Boulder: Westview Press, 1997), vii-xi.

A plethora of survey-based Canadian studies began in earnest with the Canadian Election Studies (formerly known as the National Election Studies), launched in 1965. The initial product, John Meisel, *Working Papers on Canadian Politics* (Montreal and London: McGill-Queen's University Press, 1972), was influenced by American voting studies, especially Angus Campbell, Philip E. Converse, Warren E. Miller, and Donald E. Stokes, *The American Voter* (1960; repr., Chicago: University of Chicago Press, 1976). A more consistent and systematic approach to these election studies began with Harold D. Clarke, Jane Jenson, Lawrence LeDuc, and Jon Pammet, *Political Choice in Canada* (Toronto: McGraw-Hill Ryerson, 1979). Its successors include Harold D. Clarke, Jane Jenson, Lawrence LeDuc, and Jon Pammet, *Absent Mandate*, 3rd ed. (Toronto: Gage, 1996), and Neil Nevitte, André Blais, Elisabeth Gidengil, and Richard Nadeau, *Unsteady State: The 1997 Canadian Federal Election* (Toronto: Oxford University Press, 2000). See as well the more recent Michael D. Ornstein and H. Michael Stevenson, *Politics and Ideology in Canada* (Montreal and Kingston: McGill-Queen's University Press, 1999). An older survey approach to political participation is William Mishler, *Political Participation in Canada* (Toronto: Macmillan, 1979). The left-right dichotomy is addressed in J.A. Laponce, *Left and Right: The Topography of Political Perceptions* (Toronto: University of Toronto Press, 1981). A survey assessment of Canadian opinion in the 1980s and 1990s is Harold D. Clarke, Allan Kornberg, and Peter Wearing, *A Polity on the Edge: Canada and the Politics of Fragmentation* (Peterborough: Broadview, 2000). Elisabeth Gidengil, André Blais, and Neil Nevitte, *Citizens* (Vancouver: UBC Press, 2004), offers rich and varied sources of data to assess changes in patterns of citizen engagement.

Widely cited is Neil Nevitte, *The Decline of Deference: Canadian Value Change in Cross-National Perspective* (Peterborough: Broadview, 1996). In comparing Canadian attitudes with those in other states, this uses the cultural shift and new cleavages hypotheses of Ronald Inglehart in, among other places, his *Cultural Shift in Advanced Industrial Society* (Princeton: Princeton University Press, 1990), and *Modernization and Postmodernization: Cultural, Economic, and Political Change in 43 Societies* (Princeton: Princeton University Press, 1997). Neil Nevitte and Roger Gibbins, *New Elites in Old States: Ideologies in the Anglo-American Democracies* (Toronto: Oxford University Press, 1990) examines attitudinal differences among university youth in five states, including Canada. See also Neil Nevitte, ed., *Value Change and Governance in Canada* (Toronto: University of Toronto Press, 2002).

The Institute for Research on Public Policy (IRPP) and the late Council for Canadian Unity's Centre for Research and Information on Canada (CRIC) published numerous studies monitoring the attitudes of Canadians on issues ranging from participation to policy and identity. See, for example, Paul Howe and David Northrup, *Strengthening Canadian Democracy: The Views of Canadians*, Policy Matters 1, 5 (Montreal: IRPP, July 2000), and CRIC's *Portraits of Canada* series, http://www.cric.ca/en_html/index.html. Two popular survey treatments of Canadians' values by a commercial pollster are Michael Adams, *Sex in the Snow: Canadian Social Values at the End of the Millennium* (Toronto: Viking, 1997), and Michael Adams, *Fire and Ice: The United States, Canada and the Myth of Converging Values* (Toronto: Penguin, 2003).

CHAPTER 3: CONSTITUTIONS AND INSTITUTIONS AS CULTURE

Earlier institutional studies touch on the implications of bilingualism; later ones also incorporate multicultural considerations. Peter H. Russell, *Constitutional Odyssey: Can Canadians Become a Sovereign People?* 3rd ed. (Toronto: University of Toronto Press, 2004) traces Canadian efforts at megaconstitutional change since Confederation. See Peter Russell, Rainer Knopff, and Ted Morton, *Federalism and the Charter: Leading Constitutional Decisions* (Ottawa: Carleton University Press, 1989) for the evolution of judicial constitutional review and leading cases that helped shape the direction of the federal principle and Charter jurisprudence. For a succinct review of the Constitution, see Ronald I. Cheffins and Patricia A. Johnson, *The Revised Canadian Constitution: Politics as Law* (Toronto: McGraw-Hill Ryerson, 1986). David Milne, *The Canadian Constitution* (Toronto: Lorimer, 1991) reviews the making of the 1982 Constitution; Roy Romanow, John Whyte, and Howard Leeson, *Canada ... Notwithstanding* (Toronto: Carswell/ Methuen, 1984) offers a principal player's view of the negotiations. Shedding light on the practices driving the unwritten constitution is Andrew Heard, *Canadian Constitutional Conventions: The Marriage of Law and Politics* (Toronto: Oxford University Press, 1991). Alan C. Cairns' two collections, *Reconfigurations: Canadian Citizenship and Constitutional Change* (Toronto: McClelland and Stewart, 1995), and *Disruptions: Constitutional Struggles, from the Charter to Meech Lake* (Toronto: McClelland and Stewart, 1991), offer insightful essays by a leading political scientist. David E. Smith's trilogy, *The Invisible Crown: The First Principle of Canadian Government* (Toronto: University of Toronto

Press, 1995); *The Canadian Senate in Bicameral Perspective* (Toronto: University of Toronto Press, 2003); and *The People's House of Commons* (Toronto: University of Toronto Press, 2007), illuminate those institutions.

David Docherty, *Legislatures* (Vancouver: UBC Press, 2004), and Graham White, *Cabinets and First Ministers* (Vancouver: UBC Press, 2005) present accessible treatments. C.E.S. Franks, *The Parliament of Canada* (Toronto: University of Toronto Press, 1987), is aging but authoritative. Donald J. Savoie, *Governing from the Centre: The Concentration of Power in Canadian Politics* (Toronto: University of Toronto Press, 1999), and Donald J. Savoie, *Breaking the Bargain: Public Servants, Ministers, and Parliament* (Toronto: University of Toronto Press, 2003) have deeply influenced our understanding of the evolving operational principles and practices driving the machinery of government. A solid text on Canadian institutions is Heather MacIvor, *Parameters of Power: Canada's Political Institutions* (Toronto: Nelson, 2006).

For federalism, see Jennifer Smith, *Federalism* (Vancouver: UBC Press, 2004); Herman Bakvis and Grace Skogstad, eds., *Canadian Federalism: Performance, Effectiveness, and Legitimacy* (Toronto: Oxford University Press, 2002); J. Peter Meekison, Hamish Telford, and Harvey Lazar, eds., *Reconsidering the Institutions of Canadian Federalism* (Montreal and Kingston: McGill-Queen's University Press, 2000); Francois Rocher and Miriam Smith, eds., *New Trends in Canadian Federalism*, 2nd ed. (Peterborough: Broadview, 2003); Garth Stevenson, *Unfulfilled Union: Canadian Federalism and National Unity*, 4th ed. (Montreal and Kingston: McGill-Queen's University Press, 2004); and Richard Simeon, *Federal-Provincial Diplomacy: The Making of Recent Policy in Canada* (1972; repr., Toronto: University of Toronto Press, 2006).

On the judiciary and the Charter, see Peter McCormick, *Supreme at Last: The Evolution of the Supreme Court of Canada* (Toronto: James Lorimer, 2000); Patrick James, Donald E. Abelson, and Michael Lusztig, eds., *The Myth of the Sacred: The Charter, the Courts, and the Politics of the Constitution* (Montreal and Kingston: McGill-Queen's University Press, 2002); Janet Hiebert, *Charter Conflicts: What Is Parliament's Role?* (Montreal: McGraw-Hill Ryerson, 2002); Christopher P. Manfredi, *Judicial Power and the Charter: Canada and the Paradox of Constitutional Liberalism*, 2nd ed. (Toronto: Oxford University Press, 2001); James B. Kelly, *Governing with the Charter: Legislative and Judicial Activism and the Framers' Intent* (Vancouver: UBC Press, 2005); Raymond Bazowski and Charles Smith, eds., *The Charter at Twenty* (Montreal and Kingston: McGill-Queen's University Press, 2005); and Heather MacIvor, *Canadian Politics in the Charter Era* (Toronto: Nelson, 2005). For engaged debate, see Robert I. Martin, *The Most Dangerous Branch: How the Supreme Court Has Undermined Our Law and Our Democracy* (Montreal and Kingston: McGill-Queen's University Press, 2003); F.L. Morton and Rainer Knopff, *The Charter Revolution and the Court Party* (Peterborough: Broadview, 2000); and Kent Roach, *The Supreme Court on Trial: Judicial Activism or Democratic Dialogue?* (Toronto: Irwin Law, 2001). Michael Mandel, *The Charter of Rights and the Legalization of Politics in Canada*, rev. ed. (Toronto: Thomson, 1994) offers a radical critique.

On the electoral system, see John Courtney, *Elections* (Vancouver: UBC Press, 2004), and Henry Milner, ed., *Steps toward Making Every Vote Count: Electoral System Reform in Canada and Its Provinces* (Peterborough: Broadview, 2004). *Electoral Insight* is a periodical published by Elections Canada. For political parties, Hugh G. Thorburn and Alan Whitehorn, eds., *Party Politics in Canada*, 8th ed. (Toronto: Prentice-Hall, 2001) is the longest-continuing reader on the subject. Shorter monographs include James P. Bickerton, Alain-G. Gagnon, and Patrick Smith, *Ties That Bind: Parties and Votes in Canada* (Toronto: Oxford University Press, 1999), and William Cross, *Political Parties* (Vancouver: UBC Press, 2004). See also R.K. Carty, William Cross, and Lisa Young, *Rebuilding Canadian Party Politics* (Vancouver: UBC Press, 2000). Interest groups are examined in Lisa Young and Joanna Everitt, *Advocacy Groups* (Vancouver: UBC Press, 2004); A. Paul Pross, *Group Politics and Public Policy*, 2nd ed. (Toronto: Oxford University Press, 1992); Leslie Pal, *Interests of State: The Politics of Language, Multiculturalism and Feminism in Canada* (Montreal and Kingston: McGill-Queen's University Press, 1993); and Miriam Smith, *A Civil Society? Collective Actors in Canadian Political Life* (Peterborough: Broadview, 2005).

CHAPTER 4: CULTURE, BICULTURE, MULTICULTURE, ABORIGINAL CULTURE
For cultural policy and the public administration of culture, see the Annual Reports of agencies such as the Department of Heritage and its predecessor departments, the Canada Council, and the provincial equivalents. See as well the publications of those departments and agencies responsible for culture, bilingualism, multicultural communities, and Aboriginal affairs. For example, *Multiculturalism: What Is It Really About?* (Ottawa: Multiculturalism and Citizenship Canada, 1991), and the Office of the Commissioner of Official Languages, *Language and Society* (1979-94). A landmark in the direction of cultural policy was the *Royal Commission on National Development in the Arts, Letters, and Sciences 1949-1951* (Ottawa: King's Printer, 1951). Provincial publications include *La Politique québécoise du développement culturel* (Quebec: Editeur officiel, 1978). For an alternative rationale for government intervention in the cultural sector, see Caroline Andrew, Monica Gattinger, M. Sharon Jeannotte, and Will Straw, eds., *Accounting for Culture: Thinking through Cultural Citizenship* (Ottawa: University of Ottawa Press, 2005). Eminent author Margaret Atwood surveys Canadian literature in *Survival* (Toronto: Anansi, 1972).

The bicultural cleavage was the subject of the *Report of the Royal Commission on Bilingualism and Biculturalism* (Ottawa: Queen's Printer, 1967), a turning point for language policy. See also the Tremblay Commission, *Rapport de la Commission royale d'enquête sur les problèmes constitutionelles* (Quebec: Province du Québec, 1956), and Kenneth McRoberts, *Misconceiving Canada: The Struggle for National Unity* (Toronto: Oxford University Press, 1997). A radical and provocative bestseller was Pierre Vallières, *White Niggers of America* (Toronto: McClelland and Stewart, 1971). Charles Taylor, Canada's internationally acclaimed theorist, offers his reflections in *Reconciling the Solitudes: Essays on Canadian Federalism and Nationalism* (Montreal and Kingston: McGill-Queen's University Press, 1993). For a history of francophones outside Quebec, consult Michael Behiels,

Canada's Francophone Minority Communities: Constitutional Renewal and the Winning of School Governance (Montreal and Kingston: McGill-Queen's University Press, 2004); for Quebec, see Marc V. Levine, *The Reconquest of Montreal: Language Policy and Social Change in a Bilingual City* (Philadelphia: Temple University Press, 1990). See also Graham Fraser, *Sorry, I Don't Speak French: Confronting the Canadian Crisis That Won't Go Away* (Toronto: Douglas Gibson, 2006) for a journalist's account of the bilingual story.

For multiculturalism, see Augie Fleras and Jean Leonard, eds., *Multiculturalism in Canada: The Challenge of Diversity* (Scarborough: Nelson, 1992). An alternative conceptualization of multiculturalism appears in Gerald Kernerman, *Multicultural Citizenship: Civilizing Difference, Constituting Community* (Vancouver: UBC Press, 2005). Theorist Will Kymlicka has contributed *Finding Our Way: Rethinking Ethnocultural Relations in Canada* (Toronto: Oxford University Press, 1998), and *Multicultural Citizenship* (Oxford: Clarendon Press, 1995). For criticisms of multicultural policy, see Neil Bissoondath, *Selling Illusions: The Cult of Multiculturalism in Canada* (Toronto: Penguin, 1994), and Reginald W. Bibby, *Mosaic Madness: The Poverty and Potential of Life in Canada* (Toronto: Stoddart, 1990). See also Yasmeen Abu-Laban and Christina Gabriel, *Selling Diversity: Immigration, Multiculturalism, Employment Equity, and Globalization* (Peterborough: Broadview, 2002).

The material on Aboriginals has dramatically expanded in recent decades. See, for example, the studies and extraordinarily voluminous *Report of the Royal Commission on Aboriginal Peoples*, 5 vols. (Ottawa: Supply and Services Canada, 1996). Studies include Menno Boldt, *Surviving as Indians: The Challenge to Self-Government* (Toronto: University of Toronto Press, 1993); Tim Schouls, *Shifting Boundaries: Aboriginal Identity, Pluralist Theory and the Politics of Self-Government* (Vancouver: UBC Press, 2003); Alan C. Cairns, *Citizens Plus: Aboriginal Peoples and the Canadian State* (Vancouver: UBC Press, 2000); James Frideres, *Aboriginal Peoples in Canada* (Scarborough: Prentice-Hall, 1998); Peter Kulchyski, ed., *Unjust Relations: Aboriginal Rights in Canadian Courts* (Toronto: Oxford University Press, 1994); and Thomas Flanagan, *First Nations? Second Thoughts* (Montreal and Kingston: McGill-Queen's University Press, 2000), which takes a critical look at Aboriginal claims. Another approach to Aboriginal communities appears in Jerry P. White, Paul S. Maxim, and Dan Beavon, eds., *Aboriginal Conditions: Research as a Foundation for Public Policy* (Vancouver: UBC Press, 2003). Anthropologist Michael Asch, *Aboriginal and Treaty Rights in Canada* (Vancouver: UBC Press, 1998), addresses legal biases Aboriginals face, and legal theorist Patrick Macklem's *Indigenous Difference and the Constitution of Canada* (Toronto: University of Toronto Press, 2001) is an award winner. For an Aboriginal voice, see Gerald R. Alfred, *Peace, Power, Righteousness: An Indigenous Manifesto* (Don Mills: Oxford University Press, 1999).

CHAPTER 5: REGIONS AND POLITICAL CULTURE

The most-cited article that draws on the Canadian Election Studies, Richard Simeon and David J. Elkins, "Regional Political Cultures in Canada," *Canadian Journal of Polit-*

ical Science 7, 3 (September 1974): 397-437, is survey-based. It was updated as "Provincial Political Cultures in Canada," in David J. Elkins and Richard Simeon, eds., *Small Worlds: Provinces and Parties in Canadian Political Life* (Toronto: Methuen, 1980), 31-76. John Wilson, "The Canadian Political Cultures: Towards a Redefinition of the Nature of the Canadian Political System," *Canadian Journal of Political Science* 7, 3 (September 1974): 438-83, uses vote results for elections between the 1940s and 1970s to comparatively classify provincial political cultures.

An early collection focusing on provincial politics is David J. Bellamy, Jon H. Pammett, and Donald C. Rowat, eds., *The Provincial Political Systems: Comparative Essays* (Toronto: Methuen, 1976). A more recent comparative reader is Christopher Dunn, ed., *Provinces: Canadian Provincial Politics*, 2nd ed. (Peterborough: Broadview, 2006) (all my endnotes cite the 1st ed. [1996]). See also Robert J. Brym, ed., *Regionalism in Canada* (Toronto: Irwin, 1986), for its focus on class. Two early examinations of the provincial policy dimension are Marsha A. Chandler and William M. Chandler, *Public Policy and Provincial Politics* (Toronto: McGraw-Hill Ryerson, 1979), and D.C. Rowat, *Provincial Policy-Making: Comparative Essays* (Ottawa: Department of Political Science, Carleton University, 1981). Allan Kornberg, William Mishler, and Harold D. Clarke's *Representative Democracy in the Canadian Provinces* (Scarborough: Prentice-Hall, 1982) evaluates performance. Helpful are the entries for the individual provinces in "The Provinces" sections of the *Canadian Annual Review of Politics and Public Affairs* (Toronto: University of Toronto Press, since 1961), and its predecessor *Canadian Annual Review of Public Affairs* (1901-37). So too are the chapters on the provinces in the annual series *Canada: The State of the Federation*, produced by Queen's University's Institute of Intergovernmental Relations.

Many books on provincial politics offer non-comparative chapters on the individual provinces. When one reads them collectively, comparative insights emerge. Rand Dyck's monograph *Provincial Politics in Canada: Towards the Turn of the Century*, 3rd ed. (Scarborough: Prentice-Hall, 1996) offers many tables with data on each province's political history, economy, and political institutions that make for comparative analysis. For collections with chapters on regions or individual provinces, see Martin Robin, ed., *Canadian Provincial Politics: The Party Systems of the Ten Provinces*, 2nd ed. (Scarborough: Prentice-Hall, 1978); Gary Levy and Graham White, eds., *Provincial and Territorial Legislatures in Canada* (Toronto: University of Toronto Press, 1989); Evert A. Lindquist, ed., *Government Restructuring and Career Public Services in Canada* (Toronto: Institute of Public Administration of Canada, 2000); Keith Brownsey and Michael Howlett, eds., *The Provincial State in Canada* (Peterborough: Broadview, 2001; see also the earlier edition, *The Provincial State* [Mississauga: Copp Clark Pitman, 1992]); Luc Bernier, Keith Brownsey, and Michael Howlett, eds., *Executive Styles in Canada: Cabinet Structures and Leadership Practices in Canadian Government* (Toronto: University of Toronto Press, 2005); Allan M. Maslove, ed., *Budgeting in the Provinces: Leadership and the*

Premiers (Toronto: Institute of Public Administration of Canada, 1989); R. Kenneth Carty, Lynda Erickson, and Donald E. Blake, eds., *Leaders and Parties in Canadian Politics: Experiences of the Provinces* (Toronto: Harcourt Brace Jovanovich, 1992); Leslie A. Pal and David Taras, eds., *Prime Ministers and Premiers* (Scarborough: Prentice-Hall, 1988); and Hamish Telford and Harvey Lazar, eds., *Canada: The State of the Federation 2001: Canadian Political Culture(s) in Transition* (Montreal and Kingston: McGill-Queen's University Press, 2002).

Books with regional themes include Roger Gibbins, *Regionalism: Territorial Politics in Canada and the United States* (Toronto: Butterworths, 1982); Stephen G. Tomblin, *Ottawa and the Outer Provinces: The Challenge of Regional Integration in Canada* (Toronto: Lorimer, 1995); James N. McRorie and Martha L. MacDonald, *The Constitutional Futures of the Prairie and Atlantic Regions* (Regina: Canadian Plains Research Centre, 1992); David Jay Bercuson and Phillip A. Buckner, eds., *Eastern and Western Perspectives: Papers from the Joint Atlantic Canada/Western Canadian Studies Conference* (Toronto: University of Toronto Press, 1981); David Jay Bercuson, ed., *Canada and the Burden of Unity* (Toronto: Macmillan, 1977); Herman Bakvis, *Regional Ministers: Power and Influence in the Canadian Cabinet* (Toronto: University of Toronto Press, 1991); and Lisa Young and Keith Archer, eds., *Regionalism and Party Politics in Canada* (Toronto: Oxford University Press, 2002). For regional planning analysis, see Gerald Hodge and Ira M. Robinson, *Planning Canadian Regions* (Vancouver: UBC Press, 2001).

CHAPTER 6: ATLANTIC CANADA

Ian Stewart's *Roasting Chestnuts: The Mythology of Maritime Political Culture* (Vancouver: UBC Press, 1994), is a collection of excellent essays. Two older edited collections by historian G.A. Rawlyk are *Historical Essays on the Atlantic Provinces* (Toronto: McClelland and Stewart, 1967), and *The Atlantic Provinces and the Problems of Confederation* (Halifax: Breakwater, 1979). A solid monograph is W.S. McNutt, *The Atlantic Provinces: The Emergence of Colonial Society, 1712-1857* (Toronto: McClelland and Stewart, 1965). Stephen G. Tomblin and Charles S. Colgan, eds., *Regionalism in a Global Society: Persistence and Change in Atlantic Canada and New England* (Peterborough: Broadview, 2003) examines the future prospects and policy opportunities of regional integration. A government document on the integration idea is *The Report on Maritime Union Commissioned by the Governments of Nova Scotia, New Brunswick and Prince Edward Island* (Fredericton: Maritime Union Study, 1970). See also E.R. Forbes, *The Maritime Rights Movement, 1919-1927* (Montreal and Kingston: McGill-Queen's University Press, 1979); E.R. Forbes, *The Atlantic Provinces in Confederation: A History* (Toronto: University of Toronto Press, 1993); and his edited collection, *Challenging the Regional Stereotypes: Essays on the 20th Century Maritimes* (Fredericton: Acadiensis Press, 1989). Also useful are P.A. Buckner, ed., *Teaching Maritime Studies* (Fredericton: Acadiensis Press, 1986), and Robert J. Brym and R. James Sacouman, eds., *Underdevelopment and Social Movements in Atlantic Canada*

(Toronto: New Hogtown Press, 1979). For patronage, spoils, and political colour, refer to Dalton Camp, *Gentlemen, Players, and Politicians* (Toronto: McClelland and Stewart, 1970); Jeffrey Simpson, *The Spoils of Power: The Politics of Patronage* (Toronto: Collins, 1988); and Arthur T. Doyle, *Front Benches and Back Rooms: A Story of Corruption, Muckraking, Raw Partisanship and Intrigue in New Brunswick* (Toronto: Green Tree, 1976). *Acadiensis* is the leading regional journal.

On Newfoundland, see Sid Noel, *Politics in Newfoundland* (Toronto: University of Toronto Press, 1971); James Hiller and Peter Neary, eds., *Newfoundland in the Nineteenth and Twentieth Centuries* (Toronto: University of Toronto Press, 1980); Gertrude E. Gunn, *The Political History of Newfoundland, 1832-1864* (Toronto: University of Toronto Press, 1966); David Mackenzie, *Inside the Atlantic Triangle: Canada and the Entrance of Newfoundland into Confederation, 1939-1949* (Toronto: University of Toronto Press, 1986); and Raymond Blake, *Canadians at Last: Canada Integrates Newfoundland as a Province* (Toronto: University of Toronto Press, 1994). For bureaucratic infighting, see J.D. House, *Against the Tide: Battling for Economic Renewal in Newfoundland and Labrador* (Toronto: University of Toronto Press, 1999). On the now resolved denominational school issues, consult William A. McKim, ed., *The Vexed Question: Denominational Education in a Secular Age* (St. John's: Breakwater, 1988).

Two useful journals are *Newfoundland Studies* and *Newfoundland Quarterly*.

On Prince Edward Island, see Verner Smitheram, David A. Milne, and Satadal Dasgupta, eds., *The Garden Transformed: Prince Edward Island, 1945-1980* (Charlottetown: Ragweed Press, 1982); Francis W.P. Bolger, ed., *Canada's Smallest Province* (Charlottetown: P.E.I. Centennial Commission, 1973); A.H. Clark, *Three Centuries and the Island* (Toronto: University of Toronto Press, 1959); and Frank MacKinnon, *The Government of Prince Edward Island* (Toronto: University of Toronto Press, 1951). See also Errol Sharpe, *A People's History of Prince Edward Island* (Toronto: Steel Rail, 1976).

For Nova Scotia, refer to James Bickerton, *Nova Scotia, Ottawa and the Politics of Regional Development* (Toronto: University of Toronto Press, 1990); J. Murray Beck, *The Government of Nova Scotia* (Toronto: University of Toronto Press, 1957); J. Murray Beck, *Joseph Howe: Voice of Nova Scotia* (Toronto: McClelland and Stewart, 1964); Neil MacKinnon, *This Unfriendly Soil: The Loyalist Experience in Nova Scotia, 1783-1791* (Montreal and Kingston: McGill-Queen's University Press, 1986); K.G. Pryke, *Nova Scotia and Confederation* (Toronto: University of Toronto Press, 1976).

For New Brunswick, see Hugh G. Thorburn, *Politics in New Brunswick* (Toronto: University of Toronto Press, 1961); W.S. McNutt, *New Brunswick – A History: 1784-1867* (Toronto: Macmillan, 1984); Edmund A. Aunger, *In Search of Political Stability: A Comparative Study of New Brunswick and Northern Ireland* (Montreal and Kingston: McGill-Queen's University Press, 1981); Richard Wilbur, *The Rise of French New Brunswick* (Halifax: Formac, 1989); Donald J. Savoie, *Federal-Provincial Collaboration: The Canada-New Brunswick General Development Agreement* (Montreal and Kingston: McGill-Queen's

University Press, 1981); Gary Burrill and Ian MacKay, eds., *People, Power, and Resources* (Fredericton: Acadiensis Press, 1987). On leaders, see William J. Milne, *The McKenna Miracle: Myth or Reality?* (Toronto: University of Toronto Press, 1996); Della M.M. Stanley, *Louis Robichaud, a Decade of Power* (Halifax: Nimbus, 1984); Michel Cormier and Achille Michaud, *Richard Hatfield: Power and Disobedience* (Fredericton: Goose Lane, 1992). On the tycoon, see John DeMont, *Citizen Irving: K.C. Irving and His Legacy* (Toronto: Doubleday, 1991), and Douglas How and Ralph Costello, *K.C.: The Biography of K.C. Irving* (Toronto: Key Porter, 1994).

CHAPTER 7: QUEBEC

A.I. Silver, *The French-Canadian Idea of Confederation, 1864-1900* (Toronto: University of Toronto Press, 1982), plumbs opinion via newspapers. Everett C. Hughes, *French Canada in Transition* (Chicago: University of Chicago Press, 1943) is a classic sociological study of the bicultural cleavage during Quebec's industrialization and urbanization. Alain-G. Gagnon, ed., *Quebec: State and Society*, 3rd ed. (Peterborough: Broadview, 2004) is a diverse collection, mainly by political scientists; Marcel Rioux, *Quebec in Question*, trans. James Boake (Toronto: James Lorimer, 1978) is a sociologist's historical account using ideology as a hinge; Kenneth McRoberts, *Quebec: Social Change and Political Crisis*, 3rd ed. (Toronto: McClelland and Stewart, 1993) traces the growth of the *indépendantiste* movement; Guy Lachapelle, Gérald Bernier, Daniel Salée, and Luc Bernier, *The Quebec Democracy: Structures, Processes, and Policies* (Toronto: McGraw-Hill Ryerson, 1993) describes Quebec's continuous transformation; Michael D. Behiels, ed., *Quebec since 1800: Selected Readings* (Toronto: Irwin, 2002) addresses issues related to religion, economics, language, education, and women; Paul-André Linteau, René Durocher, Jean-Claude Robert, and François Ricard, *Quebec Since 1930*, trans. Robert Chodos and Ellen Garmaise (Toronto: Lorimer, 1991) is wide-ranging as well, giving significant attention to leaders; Robert Armstrong, *Structures and Change: An Economic History of Quebec* (Toronto: Gage, 1984), and Gérald Bernier and Daniel Salée, *The Shaping Of Québec Politics and Society: Colonialism, Power, and the Transition to Capitalism in the 19th Century* (Washington, DC: Crane Russak, 1992), deal with economic development. See also Mason Wade, *The French Canadians, 1760-1945* (Toronto: Macmillan, 1955); Denis Monière, *Ideologies in Quebec* (Toronto: University of Toronto Press, 1981); Allan Greer, *Peasant, Lord, and Merchant: Rural Society in Three Quebec Parishes, 1740-1840* (Toronto: University of Toronto Press, 1985); Fernand Dumont, *The Vigil of Quebec* (Toronto: University of Toronto Press, 1971); and Alain-G. Gagnon and Mary Beth Montcalm, *Quebec: Beyond the Quiet Revolution* (Scarborough: Nelson, 1990).

For some leaders, refer to Bernard L. Vigod, *Quebec before Duplessis: The Political Career of Louis Alexandre Taschereau* (Montreal and Kingston: McGill-Queen's University Press, 1986), and Herbert Quinn, *The Union Nationale: Quebec Nationalism from Duplessis to Lévesque* (Toronto: University of Toronto Press, 1979). For a leader's political statement, consult René Lévesque, *My Quebec* (Toronto: Methuen, 1979). For a journalist's excellent account, see Graham Fraser, *P.Q.: René Lévesque and the Parti Québécois in Power* (Toronto: Macmillan, 1984).

Ronald Rudin, *Making History in Twentieth-Century Quebec* (Toronto: University of Toronto Press, 1997) is a historiographical exploration; for one that is controversial, see Fernand Ouellette, *Economy, Class and Nation in Quebec: Interpretive Essays* (Toronto: Copp Clark Pitman, 1991). Ramsay Cook, *French Canadian Nationalism: An Anthology* (Toronto: Macmillan, 1969) offers voices of dissent. See also his highly praised essays in *Canada and the French-Canadian Question* (Toronto: Macmillan, 1967), and his subsequent collection on nationalistic rhetoric, English as well as Québécois, in *Canada, Quebec, and the Uses of Nationalism* (Toronto: McClelland and Stewart, 1986). Pierre Elliott Trudeau, *Federalism and the French Canadians* (Toronto: Macmillan, 1968) is a collection of essays that appeared as he marched toward the prime ministership. Robert Bothwell, *Canada and Quebec: One Country, Two Histories* (Vancouver: UBC Press, 1995) is a collection of interviews with opinion leaders.

Claude Morin, *Quebec versus Ottawa: The Struggle for Self-Government, 1960-72* (Toronto: University of Toronto Press, 1976) offers a deputy minister's account of intergovernmental battles. Robert A Young, *The Struggle for Quebec: From Referendum to Referendum?* (Montreal and Kingston: McGill-Queen's University Press, 1999), covers a more recent period. See also David R. Cameron, ed., *The Referendum Papers: Essays on Secession and National Unity* (Toronto: University of Toronto Press, 1999). Christian Dufour, *A Canadian Challenge: Le Défi Québécois* (Montreal: Institute for Research on Public Policy, 1990) is well done and was widely read. Jocelyn Maclure, *Quebec Identity: The Challenge of Pluralism*, trans. Peter Feldstein (Montreal and Kingston: McGill-Queen's University Press, 2003) covers the nationalist and anti-nationalist camps.

Some titles *en français* include Michel Venne, ed., *Penser la nation québécoise* (Montreal: Québec-Amerique, 2000); André Lussier, *Le nationalisme québécois sur le divan* (Montreal: Fides, 2002); and Denis Monière, *Pour comprendre le nationalisme au Québec et ailleurs* (Montreal: Presses de l'Université de Montréal, 2001).

Quebec Studies is a useful journal; *Recherches sociographiques* contains some helpful articles.

CHAPTER 8: ONTARIO

Thomas J. Courchene with Colin R. Telmer, *From Heartland to North American Region State: The Social, Fiscal, and Federal Evolution of Ontario* (Toronto: Faculty of Management, University of Toronto, 1998) offers a provocative thesis that is explored further in "Is Ontario a Region-State?" *Policy Options* 21, 1 (January-February 2000): 83-105. See also Christopher Armstrong, *The Politics of Federalism: Ontario's Relationship with the Federal Government, 1867-1941* (Toronto: University of Toronto Press, 1981). For economic background, consult K.J. Rea, *The Prosperous Years: An Economic History of Ontario, 1939-1975* (Toronto: University of Toronto Press, 1975). An excellent collection is Graham White, ed., *The Government and Politics of Ontario*, 5th ed. (Toronto: University of Toronto Press, 1997), and its earlier editions by Donald C. MacDonald. An older collection, by the Ontario Historical Society, is *Profiles of a Province* (Toronto: Ontario Historical Society, 1967). See also J.K. Johnson, ed., *Historical Essays on Upper Canada* (Toronto: McClelland and Stewart, 1975); Robert Bothwell, *A Short History of Ontario* (Edmonton: Hurtig, 1986), which lives up to its title; and Ramsay Cook's acclaimed *The Regenerators: Social Criticism in Late Victorian English Canada* (Toronto: University of Toronto Press, 1985). On organized labour's stirrings, see Gregory S. Kealey, *Toronto Workers Respond to Industrial Capitalism, 1867-1892* (Toronto: University of Toronto Press, 1980), and Gregory S. Kealey and Bryan D. Palmer, *Dreaming of What Might Be: The Knights of Labor in Ontario, 1880-1900* (Toronto: New Hogtown Press, 1987). On the times of Ontario's longest-serving premier, refer to Donald Swainson, ed., *Oliver Mowat's Ontario* (Toronto: Macmillan, 1972). Roger Graham, *Old Man Ontario: Leslie M. Frost* (Toronto: University of Toronto Press, 1990), and Allan Kerr McDougall, *John P. Robarts, His Life and Times* (Toronto: University of Toronto Press, 1986), examine more recent premiers. A turbulent decade is chronicled in Randall White, *Ontario since 1985* (Toronto: Eastend Books, 1998).

The CCF-NDP, the weak sister in Ontario's three-party system, has received disproportionate attention. See Dan Azoulay, *Keeping the Dream Alive: The Survival of the Ontario CCF/NDP, 1950-1963* (Montreal and Kingston: McGill-Queen's University Press, 1997), and J.T. Morley, *Secular Socialists: The CCF/NDP in Ontario, A Biography* (Montreal and Kingston: McGill-Queen's University Press, 1984). Daniel Drache, ed., *Getting on Track: Social Democratic Strategies for Ontario* (Montreal and Kingston: McGill-Queen's University Press, 1992), offered gratuitous advice to the party when it was in office. That period is covered by Thomas Walkom, *Rae Days: The Rise and Follies of the NDP* (Toronto: Key Porter, 1994); Patrick Monahan, *Storming the Pink Palace: A Cautionary Tale* (Toronto: Lester, 1995); and Bob Rae, *From Protest to Power: Personal Reflections on a Life in Politics* (Toronto: Viking, 1996). For the Conservative denouement, refer to Sid Noel, ed., *Revolution at Queen's Park: Essays on Governing Ontario* (Toronto: Lorimer, 1997), and David R. Cameron and Graham White, *Cycling into Saigon: The Conservative Transition in Ontario* (Vancouver: UBC Press, 2000).

Three journals include *Ontario History, Great Lakes Geographer,* and *Urban History Review,* the latter dealing with many, but not exclusively, Ontario cities.

CHAPTER 9: THE MIDWEST

Many books deal with the Prairies or the West as regions. They include Roger Gibbins, *Prairie Politics and Society: Regionalism in Decline* (Toronto: Butterworths, 1980); Roger Gibbins and Loleen Berdahl, *Western Visions, Western Futures: Perspectives on the West in Canada,* 2nd ed. (Peterborough: Broadview, 2003); Donald Swainson, *Historical Essays on the Prairie Provinces* (Toronto: McClelland and Stewart, 1970); David Laycock, *Populism and Democratic Thought in the Canadian Prairies, 1910 to 1945* (Toronto: University of

Toronto Press, 1990); A. Ross McCormick, *Reformers, Rebels, and Revolutionaries: The Western Canadian Radical Movement, 1899-1919* (Toronto: University of Toronto Press, 1977); David E. Smith, *The Regional Decline of a National Party: Liberals on the Prairies* (Toronto: University of Toronto Press, 1981); and John Richards and Larry Pratt, *Prairie Capitalism: Power and Influence in the New West* (Toronto: McClelland and Stewart, 1979), which refers to Saskatchewan and Alberta. Gerald Friesen, *The Canadian Prairies: A History* (Toronto: University of Toronto Press, 1984) is outstanding, noteworthy for its treatment of the Métis. For an older collection, see Carl Berger and Ramsay Cook, eds., *The West and the Nation* (Toronto: McClelland and Stewart, 1967). W.L. Morton, *The Progressive Party of Canada* (Toronto: University of Toronto Press, 1950) won the Governor General's Award. A multi-volume collection on Prairie settlement, economy, and geography is the *Canadian Frontiers of Settlement* series published by Macmillan in the 1930s and '40s.

A regional journal is *Prairie Forum*.

The literature on Manitoba is thinner than it is for the other Western provinces. W.L. Morton, *Manitoba: A History*, 2nd ed. (Toronto: University of Toronto Press, 1967) is a magisterial account of the settlement and development of the province up to the mid-twentieth century. Another account is James Jackson, *The Centennial History of Manitoba* (Toronto: McClelland and Stewart, 1970). M.S. Donnelly, *The Government of Manitoba* (Toronto: University of Toronto Press, 1963) details the province's institutional foundations; Jim Silver and Jeremy Hull, eds., *The Political Economy of Manitoba* (Regina: Canadian Plains Research Centre, 1990) offers critical essays. D.C. Masters, *The Winnipeg General Strike* (Toronto: University of Toronto Press, 1950) is a useful treatment of the subject. John Kendle reviews the life of the province's most successful premier in *John Bracken: A Political Biography* (Toronto: University of Toronto Press, 1979). James A. McAllister examines the first social democratic regime in *The Government of Edward Schreyer* (Montreal and Kingston: McGill-Queen's University Press, 1984); Paul Beaulieu, ed., *Ed Schreyer, A Social Democrat in Power* (Winnipeg: Queenston House, 1977) conveys its leader's thinking. Nelson Wiseman, *Social Democracy in Manitoba: A History of the CCF-NDP* (Winnipeg: University of Manitoba Press, 1983), covers the left between the 1920s and 1970s; Raymond M. Hebert, *Manitoba's French-Language Crisis: A Cautionary Tale* (Montreal and Kingston: McGill-Queen's University Press, 2004), delves into the explosive world of language politics.

Manitoba History is the regional journal.

The richer literature on Saskatchewan includes John Archer, *Saskatchewan: A History* (Saskatoon: Western Producer Prairie Books, 1980); Evelyn Eager, *Saskatchewan Government: Politics and Pragmatism* (Saskatoon: Western Producer Prairie Books, 1980); John Warnock, *Saskatchewan: The Roots of Discontent and Protest* (Montreal: Black Rose, 2004); A.W. Johnson, *Dream No Little Dream: A Biography of the Douglas Government of Saskatchewan, 1944-1961* (Toronto: University of Toronto Press, 2004); David E. Smith, *Prairie Liberalism: The Liberal Party in Saskatchewan, 1905-1971* (Toronto: University of

Toronto Press, 1975); David E. Smith, ed., *Building a Province: A History of Saskatchewan in Documents* (Saskatoon: Fifth House, 1992); Norman Ward and Duff Spafford, eds., *Politics in Saskatchewan* (Don Mills: Longmans, 1968). In addition, Seymour Martin Lipset, *Agrarian Socialism: The Co-operative Commonwealth Federation in Saskatchewan* (1950; repr., Garden City, NY: Doubleday, 1968) is a masterful sociological account; James M. Pitsula and Ken Rasmussen, *Privatizing a Province: The New Right in Saskatchewan* (Vancouver: New Star, 1990) critiques the Devine government; Jim Harding, *Social Policy and Social Justice: The NDP Government in Saskatchewan during the Blakeney Years* (Waterloo: Wilfrid Laurier University Press, 1995) discusses the previous government; and Howard A. Leeson, ed., *Saskatchewan Politics: Into the Twenty-First Century* (Regina: Canadian Plains Research, 2001), reviews changes in the past few decades.

For leadership portraits, refer to Norman Ward, *Jimmy Gardiner: Relentless Liberal* (Toronto: University of Toronto Press, 1990); Walter Stewart, *The Life and Political Times of Tommy Douglas* (Toronto: McArthur, 2003); and Dale Gruending, *Promises to Keep: A Political Biography of Allan Blakeney* (Saskatoon: Western Producer Prairie Books, 1990).

The relevant journal is *Saskatchewan History.*

CHAPTER 10: THE FAR WEST

The Alberta literature is also abundant. A classic is C.B. Macpherson, *Democracy in Alberta: Social Credit and the Party System* (Toronto: University of Toronto Press, 1953). Others on Social Credit include Edward Bell, *Social Classes and Social Credit in Alberta* (Montreal and Kingston: McGill-Queen's University Press, 1994); Alvin Finkle, *The Social Credit Phenomenon in Alberta* (Toronto: University of Toronto Press, 1989); John A. Irving, *The Social Credit Movement in Alberta* (Toronto: University of Toronto Press, 1959); Bob Hesketh, *Major Douglas and Alberta Social Credit* (Toronto: University of Toronto Press, 1997); and J.R. Mallory, *Social Credit and the Federal Power in Canada* (Toronto: University of Toronto Press, 1954). Consult Lewis G. Thomas, *The Liberal Party in Alberta, 1905-1921* (Toronto: University of Toronto Press, 1959) for the province's early political scene; William Kirby Rolph, *Henry Wise Wood of Alberta* (Toronto: University of Toronto Press, 1950) on the American populist leader; Karel Denis Bicha, *The American Farmer and the Canadian West, 1896-1914* (Lawrence, KS: Coronado Press, 1968); and W.E. Mann, *Sect, Cult, and Church in Alberta* (Toronto: University of Toronto Press, 1955) on the religious influence. Two collections include Allan Tupper and Roger Gibbins, eds., *Government and Politics in Alberta* (Edmonton: University of Alberta Press, 1992), and Carlo Caldarola, ed., *Society and Politics in Alberta* (Toronto: Methuen, 1979). See also Howard Palmer, with Tamara Palmer, *Alberta: A New History* (Edmonton: Hurtig, 1990); David Leadbetter, ed., *Essays on the Political Economy of Alberta* (Toronto: New Hogtown Press, 1984); Trevor Harrison, ed., *The Return of the Trojan Horse: Alberta and the New World (Dis)Order* (Montreal: Black Rose, 2005) for critiques of Conservatives' economic and other policies; David K. Stewart and Keith

Archer, *Quasi-democracy? Parties and Leadership Selection in Alberta* (Vancouver: UBC Press, 2000). Mark Lisac, *The Klein Revolution* (Edmonton: NeWest, 1995) focuses on the colourful premier; David Wood, *The Lougheed Legacy* (Toronto: Key Porter, 1985) discusses a more substantial premier.

    Alberta History is the regional journal.

    For British Columbia, refer to R.K. Carty, ed., *Politics, Policy, and Government in British Columbia* (Vancouver: UBC Press, 1996), a useful collection. Philip Resnick, *The Politics of Resentment: British Columbia Regionalism and Canadian Unity* (Vancouver: UBC Press, 2000), offers reflections. Jean Barman, *The West beyond the West: A History of British Columbia*, rev. ed. (Toronto: University of Toronto Press, 1991); Margaret A. Ormsby, *British Columbia: A History* (Toronto: Macmillan, 1958); and J. Friesen and H.K. Ralston, eds., *Historical Essays on British Columbia* (Toronto: McClelland and Stewart, 1976) afford historical grounding. Eminent historical geographer R. Cole Harris produced *The Resettlement of British Columbia: Essays on Colonialism and Geographical Change* (Vancouver: UBC Press, 1997). Economic structures are also treated in Rennie Warburton and David Coburn, eds., *Workers, Capital, and the State in British Columbia: Selected Papers* (Vancouver: UBC Press, 1988). For tumultuous times, see J. Terence Morley, Norman J. Ruff, Neil A. Swainson, R. Jeremy Wilson, and Walter D. Young, eds., *The Reins of Power: Governing British Columbia* (Vancouver: Douglas and McIntyre, 1983); Warren Magnusson, Charles Coyle, R.B.J. Walker, and John Demarco, eds., *The New Reality, the Politics of Restraint in British Columbia* (Vancouver: New Star, 1984); and Bryan Palmer, *Solidarity: The Rise and Fall of Opposition in British Columbia* (Vancouver: New Star, 1987). Colourful leaders are discussed in David Mitchell, *W.A.C. Bennett and the Rise of British Columbia* (Vancouver: Douglas and McIntyre, 1983); G.B. Nixon and L.T. Kavic, *The 1200 Days, a Shattered Dream: Dave Barrett and the NDP in BC, 1972-75* (Coquitlam: Kaen, 1978); Stan Persky, *Fantasy Government* (Vancouver: New Star, 1989); and Stan Persky, *Son of Socred* (Vancouver: New Star, 1982). Partisan foot soldiers are the focus of Donald E. Blake, R.K. Carty, and Lynda Erickson, *Grassroots Politicians: Party Activists in British Columbia* (Vancouver: UBC Press, 1991). Donald E. Blake, *Two Political Worlds: Parties and Voting in British Columbia* (Vancouver: UBC Press, 1985) analyzes partisan popular preferences across the federal-provincial divide. The politics of resource exploitation are treated in Martin Robin, *The Rush for Spoils: The Company Province, 1871-1933* (Toronto: McClelland and Stewart, 1972), and Martin Robin, *Pillars of Profit, 1934-72* (Toronto: McClelland and Stewart, 1973).

    BC Studies is the regional journal.

    Non-region-specific journals consulted include *Canadian Journal of Political Science, Journal of Canadian Studies, Canadian Historical Review, Canadian Review of Sociology and Anthropology, Canadian Journal of Sociology, American Review of Canadian Studies, Canadian Forum, Labour/Le Travail,* and *Canadian Ethnic Studies.*

Index

Bentham, Jeremy, 251
Beothuks, 142
Berger, Carl, 138, 268
Berton, Pierre, 165
Beveridge Report, 246
Bevington, George, 242
biculturalism, 94-99, 101
bilingualism: as Canadian characteristic,
    40, 169; in New Brunswick, 139;
    promotion of, 95; Quebec secession
    and, 97
Bill of Rights (US), 64, 72
Bismarck, Otto von, 16
Blair, Tony, 234
Blake, Edward, 268
Blakeney, Allan, 75, 128, 227
Bland, Salem, 172, 232
Bloc Populaire, 172
Bloc Québécois (BQ), 114, 166, 182,
    266
blue tories, 9
BNA Act. See British North America Act
    (1867)
Borden, Robert, 227
Bothwell, Robert, 196
Bouchard, Gérard, 163
Bouchard, Lucien, 128, 163, 176, 177,
    180-82
Boulton, D'Arcy, 194
Bourassa, Henri, 161, 173
Bourassa, Robert, 181
Bourgault, Pierre, 174
BQ. See Bloc Québécois (BQ)
Bracken, John, 128
Brewin, Andy, 230
bridges, 141
Britain: British Columbia and, 251-52;
    Canada compared to, 26, 40, 66-67,
    69, 79-80, 82, 91-92; Canadian polit-
    ical science influenced by, 38; Canad-
    ian relations with, 60, 61; elite youth

in, 46; immigration from, 32-33;
Manitoba and, 219-21; Maritimes
and, 149, 154; Midwest and, 214;
Newfoundland and, 145-49; Ontario
and, 193-98; political parties in,
79-80, 157; Quebec and, 178-79;
Saskatchewan and, 223-29; symbols
of, 85, 91
British Arts Council, 92
British Columbia: Alberta and, 217, 255-
60; as Australia, 250-55; Britain and,
251-52; character of, 8; electoral system of, 79; and Far West region, 237-
44; flag of, 91; immigration to, 33,
242; political culture of, 254-55; political leaders in, 239-40; political parties in, 132, 252; politics in, 127, 244;
referenda in, 76; religion in, 255-57;
social movements in, 258-60; socialism in, 242-43, 253-54; US and,
243-44, 260
British North America Act (1867), 61,
70, 72, 91, 92, 98, 103, 115, 179
British North America Act (1949), 63
British Politics in the Collectivist Age
    (Beer), 23
Broadbent, Ed, 204
Brown, George, 150-51, 195, 196
Bryden, Ken, 230
Buddhists, 208, 255
Bush, George H.W., 81
Business Council on National Issues, 84

Cairns, Alan, 3, 109, 113, 265
Caisse de dépôt et placement, 177
Calgary, 245, 247, 250
Calgary Daily Herald (newspaper), 255
Calvert, Lorne, 227, 232
Camp, Dalton, 159
Campbell, Gordon, 81, 127, 239
Campbell, Kim, 253

Printed and bound in Canada by Friesens
Set in Giovanni and Scala Sans by Artegraphica Design Co. Ltd.
Copy editor: Deborah Kerr
Proofreader: Stephanie VanderMeulen
Indexer: David Luljak